In the Shadow of the Courthouse

Memoir of the 1940s written as a novel

By

James R. Fisher, Jr.

7/23/03

ISBN: 1-4107-1137-4 (e-book)
ISBN: 1-4107-1138-2 (Paperback)
ISBN: 1-4107-1139-0 (Dust Jacket)

Library of Congress Control Number: 2003090076

This book is printed on acid free paper.

Printed in the United States of America
Bloomington, IN

Dust jacket front cover, print of painting of the Clinton County Courthouse, reprinted with permission from the artist, Carl H. Johnson, Galena, Illinois.

Dust jacket back cover, photograph of St. Patrick's complex © James R. Fisher, Jr.

Print of painting of Clinton Downtown from perspective of Six Avenue South and Second Street looking north to Clinton Courthouse, reprinted with permission from the artist, Carl H. Johnson, Galena, Illinois.

In the Shadow of the Courthouse poem – If I were a poet....: ©1995 James R. Fisher, Jr. This poem cannot be reproduced without permission of the author.

1stBooks – rev. 4/4/03

In memoriam of Robert Lee Witt
And Deborah Ann Tharp Miller

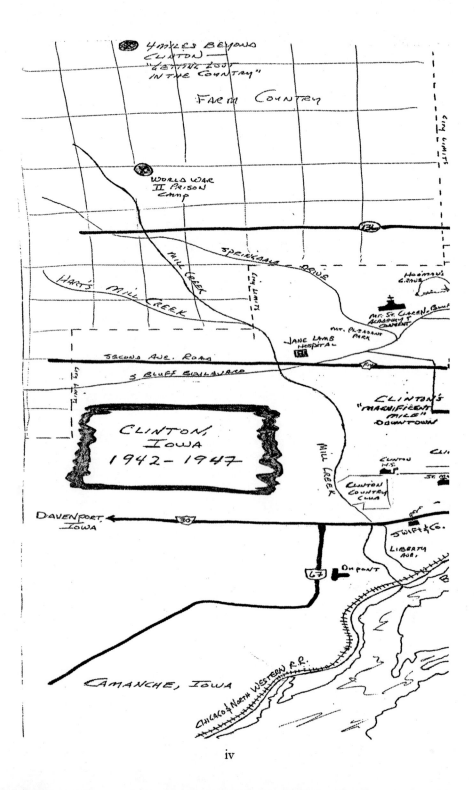

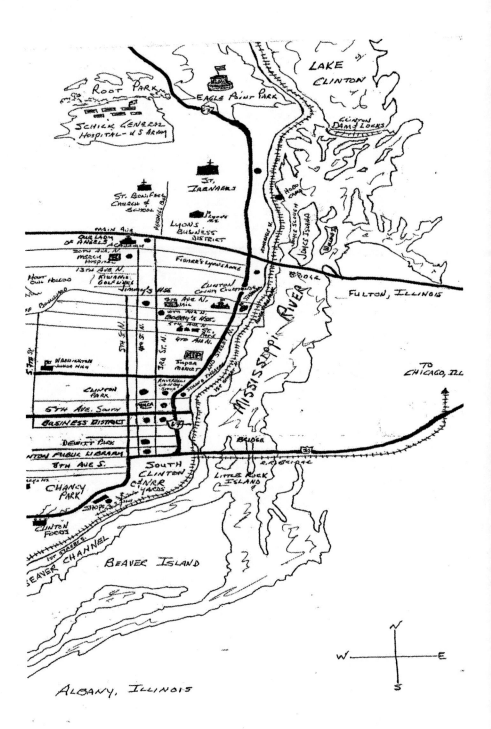

In The Shadow of the Courthouse . . .
If I were a poet . . . .
James R. Fisher, Jr.
© 1995

I *have never lost my affection for this edifice. It was like a parent that never wavered, never changed. I am sitting here now, reflecting on the fact that it is forty-four years since I have spent any time with my old friend.*

If I were a poet, I would give it metaphorical significance, like a giant knight, standing ever at attention to protect my neighborhood from itself and from the dangers outside.

If I were a poet, I would see it as a Greek god, an Adonis, a Zeus, a mighty warrior who never falters from its vigilance.

If I were a poet, I would sing the praise of this frozen music, this enchanting melody which never varies in my head, this quiet dignity, this sculptured perfection, this sensible grace as common as a pair of old shoes.

If I were a poet, I would wonder why we could have such stability, such reasoned continence against the harsh reality of tumultuous change, as it has not varied for me one iota from what it was a half century ago.

If I were a poet, I would remark that the tower and the time and the psychology of its movement is frozen like magic so that wherever I go it is stop time to my mind.

If I were a poet, I would tell the world that it has been so important in making this fumbling, stumbling, bumbling individual called "me," to always feel a mystical anchor in my roots of being.

If I were a poet, I would exalt its unique character with Vivaldi's "Four Seasons" to dramatize how the earth around may change, but the spirit within remains forever constant.

If I were a poet, I would note that men live and die, but that this structure is immortal because it exists beyond nature.

If I were a poet, I would sit here and wonder as I am now, over the happiness I feel for having the opportunity to once again ponder the regard I hold for it. And finally

*If I were a poet, I would want the world to know of the many lives that this edifice, this sentinel has influenced in the course of my fleeting life. How many young who are now old have been given succor and sustenance, and semblance of order in their lives because they have lived **In the Shadow of the Courthouse.***

Prologue

Epiphany One

Was it for this the clay grew tall?

--Wilfred Owen

The first day of my life was when I was eight-years-old and met Bobby Witt. I can remember it well. I still feel the atoms of my body rearranging themselves. It was April 1942. The winter thaw had left the naked trees shining with glistening pride. Expectation was in the wind. Happy tree limbs sprouted green buds promising a forest of beauty. The aroma of spring was everywhere. The sky was the color of my eyes, an azure blue, with mountains of puffy clouds rolling across it in silent music.

My family had just moved into our first real home. "We are no longer renters," my da said. "We have joined the capitalists." Cigarette dangling from his lips, his narrow shoulders arched with cocky pride, he failed to mention that he borrowed $300 from my uncle Arne, the down payment for this $3,000 white clapboard two-story house, money that he would never repay.

Like many Irishmen of the time, my uncle Arne never married. A frustrated cartoonist, he settled for a job at the Chicago & North Western Railroad roundhouse making boxcars. The shops employed better than 2,000 workers and stretched for ten blocks along Camanche Avenue on Clinton, Iowa's south side.

Our new home was at 318 Sixth Avenue North, in the heart of this small industrial city of 33,000, in the middle of the United States, a few blocks directly west of the Mississippi River, but only three houses from the most beautiful building I had ever seen, the Clinton County Courthouse.

This majestic structure rising more than one hundred and fifty feet to touch the sky with its magnificent copper dome weathered to a bright green, its ubiquitous head forming a four-sided clock, its collar of turrets facing all directions, its burnt orange, rustic muscular body of granite, marble and indigenous Indian red pipestone securing it to this hollow ground, United States flags flying at attention below on the well-kept lawn, proximate to WWI canons at its north and south shoulders, with second story porches jetting out from these shoulders toward Second Street, and the main nave of the building with columns like powerful oak arms standing at military parade rest, while a make shift wooden structure honoring World War II service men and women appeared at the corner, indicating with golden stars those who had died in this war, completing this visual symmetry, informing passersby, lest they forget, the ultimate sacrifice so many had made, and were making from this community in the defense of their country.

My life as a boy would be in the shadow of this silent sentinel, a shadow that was to reach well into my life. On this particular day I am buoyant. I have just performed my part in the St. Boniface School eighth grade graduation play, albeit only a third grader. It is quite a thrill to be singled out for a leading part. Sister Mary Martina chose me she said, "Because you are the right size, memorize lines well," and then as if an afterthought, "make a convincing old man." Sister's words still resonate with me. I was tall for my age, already nearly five-foot at eight, and like my mother good at remembering things. She could read a book and repeat the story practically word-for-word, or so it seemed. I don't remember the play but I do recall its essence. It was about a boy who was put upon by others and became cynical, until one day as an old man he experienced an epiphany and changed forever. Hmmm, I wonder.

I have been blessed, as have many in the courthouse neighborhood. Most of our parents were unable to go beyond grammar school, were employed in working class jobs, few owned automobiles. None of this was on my mind as I wandered over to the courthouse. Kids seemed to always be playing there, but it was quiet on this day. A boy was sitting on the concrete stoop of his front porch across from the courthouse jail, a stick in his hands, and an Irish frown on his German face as he busily oiled his baseball glove. He smiled at me as I approached, a warm smile, the smile of a boy with something unfamiliar to my restless spirit, a calm center. The warmth of that smile made me feel good. He had dark brown hair, flesh colored skin sprinkled with freckles, rosy cheeks and a dimpled chin.

His face and eyes were very Irish, but his name, Bobby Witt, was quite German. I learned his mother was an O'Brien.

"Hi," he said, "You play ball?" His directness stunned me. I didn't know how to reply. I played football with the seventh and eighth graders at St. Boniface's, German farm boys who were big and burly. In fact, I was recovering from a full-size shiner having been kicked in the head making a tackle. I expected him to comment about my black eye, like, "What happened to your eye?" The eye never came up.

Unthinkingly, I asked, "What's that?" looking at the stick beside his leg, dodging the question about playing baseball. I had never seen anything like it. The stick resembled a dark, highly polished piece of wood with a twisted corrugated grain, and was about three feet long and three inches in diameter. It looked like a cane for a midget.

"It's a fungo. Dad made it. Can hit a ball long ways with it." Then suddenly, he rose from the stoop, "Let me show you!" He tossed me his worn oily glove, and with that, we were off to the courtyard across the street. A huge patch of lawn extended from between Sixth and Seventh Avenue North, and was about 200 feet wide from the jail to a gravel parking lot with a rising hump snaking its way from the jail to the powerhouse housing underground heating pipes. The powerhouse was situated in the center of the parking lot, and I learned later, was called "the rocks." Not an ideal field, but heaven to kids of the neighborhood.

Bobby assumed I played baseball. I had never had a glove on my hand. I played football, could run fast, tackle hard, throw a spiral pass, and kick okay. That was the extent of my athleticism. He ordered me to go back about 30 yards, while he threw up the baseball, and hit it over my head. I call it a "baseball," but it was a ball wrapped in black electric tape. It hit the soft moist turf with a thud and stuck there like a canon ball. The ground was slippery and muddy. My shoes were a mess. I knew I would be in trouble when I got home. The mud seemed of no concern to Bobby. "Sorry," he said as I ambled after the ball, a few yards beyond me. I retrieved it and threw it back with all my might.

"Hey! Got an arm," he said with a broad smile as he caught it belt-high on the first hop with his bare hand. I nodded. His compliment made me forget my soaking feet. A baseball was a lot easier to throw than a football. The next ball he hit was a screaming liner that splashed off the grass and then darted towards me like a bullet. My instinct was to duck my head, close my eyes, and hope I'd catch the ball. I did, right on my chin. Now I had two chins to match my jaundiced eye.

"Sorry," Bobby said again. I wondered if he meant it. Reading my smirk, he added, "Took a bad hop. You okay?" I nodded, but gave him his glove back. The game was over.

Baseball was a contact sport outside my experience. "Have to go," I said weakly. He smiled. "Chin soon'll match your eye, huh?" So, he did notice.

"See if I can find you a glove so we can play catch later, okay?" I nodded.

In my busy adult life working in many parts of the world, I know it all started the day I met Robert Lee Witt, who was also eight years old and a third grader at St. Patrick's Catholic School. I would have limited access to Bobby and his friends, that first summer, my mother wanting to jump-start me on fourth grade, which meant attending summer school at St. Patrick's. As we walked back across the street, he asked, "How old are you?" I told him.

"Can't be! Too big."

"I'm eight," I repeated defiantly. He shrugged his shoulders.

"Have a glove?" I found that strange, as I told him before I'd never played baseball.

"Nooo," I said, unable to mask my annoyance with his stupid question.

"That's okay. We'll find you one. What position you play?"

"Bobby, I told you. Never played baseball." The hurt in his eyes made me back off. "What you play?"

"Shortstop. Pitch, too." Pounding his fist hard into his glove, then slinging his bat over his shoulder, adding in a resolute tone. "Just like to play ball."

"Wow, you sure can hit it," I added sincerely.

Buoyed by this, he exclaimed, "Ever see Three-I-League play?"

"Three eye league?" I responded dumbfounded.

"Not eye, like your eye. Like I am. That I."

"What does it stand for?"

"Don't know, just a name I guess."

I came to envy the fact that nothing seemed to bother him. Not knowing what the "Three-I-League" stood for would have kept me up nights. He seemed so free, while I felt constrained. He expected life to change around him, and it did. It was wonderful to meet such a boy in Clinton, Iowa in 1942. When I met Bobby Witt, America was at war with Japan and Nazi Germany in World War Two. A scant four months before, on December 7, 1941, the Japanese, whom I had never heard of, bombed a place called Pearl Harbor, which I never knew existed. My mother, sister, brother, and I had just come home from Sunday Mass at St. Boniface's when my da pushed the door open as we arrived with a look of terror.

"Jesus Christ, Dorothy, the Japs have bombed Pearl Harbor." My mother cried hysterically. "Oh my God Ray our Jack is there! Our Jack is there!"

She prayed. Da paced. Both smoked. My little sister, Janice, only seven months old, cried, and I had no idea what was going on. "Who are the Japs?" I asked. Some times my da ignored my questions, especially when he was upset, which was often. He was a great yeller. But for some reason, he said quietly,

"Remember the carnival on Main Avenue in Lyons last summer, where the man swung two buckets of water around without spilling them?"

I remembered. I also remembered the man looked strange.

"Well," he continued, "he was a Jap." I shuddered with fear because he was so different looking. Listening to my parents, speaking more calmly now, I learned that my cousin, Jack Clegg, was a machinist on a repair ship, the U.S.S. Vestal, and stationed at Pearl Harbor. Weeks later we learned his ship was tied up to the battleship USS Arizona on December 7th. Plans called for the Arizona to move out on Monday, December 8th, with the Vestal for extensive repairs to the battleship. When the Arizona was sunk, the Vestal was hit and my cousin, who was in the engine room, had a load of pipes fall on him, breaking his back. Only the 1940 Christmas before, he and his younger brother, Bub, had taken my little brother and me to the Eagles Lodge Christmas Party, and we had ridden on their shoulders. To this day I remember the thrill of it. The Clegg boys were like big brothers. So, I was very aware of the war from the first. It was that war, and the period that followed that some would call the end of America's innocence, but by the accident of my birth it would prove the formative years of my youth.

* * * * *

Chapter 1

In Search of Time Past

*Hide, as with winter's ice, the streams
Of your emotions and your dreams . . .*

--Fyodor Tyutchev

If school had been baseball, Bobby Witt would have been a scholar. Bobby had the brains to do anything, but only wanted to play baseball. A half-century would pass before athletics could remotely match the career prospects of an education. I was not Bobby's equal in sport or school, but had no illusions about opportunity. Bobby would graduate from college, acquire a master's degree, and become a coach of distinction. He would be elected into the Illinois High School Coaches Hall of Fame. It was not the major league baseball career to which he aspired, but in a way it was better.

Friends are our first coaches. They guide us to what we do best. Bobby was my first coach, not by what he said, but what he was. I

1

absorbed his presence. He was fun to be around, helped me relax, and showed me the way to lose myself in sport. Ed Rashke, our high school basketball coach, would tell me long after my playing days, that I was a reluctant athlete. Bobby knew this, but was never judgmental. He never owned other people's problems, accepted them at face value, and didn't waste energy trying to reconstruct their lives. This gave him amazing freedom. Where I was a grind and a pleaser in school he was a reluctant student. While I had to study for grades, he absorbed information as if by osmosis. School was a game. Sport was serious business.

My da died of multiple myeloma. A month before he passed away he spoke to his four children, me last, as I was the eldest. "Jimmy," he said pushing his shriveled hand into my shoulder blades as I knelt beside his bed, "your feet have never touched the ground." These words crushed me. I was 22; a Phi Beta Kappa college graduate, trained chemist, husband and father, home on emergency leave from the U.S. Navy, and yet I knew he was right. "Your mother tells me you want to be a writer. Jimmy you don't even write a good letter. You'll starve to death as a writer." I moved away from his touch, about to excuse myself when he pressed down harder.

"Your mother has your head so full of bullshit you think you're somebody. What you are Jimmy is the son of an Irish Roman Catholic brakeman on the railroad," then forcing the words out in a painful whisper, "not even a conductor." His jaundiced eyes with their capillary rivulets bore into me. "Look at me Jimmy for Christ's sake. Got a problem looking at people, know that?" I nodded. "Day you deny you're the son of a brakeman is the day you won't know who the hell you are."

His frail limbs were paper-thin. The bone marrow disease had reduced him from 160 to 60 pounds; nearly every bone in his body broken. Grudgingly, I moved closer to him and grasped his hand. His touch stung like an electric shock, his breath smelled like decaying food. He was dying, courageous in the face of it, still pushing the Sisyphus rock up the hill, still being buried by it. His words had the authority of pain.

"Do you want another shot?" I asked. Dr. O'Donnell authorized me to give him morphine whenever he asked for it. He opened and closed his eyes. Soon after the shot, his face was less contorted but still intense.

"Your mother thinks she understands you. Got her flummoxed." He coughed up yellow phlegm, which I caught with a Kleenex. "Don't understand you. Hell you don't understand you." He waved for me to elevate his bed to a sitting position. "Know that?" I shrugged. "Think life's a walk in the park, you do. Going to get the shit kicked out of you, and I won't be there." He took a deep, painful breath, "Nor will your mother." He grimaced to a smile. "Remember the summer you were seventeen and Eric Chalgren wanted you to hitchhike to the west coast? Do you?" I did. "Biggest mistake of my life. Might have made you a man. Don't know. Never know will we?"

My behavior through life was incomprehensible to him. Never drank, never smoked, never stayed out late, never partied. Played sports. Read books. Shared dreams with my mother. Constantly violated my da's mantra: "Never talk about race, religion or politics unless you want a get the shit kicked out of you, and one goddamn thing's for certain, you're no fighter."

In this last conversation he was making me out to be the perfect boy I never was. Forgotten was the time when I was seven and organized the kids in the block to repaint Bernie's new Ford. My parents rented from his parents. Bernie's father, a house painter, used his garage to store his paints, while Bernie used it to train to be a professional prizefighter. Our house, next door, was a small one-story wooden structure of about 900 square feet. The parlor was cluttered with only a sofa, chair, lamp, end table and radio. You were in the kitchen before you were hardly in the front door. There was one bath, two bedrooms, and no basement.

Bernie's beautiful new 1940 Ford Sport Coupe sat in the garage next door with its sparkling chrome hubcaps and whitewall tires. Nobody was at home but our baby sitter and she was busy reading a book. I collected the kids in the block. Once in the garage, I opened the paint cans with a screwdriver, distributed paint brushes, having my sister Patsy paint the whitewall tires black, Lyle paint the windows blue, Cathy paint the back fenders red, Patty, Bernie's little sister, paint the front fenders orange, while I used a ladder to paint the roof brown. I wouldn't let my little brother Jackie paint. He was only four and would get paint all over him. When the job was done, it was a Jackson Pollock masterpiece.

The first adult to see our work was Bernie. Disbelief stopped him in his tracks. Rage followed. His voice rose like thunder. Bernie's parents and mine poured out of their houses. "Goddamn vandals," he yelled. "Somebody has it in for me." He looked to his father. "Told you, dad, didn't I? Didn't I? The threats. Well, now you've got your evidence. Call the police."

About that time, we kids came out of the backyard. We were covered in paint, squinting in the sun like innocent bystanders our hands over our eyes.

"No! God damn it, no!" Bernie cried in astonishment. He loved us kids, was always letting us watch him workout, skipping rope, hitting the little bag with his elbows flared out making it sing, ratatat-ratatat-ratatat, seemingly forever. He pounded the big bag, too, until he was drenched in sweat. Then he would shadow box, which we found funny, do one-hand push-ups, sit-ups with his knees bent, leg lifts and pull-ups on an iron bar with one hand, too. I never saw such muscles. His body glistened, his muscles dancing to the rhythm of his workout. We would clap and he would give us candy.

"No!" he said again. "Almighty God no!"

You may ask why we didn't hide. What possessed us to be so bad? Obviously, I don't know. It might have been our desire to create by destroying something beautiful. Kids have been known to do that. We didn't run because we didn't think we had done anything wrong. He yelled at my father, "Get them out of here! Now!"

My mother stood between my da and me, who was choking on his cigarette. "Don't say a word Ray! I'll deal with it."

"You goddamn right you'll deal with it. That goddamn kid of yours." He instinctively knew I was the doer. "Dorothy I'll kill him if you don't get him out of here." Then he moaned like a wounded animal. "Goddamn it Dorothy how're we going to pay for this? Where're we going to live?"

He had a point. We had lived here for two years. In that time he had gone from the WPA to a day laborer at Clinton Foods to being on the extra board of the Chicago & North Western Railroad. My orchestrated mischief proved the impetus to seek housing in the courthouse area. He failed to remember this, too.

Perhaps in the back of his mind was memory of my early religious fervor. Catholicism became both my cross and refuge. My nightly prayers grew in length kneeling beside my bed. Sometimes they approached an excruciating hour of irritation to him. He never prayed, never attended Mass, not until his final days. He was quite religious in his last year of life, and found comfort in Joe O'Donnell, who was an attentive doctor and a devout Roman Catholic.

Today, I am where he had been when I was seven. My anger turned against God when he died. God took him before he had had a chance to live. He worried constantly about what never happened, which paralyzed him from taking risks. Manhood to him was physical courage, which he displayed to the end, not mental courage, which he never discovered. My life has drawn on his undiscovered account.

That same year of the car painting was the year of the great Clinton flood. The Mississippi River swelled over its banks and made our house an island in its stream. Water stretched passed Roosevelt Street and westward beyond Second Street, the main north-south artery of the city. Canoes, paddleboats, and even motorboats passed our house instead of automobiles. Miraculously, water never got in our house. My prayers saved us. My da was of another mind. "That kid of yours," he yelled to my mother watching me kneeling at my bedside praying well into the night, "has a frickin squirrel in his cage." My mother ignored him. She now said her daily rosary, twice and sometimes three times. He watched her lips move as her hands passed over the beads but said nothing. Nor was he, or my mother aware of my sexual mischief. I had an animal curiosity fed by the sexual taboos of my Catholic instruction. Catholicism was all about words. I liked getting inside words and rolling them around in my head until they made sense, which they seldom did. This obsession started with my first Confession:

Sister Mary Martina prepared me well. I knew my lines. "Bless me Father for I have sinned. This is my first Holy Confession. I am sorry for these and all my sins." I was not quite seven and sin was a vague construction. I knew it was terrible. Sister said so. I knew I could spend eternity in Hell for my sins. Father Sunbrueller said so. Hell was scary. At Sunday Mass Father made my ears hurt shouting how I could burn forever in Hell with mortal sin on my soul. I wasn't

5

sure what mortal sin was. Nor did I know what this thing called soul was. Sister explained sin but must have assumed I knew about soul. Venial sin is not as bad as mortal sin, that much I knew, but this didn't make things any clearer.

With confusion, I was off to confession standing in line with other first graders waiting my turn. I looked about the church, all those haunting statues on the pillars, Blessed Virgin Mary on the left, Saint Joseph on the right, Saint Michael the Archangel on the main altar with his legion of angels looking down on Jesus on the Cross, and below that the Sacred Host in the golden monstrance in the tabernacle. Candles flickered at the side altars. A red light flickered in a glass near the main altar. Sister said this informs the visitor that Jesus is present in the Blessed Sacrament. I was taught to genuflect and make the sign of the cross when the red light flickers on the main altar.

My eyes move about the church taking in the Stations of the Cross. Each shows Jesus as he moved through his final agony and death. He looks so beautiful, yet so much in pain. I like to come here when the church is empty and study the stations. I don't know the Stations of the Cross. I just know that I feel safe here looking at them. When I pause to study the face of Jesus at the various stations I don't feel alone. I feel He understands my confusion. Finally, I am next. The confessional is foreboding. It looks like a cage. The wood is dark and contorted into haunting patterns around sculptured doors. The priest's box is in the middle of the confessional with an embroidered door with the letters THS at the top. I have no idea what the letters mean, but I wonder nonetheless. Confessionals are on either side of the priest's box. Wooden lattice screens separate the priest from confessors on either side. The priest sits but we confessors have to kneel on hard kneelers. Sister showed us all this last week so that we wouldn't be afraid. I am still afraid anyway. The wood has a sickening smell, like sweet perfume, which makes me gag. I wonder why it smells so terrible.

The confessor's door opens and my cousin, Francis Martin Dean, comes out with a big grin. Perhaps it isn't all that bad. I enter. I hear the hum of Father in stern voice as he hears the confession of a girl on the other side. I strain to hear what she says, but I can't make out her words. Then I hear Father mumbling some Latin, then saying, "Say five Our Fathers and five Hail Marys for your First Holy Penance. Now make a good Act of Contrition." The girl responds in a high pitch muffled voice as Father continues to mumble in Latin. Then bang, bang! Abruptly, her shutter is slammed closed, and mine is opened. The bang-bang throws a shock wave through me. Sweating, tense, I smell Father's cologne, his tobacco breath, and think of my da. I can see Father vaguely through the wooden lattice. I think of Lamont Cranston, The Shadow on the radio, *"Who knows what evil lurks in the hearts of men? The Shadow knows,"* with the Shadow's eerie laugh trailing. I am terrified. Suffocating. I want to leave, but my legs won't move. Father is mumbling again in Latin. I wait. My lips tremble.

"Come, come, my child," he nearly shouts. I put my hands over my eyes as if fending off a blow.

"Well!" he continues. "We don't have all day!"

Finally, after taking a deep breath, then I begin in a stutter.

"Blessss meee, blesss meee, bless me Father, forrr, forrr, forrr I have sinned." I stop. My voice abandons me. I can't speak. If I could, I don't know what I'd say.

"Pleasssse," he says in a solicitous manner. I know that "please" well. My da says please that way when he is angry. I am afraid of my da. Still, I can say nothing.

"Well, in that case, you answer me," Father says peevishly.

"Have you lied?"

"Lied?"

"Yes, my dear child, have you lied? Have you not always told the truth? You do know what telling the truth is don't you?" I don't answer. He continues.

"Do you lie to your mother? Father?"

"Sommmmetimmes."

"How many times?"

"How many times?"

"Yes, my dear child, five, ten, fifteen times, how many?"

"I don't knowwww, Father."

"You don't know?"

"Noooo, Father." I can hear him breathing. My da breathes that way, especially when he is about to explode. Father resumes more evenly.

"Have you disobeyed your parents?" he says emphasizing each syllable as if I am slow witted. I tremble but I am angry, too. My lips move but no sound comes out. "My dear child, I am losing my patience. Do you know that?" He takes another deep breath. "Again, have you disobeyed your parents?"

"Illll donn't knnnow, Father."

"Have you had bad thoughts?"

"Illll donn't knnnow, Father."

"Have you said bad words?"

"Illll donn't knnnow, Father."

"Have you done bad things?"

"Baddd things, Father?"

"Yes, bad things."

"Illll donn't knnnow, Father."

"Have you pulled your sister's hair? Hit your little brother?"

He knows who I am! He's not supposed to. Sister said that the confessional is sacred, private, between God and me. Father has the power to forgive my sins. But is he supposed to know me? Can he see me? I feel ill. Will he tell my da? Near panic, I manage, "Yessss, Father."

"Have you touched your sister?"

"Toucchhhed my sister, Father? Touccchhhed heerrrr where, Father?"

"On her private parts."

"Prrrrivvvate pppartts?"

"Parts of her body covered with her clothing. You do understand the question?"

"Nnnnooo, Father."

"No, you don't understand the question, or no you don't touch your sister where you shouldn't touch her?"

"Bbbbooottth, Father."

"No, to both?"

"Yeessss, Father, IIII, whhhyy wouuulld I dooo that?" A terrible thought races through my head. I am in trouble. Oh, am I ever in trouble! Have I lied? To a priest? What am I to do? I help my mother change my cousin's baby diapers when she takes care of her, and gives her a bath in the kitchen sink. She is six months old. Did I ever touch her . . . . there? Did I do wrong?

8

"My child, pleassse," he says, ignoring my growing distress. "Have you stolen anything?"

"Noooo, Father." Why would I do that? I don't understand the question. Why is he tormenting me? Why is he so mad? I can hear it in his voice, like I can in my mommy's voice when she is disappointed in me.

"A pencil, someone's milk money, something that doesn't belong to you." His German accent is now much more pronounced. Next he will be speaking in German like at Sunday Mass when he explodes into rapturous Germanic rage.

"IIII dddonn't kkknnow, Father."

"You don't know? You don't know if you stole an eraser, a pencil, lunch money? You don't know? Or you don't want to confess?"

"NNNNoooo, Father, yyyyouuu'rree confusing me."

"I'm confusing you? I'm confusing you?"

My head hurts. I am angry, confused. I start to cry. My sobs grow louder. He ignores them.

"For heaven's sakes child," he says in a more soothing voice. "Let's say you steal but don't remember. Is that possible?"

I can't stop crying. The harder I try to stop the more the tears flow. I am sobbing now loudly. I pound my fists into my thighs.

"My dear child, that is enough! Do you hear me? Enough!"

His voice rises like it does at Sunday Mass. I put my hands over my ears, and say mechanically, "Yesssss, Father." I am still hiccup sobbing.

"Now that is quite enough! Do you understand?"

"Yesssss, Father."

"You have made a bad confession."

"Yesssss, Father."

"A very bad confession."

"Yesssss, Father."

"The worst first confession in all my years as a priest. Do you understand what I am saying, my child?"

"Yesssss, Father."

"You are a disgrace to your parents, to Sister Mary . . . " He starts to say her name, and decides otherwise.

"Yesssss, Father."

A seemingly interminable pause follows. I fidget. I can hear his breathing. Smell him. It is a bad smell. "Do your parents say the Rosary?"

"Nooooo, Father, IIII mmmmean mmmy mmmommmy does, Father."

"Have your mother teach you the Rosary."

"Yesssss, Father."

"The Sorrowful Mysteries. Can you remember that, the Sorrowful Mysteries?"

"Yesssss, Father."

"Say the complete Sorrowful Mysteries with your mother, and now make a good Act of Contrition."

Yesssss, Father."

I wait.

"Now! I mean now!" he hisses through his teeth.

And so I began, "O my God, I am heartily sorry for having offended Thee, and I detest all my sins, because I dread the loss of heaven and the pains of hell, but most of all because they offend Thee, my God, Who. .."

When I leave the confessional with my head down, I can hear my classmates in line sniggering. I know that no matter how long I live I will never forget this moment. And I will never forgive this priest. The rest of the day was in a fog. I couldn't wait to rush home and glue myself to the radio to listen to The Shadow, Terry and the Pirates, Jack Armstrong the All-American Boy, and Superman. My da was more comfortable with me so indulged than in my reading classic comics. I would tell him I couldn't wait to read the real classics, which mother told me were beyond me now. Da, who was a non-reader, would simply shake his head. Yet, every Friday he would trek off to the Lyons Public Library at Main Avenue and Roosevelt Street to bring back an armload of books for her, picking the books out he said by color. My mother didn't care what he brought home. She would read them all, and da would return them the following week, bringing another armload home. Mother would sit in the kitchen, a cup of coffee in one hand and a cigarette in the other, an ashtray full of cigarette butts, and a beautiful smile on her face, as she read. This is the image of her frozen in my memory as we bounced through the door after school. She would have milk and cookies out for us. Patsy and Jackie would go out to play, and I would go into the parlor, turn the radio on and listen to my radio adventures. My mother was hard of hearing and the radio never bothered her. Later, if my da weren't home, she would stop reading and tell me about the current book she was reading. "One day, Jimmy, you will be writing better stories than these. You are a handsome boy but have a more beautiful brain. It is that mind that we must not ignore."

I would ask her when I could read books like hers. "Soon," she would say, taking a deep drag on her cigarette, before lighting it with another. "I fear only too soon. You hardly look like a little boy anymore." It was 1940. My reverie was broken as my dying father concluded his assessment of me, most of which I failed to hear. "It is for that reason I am more worried about you than your brother and sisters. Now, go and let me get some rest."

Where was Bobby Witt when I needed him? I suppose he was light years away crafting his own life. Bobby always knew I wanted to write. Were he around now, he would say, "Rube, you are a thinker who could never hit a curve ball. Your dad is talking curve balls. That's all. He has scouted your weakness and is now reminding you of it. He sees people throwing curves and you striking out again and again. He's got a point. If you want to make the majors, you have to learn how to hit the curve ball. Readers are your curve ball. That's the curve ball your dad sees you missing. You love big words, big ideas. People don't. People want to be entertained, to forget, not be reminded. Not sure you understand that. Anyway, what I do know is you've got to cut down your swing, speed up your bat, not sit on your back leg, and bail out on the curve. Rube, you don't get it. Readers want to escape thinking. They want to feel smart without being smart. Big thoughts will tank you every time."

Sister Mary Martina at St. Boniface in Lyons, or north Clinton, taught me in the third grade, the year before I met Bobby Witt. She was a no nonsense Irish nun and harsh disciplinarian. St. Boniface was a German parish, serving the surrounding farm communities of the county. Father Sunbrueller, the pastor, was a small, bent man with a broad face and arching bushy eyebrows reminiscent of the priest played by Barry Fitzgerald in the film *Going My Way*, but there the resemblance ended.

St. Boniface Church epitomized authority with its dark and foreboding icons, which hugged every pillar like stationary ghosts and hovered over the pews. The church iconography filled me with dread and made my stomach churn. This would heighten as Father mounted the ten-foot ornate podium to the left of the main altar to read the gospel, and deliver his Sunday sermon. It was always the same sermon, but this did not make it less troubling. He would start quietly. The constant theme, no matter the epistle or gospel, was always about the evil in the world. His voice would rise in a swelling crescendo as he depicted the abomination of man and the constant fires of hell with horrifying clarity – "Mortal sinners, you know who you are. You shall burn forever in hell, feeling the full pain of the burning, but never be consumed by the fire. No relief. No cessation of the pain. No death to suffering. Hell is worse than your most punishing nightmare."

A chill would crawl up my spine. I would look about only to be met with hooded eyes. I wondered what people were thinking. Then, and I always knew when then was coming, Father's voice would rise, the rafters seemed to shake, and a soft hum would cover nervous coughing and breathing as he slipped into raging German. His fists would pound the podium; his small head would bob like it was detached from his shoulders. Then he would pick up his Sunday missal, slam it down with great ceremony, turn and descend the stairs to continue the Mass.

When I read the Greek myth of Aeneas, I thought of Father Sunbrueller. Aeneas went down into the underworld, crossed the dreadful river of the dead, threw a sop to the three-headed watchdog Cerberus guarding Hades, conversing, at last, with the shadow of his dead father, then returned through the ivory gate to his work in the world. Father Sunbrueller did this every Sunday without humor and my soul is now scarred for it.

The Latin Mass was a mystery to me for certain, as was Father's gibbering German, but not to most parishioners. I sensed they understood and savored every German word with nostalgia for the Fatherland. My mother thought Father Sunbrueller was wonderful even if she couldn't hear most of what he said. "Why, mommy, why does he do that? He scares me?" She misunderstood.

12

"They're mostly German, Jimmy. They love his excited German. Makes them feel at home." She would squeeze my cheek affectionately. "They think he misses the old country as much as they do."

Not me, and certainly not my little brother. Jackie didn't like Father's ranting much less the Sisters of St. Francis. He was only five and in kindergarten. A bad experience in school with Sister Martina would prove to sour him on nuns for life. Sister Mary Martina might have made a better drill instructor with the Marines in Paris Island.

Grades kindergarten through fifth at St. Boniface's were on the first floor, sixth through eighth were on the second floor. St. Boniface was an old two-story brick edifice that was badly in need of repair. The school stood high above hilly Pershing Boulevard. You had to climb 44 steps to reach the school level from the street and the steps were steep and precarious to navigate when icy in the winter. Jackie was small for his age. My sister Patsy was in second grade, and I was in third. One day, early in the term, Sister Martina left the room, and immediately the room was abuzz with talk. When she returned, she asked, "Did anyone talk?" We all looked around innocently, but my little brother raised his hand. "Come to the front of the room, Arnold John," she said. He did so with a wide smile on his face. Seeing the ruler in Sister's hands narrowed his eyes and turned his smile into a frown. A combatant little guy, he now looked at her suspiciously.

"Hold out your hands, young man, palms up," she instructed. Jackie shook his head vigorously, "No, I won't! I wasn't the only one talking. Everybody talked."

Sister looked around the room at her cherubic pupils. The veil of virtue was conspicuous. "Well, we'll see about that." She put down the ruler on the front desk, turned away from my brother, as if the matter was closed, then backhanded him so viciously that the force of the blow knocked him clear over the front desk. Fortunately, the desk was empty. A shocking gasp pierced the silence. My little brother fought back tears and looked to me for support as he picked himself up. I was a goody two shoes and turned away. My failure did not register with him until years later. To this day, he doesn't trust me.

Sister resumed classes as if nothing had happened. To add insult to injury, I volunteered to clean the board and clap the erasers during lunchtime. Sister came outside as I was doing this, and patted me on the shoulder, "Where did that little brother of yours come from?" I continued to clap the erasers and said nothing.

On the way home from school, my sister Patsy said, "Jimmy, why didn't you say something?" She had tears in her eyes. "Why didn't you defend Jackie?"

"I don't know."

"Why?" she repeated. "You're our big brother."

What could I tell her? I was frightened. Jackie held my hand all the way home. It was warm, soft, reassuring, and forgiving. St. Boniface school was at 2500 North Pershing and we lived at 1931 Roosevelt Street. We had to walk south one block on Pershing, two blocks east on Main Avenue in Lyons, wait for the stop light to change, then six blocks south on Roosevelt Street to where we lived. The blocks were long and the distance from school was more than a mile. The three of us made this trek every school day: in the spring, when it often rained, through snow and frigid temperatures in the fall and winter without ever missing a day. Mother would bundle us up like little Eskimos, then wrap our lunch buckets and books in oilcloth, and off we would go. I smile to myself today on how much this customary perseverance has changed to routine coddling.

"Do you want me to tell mommy?" my sister insisted.

"If you want to," I said with all the false bravado I could muster.

She never did. Anyway, I was confident mother wouldn't tell da. She wanted us to get a Catholic education, and she knew this would be all it would take to put us in the public school.

There were far greater secrets that my sister never told. Patty next door, for instance, once invited my sister and me to visit her attic. It was hot and muggy, and smelled of mildew. She took off her panties and said to me, "Look! Have you ever seen this before?" I hadn't. Strange feelings went through me. "Come closer," she suggested coquettishly. I did. She smelled like ammonia. "Do you want to kiss it?" she asked, spreading her legs. I hesitated. My heart was throbbing in my mouth. I felt the danger, and delicious excitement.

"Don't, Jimmy!" my sister exclaimed. "It's a sin."

"Why not, it won't hurt you?" Patty reasoned. She sat seductively bouncing on the naked mattress with some of the springs sticking out. "Do you want me to take my dress off?"

Is this what Father was talking about? Terrible things were going on in my mind. I wanted to but knew I shouldn't, but I didn't know why I wanted to. We heard a noise, and Patty quickly put her panties back on and said, "We'd better get out of here. I'm not supposed to be up here."

My sister and I, covered in guilt, never talked about that day. I often wondered if it clung to her the way it did to me. After hearing Father Sunbrueller condemn the body as the vessel of Satan, how could it be otherwise?

I remembered another time. It was during Forty Hours Devotion in which each student was given an assignment to spend an hour on Saturday praying during this period. I was teamed up with my best friend. She was quite devout as well as the prettiest girl in school. I just loved to be around her. After devotions, I walked her home, which was a little out of the way for me, but not really. She lived several blocks south on Pershing Boulevard, which was not my normal way of going home.

"Can I tell you something, Jimmy?"

"Yes," I replied.

"My two brothers took my pants off the other day and touched me with their peepees. It has bothered me ever since. Why would they do that?"

"I don't know. Honestly, I don't." And I didn't. The idea was neither repugnant nor prurient to me. It just seemed strange and troubling, and perhaps that is why I still remember it so vividly. I was to discover a totally different Catholicism in Irish Catholicism, and a new friend in Bobby Witt. For a time, I was to put my serious mind aside, my deep wondering on hold to realize my salvation, not in the Baltimore catechism, but in the religion of sport. Bobby Witt was to be my rabbi for the next five years as I found a home with the Courthouse Tigers and the St. Patrick Shamrocks.

* * * * *

James R. Fisher, Jr.

Chapter 2

Free to Breathe

*The mind is its own place, and in itself can make
a heaven of hell, and a hell of heaven.*

--Milton

We leave our mother's womb, but not the womb of the mind. The womb of the mind is culturally enclosed with walls of comfort, a floor of belief, a ceiling of hope and a door always open to the unknown, but never quite wide enough to get through without effort. Leaving the womb of the mind is therefore traumatic. Many refuse to leave, leading to experiencing the same world again and again until they return to the womb of the mind forever. My da was like that. His mother died when he was born, his father took off for points unknown, never to be heard from again. Only his Irish roots remained faithful to him. Reared by his maternal grandmother Fisher, he would abandon my sister, brother and me while my mother, 20, was in hospital suffering a nervous breakdown, parceling us off to relatives and foster care. Three children in less than four years were too much for her fragile body. She spent two years lost in an Iowa City sanitarium otherwise known as the "snake pit." My great aunt, Annie McGarrity Dean, reared me until I was four. Then "Aunt Sadie," who wasn't a real aunt took care of my sister Patsy and me for about a year. Miraculously, we became a family with our real parents in 1938 and the trauma of the mind was now part of our construction.

Looking back, trauma revisited the Fisher family as it transitioned from Lyons and the St. Boniface parish, to Clinton and the St. Patrick's parish, from renter's to homeowner's, from Lyons and the north end to Clinton's demographic center, or the courthouse neighborhood. Even so, my da held tenaciously to his Irish roots as if nothing had changed. As huge as the trauma was for my parents, it was huger for me. They developed life filters, while I was a sponge asked to accept everything at face value. Going from one Catholic school to another, on the surface, didn't seem extreme. After all, the Sisters of St. Francis taught both schools. Subtle differences, however, existed between the German and Irish parish. German Catholics tended to own everybody's problems. Father Sunbrueller was a problem warrior. He liked to strike at evil like the soldier with the bayonet; only his weapons were scathing words.

Hell was home to Father Sunbrueller and heaven wasn't in his vocabulary. His explosive hysterics gave me the feeling he hated flesh and blood people like me. He was German to the core, and set the table for parishioners' fears. To this day, when I think of German Catholicism, I think of Father Sunbrueller.

Irish Catholics were different. They were simply paranoid. They found life a living hell, so what was the point of fearing it? While German Catholics wanted to save the world, Irish Catholics wanted to forget it. An Irish wake was cause for celebration. Death to an Irishman was escape from hell, not delivery into it. German Catholics acted as if hell was home to their kind. The worst fate an Irishman could envision was Limbo, a weigh station on the highway to heaven. Now the church has taken that away. German Catholics attended Sunday Mass regularly but Irish Catholics, like my da, declared their Catholicism with a vengeance, but found it unnecessary to acknowledge the Liturgical Calendar. His Catholicism was a necessary but not sufficient condition to belief.

My Catholicism was quickly exposed at the courthouse, an alien world of mostly non-Catholics. Jack and Dick Dunmore, sons of the caretaker of the courthouse grounds, Gus Witt (no relation to Bobby Witt), son of a bricklayer, Lyle Sawyer, son of a day laborer, Dick Crider, who lived with his maternal grandmother, Ken and Dick Tharp, sons of a shift worker at Bridge & Iron Works, Sam and Russ Annear, sons of a mother on welfare, Bill Benson, son of a Dupont worker, Rock Carver, son of a milk route carrier, Walt Ferguson, son of an Allied Bridge & Iron Works worker, Chuck Holm, son of a Curtis Wood Manufacturing worker, and Alex Graves, son of a Greek restaurateur, had little acquaintance with formal religion. Even so, all were great guys.

Then there was Sheriff Ky Petersen and deputy Chris Stamp, both non-churchgoers. Irishman deputy Jim Gaffey attended Mass regularly at Sacred Heart, a German Catholic parish downtown, where Father Minehardt was pastor and already ancient, but still my favorite priest.

The only Catholics in the courthouse gang were Jim Holle, son of a house painter, Bobby Witt, son of a Milwaukee, Burlington and Rock Island railroad coal and water tender, Phil Leahy, son of a Dupont worker, Bob and Thiel Collins, sons of a barber, Dick and Loren Morris, sons of a conductor on the Chicago and North Western railroad, and David Cavanaugh, son of a saloon keeper.

Most Clintonians were Republican while most Catholics were Democrats. Out of the entire Democratic ticket only sheriff Petersen regularly won reelection. Clinton's public school system was impressive with 12 grade schools, three junior highs, and two senior high schools in contrast to five parochial grade schools and one parochial high school. There was Mount St. Clare Academy and College, the only Catholic educational institution in Clinton, which continues to thrive to this day.

Clinton's population itself has shrunk (33,000 to 29,000) in the past half-century, but the Catholic school population has shrunk even more (1600 to 350). The public school enrollment then was 5,300 compared to the parochial school enrollment of 1,600. Clinton in the 1940s had 35 Protestant churches, some of them of magnificent architectural design, and five Catholic churches. Only St. Mary's has survived today.

Catholicism in my youth was my anchor. I owe it much. With the absence of family security, Catholicism kept me together. It was not so much a belief in God, as a belief in the idea of Jesus Christ. He was pictured in my First Communion Prayer Book as a blond blue-eyed beautiful boy like myself, who had a mind of his own, and while honoring his parents, did not allow them to limit his exploration of the world beyond. I did not think of him as God, but as an outsider like myself, who had the courage of his convictions.

Then there was the adult Irish world around me, and the constant cry, "woe is me!" The church was my sanctuary from this, a place where I could express my doubts, confide my thoughts, and trust I would not be betrayed by the inanimate icons that populated it. Often, I made visits. When I couldn't visit, I would bless myself as I passed buoyed in spirit. I would feel strong as a lion, invincible. I would run and feel the delicious pleasure of my strong limbs carrying me into the wind. My Irish Catholicism was balm to my anxieties, sanctuary to my troubled soul. The courthouse would move me away from this preoccupation. I was still a loner, would always be so, but now alone among amazing people. Athleticism was courthouse joy.

Within the shadow of the courthouse was an Irish grocer, Frank Cramm, a family physician, Joseph O'Donnell, an eyes, nose and throat specialist, Ed Carey, a family dentist, John McLaughlin, a family barber, Bob Collins, family tavern keeper, Harvey Sullivan and Leon Cavanaugh, and a family mortician, Johnny Dalton. Ireland was never more insularly Irish than the courthouse neighborhood.

Da was most at home in the company of his kind. We were hardly in our new home when the coffee pot was percolating on the gas-burner, our small house filled with its aroma, my mother at the kitchen table busy singing to herself, whipping up a chocolate fudge cake preparing for the clan to arrive. The Wednesday group included railroad brakeman Bill Knight, railroad car inspector uncle Bill and aunt Blanche Clegg, saloon keeper Leo and Alice Sullivan, Cleo Hyde, a lifelong girlfriend of my mothers from South Clinton, and saloon keeper Leon and Bea Cavanaugh, lifelong friends of my da.

If two saloonkeepers seem unusual in such limited company, know that Clinton claimed in the late 19th century more than one hundred taverns along its scenic serpentine seven-mile Mississippi River waterfront. Clinton's reputation as a drinking, brawling and open town was still intact in my day. Some 50 saloons, like painted ladies, beckoned weary travelers from Clinton's city limits on South Camanche Avenue to Main Avenue in Lyons.

Regulars on Friday nights were my mother's brothers and their wives: Uncle Bern Ekland, a pipe insulator at Clinton Foods, and aunt Verna, a welder at O.D. Collis Company, uncle Frank Ekland, a maintenance man at Collis, and aunt Helen a housewife, my two bachelor uncles, uncle Arne Ekland, an electrician at the Chicago & North Western roundhouse, and uncle Ray "Snowball" Ekland, known for his white-blond hair and usually being "between jobs" as a result of his liking for the sauce. Uncle Bill and aunt Blanche might come any night, as he was equally comfortable and dominant with any company.

My parents didn't own an automobile so everyone came to them. They would sit around the kitchen table smoking cigarettes, drinking coffee, eating cake, talking and then drift into the living room. There was never any booze in the house, thus dispelling the Irish myth. I would hide behind the sofa and listen with rapture to their conversation while thought to be in bed.

The first group was rich in "going to do and going to be," but couldn't because they were too Irish or too Catholic, or both. I would peek to see their heads nodding in agreement to this refrain. Life was hell and an inescapable dilemma. Eventually, they would tire of this and turn to telling stories. That is when my ears perked up. There was never a shortage of tales. Da would mainly listen, until the mood hit him to add his two cents. My mother would busy herself seeing that everyone had coffee, cake, and clean ashtrays. She would wait to hold court when the second group arrived. The Eklands all had hearing problems, my mother the worst. They were good lip readers and my mother was a good talker. She didn't like to talk. She loved to talk, and her brothers adored listening to her without hearing her. A voracious reader with a prodigious memory, never having heard well, she murdered the King's English often with comic zest. It was fun to watch.

Uncle Bill, a Protestant Irishman, would set the stage for the story telling. He would clear his throat. The room would grow quiet.

Methodically, he would pack his pipe, light it, take a deep draw on it, and then with theatrical pause, share his current misgivings. The sweet aroma of tobacco would drift down to my hiding place, so I never minded that he always found the metaphorical glass half empty. It was his delivery that mattered. His crusty voice would rise. "The country's going to hell in a basket," he would say in the summer of 1942, "Roosevelt is not bright enough to deal with Churchill. Wilkie would handle him better. Stalin, too. As matters now stand, there's no certainty we're going to win this war." It was uncle Bill's boy, Jack, who was nearly killed at Pearl Harbor, so his words counted for something.

"Oh no!" I gasped with a hand over my mouth. His voice rolled on but I heard no more. To say anything against President Roosevelt in my house was a sacrilege; to suggest the outcome of the war was in doubt was heresy. Even so, uncle Bill was not interrupted. We had FDR's picture on the wall along with Pope Pius XII's. FDR was my da's hero, the pope my mother's. How could he not notice this?

This Catholic audience acclaimed Roosevelt and uncle Bill knew it. It was his way of being nasty and getting away with it. His people came from Protestant Belfast in Ireland. The mother of his four children, my mother's sister, who died in childbirth, had a father from Bergen, Norway and a mother from Dublin, Ireland. He saw Irish Catholics inclined to be on the dole, always adding, "present company excluded," making no attempt to hide his sarcasm.

Years later, I wondered why this group took so much abuse from him. I decided they admired his success, and fed off it. With a quarter century of seniority as a senior car inspector on the Chicago and North Western Railroad, he had made it. He was a working class somebody. Respect came from this, not from what he said.

"Your uncle," my mother would say to me later, "thinks he's an authority on everything. He forgets he wasn't working much before Roosevelt was president." This was not quite true. I don't think my da liked my uncle very much, but he never said so. It wasn't his style to knock anyone even if they deserved it. He was a stream of contradictions. He was humble in the face of authority, and cocky when physically challenged believing he could lick any man. He had Popeye sized forearms, but on a diminutive five-seven frame and weighing 140 pounds in his prime.

Uncle Bill was left with four small children to rear when his wife Marie O'Farrell died at age 26. Aunt Blanche, his second wife, raised them all. She always gave me cookies and milk when I visited her. The Clegg's lived on South Camanche Avenue one block west of Clinton Foods, the corn processing company that employed 1,500 workers, and operated without interruption during the Great Depression. Plumes of white smoke spiraled over my aunt's house that smelled like burnt food. It was hard to breathe. Everything in the house, although sparkling clean, smelled of this heavy odor. Noticing my discomfort, she would laugh, "To your uncle it smells like money." This made no sense. I let it go until I got home. I asked my mother what it meant. She puckered up her lips, inhaled the smoke from her cigarette, and then blew a perfect circle of smoke overhead, her thinking circle.

"Blanche is a saint," she answered advisedly, "to live with that man. Should go straight to heaven if Protestants have a heaven." Then raised her voice, "Wouldn't you say, Ray?" Shielded behind his Clinton Herald, he ignored her.

"Well," she added, "we need assholes like him to appreciate good people."

On the contrary, I found uncle Bill remarkable. He had a mane of thick white hair, a ruddy complexion, twinkling blue eyes, high cheekbones, a firm mouth, and towered over everybody. The Ekland clan were munchkins, standing five-four next to his six feet. No man looked more impressive in his work clothes. His blue and white striped bib overalls were immaculate with his trouser legs starched to hold a firm pleat. His light blue shirt was tapered at the neck and seemed tailored to the cuffs of his long arms. He wore a red kerchief with white dots around his neck, tied in a knot like cowboy Gene Autry's, and he wore a billed cap of the same material as his coveralls. He looked magnificent. My heart burst with pride whenever he smiled and waved to me.

"What're you doing here, Jimmy?" he asked one day, disengaging himself from two men dressed in conductor uniforms, who were waiting for their trains.

"Waiting for my da. He's coming back from Boone. I took the bus to surprise him. Mother said I could." My da's extra board job meant he worked both passenger and freight trains between Clinton and Boone, Iowa, a route covering 202 miles from the eastern edge of the state to Iowa's center. He often dead headed one way and worked the other. When he worked passenger, he sometimes took me with him. I loved it. I've always loved trains, still do. He was a different person as a passenger brakeman. He hated freight trains, hated the heavy lifting, the isolation, the boredom of it all. He would come off the job angry, and we would all suffer for it. Working passenger trains was another matter. He liked to wear the brakeman uniform, which he wore with the care of a man going to his wedding. I would watch him collect tickets, talk to passengers, get warm milk from the diner porter for mothers with babies, acquire blankets and pillows for needy passengers before they asked, and generally make travel a happy experience for everyone. He never seemed in a bad mood, always on top of the world. Bill collectors were held at bay. Passengers' welfare was a way to self-forget. It was love, vitamins for his soul. It brought out the best in him. Once home from such a trip, he would be expansive, sharing his latest adventure. Not so coming off of freight. He was another man, bowed, grumpy, and irritable. We were all verbal targets, starting with my mother.

"Goddammit, Dorothy, is it too much to expect a half way decent clean house? What'd you do all day, besides smoking and reading?" My mother would smoke her cigarette defiantly, and look daggers at him. Only five-one and barely 100 pounds, she wasn't afraid of him. She knew he was all bark and no bite. "Dorothy, you should cut down on your smoking, know that?" That was like throwing gasoline on flames. Before she could react he was in the living room surveying the mess. "Can't anyone pick up newspapers?"

Clutter was everywhere. It usually was. The house looked just as messy after my mother cleaned it as before. House cleaning wasn't her suit. She left a burning cigarette in the ashtray of every room as she cleaned, and of course, he now took note of these burned to the butt cigarettes in dirty ashtrays. "Dorothy, Dorothy, Dorothy!" was the litany, as he dumped the butts into a wastebasket. Next, it would be me. "Where's the all-American?" his arms flailing the air in exaggerated wonder. There was never any guarantee in predicting his mood swings. Yet knowing he was coming off freight was enough for me to make myself scarce. Not so my little brother. He was too young to know the game. "Jesus Christ, Jackie, look at you? You look like a little beggar. Don't tell me you've been like that all day?" Jackie's clothes were smudged with food and dirt, his face dark and grubby from playing outside; his nails caked with dirt, his greasy hair in his face. Jackie quickly retreated to safety behind my sister, Patsy, and hugged the baby, Janice, like she was his security doll. The girls were seldom touched with his wrath.

"Goddammit, I don't know." He would continue, throwing his hands up in mock surrender. Then he would start house cleaning. Out would come the vacuum cleaner, the dust mop, moving furniture and yelling and swearing, while all watched.

"Dorothy, goddammit, all I ask for is a little cooperation. Is that too much to ask?" Then he looked about for who was missing, mainly me. "Where's that goddamn son of yours? What's he done all day? Tell me! Nothing! Right? Well, thank yourself for that, Dorothy. You treat that goddamn kid like . . . oh, forget it. He doesn't give a shit, know that . . .know that, Dorothy . . . where the hell is he? Jimmy, goddammit, get your ass down here right now!"

At that point, I would descend the stairs gingerly, quietly hook up the vacuum cleaner and drown out his hollering with the music of the machine. Like Father Sunbrueller, my da's weapons were words. If there was abuse in my house, it was that. The harshness of his words lacked imagination, even violence. They were more like a wail from Dante's hell. Working freight forced him to see he had never left the womb of the mind. Migraines would follow. We had no Richter scale to register these seismic shifts, so it was always a relief when he was once again on the road. So now he is about to again come off the road.

Leo Sullivan often told spicy stories. One punch line, "so he buggered her," went right over my head. Some laughed. Not my mother. What was so funny about picking your nose?

My aunt Blanche made stuffed monkeys with red tails. One night she was stroking the monkey's tail between her legs enchanted by storyteller Bill Knight. Suddenly, he stopped, shook his index finger at her. "Blanche, naughty, naughty." Everyone looked at her stroking the tail, and erupted into laughter. I was mystified. My aunt's face turned crimson, then she threw the stuffed animal to the floor, covered her lap with her hands. "Blanche, now if you were Catholic," he continued with false sincerity, "you'd have to go to confession for that." Everyone slapped their legs and howled, except the Clegg's. Uncle Bill rose and called it a night. The Clegg's would always leave first, anyway. Once gone, everyone relaxed. Uncle Bill was a good storyteller, but his stories were never salacious, never all that entertaining either, more the informative kind. I liked them. His voice was a musical instrument.

My da's special skill was bartending. He had worked the World's Fair in Chicago in 1939, and would have stayed in the big city if he could have made a living bartending. He couldn't. This pall darkened his mind the rest of his life. He hated Clinton because it reminded him of his failure. He loved Chicago neighborhoods and the metropolitan life. Tending bar part-time was a natural to supplement his income, and often the focus of his stories. The Midway tavern downtown was a watering hole for the Clinton Giants, the professional baseball team in the Three I League. Vic Bradford, the star of the team, was a Midway regular. My da shared a conversation he once had with Vic.

"Vic, how much difference is there between a ballplayer like yourself and a major leaguer?"

Vic put his thumb and index finger about a quarter inch apart, and said, "About that much."

"You're shitting me?" my da said.

"Nope."

"How can that be? Don't major leaguers have to have a lot more talent?"

"Ray," he says, "talent counts, don't get me wrong, but talent is not the complete package. A ballplayer is a commodity. Talent is not enough to be bankrolled."

"Like what else?"

"Like can he handle the pressure, will he put fans in the seats, can he take care of himself?" Vic looked at his boilermaker, and smiled, "This shit has ruined more than a few good country ballplayers."

Then Vic got serious. "Might not think ballplayers need to be political, but they do. Have to know how to schmooze, and who to schmooze. Booze and women are the killers. Most stars are prima donnas. Don't get their backsides up. They can cause you a lot of grief. You've got to eat a lot of humble shit up there. Don't hack off anyone, especially the guy with the purse strings. Then there's the press, fans, both pains in the ass, especially when you're in a batting slump. Ballplayers want to play ball. Not be stuck with that shit. Though that shit can get in the way. Those who make it and stay know how to ride the bull."

"Does that describe you, Vic?"

"Let me put it this way, do you see me kissing ass?"

"No."

"Well, there's your answer."

My da shook his head, "Then it's no different than being a brakeman on the road."

"No, it's the same game only you don't have to suck up to 3,000 fans every night."

Vic Bradford went to spring training with the Giants, and was in the majors for a cup of coffee, but never stayed. He is still remembered by old-timers as one of the all-time great ballplayers in Clinton's history.

The women seldom entered the storytelling. If anyone did, it would be my mother. Where stories of the men had the nuance of sports, sex, or politics, stories of the women were usually about their kids. My mother waited to tell her stories when her loving brothers surrounded her. I was often the subject matter. "Jimmy wanted a pair of high top shoes with buckles instead of eyes for the laces. He pestered me for ages, but Ray said we couldn't afford them. So, I took Jimmy up to Stuedemann's shoe store on Main Avenue and got him the cheapest pair of shoes they sold, not high tops. To say Jimmy was disappointed is to beg the question. But like always, he was a jewel. It was raining the first day he wore his new shoes to school and he promised to avoid the puddles. Ray thinks he made sure he didn't miss a one, all the way to St. Boniface and back home. As he walked home, the soles of his shoes continued to swell with water. Jimmy said he felt as if he was walking on cushions as the shoes squished as he walked. Then the sole completely fell off the right shoe, with the other flapping along, until it too fell off. Now, he was walking on his socks, which, too, were completely soaked, with his feet turning blue as ice. He walked through the door, tears flowing down his cheeks, his yellow raincoat hat drawn down over his face, his shoes in his hands, and his worn through socks stretched out and about to come off his feet, looking like the socks of a leprechaun.

"'Mommy,' he says, 'mommy the soles of my new shoes came off.' That was quite apparent. His socks were caked in mud and beyond salvaging. I learned later that the soles of the shoes were corrugated cardboard with a thin leather veneer."

My da was not smiling, but everyone else enjoyed the story at my expense. This was mainly their entertainment in a time of war. Nearly everyone had family in the military. Only uncle Bill referred directly to the war, being as he had two sons in harm's way, one survivor of Pearl Harbor, the other now fighting in North Africa.

What was interesting is that these people were ambivalent about Germany but united in their contempt for Japan. "The only good Jap is a dead Jap" I heard repeatedly, but never "the only good German is a dead German." Germans were different. This sentiment was graphically illustrated one day when an elderly man walked by my house goose stepping as he did, stiff arms cutting the air like scissors, a Kaiser Wilhelm II spiked helmet on his head, his chin arched skyward. He had a German Cross pinned to his shirt, along with campaign ribbons. This frightened me. I rushed into the house. "Come quick!" I cried. Da bolted from his chair, then rushed to the screen door, looked out, relieved, ruffled my hair and smiled.

"Dorothy," he shouted to my mother, who was in the kitchen, "Klaus is at it again." My mother, with hands on her hips, looked out. "Poor man. Still has family in Germany."

"Well, why doesn't he go back? Doesn't belong here." I said defiantly. Why weren't they angry, too?

"Imagine every time he reads The Herald and there's another German setback," my mother reflected, "Must get his dander up. Wants us to know he's German."

"Isn't that unpatriotic?"

"Jimmy," and this was always the clincher. "He's not a Nazi. It's the Nazis we hate. Nazis aren't Germans. They're fascists." There it was again, words!

"What's a Nazi, fascist?"

"A Nazi is full of hate for the pleasure of hating," my da explained, "A fascist wants to rule the world."

I was sure there must be more to it. People said I was bright, yet treated me as if I wouldn't understand. "Won't he be arrested? Germany's our enemy."

"No, he won't be arrested."

"Why?"

"Who's going to file a complaint? Besides, most cops are Irish and they've no quarrel with the German people, only the Nazis."

There it was! That word meant to explain everything, but didn't explain anything. My da had always been my giant, but with such answers my image of him began to crumble. He must have sensed this as he went on to explain how Ireland had remained neutral in the war against Germany, and that the Irish people held great affection for the German people. "Many men from Ireland joined the British military, like the RAF," he continued, "but I doubt if they'd take much pleasure bombing German cities."

"So our neighbor is just crazy?"

He nodded and went back to his paper.

Little shocks were jolting my system. This was just one of them. I loved adult conversation, but rarely understood it. My mother said I was curious, my da claimed me a pain in the ass. As much as I was actively involved at home, my first ventures to the courthouse were limited to watching. Belonging was not a matter of showing up. It was a matter of winning acceptance by showing some athletic skill. That was to become my next ordeal with Bobby as my coach and rabbi.

* * * * *

James R. Fisher, Jr.

Chapter 3

Love, Truths, and Family.

People seldom improve when they have no model but themselves.

--Oliver Goldsmith

Male bonding is what I needed. My mother, who was often alone, treated me as her most intimate friend. She confided things women confide to best friends about men, love, life, God, and family. Of all this, what registered most was her abiding admiration of her brother, my uncle Leonard. "Your uncle Leonard is a Doctor of Philosophy," she announced one day. "Know what that is?" She often posed a question, and then answered it rhetorically talking to herself in the mirror, the smoke of her cigarette encapsulating her hair.

"No," I answered honestly as she took another drag on her cigarette with a mystic look in her eyes.

"Means your uncle has a love of knowledge," she paused, "knows everything about everything."

31

That caused me to wonder. I thought only God knew everything.

"Smartest man in the family is your uncle." She opened a fresh pack of cigarettes, lit one, looked at it thoughtfully, and then continued. "Len received Ph.D. degrees in psychology and economics from Iowa in 1927, went on to teach at St. Ambrose College in Davenport, then DePaul University in Chicago, and now heads Department of Finance and Commerce at the University of Detroit." She paused again, took another deep drag on her cigarette and blew a plume of smoke out her nose and over my head. "Wrote a book in 1927 predicting the Great Depression."

My mother had a capacity to enrich a story with tantalizing details that became lodged in my brain like fables. Years later, when I made reference to this great book of his, my uncle smiled knowingly. "Your mother is too generous. It was my dissertation, Jimmy, not a published book. True, I mentioned economic cycles of decline and their influence on highly volatile periods like the great depression of the 1890's, speculating it could happen again. And of course it did in 1929. Was I alone in my pessimism at the time? Hardly. Did I know the crash would come as it did? No, certainly not. Had I predicted the force of that upheaval, my career might have been quite different, but obviously I didn't. Like most market analysts, I hoped my fears were unfounded."

Seemingly mesmerized with a spot on the wall beyond me, which I saw to be peeling wallpaper, my mother gave a throaty chuckle, took another deep drag on her cigarette, and continued. "Your uncle had to quit high school in his freshman year to help support the family. That was 1913, the year I was born. For two years he worked as a telegraph operator for the Chicago & North Western Railroad, then escaped to Iowa City. There he completed four years of high school and four years of college in four years." She laughed quietly to herself. "Imagine that, Jimmy. Just imagine!"

Actually, I couldn't. I was only in the third grade and saw nothing great about going to school when you didn't have to. She seemed to read my thoughts as she studied me curiously. Whenever that happened, and it happened a lot, I knew she was about to push my buttons. "Your uncle could feel poverty climbing up his back and biting him on the neck. When you're not privileged, but only gifted, Jimmy, it's a cruel world. Len's guts were on the inside, not on the outside like your father's. He didn't have to swear like a trooper or beat the hell out of anybody who crossed him to know he was a man. He just went about his business." I winced, her throaty laugh like a nervous tic. It accentuated her remarks like a stab to the chest. I knew already a great deal about "have nots," being told constantly that I was one of them. My contemporaries would say one day they were poor but never knew it. Well, I did, and was taught to feel it as if strapped to the rail with a locomotive closing the distance. Mother knew how to get and hold my attention. "Jimmy, imagine your uncle taking the first and second year of German at the same time. German's a difficult language. Few can master it." Obviously, I couldn't imagine, but that was not the point. "One day his second year German professor at Iowa stopped him in the hall, and said, 'Mr. Ekland, you're the poorest German student I've ever had.'" She couldn't contain herself. She waved her cigarette like a torch, ceremoniously bringing the blazing butt down to ignite a fresh one, grinding the wasted butt into an overflowing ashtray as if to further penetrate my unease. "Working night and day to catch up, then focusing on mastering German grammar and vocabulary, your uncle ended the year an accomplished German student despite the many hardships he had to endure." She took my hands in hers and looked into my eyes, the way Father Sunbrueller did as he delivered Holy Communion.

"That same blood runs through your body, Jimmy, don't ever forget it. Len's not like his other brothers. Not like your father. He's special. So are you. If you're to be destined for great things, you can't afford to pay attention to anyone that prevents your escape from this place." Then the *coup de grace*. "Len didn't."

In the spring of 1941, while still living in Lyons, uncle Leonard visited us for the first time with his two sons, Robert and Joseph. They came from Detroit in the biggest automobile I had ever seen. It had a silver emblem on the hood, an inverted "Y" in a circle. I was told it was a Mercedes. The boys were older than I was. When they opened the trunk of the car, I stood back in amazement. It held tons of athletic stuff like tennis rackets, canisters of tennis balls, baseball bats, gloves, baseballs, a football, basketball and volleyball. They also had several pairs of tennis shoes and even baseball spikes. They must be really rich, I thought. But one thing they didn't have is a

33

mother.   My cousins' mother, Clara Brennan Ekland, an accomplished mathematician according to my mother, died when Robert was born, and Joseph was two. She was 26, a year younger than my mother's present age. You could see my cousins missed their mother by all the attention they gave to mine, while I had eyes only for my uncle.

He, like his brothers, was a short, round man no more than five-four with thin black hair combed straight back with a strong round face. His deep-set penetrating eyes always seem to hold the whisper of a smile. He moved deliberately with short, quick steps. His hands were small, delicate, almost feminine and carefully manicured. Even in the summer heat, he was dressed in a three-piece lightweight business suit with a silk shirt and tie. There was a *Phi Beta Kappa* key pinned to his cravat, which my mother made certain I noticed. She took me aside as the three queued to the bathroom after the long trip. "Did you see the key?" She pointed to her own chest. "Acknowledges his genius." As she said this, her voice quivered with emotion like corn in a light summer breeze. "One day you shall have yours." The key was unfamiliar to me, but again she would prove prophetic. "I'll explain later," she said with her index finger to her lips, as she busied herself making a lunch of cold cut sandwiches with fresh lettuce and sliced tomatoes, homemade potato salad, cold cubes of cantaloupe, and Danish for dessert. Kool Aid was served to the boys, and coffee to my uncle.

The stay was brief, as we had no room for them, and besides, my uncle confessed, "The boys' grandmother is expecting us in Iowa City tonight." Iowa City, a university town, was ninety miles south west of Clinton.

His voice, deep and quiet like wrapped thunder, was different, strange to my ear, not like what I was used to hearing. It was eloquent yet sparing like an actor's. Some might call it cultivated. He seemed to choose his words carefully before he spoke. They weren't big words, far from it, as I could understand every one. He didn't talk just to be speaking like my mother did. What truly set him apart, though, was that he was a listener, and he wasn't hard of hearing like his brothers. Delight was always in his eyes as my mother talked and moved about. He sipped her quietly like a refreshing beverage. My mother was the youngest of eight children, my uncle Leonard the second oldest having been born in 1899.

When they were gone, my mother poured herself a cup of coffee, lit another cigarette, and invited me to share in a critique of this brief visit. "Well, what did you think of your uncle?"

"Wonderful!" I replied sincerely. Oddly, she made no reference to my cousins whom seem to adore her.

"Yes, he is isn't he?" She looked at me closely through the haze of cigarette smoke. "But more than that, Jimmy, he's the kindest man you will ever meet."

"Kindest? What do you mean, mommy?"

She went on to explain her debt to her brother. "While Len was still a student at Iowa, he didn't forget his little sister. Not having a mother, not even a big sister, only a father and four hard to please brothers still at home, Len paid to board me at the Academy of the Immaculate Conception in Davenport." She got a nostalgic glint in her eyes. "It was 1926 and I wouldn't be fourteen until December, but was already a high school freshman," she reflected proudly. "Len wanted me to escape South Clinton like he did." She paused; stamped out her cigarette so hard the ashtray spun away, and nearly fell off the kitchen table spattering a Rorschach pattern of ash, which I thought resembled a bird in flight.

South Clinton was the poorest section of the city, the sprawling railroad yards were there, with the constant din of switching railroad cars, smoke encased chugging locomotives, and the scream of whistles long into the night. Clinton Foods was there, the air choked with sulfurous fumes of corn processing, burnt sugar, and falling debris from belching smoke stacks. Swift Poultry Processing Plant was there with the stench of boiling-processing chickens. Curtis Company was there with the grinding teeth of saws droning like tortured animals with the detritus of sap coloring Beaver Channel to lignum brown, while wood chips and silt floated on the surface to destinies downstream. South Clinton was not pretty, but it was where the work got done to keep the city alive.

In the 19th century this was where immigrant families with few skills and little education settled. They came, for the most part, from Germany, Ireland, England, Denmark, and Norway. A house in South Clinton could be painted in the spring and look like a scaling leper in the fall. There was no point in washing windows. They wouldn't stay clean through the day. South Clinton carried the fatigue of economic strain and psychological depression. It was quite literally on the other side of the tracks. My mother never was able to escape its long shadow and willed it on to me.

"I left the academy after my sophomore year and returned to St. Mary's high in Clinton. Big mistake! I thought I was missing something." She trembled as if the memory hurt her head. "It was the Roaring Twenties, the Jazz Age, Jimmy, and everyone was dancing the Charleston, partying 'til dawn, drinking, smoking, and feeling as if they'd always be young." Her eyes glowed like warm hands as they touched my face with a smile. "I left school before Christmas of my senior year. Your mother was with child, Jimmy." Tears washed away her smile and trickled down her cheeks. I was not yet eighteen, and you and I were one." She looked at me intently, as if trying to recall the moment. "I married a good looking going nowhere guy," she said with an ache in her voice, "your father," adding as an indictment, "because I loved him." Then more to herself than to me, "Sometimes love is a trap." She cleared the dishes from the table, carried them to the sink, and started to wash them. I thought she was done, but she continued with her back to me. "Not married in the church, Jimmy, but by a Justice of the Peace." Her voice dropped off as if describing a criminal act. Rinsing each dish deliberately as she washed it, and placing it in the other side of the sink, her confessional continued. "Clinton is my prison, Jimmy, like it is your father's. I married for love. So did your father, and you see what we have." She took a deep breath, and with a quivering wheeze added, "It won't be yours!"

This was not something to share with a boy, information that rolled around in your head pinging as it hit the bumpers of your brain in a subliminal pinball game, but never adding up to any score. I wasn't sure what a Justice of the Peace was nor what she meant by the stigma of South Clinton. Perhaps that explains why my body could leave Clinton 50 years ago, but why my soul stayed behind, and why I was never young.

From the time I joined my mother and da at five years of age onward, I was her confidante, and most weeks her date to the movies. I can recall my da taking in only one film with me. That was the time he paid me a surprised visit at the University of Iowa when I was in graduate school. We saw per chance *So Big*, the film version of Edna Ferber's idealistic novel about a boy growing into a man. He found it so boring he twice left to have a smoke. To make conversation after the film, I said, "Movie reminds me of Mazo De La Roche's book, *Growth of a Man*." I should have known better. He didn't read. This was another way to deepen our division. He didn't say anything. The pain in his eyes said it all. Only later did I learn the reason for the visit. We weren't close, far from it. My mother explained that he had gone to Dr. McLaughlin for a teeth cleaning. The dentist didn't like the looks of his gums. He advised him to see his family physician. Dr. O'Donnell took one look at his gums, and sent him to a specialist, who in turn took a biopsy. The diagnosis in Dr. O'Donnell's words proved "a bad actor." He was diagnosed with multiple myeloma, a form of leukemia, a terminal disease. His reaction was predictable, "Joe, how long do I have?" Dr. O'Donnell didn't mince words, "A year, Ray, fourteen months at the longest." He simply wanted to see his self-important son while he was still healthy.

My mother, on the other hand, loved the movies, especially singing cowboy westerns. We saw them all. We would take the bus to the Strand Theatre downtown. Across the street in the Revere Hotel was Rastrelli's Candy Shop. After Gene Autry, Hopalong Cassidy, Tom Mix, or Roy Rogers and Dale Evans, plus a serial of Buster Crabbe or Johnny Weissmuller, and Movie-Tone News, my mother would treat me to a "CMP" at Rastrelli's – a chocolate marshmallow peanut sundae with a maraschino cherry on top. Marcucci's, two blocks south originated this popular sundae. Marcucci's favored a more sedate, straitlaced crowd. Its clientele were mainly kids who stayed in school and echoed community standards, while Rastrelli's was more an outlaw crowd of grammar and high school dropouts with a flare for daring. Teenagers with raging hormones flocked to this place and stayed there long after curfew. They smoked cigarettes, dressed seductively, carried false IDs, and looked for excitement wherever they could find it. Around the corner was the Clinton Billiard Parlor, another lair for them but with a difference. Sam Knight was the proprietor, a no nonsense guy, who didn't allow swearing, fighting, or destruction of property. Offenders were banned from the parlor for two months. For many, the place was home. If this crowd felt especially rowdy, a more suitable haunt was the Clinton Recreation Lanes, a bowling alley across from The Clinton Herald on Sixth Avenue South. Here discipline was lax and earthy language the choice of expression.

I would eat my sundae, listen to my mother with one ear and eat the noise with the other, studying this liberated crowd with voyeuristic delight. My mother, seemingly oblivious to this carnival, would drink her coffee, smoke her cigarettes, eat my cherry, and critique the movie endlessly, unmindful of my mental dalliance.

My mother was always a delight. When I think of her now, it is with that constant prop, the metaphorical cigarette. She once confessed that she started smoking when she was twelve in 1926, and found it as soothing as conversation with an old friend, the best company in the world when there was no other. I would watch the cigarette glow, the ash build, wondering, always, if it would fall off before she flicked her finger, being relieved when the ash gently spilled into the ashtray. Sometimes, however, the cigarette would nearly burn to her fingers. I paid as much attention to the cigarette as to her words. I would follow the smoke, breathe in its vapors, regard the mess that it created, and feel a sense of disgust for the dirty ashtrays and dank smell in the air and try to wish the yellow away from her index and third finger, but it never worked. Even finger nail polish couldn't cover the yellow staining. Our little house was painted with its chemicals, the walls, the ceiling, the blinds, the curtains, the furniture, and our clothes. Yet in truth, my sense of my mother's aliveness was somehow heightened by the perpetual presence of her cigarette.

My da also smoked, but hated to see my mother smoke in public. "A lady doesn't smoke outside the home, and never on the street," he constantly reminded her. It never took. As long as I can remember, she defiantly smoked everywhere. We would go to confession on Friday night and she would smoke going to and coming from confession. She was hardened to criticism, this or any other kind. She taught me more by what she was and less by what she said. She is doubtlessly smoking in heaven. It was not until I met Bobby Witt and became a Courthouse Tiger that I took "time out" to be a boy, and yet even then, I was a reluctant one at that.

* * * * *

Chapter
4

Ancestral Voices

*The best thing, which we derive from history
is the enthusiasm that it raises in us.*

--Goethe

Clinton is a lot like me, or perhaps more accurately, I am a lot like Clinton. It is hard to get an identity fix. Clinton has the veneer of stability, which begs the question. It once was described as a quiet city of neighborhood taverns and rowdy saloons, a city where sawdust was gold, a city of millionaires served by submissive pleasers, a city with the distinction of never being as much as it felt or as little as it seemed. Clinton remains to this day a rhyme in search of a reason, a community, which continues to repeat the same errors with schizophrenic hubris. In a word, it is typically American. I write here of Clinton not as a historian, but as a person who recalls what it was like to be young in the middle of America in the middle of this community when my century, the 20th, went mad, and never quite recovered from its madness.

In the midst of this madness, there was a single oasis of sanity for me and it was in the shadow of the courthouse. The shadow is metaphor not only for a neighborhood, but also for my time. Without meaning to, I found Clinton-at-large confining and repressive because it could never quite decide what it was. I felt myself an outsider, too, born on the wrong side of the cultural spectrum, being Catholic, Irish and poor, an orphan in somebody else's home. Why Clinton remains a magnet is precisely because it has the same feeling about itself.

In the summer of 1836, John M. Bartlett settled on the site of Clinton and promptly called it "New York." He was convinced that great gold deposits abound in the area, and prepared for a boomtown to rival Chicago. Gold, alas, was not discovered, and Bartlett soon pulled up stakes and moved on. By 1839, still with no name, it consisted of a tavern, two stores, and Mr. Bigelow's counterfeit coin shop. Outraged citizens soon demolished Mr. Bigelow's shop and banished him from the county.

To the north was a place now called Lyons after the city in France, and to the south a settlement called Camanche. Lyons had its own railroad in 1852, the Lyons and Iowa Central Railroad Company. Samuel Cox and G. W. Stumbaugh did succeed in building a sawmill in Lyons in 1855, which prospered from the first. This eventually led to David Joice (Joyce) and S. I. Smith putting up the largest sawmill then known in 1869. Many ancestors of all these pioneering families still call Clinton home today.

Lyons and Camanche would lose out in the scheme of things when in the mid-19th century the Chicago & North Western Railway decided to cross the Mississippi River south of Lyons and north of Camanche, or in the heart of what would become Clinton in 1857. It was named for DeWitt Clinton, the former Governor of New York. Thus Clinton became the railroad's double track main line across Iowa while being served also by the Burlington, Rock Island, and Milwaukee Railroad. The railroad switching yards in South Clinton would eventually cover more than 150 acres, and the company's car repair shops would ultimately provide jobs for 2,000 workers during the Second World War. Clinton also became the crew transfer point for many railroad men, which found them settling their families here, and later retiring.

During the 19th century boom period, lumber was floated down the Mississippi from Minnesota and Wisconsin. What gave Clinton a peculiar advantage was its natural bottleneck to this great river. From LaCrosse, Wisconsin, the Mississippi flows southward until it gets to Guttenberg, Iowa. Then it makes an eastward detour that gives Iowa's map the nose of the pig. Midway through this protuberance the stream narrows dramatically at Clinton. Watching a pilot negotiate barges loaded with freight through this narrow strait still gives the impression of God threading the proverbial needle.

Clinton became the greatest sawmill center in the world because it was cheaper to off load the logs here than to negotiate the difficult narrows and gamble on a higher price downstream. They called Clinton, "Sawdust City," which was an accurate term. Some sections of Clinton today are built on sawdust dumps of at least 30 feet high. Meanwhile, Clinton's population exploded, wealth piled up, giving way to the good life and a touch of culture. Clinton's population of 3,000 in 1865 grew to include nearly 100 saloons but also a subscription library. To give a sense of its wealth, it boasted in the 1890s of having 17 millionaires, and a higher per capita income than any other city in the world.

During this boom period more than 6,000 American elms were planted along Clinton streets, which would eventually form a magnificent arch over Clinton's wide boulevards, blocking out the sun, and allowing a cool breeze to sift through the stultifying summer heat, only to fall prey in mid-20th century to Dutch elm disease leaving most streets embarrassingly naked.

Clinton millionaires built exquisite homes along Bluff Boulevard, where they looked over the city and the Mississippi. These grand manors were Old English, California Mission, Nantucket, and plain and fancy American architecture of the period. You can still see the touch of Frank Lloyd Wright, Louis Sullivan, and other distinguished architects in this cavalcade of homes. Estates were also constructed in what would become the central business district. These were eventually transformed into apartment houses or home to such places as the YWCA, Women's Club, and the American Legion.

The "Gay Nineties" represented a post-Civil War national economic boom. The so-called "Robber Barons" of John D. Rockefeller in crude oil and railroads, and Andrew Carnegie in coal and steel controlled the pulse of the national economy. The government did its part in this wealth creation by subsidizing railroads and allowing the formation of huge monopolies such as Standard Oil and U.S. Steel. This economic imbalance led to the panic of 1884 and 1893, followed by deep economic recessions. These national downturns failed to touch Clinton and its lumber industry. But in 1895, a year before the national Depression, Clinton, now a city of 22,000, shrunk to 16,000 overnight. The vast forests of Minnesota and Wisconsin were exhausted. Sawmills were idle. Clinton was a one-industry town, and in a state of collapse.

Leading the departure were the lumber barons. These tycoons once employed as many as 22 servants per household, and often served 9-course luncheons in their spatial gardens to a score or more of guests. They maintained luxurious entertainment boats on the Mississippi, and also flagged their cultural interests by building an opera house, a solarium, a museum, and botanical garden. Once the boom turned to bust, these vessels and manors stood deserted like naked ladies on stage without an audience, testimony to a passing era.

The few industrialists who stayed regrouped and rebuilt Clinton into a factory town. The lords of the manor became the corporate lobbyist, their servants the new factory working class. Gold was no longer in sawdust, but in dirt and grime, cold steel and hot lead, kernel corn and synthetic chemical, and finished wood products. The Joyce family continued the Joyce Lumber Company. W. E. Young stayed and pursued a number of interests including The Clinton Herald, building the Y.M.C.A., and applying his influence to the building of schools, churches, the Clinton Library, and a new post office building. C. F. Curtis stayed to create a sash factory turning out doors, blinds, moldings and windows from lumber and marketing these products around the world. Jane and Chancy Lamb stayed to build a hospital, create Chancy Park, and bequest to the city the most magnificent vista of all, Eagle Point Park. This park sits on a series of bluffs hanging out over the Mississippi four miles north of Clinton. W. F. Coan stayed to solidify the banking business to finance all these conversions, and to provide the real estate for Clinton High School and the football field and stadium that now carry his name. These men also lobbied for bridges to span the Mississippi at the north and south end of the city connecting Lyons and Clinton to Illinois.

Venture capitalists followed. Clinton Corn Processing Company was established at the turn of the century on 42 acres. Eventually, "the Clinton Company," or "Sugar Refinery," as it was known, would consist of 80 buildings with some 1,500 employees. It took Iowa's bountiful corn crop, and processed it into corn sugar, corn syrup, cornstarch, feed for livestock, hops for beer, and alcohol in the production of gin and bourbon. Central Steel & Tube Company, O. D. Collis Company, Iten Biscuit Company, Climax Company, Interstate Power Company, the Clinton Water Works, Bridge & Iron Works, North Western Railroad Repair Shops, Pillsbury Mills, Dupont, and many other industries, would combine to rejuvenate Clinton as a bustling blue-collar factory town, primed, decades later, to make a major contribution to the war effort, when the United States entered World War II.

At the same time, an attractive downtown business district was emerging. This included the architecturally splendor of Van Allen Department Store, the Wilson Building, the Howe Building, and Ankeny Building, U. S. Post Office, YMCA, and an assortment of other retail chains including Montgomery Ward, Sears & Roebucks, J. C. Penny's, Grant's, Walgreen's, Kline's, as well as local retailers including McKinley & Hummelgaard, Volckman's Furniture, Rose Gift Shop, Martin Morris clothier, to name only a few.

The years 1942-1947, when I was a boy, Clinton was a blooming, booming city to an otherwise placid countryside. World War II, like the rest of the nation, put Clinton in high gear with full employment. Goods were scarce but the stores were still open on Saturday nights and loaded with shoppers. During the Christmas season, Van Allen's was decorated to be the envy of Saks Fifth Avenue, and the street lamps of the city were covered in festive holly. Clinton had purpose and was no longer self-conscious. It was a joy from my earliest memory to walk down Second Street from the courthouse past the A&P Super Market, Machael's Auto Shop and Grill, where they made the most humongous hamburgers in the world, past Bender's Music Store, the Strand Theater, Rastrelli's Candy Shop, Boegel's Men's Wear, turning the corner at Van Allen's and heading for the cookie counter of Grant's on Fifth Avenue South. I would lift the lid on shortening bread cookies, scoop up ten cents worth, pay for them, and spend the rest of the day in heaven. I have searched the world for this golden taste to no avail.

Those who stayed were also the force behind the creation downtown of DeWitt and Clinton Park. These parks, with their diagonal walks through square blocks, landscaped with giant walnut, spruce and elms, and ornamental shrubs, with comfortable benches along the walkways, further complemented by recreational areas for children of slides and swings, and adorned throughout with antique globe street lamps gave sanctuary to young and old in the heart of the city. Spanning westward beyond the downtown to the bluff were little courts in side streets which were carefully landscaped, and adorned with globe lamps. Clinton took pride in wearing its Sunday best every day. Still, the most crowning achievement, and legacy of the lumber barons is the Clinton County Courthouse.

This majestic Romanesque structure cost only $168,000 when it was built in 1897. It remains an awesome spectacle to this day with little change to its exterior in over a century. The stately Dutch elms of the city are gone. Most of Clinton and DeWitt Park have been turned into parking lots. Downtown Clinton is scarred with empty stores, vacant buildings, and bereft of shoppers but with plenty of parking. The trees that stood as regal markers to a nostalgic past have been reduced to stumps along the main business district. Van Allen's still stands grandly in defiance of time, but with only an occasional transient occupant. Even the stately Lafayette Hotel has been reduced to a tenement house mainly for Clinton's defeated.

Once when I was about ten, doing my "Clinton walk," I came across a dapper elderly gentleman who was having difficulty opening the large double doors to the Lafayette Hotel. I rushed up and grabbed it open for him. He was dressed in a three-piece gray suit and wore light gray spats on his black shoes. I had never seen spats before. "One day, young man," he said, "I hope some young man will hold this door for you." Alas, there is no longer a door to hold.

Clinton's population has been steadily declining, yet, Clinton County has seen fit to construct a concrete behemoth, the Clinton County-City Law Enforcement Center on the courthouse grounds, the playground of my youth. In a half century, Clinton's law enforcement is many times what it was in 1945. The Clinton County Courthouse is the only talisman that remains of Clinton's halcyon days. The modernization within the courthouse has not diminished its timeless façade. It is a giant knight of Red Indian Pipestone and Minnesota granite with its grand central tower rising 150 feet waiting for Clinton to reconnect to it.

Its shadow is like the arms of Zeus stretching out to protect all that it touches. The courthouse bells sing the praises to all who would hear. It is stability in the midst of madness, timelessness in the midst of senseless frenzy, frozen music in the midst of confusion, a sanctuary for all those within its shadow. It is what is left of Clinton's poetry.

Clinton's magnificent seven-mile long waterfront is one of the longest and most attractive on the Mississippi. Because it isn't attached to the river the way some cities are, there aren't the docks and wharves and rotting boat hulks, which typify river cities. In mid-to-late-1970s Clinton demonstrated prescience. A $20 million flood protection dike was built, along with a boat marina, and the riverfront was renovated and beautified. This included decks for looking at the river, the construction of paved roads and sidewalks along the waterfront. The once state-of-the-art municipal swimming pool was modified to Olympic standards. Little League, Pony League and Babe Ruth League fenced in fields were constructed with a central clubhouse. Riverview Stadium, an imposing relic of WPA construction of the Depression era, one of the best-designed minor league ballparks in the United States, was given a face-lift. Riverview Park was re-landscaped with fountains and flowers, along with stretches of comely greens for casual strolling. A glimmering pavilion for outdoor concerts completed the renovation.

Yet, immediately west of the Riverfront, a reminder of a broken past, sits the vacant Bridge & Iron Works. Its face is pockmarked with broken windows; its shoulders crumbling with rusted girders and peeling brick supports. Perhaps to escape the omen of impotence sits a gaudily painted gambling boat at the Riverfront Dock, and along side this garish lady a showboat theater, reminiscent of when the city brought some of the most celebrated thespians to its shores including Clinton's own comic opera star, Lillian Russell, who once performed "Wildfire" in the Clinton Theatre.

Another glimpse into Clinton's past represents something of an anomaly. Duke Slater was Clinton's all-state (1916) football player, all-American at Iowa (1917-1921), all pro as a Chicago Cardinal (1927-1931) football player in the National Football League, and later a Chicago judge. Duke was a black man in a community that was 98 percent white, making himself conspicuous as Clinton's first great student-scholar-athlete. African Americans, or Negroes as they were then known, were largely confined to a three-block area from North Second to North Fourth Street and Second Avenue North, popularly known as Maple Avenue. Once all Clinton streets had tree designations, but only Maple Avenue has survived as such.

Clinton has never considered itself a segregated city, but in my recollection of the mid-20th century, Negroes worked in no Clinton factories, were clerks in no Clinton stores, never swam at the Clinton municipal pool, never ate in Clinton restaurants, never attended Clinton movie houses, and only worked on the railroad as porters. Negroes were invisible to my experience as a boy.

More visible were Clinton's own Felix Adler, the famous Ringling Brothers and Barnum & Bailey (1919-1946) clown, Marquis Childs, Washington, DC author, columnist, and Pulitzer Prize winner, and commencement speaker at my 1951 high school graduation. From the Courthouse neighborhood there was Kenny Ploen, all-state high school football and basketball player, high school state indoor high hurdle champion, member of the National Honor Society at Clinton High, Nile Kinnick scholarship winner and all-American at Iowa (1956), most valuable player in the 1957 Rose Bowl, graduate civil engineer, and all-pro and Hall of Fame Canadian football player.

Ploen and Slater were Clinton's greatest athlete-scholars, but there were others, several from the courthouse area including Philip Leahy, the first Clinton Nile Kinnick scholar-athlete, Larry Jacubsen, who attended Brown University on a full scholarship, and Dick Farwell, one of the few Clinton scholar-athletes to remain in Clinton, now as a prominent attorney.

This picture of Clinton is not complete without a sense of what it is like to enter the city from the south today. Clinton gives the impression of entering a Martian movie set, as many plants and businesses now stand like abandoned stage props. There is E. I du Pont de Nemours chemical and plastics plant, which once employed more than a 1,000 workers, but now operates with a skeleton crew. There is Hawkeye Chemical, whose pastel colored pipes and twisting tubes and cylinder tanks once pulsated like heartbeats in orange expectorating clouds, which now stands cold and quiet. Colored gases still spew out from the needlepoint towers at Nitrin, Inc., but for how long? Then you come to Clinton's Miracle Mile with Wal-Mart, Food-Mart and other retailers packed together like sardines in a can with no sense of aesthetics. No sooner are you past this and Archer-Daniels looms ahead, bellowing out white clouds of steam and its endemic perfume, cooking corn, seemingly operating in a twilight zone independent of time, place or circumstance. They place a different name on the marquee of this plant – Clinton Company, Clinton Industries, Clinton Foods, Standard Brands, ADM -- but little else changes except efficiency. It once employed more than a 1,000, but now processes twice as many bushels of corn daily with less than 400 workers. Tomorrow, with robotics and genetic engineering, who knows? It may operate without anyone.

Next you snake your way down Camanche Avenue past what was once the gleaming Chicago & North Western Shops, employing 2,000 workers, now bulldozed from memory creating an empty landscape. Then you enter downtown Clinton so empty to remind you of an abandoned movie set.

Clinton once had expectations of rivaling Chicago. The gold proved to be sawdust. Then the sawdust disappeared and the industrial revolution settled in these quiet confines, fortuitously accelerated by WWII, followed by industrial and commercial expansion during the post-war boom. That boom peaked in 1970 and Clinton, like many other communities across the nation, has failed to find its role in a post-industrial post-modern world. It has forgotten its strength and continues to mimic American society-at-large. Once it was unique and listened to its own drummer. Now the music is dying and Clinton is dying with it. The irony is I write here about one small neighborhood in this community, the courthouse area, at mid-century when it got it right. That community has produced lawyers, doctors, engineers, teachers, scientists, authors, entrepreneurs, executives, coaches, athletes, and community builders, but nearly always moving elsewhere to ply their talents. Clinton's most important product was then and continues to be its young people. Ky

47

Petersen and his deputies once had the right formula but nobody noticed. I hope this little story brings attention to this oversight.

*   *   *   *   *

Chapter 5

The Given Field

Cultivate the field that has been given to you.

--Leos Janacek

Moving so much, stability was foreign to me while native to Bobby Witt. I took nothing for granted while he was content with what met the naked eye. That comes from having roots. A boy belongs to where he is. It is who he is. Bobby was reared in a secure society. Not me. A boy without roots exists in exile surrounded by people. What we had in common was our Irish heritage. His mother had roots going back to the old country, as did both my parents. Every culture has its own gravity. It hugs people to its shores. My mother knew we did not have this luxury. I had to create my own gravity within, discover my own roots, because they did not exist without.

"Imagine," my mother once said, "that you were dropped from heaven in a foreign country fully grown. What would you do to survive? That my darling is your quandary."

Bobby would get a puzzled look on his face whenever I waxed serious. His mother must not talk this way. I wondered if it was the smoking. Mother said smoking helped her think. Bobby's mother didn't smoke.

"Fisher, why're you always so serious?" he would say in honest bewilderment.

I didn't know that I was. Just noticed stuff, and felt inclined to talk about it. That's all. What made that serious? He talked about baseball, didn't he? Well, I talked about stuff, like roots, but only with him.

We were supposed to be playing in the sunshine of our youth with no need to distinguish between necessity and freedom. This was a time of innocence. I took little solace in that. Nothing was certain, everything a splendid surprise. From the first moment, I fell in love with the courthouse and told Bobby so.

"You're kidding?" he said in disbelief. "It's just a building, an old building at that. How can you love a building?"

It was a good question. I didn't know why. The courthouse gave me a kind of peace, a kind of warmth like my mother's hug. It was strong and tall and there, always there. Besides, it was beautiful. It was God made visible in splendid wonder. Not a *He God* like in church, but a *thing god* that I could see, feel and touch, and talk to as I walked by. I couldn't tell Bobby this. He'd only laugh.

Bobby was born here. His whole life was here. He was born on April Fool's day, had a big brother, Vernon, who was older and wiser. So, he didn't have to figure stuff out for himself. He was treated like an only child. Not me, I was the eldest of four, doted on by my mother, taken to task by my da. Funny, too, I was born in April, but at the end of the month. I guess that made us sort of twins.

Bobby wanted to know why I hadn't been back to the courthouse to play baseball. I made the excuse we were not quite settled. It was partially true. I was surprised he didn't notice when I watched them play as I passed by. Closer to the truth, everything was new, wonderful, so exciting that I had to take it all in little by little. I didn't say this because Bobby would think it stupid.

School had been out for a week, but he had eyes only for playing baseball, even though the courthouse grounds were soggy and the air still held a chill. It was late May. May in Iowa is seldom warm. Didn't matter to him. He would eat breakfast and be to the courthouse by eight, take a fifteen minute break at noon for lunch, which his mother always had waiting, back to the courthouse until five, home again for a waiting dinner, which he gulped down in fifteen minutes, and back to the courthouse until dark. Once home for the night, Bobby would oil his glove, polish his fungo, re-tape his damaged balls with black tape, look at his baseball cards, and read his sports magazines. He had an encyclopedic knowledge of every major league baseball player, including their statistics, even knew about key minor league players. The Clinton Giants were as familiar to him as family. The only thing that interrupted this devotion was church. Bobby would go to confession with his mother, and then attend Novenas on Friday nights. I know because I would go with my mother and see him there. Novenas were held on nine consecutive Fridays as a devotion to our Blessed Virgin Mother. The Oblate Fathers conducted these services. These missionary priests would go from parish to parish about the country. My da loved these priests. They traveled on his trains, and, as he put it, "Were regular guys." They had their silver flasks of whiskey, smoked cigarettes, told off-colored jokes "like real men," and "weren't wimps like parish priests." My mother, listening to such bravado, would take quick puffs on her cigarette, but say nothing. She revered all priests.

Later, she was apt to say, "Don't mind your father. It's his Catholic pride showing only he doesn't know it."

Bobby didn't listen to the *Ave Maria Hour* on the radio, which surprised me. It came on Wednesday nights at 7 p.m., and was a different story each week about a priest, brother, or nun. I loved these stories. They spoke to my heart. Bobby couldn't listen because his father had *Amos and Andy* on instead. That wasn't a problem in my house as my mother controlled the radio dial.

Saturday morning Bobby and his mother would go to 7:30 Mass and Communion, and repeat the practice on Sunday morning at 8 o'clock Mass. The rest of the week belonged to baseball at the courthouse. Like my da, Bobby's father never went to Mass. "Lax Catholics" was my mother's term. We had a lot of them in the family. Only uncle Leonard of my mother's six brothers ever attended Mass.

Bobby never wondered about religious stuff like I did. I asked my mother what *oblate* meant. She said it was an order of priests. I looked it up in the dictionary. It said they didn't have to be priests. They could be laymen living in a monastery. She scoffed at that. "Jimmy, trust me, they're priests." And that was the end of that.

Still, I wondered why Oblate Fathers had to conduct Novenas. Why didn't Father Finefield? She would ignore the question as if she didn't hear it. Her hearing was bad, but always better when she wanted it to be.

I was wary of priests and was convinced I wouldn't like Father Finefield any better than Father Sunbrueller. And I was right. Father Finefield talked about money with the same scary passion Father Sunbrueller talked about hell.

"Why does Father read family contributions at the gospel?" I asked Bobby.

"That's what priests do," he replied, "ask for money. That's their job."

The reading embarrassed me. Worse than that, it humiliated me. We were poor but Father didn't have to broadcast it. I hated him for doing that. I've never gotten over being self-conscious about being poor. We gave so little in the Sunday offertory collection because we had so little, but the world didn't need to know it. We were always the last name read out of more than 100 families. I told Bobby this. He didn't notice. Bobby's folks didn't give much more. He could care less. Rather than discuss this, he would change the subject. "I can't wait 'til I'm a little bigger and can scale the fence at Riverview Stadium to see the Giants," he exclaimed excitedly. The stadium was only three blocks east of the courthouse in Riverview Park. Sneaking into a game meant paradise to him.

"Next year when I'm a lot bigger like you are now," he said looking at me with awe. "How tall are you?" I was five-three, two inches taller than my mother, four inches shorter than my da. "Boy! I'll bet you could sneak in without any trouble." Then a look of doubt. "You'd have to climb the fence. You a good fence climber?"

What a question! I'd never climbed a fence in my life, never thought about climbing a fence, and fence climbing didn't appeal to me now. I simply answered, "No."

"Too bad. You could go to the top of the bleachers and yell down what was happening. Guys would like that a lot. Tell us where the foul balls were going."

There was a constant war between ball shaggers, and kids from the courthouse going after foul balls that bounced into the stadium parking lot. A new ball was gold. So, the idea was to outfox the shaggers when one came our way. A chain developed with the surest handed kids positioned to retrieve the ball, guys like Dick Crider, Chuck Holm and Pooper Cavanaugh. They were stationed along the third and first base sides, and immediately behind the ticket office. This was directly behind home plate on the other side of the stadium bleachers. Balls would bounce off the stadium roof, hit the concrete and bounce over the fence and into the parking lot. Everyone would scramble for the ball, except the Courthouse Tigers. Behind the ball retrievers were the best glove guys – guys like Ken and Dick Tharp, Dick Dunmore, and Chang Benson -- and behind them were the runners, kids who could fly. Bobby was one of the flyers. Phil Leahy was another. They would high tail it with the ball for the courthouse jail, sprinting across the railroad tracks, up Sixth Avenue North past the A&W Root Beer Stand, across busy Second Street, making a mad dash for the jail basement as if being chased by a grizzly bear. The basement was on the east side of the jail at the corner of Third Street. They would deposit their booty and head for home. Shaggers knew who they were. Replacement runners would take up their positions and repeat the same whole scheme with the next foul ball.

Tom Clark, eleven, tall and strong for his age, once caught a foul ball on the fly and was immediately pursued by two fifteen year old shaggers, Dean Burridge and Dick Price. These guys were big, especially Price, and destined to be great Clinton High athletes. Tom was so scared he headed for sanctuary in St. Patrick's church more than four blocks away, getting there in record time. He kept the ball as a trophy to his valor.

The success ratio for retrieving foul balls was not good, even when balls were hidden under car axles in the parking lot, or thrown into the vacant field north of the stadium where rats as big as cats rummaged through city garbage. Shaggers were diligent and even brave searching in the dark for balls in the garbage dump. They made a quarter for every ball returned to the ball boy. A quarter was a lot of money. You could buy a baseball for a dollar. Shaggers regarded the courthouse gang as a nuisance. They couldn't do much about them though. They were as thick as mosquitoes.

The next generation of courthouse guys adopted a different strategy, 'If you can't beat them join them!' Thiel Collins, Dave Petersen, Marv Allendar, and Dick Tharp became shaggers. Every third ball they would appropriate for the courthouse. No one seemed to notice, until Officer Cy Robb got into the act. Cy Robb, an Irish cop, as tall as God, and ugly as sin policed the stadium. He caught Thiel pocketing a ball, and immediately expropriated it with this terrifying revelation, "By the way, lad, you're on the police blotter." Thiel didn't do much shagging after that. He wondered when the police would come to his house, handcuff him, and take him off to jail. Turns out Officer Robb was having his fun.

These night baseball games were 8 to 11 p.m. affairs, hardly the time you would expect ten, eleven, and twelve-year-olds to be out, but they were. Some were even younger. I was not one of them. I was on a much shorter leash. Besides, the thought of shagging balls had no appeal to me. Baseball, which was Bobby's life, would take some time before it would become mine. My interest was in exploring my new world. When I confessed this ambition to my mother, she said, "Fine, long as you're in the shadow of the courthouse."

"What's that supposed to mean?"

She poked me gently in the ribs. "Don't look so worried. Long as you can see the faces of the courthouse clock, you're fine." Then a caution. "No excuse for being home late, that's all."

With this in mind, I was able to explore a good bit of Clinton. I started with the neighborhood, but eventually went nearly to Lyons and as far as South Clinton, up to the bluff and down to the Mississippi waterfront. Places interested me more than people. Wariness of people comes from my mother's cautions.

"Generosity," she would say, "is a vice haves use to control have nots. In a just world, generosity is not necessary. So be leery of persons who pity or compliment you too much. You have the size and the innocent looks haves like to corrupt, and I fear you love the compliment. Know this, Jimmy, haves think themselves superior to you with a right to manipulate you to their ends, not yours."

It intrigued me when she talked like this. I would tingle as her words bounced off me. I never quite understood why, but they were said with such evenness they seemed like laws. She believed, too, that it was better to be insulted, ignored, or treated badly than to be pitied. I also took this to heart. It has kept me at a safe distance from people, but not from their world. I would look at a house and imagine the people inside.

Take Bobby's house. It was small, smaller than my own, which wasn't big as houses go. Bobby's house looked squeezed into a corner lot as if it didn't belong. It had no yard, was dark inside, the rooms so small that I felt claustrophobic, especially in his room, which was little bigger than a closet; was hard to imagine four people living there. None of this seemed to concern Bobby. Quite the contrary, it fit him. Bobby was the picture of contraction. He was small, quiet, and never gave a clue as to what he was thinking. He was well liked, even admired, with a modest disposition, so why shouldn't he live in a modest house on a modest corner by the courthouse?

The alley behind Bobby's was intriguing. Art Sheller, a garage mechanic, ran an ambulance-hearse service and automobile repair shop. The Sheller backyard was a menagerie of funeral hearses, ambulances, and automobiles in various states of health. Art Jr., who looked about fifteen, built like his father, short, muscular, and dark, was working on a wheel, and was covered with grease. Marilyn, who was my sister's age, looked at me defiantly. Her look said, 'You don't belong here!' She had fiery auburn hair and was built like a Sherman tank. I smiled, but it was not returned.

Bobby had forewarned me about her. "She terrorizes the boys who cross her and has a temper to match. Avoid her if you can." Only little Eddie Sheller was friendly, and he was a fixture at the courthouse.

Next door to Bobby's house lived the Kinney's, who were active in Democratic politics and friends of sheriff Petersen. Mrs. Kinney was always baking pies and bringing them over to the sheriff and his deputies. The Kinney's house was painted yellow. The house was cheerful and chubby like its occupants, and their two chubby children,

Don and Rosemary. Next door to the Kinney's were the Jakubsen's. Mr. Jakubsen was a huge, muscular man with a roaring Germanic voice, with a pretty diminutive wife. He would sit on the open porch of his two-story gray stucco house in an undershirt, looking as hairy and menacing as a black bear. He wore his house like a shirt. The black trimmed shuttered windows above the porch seemed like a second set of eyes staring down as he called to his three young sons to get their asses home, pronto, always in German. No matter what the boys were doing, batting, catching balls, running the bases, or talking, they would sprint across the street as if their pants were on fire.

Next to the Jakubsen's were the Leahy's. The Leahy's also had three sons, two much older than the youngest, Phil, the only one I actually knew well. The Leahy's lived in the nicest house in the neighborhood, a two-and-one-half story contemporary designed white aluminum-sided structure that spoke efficiency, economy, and utility of style. Aluminum siding was new. It was the "in" kind of construction, if you could afford it, because it was weather resistant. Iowa weather would eat wood and paint for breakfast. The house didn't belong. It was different, better. I learned Phil was like his house.

"Ray," my mother wondered, "how can the Leahy's afford that place?" My da without looking up from his newspaper answered, "Dorothy, I expect because they can."

Da wasn't competitive. Mother was. It was always a kind of race to her, but when she handed the baton off to him, he invariably dropped it -- the story of the Fisher's. It was not to be my fate if she could help it.

Phil, like Bobby, was always at the courthouse, or sitting on Bobby's front stoop tossing a ball in the air. Bobby treated him like a kid brother. Phil was small and wiry with tight blond curly hair, a strong angular face, but his eyes were different. His eyes were hardly the eyes of a boy. They had too much control. He was like Bobby yet different. With Bobby what you saw is what you got. Phil held surprise. It was unmistakable. All you had to do is look. The rhythm, balance and humor were there, but also the resolve. Such people may be alone but never lonely. Their own company energizes them. They focus without trying, and have drive without being driven. Playfulness is the source of freedom. This enables them to lead without being in charge.

Phil wasn't a talker, and blended into whatever was going on. As an athlete, he was quick, fast and agile. Like Bobby, in addition to being bright, he had sports intelligence, something that I never acquired. Sports intelligence is animal intelligence. It taps that nine-tenths buried in the subconscious and is employed instantly with skill. Animal intelligence was on display at the courthouse in choosing up sides. The one whose grip was at the top of the bat always chose the best player, and the best player was too busy being a player to think about it. Thinking is the great separator of players of equal ability. The best players always left their thinking caps at home. Chang Benson, who would eat a handful of dirt to give him inspiration, or chase a fly ball into the gravel parking lot barefooted, was always chosen high in the draw because he would come through in the clutch.

We even had a funeral home in the neighborhood, Ugarph Funeral Home, across the street from the courthouse. It was a white ominous wood structure with a veranda in mock colonial style, which for some reason found me always making the Sign of the Cross as I past by. I would scrunch my face down into my neck, making a quick rotation of my hand in the sign, hoping no one noticed. I couldn't fool Bobby.

"What you doing?" Bobby said one day in astonishment. "You're only supposed to do that when you go by a Catholic church. That's crazy. Bet it's a sacrilege."

"I know," I conceded, totally embarrassed getting caught.

"Well, why do you do it then?"

"I don't know. Just do." It disappointed me when I failed Bobby's tests. Bobby seldom pressed me to explain what I couldn't, even when he disapproved.

We had gas stations galore in the neighborhood. Across from the courthouse on one corner was the Conoco; across from it was the Coryal Gas Station with a little grocery. Alice Kiefer worked there. Down the block on the opposite corner was a Shell Station, operated by Darrell Smith's dad. Young Smitty would become in his adult life an active community leader, including stints as city councilman and mayor of Clinton. We even had Standard Oil at Third Street and Seventh Avenue, if you can believe that. Elmer Eads ran it. He hated kids. His station was directly in line with foul balls hit over the screen at home plate on the courthouse diamond. He would never return balls. We'd have to beg him for them. If every neighborhood has to have its Ebenezer Scrooge, he was ours. The next generation of Courthouse Tigers was lucky. Al Ploen and Gordy Goetzel ran the station. They loved kids. Not only did they gladly return foul balls, they often gave the guys free cokes on hot days. The neighborhood must have been a kind of gas station Mecca with few families owning automobiles and wartime gasoline rationing vigorously enforced. There seems no other explanation.

Borman's grocery next-door to the Conoco was a place where Mr. Borman always gave us more than our five cents worth of Strippers. Most of us didn't have enough money to go across the street to the A&W Root Beer Stand, the best root beer in the world. Next to the A&W was a two-story building, The Burpee Seed Company. It sold seeds around the world. Many mothers worked part-time there during the war.

Next door to Borman's were the Dean Apartments. My great aunt and uncle Annie and Martin Dean lived there. They owned the building and the Dean Roofing Company, the largest industrial roofers in Clinton. I lived with them until I was four. Uncle Mart took me daily to Harvey Sullivan's tavern down the block to have an Orange Crush, while aunt Annie let me color The Clinton Herald comics with my crayons. Next door to Sullivan's tavern was Frank Cramm's grocery. It was one of my daily chores to shop there for my mother.

Seeing the Dean Apartments again and looking up at the second story bay window, I recalled how five years earlier I would stand there, looking into the darkness, tears streaming down my cheeks, hoping my da would appear. He seldom did. I didn't know my mother, only him, and him not well. Aunt Annie had told me my mother was in hospital, and that my little sister, Patsy, whom I adored, was staying with "Aunt Sadie," a foster parent. To add further confusion, I was told I had a little brother, Jackie, whom I had never seen. He was living with my aunt Helen and uncle Frank, my mother's brother and sister-in-law in Chancy Park.

As these twisted memories surfaced, I rushed behind the Conoco station, and down the alley, and looked up at the belvedere, the open-sided roofed terrace of the Dean building. It was still as I had remembered. Then I turned and looked back at the courthouse. It all came back! The courthouse was not new to me! It was an old friend. As a four-year-old, I would venture on to this flat tarpapered roof and sit, alone, sometimes for hours in the sun, sometimes in the rain, even when it was cold, snow brushing my cheeks, studying the green dome of the courthouse as my only company, listening to its bells on the half hour, watching the hands of the clock move in staccato bursts, not wanting to ever leave. I didn't know how to tell time. Strangely, time has never been an important dimension to me.

Aunt Annie and uncle Martin, both fragile and not too mobile, never discovered my hiding place. Nor did I share this revelation with my mother. I understood without clearly knowing why that it would be too painful. When I made my neighborhood report to her, she purred, "Irish and German? Your father will be pleased."

He was more than pleased with the neighborhood. He was delighted. Howard Judd, the legendary swimming coach at Clinton High, was our next-door neighbor. His swimmers were some of the best in the nation. "Dorothy, Juddy didn't have it handed to him on a silver platter. He's a self-made man."

Self-made man. I wondered what it meant. I asked my mother while she was cooking dinner. She was boiling the noodles for my favorite, spaghetti and meatballs.

"Means he wasn't born with a silver spoon in his mouth." When I looked puzzled, she added. "He's like your uncle Leonard. Len's a self-made man but he's far more than a coach. Don't mind your father. He's impressed with men like Howard Judd."

I was torn between hearing more, and savoring my favorite dish. The aroma was competing with the smoke from her cigarette on the windowsill. It wasn't her way to leave it at that. She put a plate over the spaghetti, turned the burner to simmer, pulled out a kitchen chair, sat down, took her cigarette from the ashtray, now little more than an ash, lit another with it, then studied the twirling smoke as it rose to the ceiling.

"Don't worry your little head about such things."

"What do you mean?"

"Inside the self-made man what do you have? Nothing. Just talk. Ever hear anyone speak of a self-made woman?" Before I could answer she added, "I don't think so."

She studied her cigarette. She hadn't taken a drag on it, just watched it burn. "Jimmy, everyone is self-made who isn't born with a silver spoon in his mouth. That is what to remember."

"That's me?"

"That's you, my darling," she said, followed by a deep throaty chuckle. She inhaled her cigarette so deeply her eyes watered. "That's you." She wiped her eyes with her apron as she exhaled her head disappearing in its mist. "Everything you learn belongs to you. Nobody else. Don't listen to all that noise about self-made this or that. Listen to yourself. Trust what it tells you. Let others worry about being self-made or not. Now scoot so I can finish making dinner."

Outside, coach Judd was playing with his dog, Butch. He called to the dog hunched over the ground with flailing arms, "Come here boy! Come!" And the dog raced to him like shot out of a cannon. Butch was built close to the ground, a mixed breed, and delighted in the play. Coach Judd would step aside, like a matador, and Butch would fly by, skid to a halt, then roar back. The coach would wail with laughter, "If only I had a halfback like you, Butch," he mused, "no one could touch us." He also coached the sophomore football team. The coach's throaty laugh rumbled up from deep inside his diaphragm, scaring me a bit. He was the most powerfully built man I had ever seen. Yet, his wife Elsie who was watching this from the sidewalk with a warm smile was as thin as a rail. Coach Judd put me at ease as he laced his arm through his wife's and walked back into the house.

Next-door to the Judd's, across the alley, and on the corner of Third Street was a large white-framed house with an even larger garage. It was a Harley-Davidson motorcycle shop, and Bill Greaves was a motorcycle hobbyist. Saturday mornings there would be bikers revving up their engines with bikes splayed across the driveway, alley, and yard. The noise was deafening.

North of the Greaves across from the jail lived the Neumann's, cousins of the Judd's. Bill and Dorothy were older and Bob and Betty younger than I was. I remember Dorothy well. One day she gave me a whipping I'd never had before, and she was a girl! It was for something I'd said about her brother Bob. Never said an unkind word about him again. The good part, if there is a good part, is that she told no one and let the beating even the score. Her father worked at the Chicago & North Western Car Shops with my Uncle Arne.

Across the street from Bobby's was the plumber Herb Jaeger. He had his plumbing shop in his garage. Next door lived the Sparlin's. There were so many Sparlin girls that I never could keep track of their names. One day I saw one of the girls running. I had never seen a boy run that fast. I actually believed she could beat Bobby. When I mentioned this, he stated the obvious, "She a girl," as if that were enough said.

Across the street from the Judd's were the Lahm's. Kenny Lahm was one of coach Judd's swimmers. Mr. Lahm was a house painter and taxidermist. And across the street from us were the Johansson's. They were retired. Their son, Norman, an outstanding athlete, was in the service with the three-corner flag in the window proudly announcing this.

My other next-door neighbors were the Lange's. Walt was a milkman for Elmwood Dairy. Two doors down were the Jensen's, retired, with a son George. He was afflicted with infantile paralysis, and ran the elevator at Van Allen's Department Store. A delightful person, he never talked down to me. He was the best-read person in the neighborhood, and never made me feel dumb asking stupid questions like, "Who was Shakespeare? Why read someone dead?"

George would smile, breathe deeply, and say, "Shakespeare tells us who we are. Why read him? Because we must."

"We must?"

"Yes. Otherwise, we will never understand the human heart."

It is strange how little morsels like this stick to the mind like flies to fly paper. It was late July 1942, and I was still in summer school at St. Pat's. Bobby thought it the dumbest thing he'd ever heard of, going to school when you didn't have to. I had to agree. "Bobby thinks it's dumb to spend your whole summer in school when you don't have to," I whined when I got home. My mother paused, stopped putting food away in the icebox.

"So, your friend owns your mind. Well, I must congratulate him. How much did he pay you? A dollar? Two dollars? What?"

"What do you mean?"

"What do I mean? What do you think I mean?"

"I don't know."

"Well, that's quite apparent. Think, young man, why did I say you were going to summer school? Do you remember our discussion?"

"To get a jump start on other kids."

"Well, well, you do remember."

"But why do I have to get a jump start?"

"Because ... now help me ... because ... what?"

"Because I don't have a silver spoon in my mouth?"

She hugged me, kissed the top of my head, and then dismissed me. "Go and explore and tell me what is different about your new home." She knew this was the perfect balm to my angst. I loved exploring.

Okay. We had always been renters. This was our first real home. So, what was special? I decided to start outside. I walked from the Judd's property line to where the Lange's started -- sixty-four feet. Then I walked from the front curb to the alley -- 110 feet. The house was forty-feet wide, and the yard twenty-four feet to the Judd's. The Judd's house hugged our property line like the Lange's did. A delicious apple tree was outside the dining room window. Directly behind the house were currant bushes, a small asparagus patch, immediately behind that a crab apple tree. A crumbling cement walk divided the back yard symmetrically. Intertwined grape vines of green and purple grapes lined the west side of the walk and ended at a chicken coop. This was nestled against the alley. Across the walk was a one-car garage, a white wooden framed building badly in need of repair. We had no automobile, and my da wouldn't have the remotest idea what to do with chickens, much less a chicken coop. But there it was.

The chicken coop fascinated me. It was large and well constructed, better than the garage, with roosting bins for hens row on row, tier on tier. I knew nothing about farming. In fact, I had never been on a farm. With the happy prospects of not having to collect eggs or tend chickens, I envisioned this as my secret place. I could keep my comic books here, put pictures of my comic heroes on the wall, and write down my secret codes. I could make a small altar to the Blessed Virgin Mary and not be criticized. I looked around. The place was a mess. It smelled like rotten eggs. It would take work to clean it up, but that would be fun. I decided to name it *Nicodemas* in honor of my dog that died when I lived in Lyons.

A plum tree was directly in front of the chicken coop, and a pear tree in front of the garage. Imagine an orchard, a garden, a vineyard, and a hen house on such a small place. I laughed. My da, born in south Chicago, couldn't tell a rooster from a hen, but neither could I.

My new home was a one-and-one-half story white clapboard box-like house with a green-shingled pitched roof and a screened-in porch, ten years old and cost $3,000. Now more than seventy years after being built, people still live in it and it looks better than ever. But the chicken coop, garage, grapevines, fruit trees, and garden are gone, replaced by a two-car garage.

The house was small with many rooms – four bedrooms, formal living and dining room, kitchen, bathroom, and full basement. The basement was dank with steep steps, a low ceiling, even too low for me, opening into a large washroom for doing laundry, with a dividing wall for a fruit cellar to store homemade canned goods. The next room was the furnace room and adjoining it was the coal bin, which was under the front porch. To the right of it was an empty room for storage, which was under the master bedroom. The basement had no workbench, lathe, carpenter saw, electric drill, or any other tools. We were lucky to have a hammer, screwdriver and pliers.

The small bedroom downstairs was the radio room occupied by a reading lamp, a large padded sofa, a love seat, and a small credenza. My mother would read here while we children congregated around the radio. My da would be in the living room in his chaise lounge reading the newspaper, or taking a nap. When President Roosevelt was giving a "Fireside Chat," we all had to be as quiet as mice.

The master bedroom was out of bounds with a curtained glass door. I ventured into it anyway. It had a vanity dresser and mirror, a chest of drawers, a queen size bed, a reading lamp on one side of the bed, and ashtrays everywhere. What made the room special, however, were ceramic frescoes of Jesus and the Blessed Virgin Mother, gifts from the Sullivan's purchased in 1940 on a shopping trip to Chicago. The only defining thing in the living room, other than a three-seat sofa, two matching sofa chairs and a beat-up coffee table, with doilies on all, were framed pictures on the wall of President Franklin Delano Roosevelt and Pope Pius XII. Otherwise, the room was quite unremarkable. Leo Cavanaugh, who owned the Silver Rail Tavern, repapered the walls and I noticed that the patterns were crooked. Besides my mother's library books, there were no books, magazines or pictures. My favorite spot was the dining room table. It was mahogany, and large, nearly as large as the room itself with four mahogany chairs and a mahogany bureau. My mother had two Waterford crystal cut glass bowls and candlestick holders that were, along with the dining room set, inherited from her mother's small estate. I would sit and study the dictionary from this table with something approaching religious zeal.

"Language is the tool of the mind," my mother would say, "and since you think with words, you must master them if you are to think clearly. They are the only tools you will ever need, Jimmy. They are your silver spoon."

What started my affair with words was "aardvark." My mother was angry with me one day for breaking one of her crystal candlestick holders while I was dusting. When she saw what I had done, she said, "You don't have the sense of an aardvark." I was crushed feeling she had sworn at me. I was even more crushed when I looked up the word.

The kitchen was small and functional with country-style sink and faucet, with second hand furnishings, including a colonial style kitchen table and six chairs, an icebox and gas stove. Kitchen cupboards were built above the sink and a pantry beside the stove. I liked to stand beside my mother as she cooked and converse with her. She was especially serene when she was cooking.

As small as the kitchen was, the bathroom, which was off the kitchen, was smaller. The old fashioned tub with four legs was already too small for me. And the distance between it and the sink and mirror were no more than three feet, making the bathroom with two people in it more crowded than a phone booth.

The floors throughout the house were terrible, nothing but rough broad planks painted several times, either covered by linoleum or throw rugs. They were treacherous to bare feet; slivers were a common complaint.

When I think of the upstairs, I think of my siblings. It was practically the only place where we played together, throwing pillows, squirting each other with water pistols, or generally horsing around. It was our place to cut up. We never told on each other.

My brother Jackie and I shared the large bedroom facing the yard, while my two sisters shared the smaller bedroom facing the street. Furnishings were functional with double beds and small chests of drawers, a naked bulb in the ceiling in each room, no lamps, no pictures on the walls, and few toys. The girls had dolls but otherwise the rooms were Spartan.

It was a nightly ritual for my da to open the downstairs door and say good night. He was also checking to see if the lights were out. They always were. I acquired a small flashlight and I would read under the covers. There were occasions when he would open the door a second time as if he knew, and my heart would sink, but he never did. I would read to Jackie, sometimes Patsy would join us, especially when Janice was asleep. We would wait for da's "goodnight" before making a tent of the covers, then I would play teacher.

We were terrified of him, me more than the others, not because he hit us, which he never did, but because he was a shouter. You never knew when he would explode. It could be any time: at dinner, when mother was cleaning up the kitchen, when one of us said something, did something, or for no apparent reason at all. His mantra, "Jesus Christ Dorothy all I ask for is a little cooperation. Is that asking too much?" He would direct his anger at one of us, usually me, because I exasperated him the most. I didn't understand the irony of this until I had children, especially my boys.

Sometimes, he was justified. Once I was instructing my little brother how to do scissor jumping jacks. The downstairs door came crashing open. It was the middle of the day. The girls were playing in their room. The rafters shook with his bluster.

"Jesus Christ! What's going on up there? The ceilings about to cave in!"

Silence. We stopped our exercise. Nobody said anything. "Dorothy, hear that! That goddamn kid of yours! Jimmy, get your ass down here!" Silence.

About then, my mother intervened, who didn't hear a thing. "Someone must have fallen, Ray. Don't get your dander up. Leave them be. Isn't that right kids?"

Silence. Finally, Patsy would say, "Yes, mommy." And that would be it. Patsy was his favorite and the great appeaser. Thank God for her!

"If I hear any more of that racket, Jimmy, your ass is mine, hear me?"

Silence. Then the door would shut, and we would all tip toe around each other and snicker. "Adults!" I would say and mimic my da's roar. Janice, my little Honey-Bunny-Tinker-Fritzes, would purr like the year old baby she was.

Always a note taker, I had carefully written down my findings and anxious for praise, rushed into the kitchen to present my survey. She looked at it, tapped me on the head. "Good. I'm sure you covered everything. Keep it to yourself, one day you might find it useful." As I write these words, I think of her now. She never sat down and said to herself, 'This is what I mean to do for Jimmy today, tomorrow, next week, next month, next year.' She just did it. She had a plan without planning. It just came to her as she went along. She didn't feel the need to grade my exploits, just to get my fluids flowing. Would that I could say I did the same for my children, but I can't.

By summer school's end, I was still unknown at the courthouse. Even with the encouragement of Bobby, I still had to prove myself. That would take time.

* * * * *

Chapter 6

Translations and Transitions

He has turned into the life-giving ear of grain
Or into the gentlest rain of which he sang . . .

--Akhmatova

School is never out, was another saying of my mother. "You get a report card every day," she said. "Most generous grades come in school. Life is less obliging." She said this so often I had to finally challenge her to explain what she meant. With an electric gleam in her pale blue eyes, she pointed her cigarette at me. "Jimmy, Jimmy, don't you see the connection?" I didn't, especially when she pushes me to get grades, then turns around and tells me they don't count for much.

"Think a minute. What am I saying?"

67

I hated it when she did that. It was like taking a test. She studied my face as she puffed quietly on her cigarette. The smoke drifted above my clouded confusion.

"Do you think FDR was a great student?" I waited for her answer. "Well, he wasn't. But he's a great man." I nodded appropriately. "If polio had not struck him down as a young man," she looked dreamingly to the ceiling, blew a smoke ring into the air with rounded lips, "I wonder." Then continued. "While his 'A' student buddies at Harvard judged him as a guy with a first class temperament and second class mind, he was serving his country, acquiring experience, leaving his privileged class behind. He was embracing the American people. We would be lost in this war without him. Thank God for FDR!" I jumped as she stumped her cigarette out, then clapped her hands together like crashing cymbals. "Get A's, Jimmy, but for God's sake don't romance them. Love what you're doing. A man needs work. Otherwise, he'd fly away like a bird." She took a deep drag on her cigarette. "Hard enough holding a man to ground, I can tell you that. Remember, best moments of life are some kind of work. Choose it well. To follow someone else's ambition is to be enslaved to their demands."

St. Patrick's summer school was actually fun. Sister Mary Marguerite, the Fifth grade nun, was my summer school teacher. I was in a class with students of the fourth, fifth and sixth grade. Some students were there to acquire credits to win promotion to the next grade, others to make up deficiencies. The curriculum was more generic than grade specific: (1) Reading-Writing: had to read a biography of a saint of our choice, and make a book report; (2) Arithmetic: reviewed fractions, multiplication tables, long and short division, and participated in speed drills; (3) Spelling: had a list of 200 words each week to memorize with twenty chosen at random for testing; (4) Vocabulary: were given ten new words (from the list of 200) to define each day; (5) History: learned the history of St. Patrick's parish; (6) English: were given instruction on parts of speech, sentence structure, sentence diagramming, and grammar.

Having had some Latin in third grade was helpful with vocabulary. Sister Marguerite was encouraging and patient. Grammar, she would say, is the engine of language, and diagramming its mechanics. This foundation made both chemistry and mathematics less intimidating. My mother dampened my enthusiasm for language with a curious suggestion: "Look on English as what it is, an extension of British imperialism. Learn the rules before you break them. Too bad you don't have an opportunity to learn Gaelic." That made no sense to me, and I told her so.

"No, don't suppose it does. It's not my advice, but the counsel of the greatest writer in English who ever lived." George Jensen had told me that was Shakespeare, so I quipped,

"You mean Shakespeare?"

She chuckled. "Now where did you get that idea?"

"From George, George Jensen." She didn't know George well even though he lived two doors down. My mother was never comfortable around handicapped people.

"Well, Georgie has brainwashed you. It's James Joyce of course."

"Who's that? I've never heard of him."

She chuckled, turned her head and blew a stream of smoke away from me. "You will, my darling." And she was right. A lifetime away I would read *A Portrait of the Artist as a Young Man* at Iowa and recall this conversation.

* * * * *

It was my sophomore year taking a required core course, *Modern Literature, Greeks and the Bible,* that James Joyce and *A Portrait of the Artist as a Young Man* first came to my attention. My misfortune was to contract infectious mononucleosis and spend several days in the University of Iowa Infirmary, missing the mid-term examination on this biographical novel of Joyce's youth. Dr. Armens, my professor, decided to give me the make-up as an oral exam. Professor Armens asked the routine questions to start me off. Why did Joyce choose Dedalus as his hero? How did he create incidents to illustrate his artistic temperament (and so on)? It was clear that the professor was anxious to get home. His wife had called twice. I could hear kids in the background crying with his attempt to console a clearly overstressed mother.

"Dr. Armens," I said when he hung up the second time, "is it possible to dispense with this Q&A and let me tell you how I see Joyce?" He smiled and waved his cigarette.

"Sure."

For the next hour he allowed me to do just that. This represents the essence of those remarks.

"I see the book and the author as a single cloth. The book moved me so much I read it three times. Each time I gained a new sense of Joyce and what he was about. The book is like reading the mind of a madman where everything from casual looks, street signs, to news reports is charged with meaning. Joyce is telling the story of his own muddled youth under the guise of fiction.

"What first hit me is that Stephen Dedalus didn't belong anywhere. He existed as a warring element in a divided universe. He found himself constantly falling into the divide. He hates his Catholicism, but is obsessed with it. He is sick of his country's clerical dominance yet he reveres the clergy. He even wants to become a priest. He worships his father but hates his weakness, seeing the seeds of that weakness in himself.

"Stephen is fragile yet resolute, a romantic who insists on being seen as an enlightened realist. So, in that sense, he is a fraud in his quest to seek the real parents of his soul.

"Society, he knows, honors the man of action, not the thinker, and he wants to be honored, yet he doesn't have the temperament for action. He chooses to see style as character, and he knows he has style. He believes the remedy for his time is a return to the senses through art. This will recover society's capacity for organization against accelerating chaos generated by the duplicity of church and state governance.

"Stephen wants to soar like the mythical Dedalus beyond church heresy and Irish treason to freedom, beyond language and culture to connection with his soul. He believes both the church and state are responsible for the dislocation of his morality, and sees Ireland as a moral hell and its people captive to an immoral church, which confines them to ignorance.

"Stephen's relationship to father figures is not only critical to the book, but is the book. These relationships trigger his quest to become authentic. Simon Dedalus is the parental father whom he loves, but hates his drinking. Father Dolan is the spiritual father who brings out his masochism and deviance. Byron is the intellectual father who feeds his artistic and sexual fantasies. St. Aquinas and Aristotle are his philosophical fathers who represent the essence of what he desires to become.

"What the book keeps telling me is that what is normal is perverted in Irish Catholicism. This is a puzzle Stephen never solves. Since his taste of love at sixteen, eroticism is an overwhelming narcotic. He feels tremendous guilt for this mortal sin, but compelled to repeat it. As he studies the saints, and is bombarded with sermons on eternal damnation, he avoids confession, then finally goes to a city where he is not known to confess. There he finds a wise old priest who understands what it is like to be young and lost, who understands how natural sensuality can become compulsive sexuality, indeed, how natural love can be locked out of early experience.

"Stephen is a talker, dreamer, schemer, and fantasizer. He needs an audience to hear his own mind working. Davin and Lynch are his sounding board. My doubt is that Stephen knew as much about the world as Joyce suggests. Doubt is a powerful force in his emerging, questioning Catholic mind but it is always the mind of a Catholic no matter how much he tries to escape that reality.

"Only by leaving Ireland, he believes, can he sort everything out. He promises with theatrical solemnity never to return, and to write a book that makes clear his views on Ireland and the Irish people. This is the book, written I suspect more to quiet his Irish soul than to enlighten the Irish. I doubt though that it gave Joyce much peace."

Dr. Armens was still sitting on the edge of his desk smoking when I finished. The room was sweet smelling with the aroma of tobacco, must be a foreign brand. He put out his cigarette in a flat metal ashtray, folded his arms across his chest, and considered me. Then he got up from the desk, went to the window and opened it slightly. It made a creaking sound. The smoke followed in a swift dash for liberty. He returned, sat on his desk again, lit another cigarette, and then thought to offer me one. I declined with a nod. "You understand Joyce. How do you explain that?" I answered matter-of-factly, "I am Joyce."

Stephen Dedalus, Joyce's alter ego, was torn between being Irish and Catholic, and not being Irish or Catholic enough. He was obsessively erotic, yet painfully self-consciously chaste because he wanted to be a Jesuit. How could I not be Joyce? His pain in the classroom, anguish with priests, battles with his da, his ambivalent lustful fantasies about women, strangeness with people in authority, nonspecific anger at everything and with everybody, his sense of exile in the company of his peers, contempt for the imprisoning lies and illusions of his race, as well as his sensitivity and obsession with class were also mine. Moreover, his compulsions always favored the idea of escape, only to invariably increase his confinement, as did mine. Of course, I understood Joyce. He desired to fly the coop and soar into the sun and greatness, as did I. His life was my life.

*   *   *   *   *

St. Patrick's school was alive with activity far removed from reading, writing, and arithmetic. Workmen were everywhere. The smell of fresh paint, sweeping compound, pine sol disinfectant, boiling pots of coal tar for the roof, and new books stacked high in unused classrooms greeted the senses. School was never out in preparing for the fall schedule. Sister Mary Marguerite introduced us to the school principal, Sister Mary Flavian, and to the pastor of St. Patrick's, Father Harvey F. Finefield.

Another priest! I was waiting for this! Father was slim, short, and bespectacled with a ruddy complexion and white hair, not much bigger than I. Most noticeable was how carefully he dressed. His white starched Roman collar gleamed above his carefully tailored and well-pressed black suit, and shining black shoes. He looked magnificent and seemed to feel the same. His eyes smiled approvingly at us, and he laughed easily with a throaty rumble. His laugh was of a bigger man, like an opera singer, and came from deep within him. He was not at all the priest I saw at Mass, stern, pontific, and imperious, but cordial, even affable. Yet, his impact on me was a consuming disquiet. The two nuns smiled deferentially as he held court, principal Sister Flavian making no move to dim his light. When he left, she came over to me, smiled in a way that warmed my soul. "You are new." She looked about the room. "I know all you other children." Then she looked back at me. "What is your name?" I told her.

"Welcome to St. Patrick's, James. We are glad to have you." I felt dizzy with her presence. Sister Flavian had the kindest eyes I had ever seen. She was short, stout, peasant looking, and seemed always to be playing with the crucifix on her Rosary beads near the waist of her habit. When she looked at me, there was no sense of guile. She wasn't an actor on stage as was Father. She was all business without seeming to be. You could even tell, everyone was equally important to her. As she monitored our class participation, she seemed neither impressed with bright responses nor disinclined with dull ones. If humility can show its face in a countenance, it did in Sister's. She was a heavenly body on earth. During the next five years, under her guidance, I would never hear her raise her voice, or seem distressed. If a vocation is truly a call from God, surely Sister Flavian received hers. She was on top of things, always in charge although she had no office, conducting her business from a desk in the hall of the third floor, while doing her tutoring of students on the small mezzanine below.

On a deeper level, St. Patrick's school gave me a sense of place in space. I felt myself wrapped in trembling happiness. I soon learned why. Sister Marguerite shared with us St. Patrick's parish history, a history with which I have stayed abreast to this day.

More than one hundred years ago (1889), a young Irish priest, Father James A. Murray, one year out of the seminary came to Clinton with orders from Archbishop Hennessey of Dubuque to plan the formation of a new parish. The young priest met with immediate resistance from the "Hilltoppers" of St. Mary's on the south side. St. Mary's desired things to remain as they were with no breach in their parish authority. Clinton enjoyed, at the time, a burgeoning Catholic population with St. Boniface (1861), St. Irenaeus (1848) churches, and Our Ladies of Angels Academy (1872) to the north in Lyons, and St. Mary's (1866) and Sacred Heart (1891) to the south, but with no Catholic parish in the center of the community, the courthouse neighborhood. Father Murray, although young, was an astute observer, who recognized St. Mary's resistance as a combination of pride and control. He patiently scheduled meetings to ventilate concerns, but few showed up for these discussions. So, at the end of November 1889, with only two people in attendance, he announced that he had purchased land at the corner of Third Street and Fourth Avenue North to start a new parish with these two parishioners. Within a month, on January 19, 1890, Father Murray celebrated Mass in a small, new wooden church. This was located along the alley with the front doors facing Third Street. Even before the new wooden structure was completed, Father Murray baptized his two new parishioners on December 29, 1889. Their names were Dionysus Murray and Edwardus Lynch. The Irish had a new foothold in the middle of Clinton, Iowa. Ten years later, St. Patrick's parish was thriving. The parish was free of the debt of $8,000 in the purchase of the land, and $10,000 for the construction of the provisional church, rectory, school, and convent. Blessed with solvency, Father Murray and St. Patrick's lay leaders moved ahead to plan the construction of a new permanent church. Together they devised an austerity program and financial campaign to save $25,000 during the next five years, which they succeeded in accomplishing. The church and rectory were built at a cost of $40,000. Mass was offered in the new edifice for the first time on Christmas morning, December 25, 1905. Father Murray was not through. Along with starting the new parish, he was busy with another five-year plan. This included contracting Franciscan nuns to teach in St. Patrick's new school.

The nuns needed a home, which necessitated building a convent. This required the purchase of more land, new construction, and additional promissory notes. The Sisters of St. Francis followed Father Murray's lead by incrementally purchasing land on Bluff Boulevard between Springdale Drive and Seventh Avenue North. In 1891, Father Murray asked for five nuns of the Franciscan order to open a school at St. Patrick's. The Sisters of St. Francis recorded this tribute to him: *"Father Murray was a pastor who understood what it meant to overcome difficulties. In the mind of many Sisters, he was the benefactor and savior of their struggling community."* The first few years were indeed difficult. The lumber industry in Clinton began its precipitous decline in the mid-1890's, and with it Clinton's economy. For a time it appeared the parish might have to declare bankruptcy. But with the continued support of parishioners combined with parish austerity, St. Patrick's overcame its financial perils and once again commenced to prosper. In 1893, through Father Murray's influence, the Sisters had an opportunity to buy property owned by the Chase family. It would become the convent and motherhouse of Mount St. Clare. Although the Bishop of Davenport didn't want the Sisters to own their own property, he finally consented for them to incur a debt of $20,000. The Chase property was bought for $6,000. Two years later, the Sisters obtained permission to build an addition to the motherhouse and school for these boarding girls. By 1899, the Franciscan nuns managed to meet the challenges of debt and admission requirements to stay solvent. Having in hand this impressive fiscal record, the Sisters obtained permission from the bishop to purchase additional property from the Corbin family, the present site of Mount St. Clare College. Dr. Corbin had built a two-story home, a brick barn and other buildings on this six-acre plot. The new property was named Mount Alverno, and served for many years as a noviate for young women studying to become nuns. Through discipline, diligence and fiscal acumen, the Sisters were able to retire all debts in six years, which gave them the credit line to purchase an additional 12 acres from the Upjohn family. This property, which was essentially a pasture, joined Mt. Alverno and seeded the acquisition of more property along Springdale Drive. By 1904, Mount St. Clare was able to add a music room, a 12-bed dormitory, a recreation hall, and art rooms to its ever-expanding facilities. Even so, the Chase buildings were becoming too confining. They were also gloomy, poorly ventilated, and unsanitary. So, in 1910, the Sisters took on a $200,200 building project to finance the building of a complete new facility. This was completed in time to open classes in the fall of 1911. Adversity was to confront the good Sisters their first year in the new building. First, diphtheria struck the academy in February 1912, followed three months later, with an epidemic of scarlet fever. Fortunately, no one died of these outbreaks. In 1918, Mount St. Clare chartered the new college. By 1924, the Sisters were blessed with normal routine and able to finally focus on education. Summer school was held each year at St. Patrick's. College students, all women at this time, were able to obtain associated degrees from the College. By 1931, Mount St. Clare was accredited by the North Central Association. Its first commencement exercises were held in 1930 with 20 people graduating, of whom 12 were nuns. In 1950, the foundation was laid for nuns to continue graduate education in other institutions. Scores of Franciscan nuns have earned their PhD's in diverse disciplines and have become specialized educators. In 1959, a new library and gymnasium was constructed at Mount St. Clare as well as the establishment of a Speech and Hearing Center. In 1960, a new college dormitory – Durham Hall – and science building were opened. And a new preschool was established. In 1967, young men were admitted to classes for the first time. In 1979, Mount St. Clare College was accredited as a four-year co-educational liberal arts college offering a degree in business administration. Today the college offers 17 majors and 50 areas of specialization with a student faculty ratio of 12:1, and a placement success rate of 96 percent. In 1980, as the parochial school system in Clinton all but vanished, Mount St. Clare came to the rescue, merging its academy to form Mater Dei High School in the former St. Mary's buildings. In 1989 the Flavian Center was created in honor of Sister Mary Flavian, principal at St. Patrick's grammar school from 1931 to 1958. It was Sister Flavian's belief that no student should be left behind, and that all students had a unique key to their development, which was the responsibility of educators to decipher. The Flavian Center, a tutoring program, is legacy to her philosophy. Mount St. Clare is embarking on a new identity today, as *Franciscan University*. The good nuns are indeed gifted at the business of education.

As Father Murray seeded the formation of this institution, he had a hand in the establishment of St. Joseph Mercy Hospital. In 1892, he saw to the purchase of the Phillip Deeds residence, which became the first home of Mercy Hospital. Later, he spearheaded the purchase of the adjoining Disbrow property to form a 146-bed hospital. Mercy Hospital, run by the order of the Sister of Charity, BVM (Blessed Virgin Mary), followed the acquisition and expansion model developed by the Franciscans. Today the hospital is called Mercy North as the former Jane Lamb Hospital to the south is now designated Mercy South. In 1913, two years after Clinton County became part of the Diocese of Davenport, Father Murray received his first assistant, another Irish priest, Father M. A. O'Connell. For 24-years the good priest labored alone. Pastors and their assistants through the years were all Irish until my time at St. Patrick's – 1942-1947. Father Finefield, pastor of St. Patrick's from 1932 to 1955, received his first assistant, Father Geerts, in 1947. Father Geerts was only 27, a balm to his more acerbic boss. Father Murray died on July 8, 1928 after 39-years of service to St. Patrick parishioners and to the larger Catholic community. By a twist of fate, Father Finefiled would also die on July 8 (1955) after 27 years of devoted service to St. Patrick's parish, and like Father Murray before him, while still pastor of this church.

On Father Murray's tombstone in St. Mary's Cemetery is this simple tribute: *"Founder of Mt. St. Clare, Mt. Alverno, and Mercy Hospital."* No mention is made of the establishment of St. Patrick's church, rectory and school. This prophetic bit of exception is ironic as the St. Patrick's complex was being razed in 2002 to make way for a Senior Citizen Home, as if it never existed.

* * * * *

St. Patrick's school was on three levels. The basement housed kindergarten and first grade. Ground level was the school banquet-basketball court & recreational hall. The second level housed second and third grade. A mezzanine between the second and third floor was used by Sister Flavian to tutor students with special needs. Fourth, fifth, sixth, seventh and eighth grade were on the third level. Seventh and eighth grade were combined into a single room, the school's largest. Class sizes were small varying from 12 to 14 per class with 7-8th grade together only 27 students.

What a joy to be on the top floor of the school with the other "big" kids, and no longer in a classroom of multiple grades. At St. Boniface, kindergarten, first, second, third and fourth grade were all in one room on the first floor. The design of St. Patrick's second floor lobby was interesting. The north wall was closed off from the gym below by three large wooden corrugated shutters. Once opened, they gave a grandstand view of the gym. The basketball court was about twenty feet short of regulation size and the basketball hoops were attached to the west wall and to the stage at the east end with wooden backboards and conventional hoops. The hoop attached to the stage came down when the hall was set up for bingo, a play, awards banquet, or teachers' conferences.

These buildings are now viewed through admittedly tired eyes but with the same rapture as first observed in 1942. Now, the picture is only in my mind, as St. Patrick's is no more. After a century, the mind still sees St. Patrick's bricks glistening in the sun with the sheen and brightness of their nativity, the church, rectory and school apple red in my ageless conscience. I see the sky blue twin domes of the church, the single sky blue dome of the rectory standing in the shadow of the courthouse, connected to a secret past, a past that cannot be buried. Four white pillars stand like silent sentinels on the rectory's porch while a commanding bright red brick structure rises from this porch two stories into the sky and beyond to a cathedral windowed dormer and a steeple dome. This building was as majestic, as its occupant, Father Finefield, was mysterious.

St. Patrick's school, itself, was less spectacular, a Lego block construction to a functional purpose with no need to impress. Utility was an understatement, starting with sets of double-framed windows on either side of the metallic gray double front door, with the windows rising to three levels. Above the front door was the cornerstone of "St. James Hall." Entering the school, you would climb ten marble steps to the main marbled floor with second grade to the right and third grade to the left of the main lobby. The west end of the hall had steps going both up to the mezzanine and down to ground level, with additional steps at ground level down to the kindergarten and first grade, the janitor's room and the boy's locker room. The parish hall-gymnasium was at ground level with a ten-foot door into the facility. At the basement level on the street side were double windows, both to kindergarten and the first grade. And at ground level at the west end was a double door and second exit from the school. An attached brick garage outside this exit housed Father Finefield's 1938 Oldsmobile, while a cement driveway extended to the street.

Sixth grade was the first class room on the third floor with large double windows to the street side. Fifth grade was in the middle with a single window to the street, while seventh and eighth grade were at the east end of the floor with double windows to the street. Fourth grade was situated on the north side of the third floor with no windows, and was of similar size to fifth grade.

The playground to the back of the school was limited to swings, a slide and teeter totter on one side of a ten foot wire mesh fence with a recreational area for playing softball and touch football at the other. This area was small – about 20 yards wide and ten yards deep to the alley. Its surface was rough, a combination of gravel, cinders and compacted dirt. Boys played here, but girls had no real place to play, or to sit for that matter, other than in swings.

Yet, as I digest the visual apparition of St. Patrick's, I imagine myself once again back there, once again trembling with the happiness of this place. Does everything start with the imagination?

Or does it start with the eyes, then the imagination kidnaps it to the heart? If so, does the heart make it real? Or does the heart help us forget, to start over, to ever start over again? So sixty years later, I come here to nowhere, looking for the next avenue out. It is as if I never left, that in this old body, a child still lives boxed in to a time and a place that is more real than I am to myself. Aeschylus said, "Man grows against his will." Perhaps in translation and transition so do institutions.

* * * * *

Chapter 7

Fighting for Air

Pride grows in the human heart like lard on a pig.

--Alexander Solzhenitsyn

If the child is parent to the man, I got my baptism to this fact at the end of August 1942, a week before I would start fourth grade at St. Patrick's school. My da was not known to take an interest in child rearing. That was a mother's work. Yet, one day he stepped out of character. "Dorothy, I'm taking Jimmy downtown to get him some school clothes." His euphoric mood is immediately suspect.

"Ray, are you sick or something?"

He rolled his narrow shoulders to cover his unease, and clenched and unclenched his fists. His Popeye forearms, looking like piano legs, rippled like piano keys. I loved to watch him sharpen his straight razor in a glass, working the blade hard against the surface with his fingers pumping up and down to sharpen the cutting edge. It was piston power on display. If he wore only an undershirt, it was a double pleasure. His large, well-defined bicep would bulge, then recede like a coiled corded ball with a prominent vein running down its center. Fully dressed, you might confuse him with Mr. Milquetoast. If you did, it would be a mistake as he was a compact package of anger waiting for an excuse to explode.

"What's the big deal? Can't take your goddamn kid downtown? Tied to your apron strings, is he?" I was always my mother's child when conflict surfaced. My mother was a slip of a girl of seventeen, he an irresponsible twenty-two-year-old man of the world when lust and innocence collided to produce the accident, me.

"All right, all right," she replied waving her cigarette in mock surrender. "Got money?" She knew he didn't. She controlled the threadbare purse strings.

"Some."

"Some?"

"Enough." She delighted in grilling him. Where it worked with me, it could set him to boiling, which he was about to do now, when she said,

"Splendid. Be good for both of you."

I watched this parry riposte like a spectator to a fencing match, not knowing for sure the outcome. Soon, to my surprise, we were off for downtown. Perhaps because of this awkward bonding I noticed everything as we walked south to downtown, a little more than a mile. As we walked, my mind left me and went back five years. I am waiting for my da looking to the street below from my aunt Annie's second floor windowed dormer, tears welling up in my eyes. My love for him is like a fever with no will of its own involved in the process. He is my blood and connection to the world while strangers surround me. I jump for joy when I see him, "Annie, Annie, da's here!" She smiles and goes back to her knitting, filling the rocking chair with her amorphous girth as if she were part of the fabric. I never saw her in anything but a housecoat, which covered her from her neck to her shoes. Nor do I remember ever seeing her not in that sturdy rocking chair. She was like a queen on her throne rocking away, but never missing a thing. They speak to each other briefly, then he takes my hand, and we walk down Second Street to downtown. Once there, we wait in line with scores of other people for a free lunch of chili and coffee. At four years of age, coffee is more available than milk, so I have already acquired the taste. There is rain in the wind and I feel a cold chill up my spine. Noting this, he gives me his scarf. The scarf is large, red and warm and I ask him if I can keep it. He looks at me curiously, tousles my blond hair, and then makes a careful knot in the scarf, "Sure." Like a talisman, I take the scarf to bed with me. I even make a belt of it until aunt Annie says it looks silly as it hangs almost to the floor once wrapped around me. On this day, we find ourselves just south of the Clinton Public Library near the Chicago & North Western Depot where Third Street jogs west to Eleventh Avenue South and then turns south into Camanche Avenue. Mostly men are in the line. They talk easily of how tough work is to come by, wondering how much longer the Depression will last. It is 1937. Far from being a gloomy lot, the men laugh, tell jokes, smoke cigarettes, and seem somehow united in misery. I find it strange that I am the only child with a man; others are all with women.

It was this memory that caused me to seek my da's hand. Surprised by the touch, as if by an electric shock, he moved away with a start, and then dug into his pocket for a cigarette. As we walked on, I covered my hurt by observing landmarks as if I were a dead reckoning pilot. Third Street in 1942 was mainly residential with a haphazard smattering of businesses along the way. We first passed Thiesen's grocery across from St. Patrick's Church, then Bosen's grocery and Turner Junk Yard at Third Avenue, then on Maple Avenue we came to Gus's (Turkus) Phillip 66 Service Station with a Standard Oil Station across the street. Negro children were playing stickball in the street, laughing and jumping about. I watched with fascination. I seldom saw Negroes; never saw them at the courthouse, or anywhere but here. My da waved to deputy sheriff Jim Gaffey who was in his yard on First Avenue. A big man with a broad Irish face, he yelled back, "Got the kid, have you? We're going make ballplayer of him." My da laughed, "Maybe you could get him a job while you're at it." I don't think he was kidding. Martha Washington Candy Store comes up next, then Snell Funeral Home and Bethel African Methodist Church. They are kitty-corner across the street from each other. As we passed Clinton City Park, I saw kids my age playing around the fountain in the center of the park. Finally, we were on Fifth Avenue, the main business district. The YMCA, U. S.

Post Office, Milo John's Drug Store, and Walgreen Drug Store were on the four corners of Third Street. Walgreen's was in the Jacobsen Building with Clinton's only radio station, KROS, located on the second floor.

I was only remotely aware of my da. He would comment, "Leon Cavanaugh lives up a couple blocks," as we passed Second Avenue North. I would nod but say nothing. He was always telling me things I already knew, never thought provoking things like with my mother. He never asked me what I thought, or how I felt. My mother did all the time. I was busy anyway with my own private study. Still, I cherished this walk, not knowing when there would be another. When I was four, I had to run to keep up with him. Now, I could match him stride for stride. Some said we even walked alike, a kind of cocky walk that spoke to a confidence that neither of us had. It was a shuffle with our feet darting out and up and down as if we knew what we were about, which might only be in a hurry. When I was four, all I wanted was to be a man like him. I looked at him with that handsome face, those powerful arms cutting the air in rhythm with his long stride, a stride more common to a bigger man, and I would explode with pride. When he was not at home, he seemed to laugh easily, to call out to acquaintances along the way with charm, and disarming digs. "How you making it, sport," he would say, "catching any grief?" Then he would laugh. Anyone he liked was "sport," anyone he didn't was "fella" – like "Don't push your luck, fella!" He seemed to know everybody, the picture of confidence on top of his game. Why, I wondered, did this disappear once home? Anger seemed a painful presence behind the eyes, which could quickly turn to a verbal explosion, over nothing, once he was home.

When I registered for summer school, Sister Flavian gave me a form to have my parents fill out. It asked for my father's income. Seeing that request, he went berserk. "Dorothy what goddamn business is it of theirs? Jesus Christ is there no peace? No privacy?" The harangue continued and eventually settled on me, forgetting he had two other children scheduled to attend St. Patrick's in the fall. "Kid should be in the public schools know that Dorothy? But no, we can't have that. Jimmy's special. Jimmy needs devoted nuns." His hands would go up in mock surrender. "I Jesus Christ don't goddamn get it. Know that Dorothy?"

He would eventually collapse into a chair while the rest of us shuddered in a nervous rattle, which was actually our breathing. Since society measured identity in terms of money, security in terms of income, he saw himself always coming up short. The pain of this triggered these spontaneous verbal explosions. "Ray, have a cigarette," my mother would say, as the perfect palliative. "I'll get you a cup of coffee." He would continue to fume while she smoked and read. It was as if his happiness dissipated once he entered the house. All the stored up venom in his soul burst like a lanced boil once he crossed that threshold. The rage would continue until it became only tired pain.

Violence was always there under the calm, and yet the violence had a focus. Family meant everything to him, never having been part of one. He worshipped my mother with Madonna-like zeal, while being exasperated by her easy strength. The primordial beast was activated whenever he felt his family threatened. The threat could be real, or imagined. It was a weakness born of strength for his heart ruled his head while my mother's head ruled her heart. He reacted to things. My mother anticipated them. He loved us. My mother used us. A distinction I never understood until they both were gone.

One day earlier in the summer of 1942, his repressed anger became physical. My uncle Snowball was invariably drunk when he came to visit us. On this occasion I was playing the radio when he came into the sitting room and started to talk to me. I ignored him. "I'm talking to you, Jimmy," he said as he turned my head towards him. "Do you hear me?" I turned away. Then he slapped me gently on the cheek, first with his palm, then his backhand. It surprised more than hurt me. I yelled to my mother in the kitchen, "Mommy, uncle Snowball hit me."

My da, also in the kitchen, rushed out, grabbed my uncle, pulled him out of his chair, hit him with a short jab to the chin that sent him through the screen door onto the front porch. He then picked him up again and hit him with another short jab sending him through the screened-in porch onto his back in the front yard, out cold. It was more dramatic than a fight scene in a cowboy movie. I couldn't believe a short punch could send a five-four, 150-pound man through the air like a projectile, but it did. This bizarre explosion was typical of that dichotomous summer of '42 with a series of contradictory events, which have stayed with me all my life.

We took a brief vacation to Chicago, the first in my memory, the middle week of August. Although a train trip from Clinton to Chicago was less than 150 miles, it was enough time to see him in his element. He talked chattily to people on the train, telling them that he was a brakeman on the Iowa division, was even patient with us kids, and clearly happy for our company. He loved Chicago with a passion born of dreams, but with an equal hatred formed of failure to make it there. All this was forgotten once on holiday with a free railroad pass in the company of his family.

Spontaneous violence was to show its face again. My mother and three-month old Janice in a stroller embarked across the busy street outside the Chicago & North Western Railroad Depot, only to be nearly hit by a truck that tried to beat the light, then stopped abruptly nearly hitting them as they crossed. My da, like a soaring rocket, leaped on the fender of the cab, grabbed the driver by his hair and slammed his fist into his face. My mother was screaming, Janice was crying, my sister, Patsy, brother, Jackie, and me were frozen as if struck dumb. The driver -- blood running from his nose, his arms up to fend off more blows -- was choking in sobs, with a cacophony of terror, "Sorry! Sorry! Don't hit me anymore! Please!"

Fist cocked like a gun, face red as a beet from the neck up, ears white as snow as if all the blood had left them, he was yelling in a coarse voice, "You goddamn sonofabitch! You rotten bastard! Fella, I ought to kill you!" The man moved his lips to speak. "Keep your goddamn mouth shut!" And he did.

But little fight was left in my da, as he could see the driver was as defenseless as an armless man. He stepped down from the fender still with his fist cocked, daring the truck to move. The driver turned his face away as my da guided us across the street. Cars passed. People walked by, all seemingly oblivious to the one-sided fight. No one spoke until we reached State Street. My mother broke the silence. "Look, Ray, one of your favorite entertainers is at the Chicago Theater. We could catch a matinee. What do you think?"

He looked up at the marquee, Billy Eckstein, the Negro rhythm and blues singer, was there in person. He loved Eckstein's rendition of "Old Black Magic," and would sing it, off key, when the mood struck him. "Think it will be okay for Janice?" he said hesitantly, anger leaving him like a deflated balloon.

"She'll be fine. I'll nurse her. She'll go to sleep. Besides, it'll give us a chance to get our legs under us." No mention was made of the incident. Once in the theater, the handsome entertainer on stage, the air cleared in a surging wave of relief, I watched his face light up like a little boy's as Eckstein and his ensemble moved about the stage. It was the first time, but not the last that I felt older than he was. Afterwards, we lunched in the Forum Cafeteria with the assertion we could select whatever we wanted as long as we ate it all. Already a big eater, I managed to take two trays and to fill them generously with entrees, salads, beverages, and deserts. My mother smiled, but not my da. "You heard what I said. Eat it all, or you stay until you do." I not only ate all my food but helped my little brother dispose of his.

"What's next?" my da asked.

"How about St. Patrick's Cathedral?" I suggested.

"What about the Chicago Museum of Fine Art?" my mother chimed in.

"When we going to the hotel?" my sister Patsy asked. "My feet hurt." My little brother, Jackie didn't seem to care where we went. He couldn't stop looking up at all the tall buildings with his hands in his pockets.

"Jesus Christ, Jackie," my da said, alarm in his voice, "get your goddamn hands out of your pockets! How you going to defend yourself if somebody tries to grab you?"

Stunned by the charge, confused by what it meant, Jackie started to cry. My da patted him on the head, and then took him in his arms. "Didn't mean to scare you, son. This is Chicago. Dangerous place. Not Clinton. That's all I meant. Sorry. You okay?" Jackie's uncertainty melted into quiet sobs as he snuggled into my da's arms, a man who could go from ice cold to warm milk in a minute. None of us could resist these mood swings.

"How about Lincoln Park Zoo?" he suggested as if all was well again, and that is where we went. As we rode the bus on Chicago's North Shore, my da squeezed my shoulder. "Isn't this beautiful, Jimmy?" I agreed as my spirits rose like dry leaves in a wind. Lake Shore Drive was abuzz with activities. A myriad of white dots were stenciled on the aqua waters of Lake Michigan against a cerulean sky.

I soon realized these were sailboats, seemingly hundreds of them. People along the beach were sunbathing, playing tennis, jogging, listening to a concert, playing volleyball, and walking along the boulevard -- a Degas painting in motion. Once at the zoo, my da surprised me when he wouldn't go into the snake world exhibit. "Your father's terrified of snakes, imagine that," mother kidded, "an Iowan about as close to nature as a Chicago cabby."

I looked to see his reaction. His face said I'm not an Iowan! Instead of saying anything, he lit a cigarette and turned away. People always think Iowans are farmers. I don't know one cow, pig, or chicken from another. I've intense pride in being an Iowan, and regret my lack of agricultural education. My da, on the other hand, seemed to take a secret pride in his ignorance.

We next visited the koala bear enclosure. There, a mural painted on a tall pink wall expressed the forest in which the bears would have lived in the wild. Simulated eucalyptus trees were formed by crisscrossing branches that rose out of the floor. A single diminutive bear slept in the "V" of two of the branches. Nearby was hanging a bucket that contained the leaves he was to eat. The forest floor beneath the bear was concrete, and there were no bushes, no diversions, and no toys for him. He had no companion to break his solitude, only visitors to his enclosure, who whistled and called out to him, frustrated that this nocturnal creature would not accommodate himself to their timetable. I looked at this and felt heaviness settle on me. "Mommy, why do people come to zoos?"

"To look at the animals, why else?" my da said as if it were a stupid question.

My mother tapped a cigarette out of her purse, and then lit it. "I don't think so, Ray. I think it is to remind people of their freedom."

I kept my gaze on the pathetic koala, a ball of fur unmoving in the embrace of the wood that posed as branches from his native land.

"You think?" my da reflected, and then smiled. "That's pretty pro...found, Dorothy," he added sarcastically, "sounds more like brother Len."

Not dissuaded, she continued. "A zoo is a place people can go to wallow in their superiority." Then she turned to me. "Zoos are not happy places, Jimmy. We have them, I suppose, because we need to delude ourselves into thinking we're not in cages."

88

"Jesus Christ, Dorothy, we came here to have a little fun." He shakes his head in disgust. "For Christ's sake, I don't goddamn get it! Do you understand? Why do you have to give the kid that crap? He's confused enough."

"Now, Ray, you're wrong. He's not confused at all."

That seemed to put a pall on the zoo, as a frigid silence accompanied by a scuffling of feet marked the stroll through the park, until we came to the elephants. A keeper was hosing an elephant off. We watched as sheets of water cascaded down the side of the enormous creature. Sprouts of hair along the elephant's backbone bristled like wires as the water hit them, and the animal shifted its weight from foot to foot.

"Odd looking sort, don't you think?" by da said trying to put some levity back into this excursion.

"He's probably thinking the same of us," my mother replied. My da shook his head again in surrender. It was my mother's way of getting back at him for beating up the driver. She was never direct, never obvious. My da was being punished for no other reason than to remind him of what he lacked.

"Have it your way, Dorothy. You didn't want to come here in the first place. Okay. My mistake." He looked to her for some sign of concession.

She smiled, touched his face with the palm of her hand. "Ray, it's fine. Don't worry about it." This gesture was enough. He was himself again, as he picked up Janice from the stroller. "How's my girl?" She cooed, and his face lit up with love.

The aspect of the zoo, not to my mother's liking, was the pervasive odors. The atmosphere was redolent with the smells of urine, droppings, and spoiling hay, which seemed to cause her to smoke even more. To my da's credit, he abbreviated the zoo tour and had us back on a bus within the hour. We stayed in a modest hotel near the Forum Cafeteria. Our room was a veritable barracks with six bunk beds, not like a hotel room at all. The first night we were there our parents went out and I was left in charge. We had tons of pillows. So, while I was giving Janice a bottle of warm milk, burping her, and changing her diaper, Patsy and Jackie were having pillow fights. Once Janice was asleep, I joined them. Feather down was everywhere.

Only I was awake when my parents came in. It never occurred to me to clean up the mess, or to imagine us being in trouble. But my mother seeing the white feathers covering the floor put her hand to her lips. "Oh my God, Jimmy, what happened?"

"We had a pillow fight," I said nonchalantly. "Some of the pillows came apart."

"Nooo!" she exclaimed in disbelief. "Jimmy, I trusted you. How could you?" I thought she was going to cry.

"I'm sorry, mommy."

"Calm down Dorothy," my da laughed, "looks like there's some spunk in your kid after all!"

"Not funny Ray." She narrowed her eyes in clear bewilderment. "You think it's all right to tear the place apart? Ray, sometimes, I ..." Then she turned to me. "I'm disappointed in you, Jimmy. Truly am. Thought you were more responsible."

"Dorothy, we're on vacation. It's okay," he said, taking off his suit coat, folding it carefully and laying it on an empty bunk bed. "They're kids. Remember being a kid?"

She shook her head. "Well, it's not all right with me. Give the maid a nice tip in the morning. Explain this to her. I don't want any trouble."

"Fine. So let's get some sleep. We have a busy day tomorrow."

My mother was a great Chicago Cub fan. Even during the war years, she still followed the Cubs religiously. To my da's relief the Cubs were out of town. "Besides, Dorothy," he said trying to lessen her disappointment, "all the good players are in the service. Be like watching the Three-I-League." This didn't appease her.

"Well, good or not, if they were in town, we'd see a ball game," she said defiantly.

There was no point in arguing. "Of course," he replied savoring his small victory.

My da judged athletes only in the quality of their excesses. "I remember when I was bell hopping at the Palmer House," he reminisced. "Hack Wilson was a bar regular. Good drinker. Amazing what that guy could drink, then go to Wrigley Field and hit three homeruns." Although he didn't drink anymore, my da remained genuinely impressed with men who could hold their liquor. It defined a man.

If Chicago was my da's religion, downtown Chicago was his church. He loved everything, the traffic, the commotion, the anonymity, Marshall Fields, Carson, Pirie & Scott's, and all the landmarks. He gave us a running commentary on the Old Water Tower, and how it was the only thing standing after the Great Chicago Fire. "Chicago rose from the ashes of that great fire started in 1871 by Mrs. O'Leary's cow," he stated like a tour guide, "to become America's second greatest city." People smiled as they walked by seeing all of us clustered around him listening.

We visited Grant Park, the Chicago Library, took a ride up the elevator in the Chicago Tribune Building on Michigan Avenue. He then allowed my mother to peruse the books at Brentano's for what seemed like forever. She bought a copy of Ellen Glasgow's bestseller *In This Life*, and beamed at the purchase. My mother owned few books, and cherished them like expensive jewelry.

We seemingly went through every department in Sears & Roebucks and Montgomery Ward, Marshall Fields, and Carson, Pirie & Scott's. What was funny is that people often mistook my da for a floorwalker. He would stand in place with a bemused expression on his face, arms folded across his chest, watching us run about like an overseer of the store's operations.

It was amazing how much you could do with little money. We stood on the bridge and watched tourist boats go up and down the Chicago River, and spent our nights in Grant Park. There, we could feel the cool breezes of Lake Michigan, watch the lights of the city come on, listen to the up-tempo of vehicular traffic creating a chiaroscuro radiance and contrasting sounds. Then too, there was always an outdoor concert in the park. Ice cream vendors were aplenty. There you could get caramel apples and candy canes, soda pop and popcorn for a dime. Downtown Chicago was like Clinton's 4th of July, only it happened every night. Then, of course, there were those giant buildings standing like silent gods to circle and shelter us from all harm. I could feel why he loved the place. He needed the city like lungs need air to breathe. Chicago revived him with its caustic wit and nervous dance. Country life killed his humor. His Irish soul remained in Chicago while his body settled in Iowa to die.

On this balmy August afternoon in 1942, fresh from this revitalizing Chicago vacation, with a bounce in his step, he set out for a shopping spree with his son. Martin Morris Men's Wear was the destination, which stood proudly in the center of the block on Fifth Avenue. It was Clinton's most exclusive men's and boy's casual apparel clothier, a store that had managed to survive the Depression. It was now in the process of renewal as the burgeoning professional middle class was rushing into Clinton in support of the war effort and would come to dominate all aspects of the community. This was my first time ever in the store. I felt a sense of intrusion the moment we passed through its doors.

We immediately headed for the boys' department, which was in the center rear of the store. The salesman, Ralph, turned out to be a boyhood pal of my da's, whom he hadn't seen since the days they were raising hell. They immediately reminisced about "the good old days," while I watched them. Ralph had a decided limp. I noticed that one of his shoes was built up about three or four inches. He was taller and heavier than my da with a pale pallor that made me wonder if he ever got out in the sun. It was hard to imagine them as friends. His speech was stilted as if he was trying to impress, while my da's nasal twang was, well, my da's, spontaneous and full of earthiness. He seemed to enjoy the renewal. I wondered if the opposite were true. Ralph gave the impression he was terribly busy, checking the register, looking through receipts, making notes, when in fact there wasn't another shopper in the department.

They talked about getting "shit faced" at dances in such places as Low Moor, Preston, Sabula, DeWitt and Grand Mound. Liquor by the drink couldn't be sold in the State of Iowa, but this was apparently ignored out in the country. They also talked about dances at the Modernistic Ball Room. The air was full of names as Ralph went down memory lane. "Remember that drummer Tony Bellsons and the organist Bill Tombin at the American Legion?" He laughed. "The manager used to urge everyone 'to get drunk and be somebody,' remember that, Ray?"

"Oh yeah," he replied with a dreamy look in his eyes. "I remember when Duke Ellington came to the Mod and jazzed up the place."

"Yeah, that was upstairs. That was something. Then there were bands like Tiny Hill from Lincoln, Illinois of 'Angry' and 'Please Don't Talk About Me When I'm Gone' fame . . . Eddy Howard of 'To

Each His Own' renown . . . then there was Art Castle and his 'Castles in the Air' . . . the bands of Ted Weems and Russ Morgan, and then of course Sammy Kaye . . . oh, and don't forget Clinton's own Wayne King, the Waltz King . . . King was born in Savanna, Illinois but raised here ... God, Ray, those were the days!"

This litany meant nothing to me, but I could see my da's eye water with happy recognition. He was mainly the contented listener, as Ralph seemed only comfortable when he was talking. "I remember when that guy came at you with a broken beer bottle in Low Moor and jabbed it in your face. God! Never saw so much blood. Thought he killed you, but you were still able, bleeding and all, to deck him." He shook his head in awe. "Ray, you were some mean sonofabitch. How many stitches did it take?"

My da, clearly uncomfortable with this hero worship, lit a cigarette. "Fifty-six. Thought I was going to lose my eye."

"Good thing you were drunk," Ralph chuckled inanely, "more like shit faced."

"Don't know," my da said earnestly.

"Did you know the guy?"

"No. Think he was just looking to hurt somebody for the hell of it, and I was there."

"Oh! I think it was more than that, Ray. You were a fighting machine in those days. Somebody look at you cross eyed and you'd pop 'em." He gazed at me, blond, blue-eyed, what some called a "pretty boy," raised an eyebrow trying to see evidence of brazen courage in me, and decided there was none. "Your dad was the toughest guy in these parts. He wouldn't back down to nobody no matter how big they were." He lifted his gimpy leg. "Then there were guys like me with a lame leg who were afraid of their own shadow. God, I envied your old man's courage in those days." Then he looked back at my da. "Now married. Behaving, huh?" He shook his head in disbelief. "Times are a changing."

"Got four kids."

"No shit?"

"Yep. This is my oldest." He tousled my hair. "Needs some school clothes."

"Well, that's what we've got."

"Jimmy, pick out what you need."

I hesitated. He knew what I was thinking -- what we were going to use for money. Reading this in my look, he pushed me away. "Get! Don't worry about it."

So, I picked out a plaid cotton shirt with a collar and long sleeves. It was a beauty. It had a red collar and red cuffs in a Scotch plaid. I added a blue pair of corduroys, a pair of argyle socks, a white tee shirt and a pair of jockey shorts. I thought about getting a belt but didn't want to push my luck. When I returned with my booty, they were still talking animatedly. I placed the clothing on the counter gingerly.

"That's all?"

I nodded.

"You sure?"

I nodded again.

"Get yourself another shirt, pants, two more sets of underwear and another pair of socks. Don't you need a belt?"

"Yes."

"Well, get that, too."

When I returned with the rest of the clothes – it was more than I ever got for Christmas -- my da said to the clerk with the gimpy leg. "Bill me for it, Ralph."

The words were like bullets. Ralph turned ashen. He reacted as if it were a hold up. He literally went into shock. Not the normal sort of shock when one's system undergoes a physical trauma like a car accident, or a fall from a roof, but the sort of shock that shatters the psyche so that one can take in only a single detail. "Charge it?"

"Yeah, charge it. Any problem with that Ralph?"

"Well, Ray, have to check your credit." With that he limped away to take shelter behind the door marked "Employees Only."

It seemed an eternity before he returned. My da whistled and did a little shuffle like Fred Astaire. "You all right, Jimmy?"

I was far from all right, but I lied. "Fine. I'm fine." Something was wrong. I knew it. I felt it. Why didn't he?

"It won't be long," he said to put me at ease, "these things take a while."

Just as he said that Ralph reappeared with the expression of the Grim Reaper. "Sorry, Ray. Can't do it. Your credit, ah, you know, well you know" and left the rest to my da's imagination.

Clearly, this was not expected. My da was looking at me, but not seeing me. "I don't know why that should be a problem." He seemed to be talking to himself. His voice was little more than a whisper. Self-loathing twisted his face into an ugly frown as if he had done something stupid. And his insides seemed to tighten like a wrung-out dishrag. It was horrible to watch him disintegrate. I stood as erect as I could make myself, looked Ralph in the eye, and said in a quivering voice,

"Don't need these things anyway," and pushed the mountain of clothes to his side of the counter.

My da rubbed his eyebrows as if trying to stimulate his memory. When he dropped his hand, he looked up at the ceiling instead of at me. I could see his eyes had become red-rimmed. I felt a pang, as he said, "I don't understand."

Something in me jarred loose at that moment. My da was bent forward as if hit in the stomach with a cheap shot. He seemed to fade into himself, to collapse without falling. I had never seen him like this before. He couldn't speak, couldn't move, and seemed suspended in shock. Ralph also appeared as if frozen in place. I watched them with alarm, then with something like revulsion, took my da's hand. "Thank you for your time," I said to Ralph forcing a smile, and then marched my da out of the store. I didn't look back, but held my head high and rallied my confidence with a self-conscious bounce in my step that felt more like wading through sewage.

Once on the street, I directed him toward Second Street with my hand still in his. He made no attempt to reject it. We passed the Wilson Building and a man said "Hi Ray," but my da made no reply. A woman coming out of the United Cigar Store on the corner gave a look of recognition then moved on. Could she sense our shame? We crossed the street to the Van Allen side, and walked more swiftly passing the Clinton Cigar Store, Boegel's Clothier, the abandoned old City Hall, Espey's Jewelers, and Bickford's Barber Shop. Somebody across the street coming out of the Midway Tavern waved to us. I waved back. My da broke from me, lit a cigarette, then took my hand again. My heart swelled. We passed the Revere Candy Shop without a hitch, then Becker's Café on the alley and Burken Bros. Men's Wear. Beta Hass Grocery was next. A man was setting up displays outside with his head down and his hands stretched forward diligently straightening out crates of produce. As we passed, my da turned his head away to the street. "About back there," he said finally motioning with a slight dip of his head as we crossed Fourth Avenue North. "I'm sorry. You didn't need to see that."

"It's okay, really it is. I didn't need anything. I'm fine. Really!" He squeezed my hand hard. "Notice that man back there? The one working in front of the store?"

"Yes."

"Well, that's Beta Haas. Beta once was a friend, turned my name into the credit bureau during the Depression. Owed him $25 for groceries. Couldn't pay it. Lots of money then. When I could, never got around to it. Guess it's still on the books. Why Ralph couldn't make the sale. Not his fault. Got bad credit, Jimmy, know what that is?"

"Yes. You have to pay in cash for things."

"That's right. Well, thought it was forgotten. Guess not. Your mother and I pay our bills best we can, Jimmy, know that?"

"Yes."

He didn't say another word the rest of the way home, just held my hand in his warm palm as if we were one.

* * * * *

Chapter 8

Into Battle

It is the cause, it is the cause, my soul . . .

--Othello

The individual we become has much to do with the accident of our birth. We enter a culture with its predominant themes, myths, and biases without conscious thought. In a sense, we differ little with the turtle egg buried in the Florida sand. The egg hatches, and by instinct the baby turtle moves to the light of the sea. Should the first light emanate from vehicular traffic, this waddling baby is more apt to move to the highway and extinction, accident of false stimulation. Eco-minded persons come to the rescue, place these turtles in buckets, and lovingly return them to the sea where they might flourish. Divine intervention often has a human face.

My entering St. Patrick School's fourth grade was like that. Up to then, I had been floundering in the traffic of life, buried in the gloom

97

of St. Boniface German Catholicism.   Like Dedalus, I was programmed toward, not away from Byronic hedonism by the exhortations of Father Sunbrueller and the manic control of Sister Mary Martina.   The irony was that I was Sister's pet, while my brother was not.   Already, I was a weary cynic distrustful of adults with the exception of my mother, and suspect of all men.   I saw women strong and men weak.   Men strutted, while women coped.   I lived in an Irish culture of gonna do's and gonna be's, where men saw themselves as ruling the roost but didn't, where they wore the long pants and demeanors of victim as if lacking the free will to act. Weakness in men was everywhere, except for my uncle Leonard and Dr. O'Donnell.   Our family doctor had the gentleness of a woman, while uncle Leonard was a man of cerebral courage who escaped his Irish-Norwegian indifference.   I realized, years later, they were in touch with their feminine side.   They didn't have to act brave to be brave.

Sister Mary Helen was my fourth grade teacher.   Tall, slender, young, with perpetually laughing eyes and expressive lips, even as a fourth grader, I imagined her beautiful without her habit.   She listened attentively with hands folded beneath her bib, her steel blue eyes riveting.   She had a peach cream complexion and wore thin rimless spectacles, like granny glasses.   When she was annoyed, her fingers reached for the rosary beads that circled her waist and hung down her side.   When angry, she would plunge her hands into the cavernous depths of her pockets, bring out a crumpled tissue, and press it to either side of her mouth.   When delighted, her hands would slide out from beneath her bib, and resound with energetic clapping, "Right! Right! Very good! Very Good!"   Sister gave you the sense she enjoyed the moment.   I melted to her commands from that first day. What a contrast with Sister Mary Martina, who would brook no nonsense, and believed a ruler to the knuckles was a learning tool.

You could tell Sister Helen had the calling as she handled 18 rambunctious nine-year-olds with consummate ease, and without cracking a whip.   She had auburn eyebrows, which always reflected her mood, arching to express wordless joy and narrowing to weighty concern.   I wondered if her hair was the same color.   My mother claimed most redheads were Irish.

Sensitivity is often derivative. Mine was from my mother's reading. A book, cigarette, and cup of coffee were her props. One day I saw she was reading *The Little Flower*. The title intrigued me. When she put the book down to turn off the teakettle, I opened it. "It's about Saint Therese. She was French," she said as she returned from the kitchen, "from a family of daughters, no less." She picked up her cigarette, which was smoldering, took a deep drag then stamped it out. "Imagine, Jimmy, Saint Therese was what they called a cloistered nun. Meant she took vows to deny the warmth of human conversation, even the love of family, then to add misery to sorrow, confined herself to a dreadful cell with no heat and few blankets for warmth. Get the picture?" She tapped another cigarette out of the pack but didn't light it. "French winters can be like ours. No wonder she died young. Several times nearly froze to death. Took vows to endure all this without complaint." My mother rolled her fingers around the cigarette between her index and middle finger thoughtfully, then lit it with a match. "Hmmm. Come to think of it, we women haven't made all that much progress in our cells." I was about to speak, but before I could she held up another book. "Book's on Saint Clare. The Mount is named for her. She was an early follower of St. Francis of Assisi. Gave away everything and founded an order of nuns, lived a life of chastity, and died in poverty. You are blessed, Jimmy, to be taught by truly good people. Nuns ask nothing for themselves but only to serve God by serving you. Whenever a nun puts you down, and anger boils up, as surely it will, you being your father's son, remember this."

Now in the autumn of my years, I remember these little homilies with the perspective of age. How these have provided oxygen to my soul. One might think I shared them with Sister Helen for advantage, and perhaps I did, but I think more for clarification. "Your mother must be some woman," Sister said as she was erasing the board. This only made me more anxious. I wanted to know why suffering was good. How could nearly freezing to death be saintly? Or poverty, good? We were poor and I failed to find it comforting. I didn't know how to be direct. Instead, I asked to be excused. Sister smiled. "Of course. Keep me posted on your mother's reading." I nodded. "Fine," she said and disappeared into the cloakroom for her shawl and

The Mount. Alone now, I didn't move, pounding my fist into my hand for not asking Sister the questions tormenting me.

With Sister Helen, I didn't have to be subtle. The climate in the classroom encouraged spontaneity. She conducted class in a style almost like play. We covered each subject, but where Sister Helen was different, each person assumed a role. One would collect homework, another would post discussions on the board, and a third would lead class discussion with Sister monitoring. Some didn't want to do anything. Sister had a way of bringing them out of their shells, too. She would form them into a group, and have them lead an exercise in reading, or some other subject. Eventually, everyone became comfortable with these assignments.

Sister had a way of corralling our energy without dissipating creativity. Today this is assumed a progressive learning style, but then it was a natural approach to her teaching. Take my run-at-the-mouth inclination. Like many others, I had relatives in the military, and would go off on a tangent about the war during class discussion. Rather than put me down, she used it.

"James, no matter what we're discussing, you manage to bring up the war." I scrunched down into my seat. A muscle worked in her jaw. "No need for that. Now sit up!" I did. Then she turned to the class with a relaxed expression.

"Well, class, think James is trying to get us off the subject?" Everyone laughed. "I think so, too, but still," she paused, bringing her crumpled tissue out of her pocket to her lips, then taking a bead on me. "James, maybe we can find room for your war news." She took off her glasses, pulled a large white handkerchief out of her sleeve, and polished the lenses studiously. "Let's see. Why don't we have James read The Clinton Herald on the latest developments of the war, give a brief report to us, say on Wednesdays after recess, would you like that?"

"Yes, Sister!" rose from the class.

Then Sister turned to me. "Now, James, this report is to last no more than ten minutes, five minutes for questions. That's it! Understood? No mention of the war beyond that . . . any . . . other . . . time. Is that clear?" She studied me. I nodded happily. "Fine, now let's get back to work."

Given this liberty, I got off on the wrong foot. I thought there should be some introduction. So, I told the class about Pearl Harbor and my cousin being on the USS Vestal when the Arizona was sunk, and was about to launch into a story about another cousin when Sister interrupted.

"James, James, James!"

"Yes, Sister?"

"What has the class learned thus far about the progress of the war?"

"Nothing I suppose, ster."

"Now why is that?"

"Because I'mmm rambling?"

"Because you're off on a tangent already." Laughter. She put her finger to her lips. "You have four minutes, and, James, it's a lonnnng time until next Wednesday. Cap it or I'll put a cap on your lips." Laughter again. I got better after that.

Recess proved a new learning experience. There was only one other boy in my class equal in size to me, Donny Costello. Everyone admired Bobby Witt, but feared Donny. He looked strong and probably was. When he found something funny, everyone laughed. When recess began, he was first to bat, no argument. I found his influence strange. I had never run into it before.

Recess was a ritual that had unwritten rules. Since it lasted only 20 minutes, everyone was in position almost immediately. Bobby Witt was the first pitcher, and Donny the first batter. When a batter made an out he went to play the outfield, and the pitcher was the next batter, and the first baseman became the pitcher, and so on. Being new, my chances of batting were between slim and none. I wasn't very good so I didn't mind. What I did mind was Donny's picking on John Knoernschild. John was a child prodigy and the smartest boy in class. John, like me, was new to St. Pat's. It was apparent he had been sheltered from the rough and tumble give and take of boys. He had a delicate physique, wore think glasses, and seemed as coordinated as a rag doll. This was evident as we returned from recess. Donny said, "Look guys!" as he tossed the softball underhand to John. John covered his face with his hands, and cowered like a three-year-old might. Everyone laughed except John and me. Donny picked up the ball again, only throwing it overhand this time. It hit

101

John in the chest and he stumbled backward and fell down. Everyone laughed again. I picked John up and said, angrily, "Don't ever do that again!"

You would have thought I said a swear word. Everyone stopped. They looked at me as if I was crazy. Only Donny remained calm. "Well, smart ass is a tough guy." He gave me a shove. I didn't shove him back. "After school, we'll see how tough."

What had I done? I wasn't tough, certainly not like my da. I wasn't even interested in being tough. I wanted to be smart like John. Each day I sat in amazement listening to him recite in class. He was beyond smart. He was a genius and the youngest person in class. I was clearly awed by him in every way. Sister accepted his little barbs in good humor. "Sister, you said 'gleam' when I think you meant 'glean,'" he would say with a guileless giggle. The meanings of both words were foreign to me.

"Did I now?" she pondered. "Well, if I did, thank you for listening so intently. I stand corrected." Then, she asked John to explain the different meaning of the two words. Delight burned in his eyes as he did. I looked around the classroom to see if others appreciated his genius. Their boring looks told another story.

Sister informed us John would be giving a piano recital at Mount St. Clare, and we were all invited to attend. She passed out a program. Sure enough, there was John's name with the pieces he would play: Edvard Grieg's piano sonata in E minor, Franz Schubert's piano sonata in B-flat; and Johannes Brahms's concerto for piano and orchestra No. 2 in B-flat. I knew nothing about classical music, but loved it when I heard it on the radio. My da would tell me to turn off that noise. How could such soothing music be considered noise? It was my astonishment at John's intelligence and respect for his talent that caused me to defend him. I expected Donny to clean my clock after school, and was wondering if John was worth it.

Sure enough, Donny was waiting for me behind the school at the end of the day. Every boy in my class was there, too, forming a ring around us. "I hope this teaches you a lesson not to butt in when it's doesn't concern you," he said, as he swung hard to my stomach. The blow knocked me off my feet. He laughed, "Had enough?" To my disbelief, he didn't hit me on the ground, actually waited for me to get up and fight or concede. "Fair fighters don't win fights," my da would say. "Only advantage you have when overmatched is surprise. Kids don't like to hit kids in the face, even mean kids don't. They go for the belly, leaving the face open. That's your target. Get in a fight Jimmy hit him in the frickin face hear me? That'll end it quick like."

No one was further from a fighter than me. My size up to this point had been my protection. Now, it was put up or shut up time. Getting to my feet, Donny did the rub-a-dub-dub my da predicted, so I hit him in the face with a left jab with a spectacular result. Blood poured out of Donny's nose and dripped down his white shirt. "God darn! Look what you did!" he said in shock, throwing his arms wide as if in surrender, "You busted my nose!" Something came over me. Defenseless as he was, I hit him again in the same spot, only harder this time. I discovered a taste for violence. Once I made him bleed, I couldn't stop. I hit him again and again blacking his eye and putting welts on his cheeks, and didn't stop until Bobby and Dick Morris pulled me back. "That's enough!"

My heart was pounding, head aching, ears ringing. I was on fire. This was a new feeling. It felt delicious. I was, after all, my da's son. Violence brought me to a peak of pleasure I had never felt before. It frightened and sickened me, too. I was out of control. John told me later as we walked home that he thought I was going to kill Donny.

"You're kidding?"

"No, I'm not, James."

"I didn't mean to hurt Donny."

"Yes you did. You have a terrible temper. I hope you learn to curb it or you will kill somebody someday."

"This is your way of thanking me?"

"I didn't need you to defend me."

"Oh, you didn't?"

"No."

"No?"

"No, James, I don't think you understand. My strength is not physical. Donny's is. That is why he's popular and I'm not. Do you want to be like Donny or me?"

"I want to be like me. You're confusing me though and making me a little mad."

103

"See? Anger boils under your skin. I see it in your eyes. You going to hit me?"

"No."

"No what?

"I'm not going to hit you. I don't like hitting people."

"I think you do. The test will be tomorrow."

"Tomorrow?"

"Tomorrow you will take Donny's place as the class bully, wait and see."

And he was right. I got to bat first in recess and Donny took my place in the field. Nothing was said. It was just how things were. Later, I tried to teach John how to catch a ball without success. He was comfortable in his genius. John lived in the 900 block on North Third, which was three blocks beyond my house. I would walk with him to the county jail and stand and talk to him. He seemed to know everything, and he was only eight. His superior intelligence was like a magnet. I'd never met anyone so smart. His seriousness, far from turning me off, was an attraction to my own confused mind. If anything, I felt terribly slow-witted and a plodder. I wonder now, these many years later, if his life fulfilled that early promise.

* * * * *

School hummed along and Donny Costello and I became good friends. He was Irish like me with what people thought an Italian name, while most people considered Fisher as being English or German. Surnames and heritage can get a bit confusing. I met Donny's uncle one day who claimed to have worked around the world, speaking several foreign languages. I asked for a sample of his language skills. What was meant to be French, German, and Italian all sounded like gibberish, or exactly the same. I had heard Father Sunbrueller speak German and Donny's uncle wasn't close to sounding like him. Donny beamed with innocent pride at this blatant deception. I wondered why adults had to lie to impress kids. Later, I learned Donny's uncle was from the east coast of the United States, and not a Midwesterner. My mother told me Midwesterners couldn't afford to get too big for their britches, while Easterners never found pants big enough to fill theirs.

* * * * *

One day I was rushing down the back steps of St. Patrick's after school, anxious to walk in the falling snow, when a voice stopped me at the door. "Hey, kid, why aren't you out for basketball?" That simple declarative statement was to change my life again. The voice didn't wait for an answer. It informed me that a kid my size should be playing basketball. "How old are you? What grade you in?" I told him. He smiled broadly, "You're going to be a big fellow. How tall are you?" My mother had just measured me the day before. Since last June, I had grown two inches. "Five-six." He shook his head and laughed, "Know you've got to play basketball."

"Bring a pair of sneakers Monday and we'll see where you are."

"Where I am?" I answered stupidly. I had no idea what he meant.

"Yeah, basketball-wise."

"Basketball-wise? I've never played basketball."

"Just be here Monday with your sneakers. Don't worry about anything else, okay? Practice starts at 3:30." With that he disappeared into the gym. I saw some of my classmates shooting around. There was Donny Costello, Jimmy Halbach, Joe Zimmer, Jim Rederer, Joe Moldt, and Bobby Witt. Bobby Witt? Was he a basketball player, too? He never told me he played basketball. Knowing he played excited me. I had to play basketball. I just had to. I was sorry I didn't get a chance to play much baseball with Bobby last summer with summer school and all. Besides, the other guys at the courthouse didn't warm up to me the way he did. Then my da didn't allow me out until my dinner settled, which meant I never got there until after they had chosen up sides. Plus, I never got to go to Riverview Stadium at night and shag flies with the courthouse gang. I couldn't hit the darn baseball anyway, and Bobby could hit it every time. I couldn't throw or catch very well either. In fact, I was a little afraid of the baseball. The only thing I was good at was throwing and catching a football. That was different. Baseball was more a finesse sport. You didn't have to be big or strong or anything. You just had to know how to play, and I didn't. Would basketball be like baseball? If so, maybe I wasn't cut out for it either.

All these thoughts were assailing my senses as I walked through a snowy afternoon. Usually, I was happy spinning and dancing through the snow, taking my time, enjoying every minute of the short walk home. But not today. Today I had questions. Once in the house, the snow melting on my face and clothes, I could feel almost immediately that my timing was bad. My da was on the phone, his face drawn, his brow narrowed, his eyelids leaden like they were too heavy to open completely. He whispered to my mother as he put his hand over the phone. "Thought it was the railroad calling. It's a collection agency." The color was drained from his face.

"Now listen here goddamn it," he said into the mouthpiece weakly. I knew he swore to booster his confidence. A barrage of curse words was directed at the inanimate mouthpiece and would have been funny if it wasn't so tragic. My mother, leaning against the door to the kitchen, her left palm under her right elbow, was quietly smoking. My da was now shaking and nearly out of control. It was then that she moved to the phone, put her hand gently on his shoulder, and took the phone from his feeble hand. Once free of the phone, he colored the air with more cursing. Mother waved him to be quiet, but not sternly, then turned up her hearing aid, and listened intently.

"Well, ma'am, I don't blame you for being upset. You're just doing your job. You're right you don't deserve that kind of treatment. I couldn't agree more. No, my husband has no right to talk to you that way. He hasn't been well, you see, and isn't quite himself yet. I know. I know. That doesn't justify any of this. True. You're not well yourself? Well, then, I can see how this would be upsetting." She then takes a long deep drag of her cigarette that is not much more than an ash, waves to my da to get her another. He brings a pack over. She hunches up her shoulder and cradles the phone between her ear and neck, then shakes one out and lights it with the fading butt.

"I'm sorry to hear that. Obviously, you haven't received our check. Are you absolutely sure? You've checked. You are sure. Fine. Well, we'll have to remedy that, won't we? Otherwise, we'll never get well, will we?"

Listening again. "Hmm, yes. Well, thank you for bringing this to our attention. No, it's quite all right. No, you didn't act out of turn. Just doing your job. Thanks again. Goodbye." My mother then hung up, lit another cigarette with the butt of hers, handed it to my da, who by now was wringing wet, sweat beading on his brow with damp patches under his armpits and the front of his shirt in a Rorschach pattern. He looked as if he had gone five rounds with Joe Louis.

"Dorothy, you know we can't pay that bill. There's no check. There won't be any check." His powerful arms flailing at shadows while his voice, now dry, husky, and shallow, had lost its steam.

"Ray, don't you think she knows that? Can you imagine having to make such a call? Think about her. That call was as hard for her to make as for us to answer. She'll tell her boss what I said."

"He won't believe her!"

"Of course not. Not for a minute but Ray, she did her duty. Besides, they have no choice but to be patient. They get half of what they collect. Half of nothing is still nothing."

He was still feeling his rage. "What will we do when she calls back?"

"We'll deal with it then, won't we?" She lit yet another cigarette on the end of her still glowing one, finally noticing me in the doorway. "Now, Jimmy, tell me why you're standing there with your clothes dripping wet?" I felt like Little Abner with a dark cloud over my head, knowing there never is a right time for asking, certainly not now for a pair of sneakers. The image pulsating through my mind was not this, nor was it my parents fighting on the phone with a bill collector. I was still abuzz with my brief encounter with St. Pat's basketball coach.

He was 15 and a freshman at Clinton High. His name was Dean Burridge. Dean was handsome with dark curly hair, olive skin, piercing brown eyes in sunken sockets, a strong chin, a thin straight nose, white teeth, and a warm smile, which gave me the feeling of his being both serious and sincere. His v-neck, cream color sweater clung to his somewhat rounded but powerful shoulders and chest with the sleeves pulled up to reveal hairy, muscular forearms. His brown slacks were form fitting, and pressed with a sharp crease, while he wore brown penny loafers. I noticed that he walked bent slightly forward like athletes do. He wasn't even half a head taller than me, but there was something in his voice that I found magnetic. It was soft yet deeply masculine while his demeanor exuded confidence. I guess I felt all this before I knew it. Whatever he wanted of me, I knew I would give him. Yes, I would play basketball. Being around the energy he radiated was soothing like being wrapped in a warm blanket. I trusted him before I knew him, which gave me confidence in myself. There was no strutting. He was all business. He was the most celebrated athlete ever to come out of St. Pat's, but there was no sense that his power would be used to diminish mine. He was the first person, other than my mother, who had power over me but didn't flaunt it. He had no need to bend me to his will. I loved him. I know that now, but I only felt it then. I have throughout these years loved the image of him from that initial encounter. Wherever I have gone, whatever I have done, he made me more than I am. He was a god in human form, and I never met his kind again.

Coach Burridge lived with his uncle, Timmy Burns, on Fifth Street off Second Avenue North. His mother, Timmy's sister, was a Justice of the Peace out west somewhere. I never heard mention of a father. Timmy Burns managed the Clinton Liquor Store. The state controlled the sale of liquor in those days with only two liquor stores in Clinton, one in Lyons and the other near the Modernistic Ballroom downtown. A passbook was required to buy liquor. Timmy was quite a Clinton celebrity in his own right, supporting athletes like Therol Petersen, Harold Lutz, and Dick Price with pocket change when they needed it. He hung out at George D. Reynolds's Cigar Store, where he held court on sports book. Reynolds was a coffee shop and cigar emporium, serving breakfast, lunch, and dinner and selling the finest Havana cigars.

It was exciting to think of playing basketball with Bobby Witt. He was the class leader. He didn't assert himself but simply led by example. Bobby was quick-witted and intuitive, gifted with both compassion and humor, a boy liked by his classmates and respected by the nuns. I knew from the first how lucky I was to call him friend and how deserving he was of my trust. He put up with my mood swings and seriousness, stoically listened to my ravings even when directed at him. He was unlike anyone I had known. His baseball playing was so natural and fluid that I could imagine him equally good in basketball. In contrast, I was clumsy, tentative, and aggressive. The aggressiveness got me into trouble with Donny. After that fight, Bobby kidded me,

"Congratulations, now you're the class bully. How's it feel?"

"No I'm not!" I replied loudly, remembering what John Knoerschild had said. The idea of being a bully was disgusting. Mother said bullies were cowards and Bobby was accusing me of being one. "I'm not a coward! Take it back!" I grabbed his arm as if to hit him, but he knew I wouldn't.

"Not what?" he said, shaking free of me nonchalantly.

"You just called me a bully. Bullies are cowards."

"Not where I come from. Where'd you hear that?"

"My mother."

He scratched his head. "Boy, I never heard that one before." Then he smiled. "You calling Donny a coward? That's a good one. Bet that'll get his dander up again." He poked me in the arm. "I can see it now, round two," putting two fingers up and dashing ahead of me, laughing hard.

"No, that's not what I'm saying. I'm saying he's not a bully. Neither am I."

"Okay. Have it your way."

All of this poured into my mind in milliseconds as I stood in the doorway, dripping wet trying to decipher the mood of my parents. Most of the sidewalks had not been shoveled and I raced home punching my feet through snowdrifts up to my knees. The courthouse clock was singing to me, striking four o'clock as I rounded the corner at Bobby's house. Oh, no! I forgot my boots! They were still at school beside the door where coach Burridge stopped me. I stomped my feet hard on the porch but my shoes and pants were still caked with snow as I stepped inside, dripping wet.

"Jimmy, look at you! Where're your boots?"

"Mom, they want me to play basketball! You'll have to get me a pair of sneakers this weekend!" I said in a rush.

"What the hell did he say?" My da stormed out of the kitchen a cup of coffee in his hand. My mother still had her hand on the phone as if it were a magnet. I would imagine it was still warm. She put up her hand like a stop sign. "Ray, let me handle this." She helped me off with my wet clothes in the doorway, pulled my shoes and wet socks off, and wiped my feet with a towel. I unbuckled my belt and lifted my legs, first one, then the other as she took my pants off. There I stood with no pants on still in my coat and hat. I felt naked and a little cold as I took them off, and threw them on the floor.

"We don't have any money, Jimmy, you know that, you heard us on the phone, for sneakers or much of anything. Things are slow right now."

"You goddamn right they're slow. Kid is big enough to get a job. Help out around here," my da said punching the air with his coffee cup and splashing coffee on the dining room linoleum.

"But mom," I said feeling crushed and a little dizzy from a whirl of her cigarette smoke and a vigorous toweling, "can't I have them?"

"Look at your shoes!"

"I can't play basketball?" The question hung in the air like cigarette smoke.

"I didn't say that." She turned to my da who was about ready to rupture a blood vessel. "Ray, you still have that pair of bowling shoes Tony Tonzig gave you?" He nodded. "Well, there you are. They're almost new. Tony hardly worn them, and they're about your size." She went to the closet, threw things left and right, and down behind everything was a green box with a big black bowling ball insignia on the side. "Here they are," she said triumphantly, "try them on."

First, I looked at them with my heart sinking. They were leather and didn't look like sneakers. I turned them over to look at the soles. "Mom," I said in horror, "one sole's leather!" She scooped them out of my hands and placed them on the dining room table. After a level look, she bit her lip. "Hmm, is isn't it? Now that won't do will it?" Turning the shoe over and over again in her hand as if that would change leather-to-rubber, she finally went to the hutch and brought back a pencil and piece of paper, and made a note. "Take this to Cramm's and pick up a package of Cat's Paw." I narrowed my eyes in puzzlement. "They're rubber soles made to be glued to shoes."

Excitedly, I started for the door.

"Make sure it comes with glue, and charge it."

That caused me to hesitate. "Go on! Go on!" She knew why I hesitated.

"Charge it," those hated words. A grilling was bound to follow when I uttered them at the grocery. It was a game between mom and the grocer with me always in the middle. Mom would hand me a list: 4 loaves of white bread, 2 pounds of butter, 3 pounds of ground beef, a 2-pound can of Maxwell House coffee, and 10 pounds of potatoes. She saved up her rationing books for this booty, but that didn't matter. Frank would always ask, "Did your mother give you money to pay on the bill?" I would shake my head, "No." Frank would turn, put his hands on his hips, look to the ceiling, walk away, come back, and then examine me from my shoelaces up as if I were a suspicious character.

"Here's all I can do, Jimmy, and I shouldn't be doing this. I can give your mother two loaves of bread, a pound of butter, a pound of ground beef, a small can of coffee, and five pounds of potatoes. That's it! Tell your mother this is the last time I can fill her order until she pays me something. Will you tell her that, Jimmy?"

A dull flush would creep into my cheeks. I'd shift my weight from one foot to the other, and look so ill at ease that Frank would feel sorry for pressing so hard. With an edge of despair in his voice, he would add, "Times are hard for us all."

I would nod, take the two sacks, and thank God once again I escaped with the groceries. When I arrived home, and shared my woe, vowing never to go to the store again, my mother would smile through blue smoke. "God bless Frank. That's exactly what we needed, Jimmy."

Nothing ever seemed to daunt her, but the Cat's Paw proved a failure. No matter what she tried, it wouldn't stick. She heated the sole over the gas burner, made grooves in the sole with a kitchen knife, even tried to nail the Cat's Paw to the leather with tacks. Everything failed. "That's it, Jimmy. Now we have a choice, don't we, basketball practice in bowling shoes or no basketball, what's it to be?" I took the shoes from her with tears in my eyes, and whispered, "Basketball," then headed upstairs to my room, stopping at the door. "Thanks, mommy."

She waved with the salute of a stream of smoke. "Jimmy, as I've told you many times before, if it's meant to be, it's already been. You can't fool Fate."

Monday came. The hours passed as if the gears in the hall clock were stuck and had to overcome immense inertia to move forward. Finally, it was time. After removing my shoes and putting on the bowling shoes in the boys' locker room, I slipped and slid on the cement floor even before reaching the basketball court. If that wasn't bad enough, I found I couldn't dribble. I patted the ball like a girl. The guys turned away and laughed. Bobby Witt, I noticed, had large hands and dribbled the ball with a slight roll and gentle touch. It seemed as if an invisible tether connected the ball to his hand, and when he shot the ball, it was poetry in motion. Once I got past him I could see the skill level of the others fell off drastically. Perhaps that is why I wasn't embarrassed. I was indifferent to what they might think. So when they laughed at my shenanigans, I laughed with them. Why not? What choice did I have? I was terrible. Clearly, my performance was a fiasco, after all, what will be has already been.

Coach Burridge came in while I was making a fool of myself. He didn't laugh. Instead, he took me aside. "What size shoe do you wear?" I told him. He smiled. "You've got a big understanding for a 4th grader."

"I know," I smiled back, "feet are already bigger than my da's."

"No kidding?" he smiled. "Well, think I have a solution. I'll bring you a used pair from high school." And he did.

The second night of basketball practice is embossed in my memory. The initial drill was how to properly make lay ups to the basket. Right-handed shooters, coach explained, should go off the left foot and lay the basketball against the board with a gentle roll to the right and above the rim. Sounded easy, as he demonstrated, but it wasn't. I couldn't do it. The drill was hard enough but I had another problem. I was naturally left-handed and had been forced to be right handed. "Girls can be left-handed," my da declared, "boys are right-handed. Left-handed men are weenies." Coach Burridge bounced the ball to me at the head of the line. Clumsily, I dribbled to the basket and went off the wrong foot. He retrieved the ball, demonstrated the move again with ballet precision, then said, "Left foot! Left foot! Plant the left foot!" Easy for him to say. I couldn't do it. This went on for at least twenty minutes with the other boys patiently waiting their turn to shoot. About the 40th time, I finally went off on the left foot but missed the basket, but never got the feet wrong again.

Basketball, after that second night, became a passion. I found something I loved. Every available moment that I could, I spent in the gym. At home, I put up a two-pound Maxwell House coffee can with the top and bottom lids cut out and mounted it to the basement wall. Bobby would come over almost every night during the winter and we would play games with a tennis ball, pretending we were high school stars.

The St. Patrick's gym was also the St. James parish hall where bingo was played on Friday and Saturday nights. If we wanted to use the gym on the weekend, it meant cleaning up before playing. The gym could be freezing, with no heat, but we would ignore the cold. We loved playing. Chuck Holm, a Courthouse Tiger, who lived across the street from Kirkwood School, also loved basketball, but he didn't have access to a gym. He played on an outdoor snow-packed court with the basketball hoop a rusty iron ring and no net, the air so cold the basketball often wouldn't bounce. Persistence paid off. He became the purest of shooters.

Although we had the advantage of a gym, we had another problem. Someone had to get the key from the rectory. That meant confronting Father Finefield in the midst of having his breakfast after saying Mass. My selection to get the key came as a result of the Donny Costello showdown. It had been Donny's role. Now it fell to me. Father liked Donny. Donny lived only two doors north of the church, and was always doing little chores for Father. It helped, too, that he was dutiful by nature, whereas I was not. No surprise, it went wrong from the first. I knocked at the back door of the rectory. No answer. Then I used the doorbell. Still, no answer. I waited, cold as it was, the guys huddled by the school door expectantly. I wasn't about to leave. I could smell the aroma of bacon and coffee. After another minute, I knocked again. This time I heard the rustle of fabric noisily moving toward the door. It was the housekeeper.

"Do you know what time it is?" she barked.

"Yes, ma'am, it's noon," I said as evenly as I could, forcing a smile, "I've come for the key to the school. We have to practice basketball." From the dining room, I heard the gruff voice, "Who is it?" He knew very well who it was and why I was there.

"Tall blond boy, Father. What's your name?"

"Jimmy Fisher."

"Jimmy Fisher, Father. He wants the key to the school to play basketball."

Father stormed to the door, white napkin clinging to his Roman collar, his white hair contrasting with a flushed face and flaring nostrils. "Such impertinence." He shook his head vigorously. "Such bad manners, can't you see I'm dining?" He looked me in the eye, and I could see his eyes were bloodshot through his thick glasses. We held eye contact until he finally looked away, ripping the napkin from his throat. Obviously, he didn't like me much. Well, the feeling was mutual. So, what's it going to be, Father, I thought. He wasn't a bad looking man, bespectacled with gold rimmed frames, piercing flint blue eyes, thin nose and lips, but with everything about him small. He was fine boned with classic features and delicate feminine hands, which I noticed were carefully manicured. He was obviously meticulous about his dress with his clothes smelling as if fresh from the dry cleaners and his shoes as shiny as those of a US Marine.

"Do you have any consideration of people?"

Why ask someone such a self-deprecating question? Feeling my temperature rising, instead of answering I maintained my control with practiced blankness.

"I don't believe you do," he answered for me.

It was hard for him not to notice my foot was inside his doorway. What is it going to be, Father, I thought, balls in your court.

"Does your mother have any idea . . . " He trembled with disgust, but moved to the wall, yanked the key from the rack. "Here, take this. Make sure you lock up and return it. The very idea. . . " His voice fading as I moved swiftly away.

"Thank you, Father," I said leaping in one jump from the five-step porch to the ground, jubilant that once again good had triumphed over evil. In retrospect, I think Father owed us gratitude rather than scorn. After all, we provided janitorial service without compensation for those many winters, and were never thanked for it. Before we could play, we had to clear the gym of hundreds of chairs and fifty or more tables. Then we had to sweep the floor with chemical compound to restore it to its original polish. This was done every weekend during the basketball season or winter months without fail. Our efficiency was motivated by the short afternoon light of winter. Father would never allow us to use electricity. Everyone knew his assignment and did it with dispatch. One folded the chairs, another carried them to the stage, a third, stacked them properly, a fourth folded tables, a fifth and sixth carried the tables to the stage, a seventh and eighth stacked them on the stage next to the chairs. The ninth and tenth guys put down the chemical compound and swept the floor. Within twenty minutes, the gym was again ready for basketball. Given the diminishing commodity of daylight, the tempo of play was hectic and exhilarating. I still remember the studied concentration of Dick Morris dribbling the ball down the court, with little Jimmy Halbach in quick pursuit. We called him "Super" because his hair would stand straight up as Dick crashed him into the stage going in for a lay up. Jim Rederer was nearly as tall as I was but a lot bulkier. One time he crashed into me as I was going in for a lay up and caught me with his knee to my groin. I never knew such pain. I ran outside and dove into a snow bank hoping to put the fire out of my loins. Guys laughed at the angel I made in the snow bank.

By the end of scrimmage on Sunday, we were all pretty beat up. Only Bobby had the finesse to avoid all this bumping and bruising. I can still see him coming across the key and shooting the ball behind his ear in a hook shot that I could never block. He wrote the definition of finesse. We would play until we couldn't see the ball or each other very well. I would return the key at sundown, and suffer the customary rebuke of the housekeeper, whom I knew was only doing her job. "Try to be a little less impish next time, young man. It doesn't serve you or your interests to provoke Father." She was right. It didn't. What she didn't know is that we were kindred spirits exercising similar demons. She was nice, like a grandmother I never had.

"Yes, ma'am," I would say and mean it for about twenty seconds.

* * * * *

James R. Fisher, Jr.

`

Chapter 9

Sacrifice

Finish, good lady! The bright day is done.

--Antony and Cleopatra

It is June 6, 1943. Feeling the sun through the soot-encrusted windows of St. Patrick's gym, where we are in our final assembly, warms my face. I smile, lean back in my collapsible chair, close my eyes, soak up the rays, and squeeze my mind into quiet jubilation. School is over!

What a year! I made the basketball team, first team sixth grade and I'm only in fourth grade. Bobby Witt made it, too. We played with fabulous Jim Junker, who could shoot the eyes out of the basket, and Tom Clark, who seemed nearly as tall as God. Tom shot left-handed. I loved to watch him cross the key and put the ball up. Bill Christiansen, a fifth grader, a fancy Dan with his body going in all directions at once, completed the line-up.

Basketball was still on my mind even though baseball season was here. Thinking about it gave me shivers. Bobby and I got to see Dean Burridge play at Clinton High. Only a freshman this past winter, he got some playing time on the varsity. Next basketball season he'll be a starter. Never happened before. But it will again when Bobby starts there as a sophomore. Two St. Patrick's boys!

It was fun to watch coach Burridge play, but it seemed more than fun for Bobby. "Notice how he drives hard to the basket," he said jerking my arm. "See him pull up with his defender stumbling backwards leaving him unguarded to shoot?"

"No."

"Come on! You saw that, didn't you?"

"I guess."

"I'm going to do that!"

"Why?"

"I'm not too big now. Might never be too big. Doesn't hurt coach." His face twisted into resolve. "Not going to hurt me!"

He was right on both counts. Bobby would never reach six feet, and it didn't hurt him. What amazed me about Bobby is that he didn't just watch a game. He coached a game. It could be basketball or baseball. Didn't matter. He would study every move. "Know the difference between a zone and man-to-man defense?"

"Yeah," I lied. I know coach Burridge talked about them, even showed us the difference, but I wasn't paying attention. Bobby was. I liked to shoot baskets, and hated to play defense. Soon as you mentioned defense my eyes glassed over. Bobby already excelled at both offense and defense. Another thing Bobby was apt to lecture was free throw shooting.

"Can't you see," his face very serious, "that's why they're called free throws, nobody's guarding you. Only a moron wouldn't take advantage of that."

Well, I guess I was a moron. Coach Burridge, I noticed, was great on defense, stealing the ball, and driving the full court for easy lay ups. Everything the coach told us he did. This wasn't lost on Bobby. It was funny in a way. Bobby was a good student, but he treated schoolwork the way I treated sport. I was a coach in the classroom, studying the teachers, seeing what they thought important, more observant of students who were really smart, guiding my efforts to be in sync with theirs. Could we say the die was cast when we were nine-year-olds? Bobby would move gracefully from grammar to high school to college in athletics, and then coaching, and me a more academic route into industry.

The spring of 1943 was frustrating. The Fisher's had a ritual. We ate dinner promptly at 5 o'clock. Clean up was over by 5:45, but I was not allowed to go to the courthouse "until your dinner's settled!" This meant not before 6:00. By then they had chosen up sides, and were playing. Bobby Witt and Dick Crider were typically the captains. One would throw the bat to the other, where his hand caught it was where the hand-over-hand started to see who had first choice. I never got considered because I was always too late.

It was painful to wait for my dinner to settle. I would count the seconds off, one thousand one, one thousand two. To cover 15 minutes meant going to nine hundred, but sixty was my limit. Even then, I cheated. Once I hit one thousand forty, I would rush to get to a minute. Fifteen minutes! An eternity! It seemed longer than the school year. There was absolutely nothing I could do. I would pine, pout and brush by my da's sofa chair, where his face was blanketed behind The Clinton Herald. He wouldn't raise an eyebrow. You would think I was invisible, that I had suddenly vaporized into Lamont Cranston, the Shadow, only to materialize when my mother said,

"Ray, it's six. Can the kids go out now?" He would do a Father Finefield roll of his eyes as if in excruciating pain. "I suppose, but back by 7:30."

On, no! 7:30? That's when the guys are through playing and kidding around, go to the A&W Root Beer Stand, ride their bikes, or go to the stadium to shag flies. 7:30? Things are just starting to happen. Why 7:30? I'm bigger than any of the guys, so why can't I stay out later? That's what I'd like to know. So I don't have a bike. So I don't have any money. So I don't know anything about shagging. So what? So "No!" he yells, "and that's the end of that." He must be related to Father Finefield.

What the guys didn't mind when I got there, was for me to be steady catcher for both sides. Nobody likes to be catcher anyway. Incredibly, I fell in love with the position. I loved everything there was about catching, putting on the catching gear – shin pads, chest protector, and mask – handling the pitcher, catching the ball when the batter missed, feeling the pop of the ball in my glove, throwing to second base when the runner tried to steal, being able to watch the play of the entire field, but most of all, being in control. No other position in sport exhilarated me to the level of catching.

Watching older guys play at the courthouse, like Ramey Baker, was an inspiration. Ramey was a catcher, and Ray Jorgensen was his pitcher. Ray only had one arm but he was very fast and had great control. He would tuck his glove under his arm when he was about to throw, then grab it and place it on his only hand when he followed through. It was something to see. I would watch Ramey squat behind the batter, signal Ray with the fingers of his right hand between his legs, using his glove to hide the signal from the third base coach. He would stick his right hand down with his elbow out to prevent the first base coach from stealing the signal. We didn't have any coaches at first and third, but I always pretended we did. I studied the way Ramey dug balls out of the dirt, blocked wild pitches, and moved his legs to the right or left to handle wide pitches, still in a crouch, and copied this, too. I even learned to throw like Ramey, bringing the ball back behind my ear and breaking my wrist to send it back on a line to the pitcher, or straight to second base when a man was trying to steal. My arm wasn't nearly as strong as Ramey's, and after a while, my elbow started to hurt, but I ignored the pain. Three years later, I was to pay for this.

I'm ten now. I'm tall and husky without being fat. I could easily pass for 12 or 13. Proof that I'm only ten is that I notice girls, but prefer playing baseball. It's impossible not to notice Iowa girls in the summer. They seem to bloom like flowers and to float like butterflies. Their corn silk flaxen hair hangs loosely around their shoulders, their sky blue or dusty brown eyes seem like jewels in the sun, their trim figures clothed in pastel colored starched pinafores show freckled arms and backs, and their lanky legs like corn stalks tapering to shapely ankles make my heart beat faster without knowing why. These blooming flowers float by me without noticing me, laughing, bouncing, happily skipping along without a care in the world. I stare at them when they aren't looking. They seem to understand a lot more about everything than I do. Why is that? They're not any smarter in school. Outside school, they seem to live in a different world than mine. The looks they give me, like drop dead, creep! Then giggle. I don't have a clue. I really don't. I'm glad I've got baseball. They make me crazy.

"Girls are dangerous," my mother tells me. "Risky business. Can turn your head so you don't know what side's up. Don't let them push you down and kiss you."

"That's funny. Girls don't even notice me."

"Funny, huh? Don't kid yourself. They notice all right. Your sister's friends have got their sights on you, boy, so be wary!" Mother always called me "boy" the way da called people "fella" when she was aggravated. What did I do? She taps out a cigarette, goes to the hutch, opens a drawer and takes out a box of matches, lights her cigarette, then takes a long thoughtful drag on it looking to the ceiling, a twirling spiral of smoke follows her eyes. "With that baby face and big body you'll attract them like bears to honey."

"Baby face? I look like a baby?" What could be more humiliating?

"No, just happen you have a pretty face with that husky body. Soft, not hard looks. You have the best of both sexes." She draws in on her cigarette forming a big ash, goes to the window and moves the curtain away from the glass. The ash falls to the floor but she doesn't seem to notice. Elsie Judd waves to her from her kitchen window next door. She waves back with her cigarette.

"You're beautiful, Jimmy," she says with her back to me, "you've a beautiful figure." Her voice is husky as if she is about to cry. "You're something of a peacock, you know," smiling through liquid eyes, "a strange but beautiful bird. It won't be easy for you. It never is for beautiful people who don't belong to anyone."

It was such conversations that disturbed me. Later, I learned men had physiques and women figures, women were beautiful and men handsome. I've wondered if my mother preferred for me to be a girl. Perhaps that explains my da's anxiety about me.

My mother, sitting on the chintz-covered sofa, her arms cradled in front of her, hands cupping her elbows, said, "I've received a letter from Sister Helen."

The hair on the back of my head rose like bristles in the wind. "Sister Helen?"

"The same," she said, taking a long drag on her cigarette producing a long flaming ash, which I was certain would fall in her lap, but she stamped it out in the ashtray before it happened. She took the red cellophane wrapper off a fresh pack, tore a corner off, pounded the pack on the coffee table, pulled a cigarette out, and lit it meditatively.

"Want me to read it?" Her eyes narrowed to make a "v" on her forehead.

"Sure." What else could I say?

With that she took the letter from a pocket in her apron and read it to me.

Dear Mrs. Fisher,

It has been a delight to teach your son, James, this past year. But I feel it would be remiss of me not to voice my concern. I see trouble ahead for James if he doesn't curb his bold spirit and carefree individualism. Peer pressure is a normal influence on young people. Not your James. He seems to delight in being his own person. This tendency surfaces in a selective rather than general disregard for authority. I apologize if I seem vague. Permit me to be more specific. He respects me and abides by my rules but seems to delight in aggravating Father Finefield, and of course Father is pastor of St. Patrick's.

You are his mother. It is for this reason I share this concern with you. Please feel free to call me at Mount St. Clare if you would like to discuss this further.

Sincerely yours in Christ, Jesus, I remain ever,

Sister Mary Helen, OSF

Still standing in the doorway, all the sunshine of my spirits zapped, I held on desperately to that first line of the letter. "I told you Sister liked me, didn't I?"

My mother locks her eyes on me, which means trouble. Still, she says nothing. She grinds her half-smoked cigarette into the small crystalline ashtray, gets up, and takes the ashtray with overflowing butts into the kitchen, and dumps them into the garbage bin. She removes her crispy apron. Hangs it over one of the chairs. She smoothes it into pleats, then comes back into the living room, sits down, and pats the sofa for me to join her there. I move hesitantly to the far end. "I was only eighteen," she begins, "when you were born.

I thought I could be a proper mother without anybody telling me what I was supposed to do to be one. It came natural to women, I thought. A guy gets a girl pregnant, and her body changes, and so does the rest of her with it. I didn't want anybody telling me how to be a mom to my little boy because I knew. I had this grand picture of things. Me spooning baby food into your mouth, and your father looking on with love and devotion. I decided to make another baby fast as I could because I believe kids aren't supposed to grow up alone. I wanted to do things the way a mom is supposed to do things. So, we had your sister on your birthday. I was alone with two babies with a husband off in Chicago living it up with his brother. Your father came home long enough to get me pregnant with your little brother. It was at this point that I had a physical and emotional break down. I spent the next few years in hospital with you three kids farmed out to relatives and, when they tired of you, to foster parents." The sofa pillow I crush to my chest, making a sound into it, which was more a whimper than a cry. My mother didn't notice.

"But I didn't know, see. That was my problem. I thought you had a baby and you loved him and he grew up and had babies of his own. I didn't think about the other parts, the talking to him, listening to him, scolding him when he'd done wrong, not flying off the handle when you wanted to scream to high heaven, or smack the daylights out of him for doing what you told him a hundred times not to do. I thought of birthdays, of Thanksgiving, Christmas, of going to church as a family on Easter Sunday. We'd have such good times, I thought. I'd be such a good mommy, even though I lost my mother when I was still a little girl. I thought we'd love each other, respect each other, and be there for each other." She opens her arms to have me move toward her. I do, resting my head in her lap. I can feel her warmth and her heart beating through her pulsating thighs. "I guess what I'm saying is that I haven't done right by you, Jimmy. I thought I knew everything, so I didn't want to learn. What I'm saying is that I'm a failure, but I didn't mean to be. I've treated you too much as my friend, a person I could unburden my heart to, forgetting you were only a little boy. I robbed you of that, Jimmy, and I'm sorry. I've made you so serious, so driven, and now you're starting," she sighs, "to run into walls for my indulgence."

My body is tense, but not quite as rigid as it had been before. "Mother, why are you telling me all this?"

With tears in her eyes, she smiles oddly, "I guess it means you're not as perfect as I thought."

"Now you sound like da," I wax hurt, and it makes her smile. I'd seen her Irish side before. "Your mother has Celtic guilt and Viking resilience," uncle Bill said to me one day when I was older, "both gifts of her parents. Viking Protestantism buoys her up and Irish Catholicism pulls her down." Perhaps without meaning to, that explained how he felt about my parents.

Even at ten, I didn't believe her words, didn't think she saw herself as a failed mother. That was her Irish talking. She said it to make me say, "No, mother, you're not a failed mother, you're a great mother," which I always did. I didn't understand her rocky life; the impact of her mother's early death, the neglect of a husband who still had to sow his wild oats, because what I saw between them was savage love. If anything, he adored her. He was a much more loving man than she was a loving woman. His heart was on his sleeve. Hers was in her head. As for my early life, I remembered foster care, when my only family was my little sister, Patsy, but I didn't feel disadvantaged. How could I? It was all I knew. I had nothing to compare. It was confusing to be told I was neglected, and then in the next breath I was blessed beyond measure.

"Are you going to call Sister?"

She rises from the sofa, goes across the living room to the window, and lets the curtain fall back into place where she had before pushed it aside. She is very beautiful, slender but with round curves, a round face with piercing blue eyes, full lips and a Norwegian pug nose. She has harvest wheat blond hair like all her brothers, and what my da calls "Betty Grable legs." She picks up a Life magazine, and perches on the edge of one of the cushions on the sofa, then sits on a cushion. It is so worn that its stuffing has long ago been packed into tight little pellets. They afford all the comfort of having to sit on a patch of wet sand on the banks of the Mississippi. She opens the magazine to an article, I can see war pictures, and appears to be reading, but isn't.

"God, Jimmy, what am I to do with you? Sometimes I think you've mush for brains. You're sure we're related?" I study her face to see if she's joking or serious. She doesn't smile.

"You're not going to call Sister?"

"I called her." The burning tobacco of her cigarette glows, fades and quivers like a firefly. She punishes me with a pause. "She let you off the hook," she says finally, "Sister Flavian talked to Father Finefield. He says you're arrogant. Sister Flavian claims you're spirited."

My mother breaks into a wide grin, putting her hand over her mouth to stifle a laugh. "Spirited?" she resumes, making like Father Finefield's grumpy voice, "he's unbearable is what he is, Sister."

Quite the actress, she now displays the radiance of the storyteller. "Sister Flavian agreed with Father that you can be burdensome, but she added, 'he does get the hall cleaned for bingo, Father.' That seemed to break the ice. Father gave a guttural chuckle of concession. Sister Helen said Father respects Sister Flavian and enjoys bringing a twinkle to her eye. As for you, Sister Helen said, once she wrote the letter, she felt everything would work out fine." Time would prove her concern more accurate than her prophecy.

$$* \quad * \quad * \quad * \quad *$$

James R. Fisher, Jr.

Chapter 10

A Sense of Place

The place is dignified by the doer's deed.

--Shakespeare

The Clinton County Courthouse stands tall in its rustic dominance, it towers over everything in town. It is like a watchful god, giving me a sense of place. As long as I can see the courthouse, which is even lighted at night, I am never lost. It appears beyond time's restraints, unchanged, constant in my haunted memory. I am anchored to it and am home. The courthouse is sanity in a world gone mad, a world restless to change. It is at peace with its past and not anxious for its future. Were it not for the courthouse, I would feel shipwrecked in a senseless sea. It is at the courthouse that life takes on the music of the day, where I am teased, cajoled, and shaped into a boy. It is where I am daily baptized into the give and take of life, where the delicious fragrance of freedom touches freedom's limits,

127

where I grow atom-by-atom, not in an explosion of growth, but in joyful participation in the sorrows of the world.

The summer of 1943 is especially distinctive because it is a season without summer school. It is also a summer with America at war. Clinton men and women are in uniform overseas, in some military camps, in uniform on leave here, or working in Clinton industries to support the war effort. You hardly ever see anyone between twenty and thirty who is not in uniform. I love seeing the uniforms, especially of U. S. Marines. Marines wear their uniforms so tight fitting that they seem painted on: dark blue jackets, light blue shirts with red ties, and blue pants with red and yellow stripes down the seams of their trousers. Campaign ribbons and medals are carefully placed over the left breast pocket, with caps and white gloves held in hand. Their shoes shine like patent leather, but I know they're not. Marines walk like they have steel in their spines; topped off with clean-shaven faces with no sideburns, burr haircuts, sharp eyes, straight noses, firm lips, and strong chins. Some of these young men I had seen around town before they went into the Marines; then they looked different. Now, they look as if melted down, poured into a mold, and made to come out the same. I gawk at them like an idiot wondering where they left their Superman capes. They always smile back as if they understand my awe, and wink with affection. I blush with pride knowing no harm can come to me with Superman as my protector.

It is the first summer when my da is gone more than he is home. He is on the road constantly deadheading to Boone to bring troop trains of wounded G.I.'s from the South Pacific to hospitals in the east. This is also a time when Schick Army Hospital is being completed in Lyons with a capacity of 2,500 patients. The facility is being built on 28-acre Root Memorial Park with an additional 80 acres adjoining the park to provide the most advanced medical technology in surgery, rehabilitation, and convalescent care and treatment available. Schick Hospital will also have an Olympic size swimming pool, a professional size gymnasium and basketball court, an athletic field, a fully equipped weight room, and all the trappings of a small city.

We have two carpenters from Peoria boarding with us who are working on the hospital. Of an evening, they drink coffee, smoke cigarettes, and tell stories of their daily adventures. I love listening to them, except when there is a game at the stadium. It is a time when, with my da's frequent absences from home at night, my mother is in charge. What luck! She allows me freedom never allowed by him. It finds me up at 7, splashing water on my face to wake up, a quick bowl of hot cream of wheat, along with two slices of buttered and jellied toast, a glass of orange juice, and a cup of coffee. I'm out of the house by 7: 30, and over to the courthouse by 7:31, ready to play baseball all day, or until I get ungodly hungry, which usually occurs about noon. My mother makes me a bologna sandwich and pours me a glass of milk, and then it is back to the courthouse again until dinnertime. I eat my dinner in record time, don't rest it, and am back to the courthouse until dark, which is now almost eight. If there is an Industrial League game at Riverview Stadium, I am off to the ballpark with the guys, sneaking in over the fence, and staying until the last out, which is usually not until about 11 p.m. It is truly a glorious time! After a game, I can't wait to tell my mother of my latest discovery, how the catcher camps under foul balls, and uses his glove to shield his eyes from the lights to catch pop ups behind the plate, or how he blocks home plate to prevent runners from scoring, who have tagged up at third with a fly ball to the outfield, stuff like that.

Even with my mind on baseball, it was impossible not to notice changes in the neighborhood. Everyone's lawn, with the exception of ours, has been converted into a victory garden. My da is gone most of the time. Besides, gardening isn't his thing. The front windows of many homes display red triangular flags, which mean a member of the family is in the military. The Judd's next door have a flag because Sonny's sister, Laverne, has a husband in the service. Flag with a gold star in the center means the serviceman is missing in action or killed. Right besides these flags are often cardboard signs to give notice to the iceman to deliver 25, 50, 75, or 100 pound cubes. Everyone in the neighborhood has an icebox. Many homes have American flags on their front porches jutting out proudly at forty-five degree angles from wooden poles. There is great reverence for the flag. Everyone takes care to see that the flag is secured before dusk, as it is not patriotic to fly a flag when the sun sets.

Racing over to the courthouse, I see Mr. Yeager the plumber loading his truck, nod to Mr. Jakubsen who is coming off his shift at

Clinton Foods, say "hi" to Heinie Witt, Bobby's father, who always
has a big smile as he goes to his railroad pumping station on First
Street by the stadium, and wave to the milk man who is delivering
milk along the avenue. Everyone seems in good cheer. My job is to
put as much fun into the day as my energy will allow, and so I am
happy, too.

* * * * *

Bobby could care less about catchers. He was a pitcher and a
finesse player at shortstop. He laughed at my being so nutty about
catching.

"Rube, you love those tools of ignorance, don't you?"

"Yeah, I do."

"You ought to work on your hitting. Forget studying catchers.
Study hitters. You're already a good catcher. Hitting's your
problem."

Bobby could cut me like that and not hurt my feelings, because he
was right. Still, I ignored his advice. Why not? I could never hit like
he does anyway!

Gussie Witt was always talking about eye-hand coordination and
body rotation. To him, hitting was a science; to me it was a skill, you
either have or don't. One day he studied me as if a specimen in a
bottle, stroked his chin, and said, "Rube let's try something, okay?
Let's see if we can make you a switch hitter."

A switch hitter bats right when facing a left handed pitcher, and
left when facing a right-handed pitcher. Incredibly, it did help. It
didn't make me a great hitter, but it sure improved my batting
average. I found I could pick up the ball much better when I batted
the opposite side to the pitcher's throwing arm. I also discovered that
I had more power batting left than right.

Rube is my nickname. Gussie came up with it. Rube Fischer
pitched for the 1940 Clinton Giants, and now pitches for the 1943
New York Giants, and Rube Walker catches for the St. Louis
Cardinals. The combination of a pitcher named Fischer (with a
German "c") and a catcher named "Rube" seemed a logical choice.

Dick Crider was born to play baseball. He has an eye for the ball
like Joe DiMaggio, and power like Ted Williams. His hitting skills
play right into the courthouse ritual, which starts every morning with

a game of pepper. Someone bats, usually Dick, and the guys surround him in a semi-circle, and throw the ball to him, and field groundballs hit back. The purpose of the batter is to keep the ball in play sprayed about the fielders alerting them to play the ball rather than have the ball play them. This lasts about fifteen minutes. Next, someone hits fly balls with a fungo bat to guys in the outfield. This goes on for another twenty minutes. Then, if there are not enough guys to play a game, we play a phantom game of baseball. Dick knows the rosters of every major league team. He can invent a game of All-Star players right on the spot. Amazing as it may seem, each phantom game has a new roster. This diversion prevents any lull in the courthouse day. Dick bats, I pitch, Bobby plays shortstop, Phil Leahy and Bill Benson the outfield. These are the core guys who show up every day, rain or shine. If others guys come later, and they usually do, they fill the vacant positions in the infield and outfield.

There are rules to this phantom game. A grounder to short that is handled cleanly is an out; if not, it is an error and puts a man on base. The same with fly balls to the outfield. A ball that can't be reached on the ground at short is a single, a fly ball that can't be reached in the outfield is a double; if it hits the backstop screen on one bounce, it is a triple, and if it hits the screen in the air, it is a homerun. Dick has such good bat control he can spray the ball all over the field. He can even tomahawk a shot over the screen and into the street if he wants, which is 300 feet away. This he tries to avoid, as old man Eads doesn't take too kindly to baseballs bouncing against his house, or on top of his customers' cars. All the same, if Eads keeps the ball, chances are the phantom game is over.

We play a full nine-inning game, and sometimes double- and triple-headers, or until the sun goes down and we can hardly see the ball. We have played by moonlight but it can get pretty scary when you don't see the ball until it's in your face. We'll break up this phantom game any time enough guys show up to play a regular game.

The courthouse gang has no adult supervision, nor any adult involvement to speak of. Gussie Witt, Jack Dunmore, and Lyle Sawyer are teenage coaches, and not always there. We are always there! Our rules are implicit rather than stated. No one ever steps out of line because you know the next time you won't get to play. Prominent parents have no leverage in seeing their sons playing at the

131

courthouse, nor is any allowance made for handicaps. Chuck Holm lives a block from the courthouse on Fifth Avenue North, across the street from Kirkwood School. He never came to the courthouse in 1943, although he was eleven. Chuck was struck with polio when he was five, and had to work hard during the intervening years to strengthen his arms and legs to match his will to compete. Dave "Pooper" Cavanaugh wheeled him around the neighborhood in a wagon before he could walk. It was tough for Chuck. But he was determined to ready himself to play at the courthouse. That meant spending the summer of 1943 having Gussie Witt hit ground balls to him every day on the Kirkwood school grounds. Chuck didn't come to the courthouse until he felt ready to compete.

Bob "Ripper" Collins, nicknamed after Ripper Collins of the St. Louis Cardinals, turned courthouse Darwinian cruelty to his advantage. Ripper was not a talented athlete. Instead of standing around watching the Courthouse Tigers play, he fielded his own team, the Cardinals. He used the softball field behind Riverview Stadium, and below the Clinton incinerator as his home field. It was a time when Clinton had no organized summer recreational program in youth baseball. Ripper filled this void by creating his own league. Ripper Collins was also a savvy promoter persuading The Clinton Herald to print standings of the teams in his league, and to report on his league's All-Star game. What welcomed him to the Courthouse Tigers was his keeping baseball statistics on them, something every player loves. Only a lad himself, Ripper Collins, with his genius for organization, was the de facto summer recreational director in Clinton in the summer of 1943.

If Bobby Witt is the soul of the courthouse, Dick Crider is a fixture. He lives just north of the courthouse with his grandparents and sneaks out of the house before breakfast, sometimes as early as 5:30 a.m., and settles himself in sheriff Petersen's kitchen to chat with Sybil Keeley Johnson, as she prepares breakfast for Ky and the prisoners. Sybil lives with her brother, Cab Keeley, who lives across the street from me and next door to the Johansen's. Deputy sheriffs Jim Gaffey, Chris Stamp, and Frances Ryan usually wander in after breakfast. Sybil is also Ky's secretary. Dick brags about his tasty breakfast of fried eggs, pancakes or waffles, hash browns, link sausage or bacon, and sometimes fried ham or steak, buttered toast and jelly, caramel pecan rolls, hot from the oven of Mrs. Johansen, a grapefruit or banana, orange juice, milk, dry or cooked cereal, and coffee. Most of this food is rationed, but somehow available to the Clinton County Sheriff's Department.

By 6:45 a.m. Dick is sitting pretty with a sumptuous breakfast consumed, a cup of coffee in his hand, and the Sports Section of the *Des Moines Register* propped up on the table against the syrup bottle, reading away. Dick not only reads about sports, he memorizes every detail on baseball as if he is to be tested. Then he comes out of the kitchen smiling like a Cheshire cat as the guys start to arrive. This sneaking out early in the morning goes on for about three weeks without incident. Then his grandmother's 1937 Buick roars to a stop in front of the jail, bellowing smoke. She gets out, keeps the car running, opens the trunk, and throws a suitcase full of clothes against the jail's steps. It flies open with shirts and pants, shorts and tee shirts, hankies and socks flying across the lawn, making quite a sight.

"If you like this place so much, Mr. Crider," she screams to no one in particular, "then you can live here." She then jumps back in the car, revs the engine with another plume of smoke coughing from the exhaust to accentuate her rage. Dick never notices, as he is too busy having his breakfast, and we have yet to arrive. We all know she has been here again, however, as we see the evidence everywhere.

About that time deputy Jim Gaffey ambers in from his home, and a new segment of the ritual unfolds. "Boy, your grandmother been here again?" deputy Gaffey bellows. Dick looks up from his paper with a bored expression. "I suggest you take your nose out of that newspaper, get off your ass, pick up your clothes, pronto, and make ready to eat humble pie. She'll be back in a minute if she's not here already." Sure enough, about the time Dick is through picking up his clothes, she roars up to the curb, still angry, looking daggers at him, waiting for him to make his move. With bowed head, he picks up his suitcase, climbs into the car, and says nothing. His grandmother, looking straight ahead, peels rubber as the old buggy takes off. Dick is absent from the courthouse for a day or two, and then the routine resumes.

"What are we to do with that boy?" she complains in frustration to Dick's grandfather. "We lock his door and he climbs out the window, slides down the tree and off he goes. We bar his window and he has a key made for his door, and walks out the house as we sleep, good as you please. He's heading for trouble, I tell you."

Dick's grandfather has heard this all before. "Mother," he reminds her, "your grandson has a passion for the courthouse, a passion for baseball. Can you name me a better place than under the watchful eye of the law to keep him out of trouble?" These consoling words seem to work for a while, but then the suitcase comes down from the closet, is hastily packed, and the ritual is repeated.

The jail and the courthouse are Dick's sanctuary and baseball is his laboratory. Here in the jail house Dick and Walt Ferguson can be seen spending many rainy afternoons creating a baseball game. A piece of cardboard is cut into a square, and then they draw carefully pie-shaped segments to extend to a circular circumference, placing a spin dial in the center with a red arrowhead pointer. The pie shaped segments indicate strikes, balls, errors, fielder's choices, sacrifices, groundouts (to first, second, or third base), fly outs (to first, second, third base, or right, center, or left field), singles, doubles, and homeruns. Carefully cut out pieces of cardboard identified every player on the roster of the major league teams. Each contains the vital statistics for that player. The information is acquired and updated from *The St. Louis Sporting News*. This amounts to cards for hundreds of ball players.

A rainy afternoon would evaporate into what seemed a matter of minutes with this engagement. This diversionary game, which neither Dick nor Walt ever thought of patenting, was developed decades before such commercial games were widely available. Actually, no one thought of purchasing an afternoon's diversion. No one had any money. Recreational inventions were for the courthouse use and that is where they stayed. I've never been into games, and must confess I never played this one. Bobby Witt and Dick Crider, however, could be seen playing it for hours during a summer thunderstorm. I would be at home, up in my room with a stack of traded comic books in my lap, along with a dozen oranges. At first, my favorites were *Captain Marvel, Terry & The Pirates, Flash Gordon, Spider Man, Batman, Superman,* and *Buck Rogers*. Once I discovered Classic Comics, this changed. The problem was guys at the courthouse didn't own Classic Comics, and the guys that did didn't like to trade for *Captain Marvel*. I managed, with some difficulty, to get *The Count of Monte Cristo,*

The Last of the Mohicans, Moby Dick, Robin Hood, Gulliver's Travels, Swiss Family Robinson, Black Beauty, Treasure Island, and *Joan of Arc.* Classic Comics guys all seem to be collectors. If you didn't return a comic in the same pristine condition that it was lent, the word got out and that was the end of trading with anyone. So, I was extra careful of not getting orange juice stains on these comics.

Dick Crider was a big collector, too, but of baseball cards that came with one-cent bubblegum packets. He never took the cellophane off the baseball cards, kept hundreds of them in mint condition in boxes in his closet. When he left Clinton to live with his mother in Cedar Rapids, his grandmother threw the boxes out. Bubblegum baseball cards of the early 1940s, in mint condition, sell today for as much as $1,000 per card at baseball collector shows.

* * * * *

Sheriff Ky Petersen makes everything happen for the kids at the courthouse with the able assistance of deputies Chris Stamp and Jim Gaffey. The sheriff is built like a Sherman tank. He is as wide as he is tall with a round face and smiling eyes with thin blond hair, which he wears quite short. His eyes are gray blue with a tinge of green in the iris. When he smiles, his face lights up like a Christmas tree, and you can't help but think of Santa Claus. In a way, that is what he is. You sense his athleticism as he moves lightly on the balls of his feet. He stands about five-eight and weighs 220, and is only in his late forties, but that seems old to us. The sheriff played football at Clinton High. His daughter Carleen proudly wears his gold football on a chain around her neck, which reads, *"Iowa High School Champions, Clinton, 1910, C. Petersen, end, All-Iowa."*

Sheriff Petersen went on to play semi-pro football in the 1920s for the June Van Meter post of the American Legion. All-American Lester Belding, who also directed many winning football teams at Clinton High, coached the team. Belding, incidentally, out punted the legendary Jim Thorpe in a 1924 contest held at Riverview Stadium. Moreover, he was a member of the Clinton semipro team that won the Iowa State Championship in 1924. One of Clinton's opponents in the late 1920s was Rock Island of the National Football League. Ralph Holden and Duke Allen played for Rock Island. The Rock Island team eventually became the Chicago Bears.

From the 1920s into the early 1940s, Ky also refereed Clinton High football games. The Clinton Herald always listed his name with "U of I" after it, as if he was a graduate of the University of Iowa. He wasn't. Ky never attended college. When his daughter asked him about this, he laughed, "All the other refs have schools listed after their names so The Herald wanted me to have one, too." He got a big kick out of that. She remembers him often coming home from those games as bruised up as if he had played. "As you know," Carleen adds, "he was rather overweight, and eventually couldn't keep up with the young players, or get out of their way fast enough. I saw him get knocked down several times but he always bounced right back up. The next day all you could smell was the eucalyptus balm applied to his sore muscles. He finally had to quit."

To illustrate his natural magnetism with people, she adds, "Many times when I was walking downtown with my father, he would be approached by someone asking for money to tide them over. He always gave them something, and never expected it back. But this one time a man asked for money, and my father said no. I asked him why? He said, 'he'll just go to a tavern and get drunk.' My father never drank or smoked."

"He wasn't always a sheriff," she points out. " When he was young, he ran several gas stations in Clinton, and for a time, drove a semi-trailer truck. But what he always wanted to be was a farmer. After he married my mother in 1915, at the age of 21, he set out for Texas to realize his dream. But the land he rented was just a dust bowl, and he couldn't make it as a farmer. So, he returned to Clinton and opened a gas station. This is how he made his living until he turned to Democratic politics. He was Clinton city treasurer from 1934 to 1936, and served as sheriff from 1936 until his death of a heart attack on September 29, 1950. He was 56."

No one was more popular in Clinton County politics than sheriff Petersen. In countless county elections, he was the only Democrat to win office. I can see why. The sheriff has an amazing face, the map of sincerity with a long straight nose with a slight pug curl at the end, and a square chin that gives it strength. Most remarkable are his eyes, kind yet knowing, which he fixes on you when he is talking as if nobody else exists. That makes you feel special and his calm makes you feel safe. He is always in charge without appearing to be.

Deputy sheriff Jim Gaffey is an Irishman, and carries the bluster in his walk. He is over six feet tall, with an ambling bony frame, long face, prominent jaw, and dark eyes, which appear almost black behind horn-rimmed glasses. His hair, what he has of it, is dark brown with a touch of gray, which lies in thin strands across his broad forehead. Perhaps that is why he prefers to wear a hat even in the hottest weather. It is an Irish face with the glint of the practical joker in his eyes. Jim walks to work from his Second Avenue South home on Third Street kibitzing with neighbors along the way. No telling when he will roll in, but nobody seems to mind.

My favorite is deputy sheriff Chris Stamp. He, like Jim Gaffey, is about forty, but there the similarity ends. Deputy Gaffey wears his clothes about two sizes too big, while deputy Stamp prefers tailor made attire. His shirts are form fitting and his trousers heavily creased and impeccably maintained. He prefers tans and browns like the uniforms of naval officers at sea but with a preference for polished brogans. He parts his thin brown hair in the middle which tops a round face with bright blue eyes that seem to always be thinking of some mischief for us. His pudgy face is actually incompatible with a five-ten athletic frame accentuated by a flat stomach and strong arms that show through his tailored shirts. You can tell he is devoted to the courthouse kids by the attention he gives. It is a common sight to see him in his fine clothes marching down the sidelines wheeling the limestone bucket chalking the left and right field foul lines readying the baseball diamond for a courthouse game. It was he who named us.

"Why not call yourself the Courthouse Tigers?" he suggested, a clear reference to the Detroit Tigers, one of the major leagues premier teams of the era with slugger Hank Greenberg and his favorite team.

* * * * *

The Clinton County Courthouse faces Second Street or the east end of a square block, while the Clinton County Jail is opposite it at the western end of the same square block on Third Street. These grounds were not designed to be a city park or recreational area, but none existed for the courthouse neighborhood. Sheriff Petersen found this shameful. He didn't make it a political issue, didn't go to the mayor and city council and plead his case for the courthouse kids. He acted. He created a playground.

To give you a sense of his heart for us kids, several visitors to the courthouse complained to the sheriff about baseballs hitting and denting their cars in the courthouse parking lot on the north side of the powerhouse, where we played our baseball games. He listened to these complainers politely, and then asked a question. "Did you see the posted sign? It suggests that you park on the south side of the powerhouse when a game is in progress." Visitors would either claim ignorance of this posting, or insist that they preferred to park on the north side. Sheriff Petersen would smile, and say, "Then I hope you have good automobile insurance."

Even as we were playing baseball in the summer of 1943, the sheriff was busy planning new activities for the fall and winter. He arranged to have the Clinton County Street Construction crew use a heavy roller to form an earthen floor for a full outdoor basketball court with regulation baskets and nets at opposite ends and parallel to Sixth Avenue North between the south parking lot of the courthouse and the county jail. Perhaps the sheriff's greatest legacy is his creation in that fall of the Halloween Mardi Gras Parade. This annual outing provides a constructive outlet for youthful enthusiasm. Kids throughout the city, sheriff Petersen reasoned, would prefer creating floats for a parade to senseless vandalism. Before 1943, it was common for kids to run up and down alleys and turn over garbage cans, throw eggs at people's houses, and even dump paint on lawns, vegetable gardens and sidewalks. He was right. Kids did prefer a constructive outlet. Nearly every neighborhood in the city constructed a make shift float, including the courthouse gang, to celebrate neighborhood pride, mounting their floats on trucks and parading them through the city. Bobby Witt, Bill Benson and Dick Crider, big boosters of the sheriff, walked along the parade route in that 1943 Mardi Gras Parade, passing out Ky Petersen reelection stickers to the crowd. They wanted everyone to know who had made this happen.

When fall gave way to winter, Ky flooded the lawn formed by the barrier of the grassy mound between the powerhouse and the jail, to include the baseball diamond north of this barrier, and extending from the north side courthouse parking lot, west along Seventh Avenue

North, and south on to the jail garage, completing a good sized ice skating rink. The sheriff also provided music for skaters from loud speakers mounted on the jail garage, along with floodlights for night skaters. Young people from all over Clinton County were invited to this winter wonderland.

I was never an ice skater, but my sister Patsy was an excellent skater, and so I would stand in the cold and watch and envy her. Bobby Witt was also an exceptional skater. He would glide across the ice like the wind, spin around, then dash towards me like a bullet, turn his skates sideways and stop abruptly, spraying me with ice. He would grin magnificently, his breath a condensing cloud about his face, laugh joyously, then taunt me. "Get yourself some skates, chicken!" Without waiting for a reply, he'd dig his skates into the ice, then skate away, his cheeks as red as his stocking cap. I never saw Bobby happier than on ice. It was as if his body was lighter than air, and he could fly. Why did I not skate? What I needed were hockey skates for supporting my weak ankles. I had a choice between basketball sneakers or ice skates. I chose sneakers.

*   *   *   *   *

Gussie Witt, Jack Dunmore, and Lyle Sawyer, all sixteen, and our coaches, are more different than alike. Gussie is an eternal kid. I don't think he will ever grow up because he's having too much fun being a kid. No one was ever more gifted with athleticism than Gussie. The only sport that registers any discipline over his free spirit is baseball. He made the high school basketball team, but preferred ice-skating at the courthouse to playing road basketball games. Better yet, when the Mississippi froze over in the channel, Gussie liked to skate there jumping as many as four barrels at a time. Wherever Gussie is you are sure to find his dog Hoiman beside him. Hoiman is named after the dog Herman in the comic strip, which Gussie misspelled from the first. Hoiman is a rust colored longhaired mongrel weighing about sixty pounds with a knack for the dramatic. One day in the summer of 1943 someone brought a giant turtle to the courthouse. Hoiman had to inspect its shell with his dripping nose, when suddenly the turtle's head popped out, snapped at Hoiman, taking a chunk out of his nose, then disappeared into its protective cavity.

This enraged and frightened Hoiman. Hurting and terrified, Hoiman pawed the earth viciously like a bull, and then pounced on the shell, trying to get his teeth around the huge turtle's hard surface, but to no avail. The turtle was eighteen inches long and twelve inches wide. The more Hoiman tried to take a chunk out of the turtle the more frustrated he got, howling, barking with a bleeding nose, and blood dripping from his mouth. Guys were egging Hoiman on, yelling encouragement like fans at a sporting event. Hoiman, covered with sweat, tried to respond to the cheers, but without success. His blood all over the turtle's backs, his eyes unfocused, his head slumping between heavy sighs, Hoiman looked beseechingly to Gussie for some sign. His teeth were chipped and bleeding, his head cowering as if in shame at letting his master down. Gussie bent down and hugged his dog, then picked him up and carried him to the jail to tend his wounds, whispering soothing words in the dog's ear as he struggled with his heavy load. The turtle, totally intact, wandered away as if survival were its primordial destiny.

* * * * *

Jack Dunmore is an adult in a teenager's body. He stands over six feet tall with an angular face, and slender but powerful frame of sinewy long arms and legs. If there is a word to describe Jack, it is maturity. He has the understanding that generates followers and we all listen when he speaks. Yet, he is as much fun as Gussie, who is his best friend. Like Gussie, he is a superb athlete in all sports, but baseball is his favorite. Whereas Gussie often acts like a kid, Jack plays the adult and nudges us in the right direction without seeming to. From the start, he perceived I was naturally serious and not comfortable with horseplay. "You didn't like that," he said to me, when I cringed at seeing Hoiman all bloody. "You feared that Hoiman was going to kill that turtle, didn't you?"

I started to cry. How could he know that? Yet, he did. Even as a boy, I hated any form of cruelty. My chest heaved violently. I couldn't hold back the tears. I was terribly embarrassed. Why did he have to know? I couldn't stop crying. My only salvation was that the guys had wandered off to see how Hoiman was doing.

Jack said nothing. He didn't move to reassure me. His eyes spoke volumes. He was going to stay with me until I was all right.

140

That seemed to close my floodgates. He waited. "Are you okay now?" he said finally. I nodded. "You sure?" I nodded again. No lecture. No reassuring words. He walked towards the jail, looked back. I dropped my eyes. When I looked up again, he was gone.

*   *   *   *   *

Lyle Sawyer is an enigma. He lacks the grace or the athleticism of Gussie and Jack, yet possesses his own brand of dignity. Nothing seems to come easily to Lyle. He doesn't see well, and his thick glasses often steam up in the summer heat, and therefore, fielding and hitting a baseball are difficult for him. At sixteen, he isn't much taller than I am at ten and can't weigh more than 130 pounds. But like Jack, there is a kindness about him as well as a mystery behind the eyes. He listens more than he talks, and demonstrates what he is by what he does. Lyle was into self-improvement years before it became popular with progressive educators. In the summer of 1943, I had never heard of cross country runners or joggers, but Lyle was both. Eagle Point Park is about eight miles from the courthouse. Lyle would run up and around the park, then return and run around the perimeter of the courthouse and jail in 100-degree heat, lap after lap after lap. Dick Crider liked to taunt him, throwing cold water on him as he passed by, but Lyle never got upset, or ever tried to put Dick in his place. Accepting was the word that best described Lyle. He accepted his lot in life and made the most of it. He remained always quiet, never boastful, but most notable of all, never vindictive. He liked being part of the courthouse gang and took the joshing in stride as part of the price of belonging.

Most of us were poor, but Lyle's poverty made us seem rich. It wasn't his poverty that bothered him, however, it was his lack of athleticism. Yet he had a knack for being helpful to those with more athletic talent than himself, and never complained or looked for sympathy. He wanted so desperately to be a good athlete, but his failing eyesight, slight frame, and lack of quickness assured him to be an "also ran." He did hit on something that he felt could distinguish him from others, and that was his incredible endurance. He seemingly could run forever.

Larry Jakubsen in 1943 still was forced to take naps. He would go upstairs to his room, look out his bedroom window, which was

141

directly across from the courthouse, and watch Lyle and his little dog ambling along in the summer heat. When he woke from his nap, and looked out his window, there was Lyle still running, but his little dog had chosen to sit in the middle of the courthouse grounds moving its head to follow Lyle's progress around the courthouse acreage, but without moving a single leg. The little dog had had enough.

* * * * *

One day in late June 1943, Gussie asked me to warm him up. I was flattered. The big guys were going to play a game at the courthouse, and Gussie was going to pitch. I was catching him like a big guy, handling his pitches with ease, that is, until he made a gesture of breaking his wrist in a semi circular fashion then throwing the ball. It was a curve ball. I had never caught a curve ball before. I didn't know that bending the wrist meant a curve ball was coming. Instead of catching the ball with my glove, the ball split my fingers on my open right hand all the way to the bone. In shock, I looked at my right hand. There was a deep split between my index and middle finger to the center of my hand with blood pulsing in staccato spurts. I was so traumatized I didn't cry, didn't move. Gussie dropped his glove, grabbed a towel and wrapped my hand in it, then took me home, putting his game on hold.

All I could think was 'thank God da is on the road.' My mother came to the door with a cigarette between her teeth masking her face. She nearly dropped it on the porch when she saw my wrapped hand with the white towel drenched in red.

"Oh my God, Jimmy!" she said with her hand to her mouth in stunned disbelief. "Your hand? Jimmy, your hand! What happened?" Gussie intervened.

"He caught the ball with the wrong hand, Mrs. Fisher, and it split his fingers. This happens with baseball players." I was impressed with Gussie's calm. He was in charge. "What we need to do, Mrs. Fisher, is clean the wound, then disinfect it, iodine would be good, then create a splint, a small piece of balsam, a tongue depressor would be good, then wrap the index and middle finger together with a sterile bandage, and secure it with tape. Do you have a First Aid kit?"

My mother nodded, completely under Gussie's spell.

"Good, then we can stabilize the fingers, and start the healing process. No need to go to the doctor's. What I suggest you do is change the bandage every day, and Rube, I mean Jimmy, will be fine in a couple weeks." Then he took my towel wrapped hand into his. "Show me where the First Aid kit is, Mrs. Fisher, and I'll take care of this right now."

My mother moved away from the door to let Gussie and me in and then went quickly to the bathroom. "Is this what you need?"

Gussie inspected it and smiled. "This will do just fine."

Like a doctor, Gussie went to work. My spine tingled with pleasure watching him take care of me. I was amazed that I was in so little pain. He managed to totally calm my mother down. There was no yelling. No swearing. No histrionics. Just calm attention to an accident. How different it would have been if da were home.

When Gussie left, my mother lit another cigarette, looked at me pensively. "When your father comes off the road tomorrow morning, he'll notice your hand. You won't tell him you split your fingers. He'd go through the roof. You'll tell him you sprained them and that I've bandaged them with a splint so that you won't re-injure the fingers again.

"But mother that's a lie!"

"No, Jimmy, it's not a lie. It's prudence."

* * * * *

James R. Fisher, Jr.

Chapter 11

Crosses

He that has no cross will have no crown.

--Francis Quarles

There is something positive about being injured that suspends you from duty, and puts you in the bleacher seats, so to speak, to see what's happening. Otherwise, you're so caught up in what you're about that most things whistle by you without so much as a "merry-thee-well." I must confess this passive role suits me. I'm more comfortable observing than participating. Oscar Wilde in my Classic Comics cautioned against this in *Portrait of Dorian Gray*. Said it wasn't healthy. Imagine staying young on the outside, while your portrait rots away in the attic like his did. I know it's just a story, so why does it bother me? I wish I could ask Bobby, but I know what he'd say.

"Rube you worry too much. Why read that dumb stuff anyway?"

So I keep such things to myself.

There is no way I can climb over the fence and sneak into the stadium with this bum finger, so I'm home most nights, even when my da is on the road, listening to the grown ups talk. They seem to be here every night. Just last night, the two carpenters joined my uncles and aunts in talking about Clinton and the war effort. It never occurred to me that Clinton was a war machine, as uncle Bill declares, or that women are soldiers on the home front. True, some of my aunts are working in factories. They aren't shy about speaking their piece. Doesn't include my mother. She smokes, listens, serves coffee and chocolate fudge cake, and empties ashtrays. Her war zone is putting up with us kids. I find the talk strange. There are signs all over town picturing Uncle Sam with his index finger to his lips saying, *"Loose lips sink ships!"* Lips are pretty loose here.

Uncle Bill reports more than 7,000 Clintonians work in Clinton factories in support of the war effort. Aunt Verna who is a welder at Collis says with her delightful chuckle, "Well, Bill, then guess I'm one of those soldiers." They all say stuff like that. It's fascinating to learn what's going on in Clinton, but isn't it dangerous to talk about it? *The Shadow* is always chasing spies who look like everybody else. Could one of them be a spy? I learn a lot by listening. *The Clinton Garment Company* suspended its dress production to manufacture insect bars. Cleo Hyde who works there explains that these are tent and cot coverings made of mosquito and sand fly netting. Garment company workers are working around the clock to produce this top priority item for the North African Campaign, which is critical to the Allied Forces success. Urgently needed shipments of these insect bars are being hauled from Clinton by cover of night directly to merchant supply ships on the eastern seaboard. *The Climax Company* converted its manufacturing processes to wartime production, producing small generators for the Signal Corps and heavy generators for the Seabees and U. S. Engineers. *Dupont* centered its cellophane production to package G.I. food rations, protective coverings against possible gas attack, and as wrapping material for small mechanical equipment shipped directly to battlefields located all over the world. *The Collis Company* suspended making its commercial and industrial wire shelf products for applications to making M-54 time fuses for the U. S. Army. *The Bennett Box Company* suspended its products for peaceful applications to making ammunition boxes for the U. S. Army, U. S. Marines, and U. S. Navy. *Clinton Foods* in spite of losing more than a quarter of its employees to the armed forces, has increased its production to record levels. Corn sugar and corn syrup are now important food substitutes to cane sugar and maple syrup. *The Clinton Alcohol Plant*, located in the old Pointer brewery, is making industrial alcohol products for the manufacturing of synthetic rubber and the synthesis of rubber for military jeeps. *Pillsbury Mills, Inc.'s Feed and Soy division* is producing products for the food supplement and livestock market. The company is dealing creatively with a wartime manpower shortage by using *Clinton High* athletic squads to work part time to get the job done. What seems even more amazing is that *Pillsbury* has contracted with the federal government to use German prisoners of war as well. More than 50 German prisoners are being trained to work in the mill. Uncle Frank says these prisoners are quiet, submissive and forbidden to engage in "Heil Hitler!" salutes. *Pillsbury* is paying the federal government regular labor rates for their services. *The Chicago and North Western Shop* is hiring women for the first time to perform maintenance jobs previously reserved for men. I have three uncles and an aunt working there. *Clinton High School* has created a wartime technical training program to train workers in metal working machines, electronics, and other specialties critical to local manufacturers including the *Clinton Bridge & Iron Works, Central Steel & Tube, Clinton Engineering Company, Climax* and *Collis*. Nearly 80 percent of these students are women. *Burpee Seed Company*, across from the courthouse, has gone to three shifts to keep up with the victory garden demands throughout the United States. With my eyelids getting heavy, uncle Bill takes the floor again, and starts to spiel off with obvious pride, canteen statistics of the *Clinton USO*, where he is a volunteer. He rattles off how many servicemen have enjoyed canteen hospitality, and it is in the thousands, to how many tens of thousands of pounds of meat and bread have been consumed, to the millions of cups of coffee served, to the thousands of gallons of salad dressing and butter used, and of course how much it all cost. It's past my bedtime. I'm going to sneak upstairs. I guess even spies would be bored with all this information.

* * * * *

The courthouse neighborhood is neither inhabited by little angels without wings nor little devils without horns, just darling miscreants. Low and high jinx are common fare. Bill "Chang" Benson, although devoid of Oriental blood, has the look and shuffle to give it credence. He doesn't mind. No one is more competitive. He lives in the upstairs apartment of the Leahy's. Chang is four years older than Phil Leahy. Often their respective parents mosey over to Sullivan's tavern for a few brews and Chang baby-sits. Sullivan's is an after work neighborhood hangout, and within walking distance of the Leahy's home. Smokey Benson and Art Leahy, Chang and Phil's dads, are good friends, and coworkers at Dupont.

On this warm, humid July 1943 night, Chang and Phil are playing war games running through the house, jumping up and down the back steps of Chang's apartment like commandoes, when Chang stops. "Why don't we dig a foxhole in the yard like the Yanks did in the movie, *Sergeant York?*"

Phil, only eight, cautious to Chang's rashness wasn't sure. "Don't you think we ought to call our parents?"

"Sure, why not, all they can say is no, right?" Chang looks up the number and calls the tavern. "Mr. Leahy, me and Phil are playing war games," he states without overture, "and were wondering if we could dig a trench in the backyard."

"A trench? In the backyard? Hey, Smokey," Art Leahy yells to his friend, "kids want to dig a trench in the backyard!"

Smokey, who is bringing back drinks to the table, shakes his head, "What these kids won't think of," then adds, "might keep 'em out of trouble."

"Sure, Billy, but don't take any prisoners," Phil's father laughs.

Elated, Chang replies, "No sir, we won't."

Next morning about six a.m. as Smokey and Art are about to car pool to work, they spot the huge hole. The trench is five feet deep and a good eight feet long, a mountain of dirt piled beside the house. They look at each other scratching their heads, smile, then roar with laughter. "A real shitter," Smokey Benson says,

"A bitch," chirps Art, "can you believe that?" looking down into the hole. "Wonder we didn't fall in it last night. Wouldn't that have been a pain in the ass?"

"Not so funny then!"

Art rubs his chin. "No, not so funny."

"Knowing my kid," Smokey says easing the shock of it, "if I asked him to dig a ditch he'd hardly turn the dirt over." Then getting serious, "What're you going to do, Art?"

Art grins, "Let them enjoy it today, fill it in tomorrow, plant some grass seed, set them to watering it every day." Shaking his head, "Smokey, can you imagine how much work that took?"

"Yeah, I can. I've been there."

* * * * *

Chang had another side he kept to himself that summer. He did lawn work for families on Springdale Drive. These lawns were often huge. It wasn't unusual for a single lawn job to take up to eight hours. Chang would take his earnings; usually $15 per lawn job, buy cigarettes and gum for patients at Schick Hospital, and then pass them out to wounded GI's on alternate Tuesdays and Thursdays, thanking the soldiers for making it safe for him to play ball at the courthouse.

* * * * *

1943 Clinton was a trusting society. No one locked front doors at night. Since there was no air conditioning, windows in the summer were open wide to let what little breeze there was be moved around with small electric fans. Young people escaped the heat by swimming at the Clinton Municipal Pool, or attending a matinee at the Strand, Rialto, Capital or Lyons Theater. If they had bicycles, they would leave them outside the pool or theater unsecured as they had little fear of them being stolen. Sometimes the nights were so suffocating that families would take blankets and head for Riverview Park, and sleep under the stars, serenaded by the foghorns of the passing barges down the Mississippi with no thought of danger. Often, a summer concert would be held in the park and folks would combine this entertainment with a night under the stars. Others might spend time at Eagle Point Park, which overlooks Lake Clinton, the widest point in the Mississippi River, and nearly three miles across. The park has nature trails, a rustic pavilion, and a Celtic-like viewing tower built by the WPA in the 1930s, which sits atop the highest point of the bluff. Eagle Point also has botanical gardens, recreational and picnic areas along winding roads, which snake their way through the park.

* * * * *

Sometimes a trusting society is too much for a young boy, especially when it comes to Riverview Stadium in the form of baseball bats, balls, gloves, and catcher's equipment. The Industrial Baseball League started up in 1943 with eight teams: *Bridge Works, Central Steel, Collis, Curtis, Dupont, Clinton Foods, Savanna Ordinance Depot,* and *Schick General Hospital.* Games were scheduled at 8 p.m., but the courthouse gang would show up at 5:30 p.m., or about the time teams scheduled batting practice. We were allowed to shag flies, chase foul balls, and hang out in the dug out until the game was ready to get underway. Teams would give us broken bats, which we would nail together, then wrap with electric tape, and baseballs where the leather stitching was coming undone. We would put tacks in these balls, and wrap them with electric tape, too. We even accepted water soaked balls so heavy they felt like shot puts. Ever the optimists, we were certain we could dry them out and recover their resilience. Never happened, but we always held out hope for the next water soaked ball.

I sit this July evening at Riverview Stadium on the edge of the right field dugout, two hours before game time, feeling the tingle of my healing fingers. Stacked on the corner of the dugout next to me are four 12x16 inch boxes. Marked on the top cover are "Official Clinton Industrial League Baseballs" with a big black "Twelve" circled in red, the number of balls in a box. Guys are out on the field shagging balls for the team having batting practice, while I'm nursing my split fingers. I look around, everyone is occupied hitting, throwing or catching baseballs. I take the top box, put it under my arm, and quietly saunter out of the dugout, through the side gate by the right field bandstand, and through the open fence where a groundskeeper is bringing in a tractor to prepare the infield for the game. No one pays me any attention, not even the ticket taker, who is busy talking to someone.

Once out of the stadium, I walk rapidly through the parking lot, across the railroad tracks, and Second Street, then barrel ass to the courthouse jail. Once there, breathless, I open the box on the jail steps. Gleaming up at me are twelve highly polished leather covered white baseballs with red stitching. I take one out and put it to my nose. It smells like freshly polished white shoes. I have never seen anything so beautiful. My heart is pounding so hard in my chest I think it might explode. I squeeze my eyes shut, and hold back a shout. God, the guys are going to go wild over this! They won't know how to act. Twelve new baseballs! Not one, not two, but t-w-e-l-v-e, twelve! They'll last forever! Boy! Won't it be fun to hit a real honest to goodness baseball? Nobody is around to share my excitement, not even the sheriff. The sheriff? Oh, my God! The sheriff! He'll know. He'll pick up a baseball that bounces his way, see the official stamp on it, and ask questions. Guys will say, I found it. He'll ask to speak to me. Where did you find this ball, he'll ask. I'll lie. He'll know I'm lying. He'll make a call, and find out I stole it from the ballpark. Then I'll be in real trouble, trouble with the law.

Sheriff will never let me play here again, never smile at me, never muss up my hair, never be there for me again. I won't be a Courthouse Tiger anymore. I rush to my house with the box under my arm. Thank God nobody's home. Go to the phone book. There's his name and home address, general manager of Clinton Industrial Baseball League. Need a bike. Darn it! Don't have one. How far is it to his house from here? Count the blocks on the phone book map. Eighteen blocks.

With the box under my arm, I run like a halfback going for a score. Stop, winded. How much farther? Eleven blocks. Start walking. My clothes are sticking to my skin. Mind full of terror. Why did I do this? Stupid, stupid, stupid! I've never stolen anything before. Why now? Somebody on a bike waves at me. I put my head down as if I don't see him. Start running again. Please, God, forgive me! If I escape this, I'll be good the rest of my life. I will. No kidding! God should know I couldn't lie to Him.

There it is! There's his house. Nice house. God! Is it big! Pretty yard. Why no victory garden? Oh, well. I ring the door bell, place the box on the steps, jump over the hedge of the house next door, then leap over a low wrought-iron fence separating the next yard from its neighbor's, both yards roughly the same size as the general manager's, rich people, though not as well landscaped. I take an enormous chance of being seen by someone, but no one calls out to

151

me. I run around the far side of the last house, then scurry down the alley, and out into the street, running again until my lungs tell me to stop. It is dark now. This part of town is not familiar to me. I walk in the middle of the street. It feels like walking down the main nave of a cathedral. Giant Dutch elms form an arched canopy over me. This is Fifth Avenue South where some of the richest people in America once lived. Looks like they still do. Houses are mansions. The trees mesmerize me. They are gigantic, much taller than the two-story houses along the street. I wonder how old they are? I walk westward now more calmly, not thinking, find trees go almost to Bluff Boulevard. I look upward at the cathedral ceiling. Can't see the moon through the trees; wonder if the sun gets through this canopy in the daytime. Promise myself one day I'll come back here on a sunny day and see if the sunlight hits the pavement. Bet it doesn't. Walk north on the bluff toward home, promising myself I will never tell a living soul what I did, me, of all people, me, perfect me, me who is supposed to be so good, me who has the nickname of two famous ballplayers, me, who everybody thinks is principled.

Advantage of being a loner is no one else knows the corrosion of your soul. Now, some sixty years later it surfaces. Why? Perhaps it is because I am thinking about the catcher's equipment that I wore with such immense pride, not knowing it was stolen, and that it actually belonged to the Clinton Foods baseball team. While I became a cowardly thief stealing, then returning a box of baseballs, Jim Long, the son of Ted Long, Clinton's chief of police, followed through on his thievery. He walked away from the dugout with complete catcher's gear -- mask, chest protector, and knee guards -- and sold it to Pooper Cavanaugh for five dollars. Pooper got the money from Sheriff Petersen, who never asked Pooper where he got the gear. *The Clinton Herald* ran a column on this stolen equipment, even offered a reward. No one ever laid claim to it. Deputies Stamp and Gaffey, who found out about this shady purchase after the fact, remained mute. They decided it was prudent to do so, not reflecting too well on the Clinton County Sheriff's Department. Sheriff Petersen, ignorant of the whole affair, was much involved in his re-election campaign, and was saved from the embarrassment. Nor was I aware of where this equipment came from, never asked, never thought about it. It could have come from heaven for all I cared. I just loved to put the gear on, and pretend I was a great catcher. Complicity has many deviant names.

Makes me wonder, though, about the box of new baseballs. After a day of use, a new baseball looks old. It is scuffed up; its markings erased, with no one the wiser, not even the sheriff could tell that it was new, much less stolen. Would that I had thought of that then. Might I have hidden the balls in my closet, scuffed one up with sandpaper, and brought it over to the courthouse, one ball at a time? I think so. Might have done that if I had thought of it; must be only a tiny criminal in my heart.

How to handle my guilt? One option, have Father Minehardt at Sacred Heart downtown hear my confession. Confess that I took some baseballs from the ballpark, no need to be specific, but kind of implying without saying it, that they were discarded practice baseballs anyway. I could make this implication credible by saying; truthfully, that I took them during batting practice before the game. Father Minehardt, a trusting soul like the Bishop of Digne in *Les Miserables*, would give me the benefit of the doubt. That is his way. Wouldn't be exactly a lie, just kind of misleading. I'd get away with it.

* * * * *

The Clinton County Jail, along with the Clinton Police Department Jail, had a combined space for 40 prisoners, and neither was ever filled to capacity. There were no drug dealers, no traffickers in pornography or peddlers in illicit sex, no murderers or rapists. The prisoners were in the main petty burglars, shoplifters, drunkards, and bar brawlers. My uncle Snowball spent a good number of weekends in the city jail, as city cops would see him staggering along a street, talking to invisible people. He would be released on Monday, sober and ready to go back to work.

Carleen Petersen Wood can attest to the atmosphere of the times. While Carleen was in high school in the 1940s, there was a party that she had to attend, and she didn't have a ride. She called her father, the sheriff, at the jail and told him of her plight.

"Don't worry, honey, someone will be out shortly to take you to your party."

Sure enough, within the half hour, a large sedan with a siren mounted on the fender drove up to her door. A young man got out and ushered her to the car. He was tall, and clean cut with ginger hair. He drove her to the party, but proved not much of a conversationalist. *"What time should I return to pick you up?"* he finally said.

Elated at her good fortune, giggling inside at having a chauffeur, Carleen's face grew crimson, *"Oh, I don't know, let's say elevenish."* Once the words were out of her mouth, she felt silly.

Promptly at eleven o'clock the large sedan was again there with the same driver. When she got home, she couldn't wait to thank her dad. *"I'm glad it all worked out fine for you, honey, Red is one of my best trustees."*

"Trustees?"

"Prisoners, precious."

* * * * *

The Clinton County Courthouse tower is kind of sacred to me. Why, I don't know, but apparently not to the other guys. Almost every day, we talk about what it would be like to go up into the tower. Then one day Pooper Cavanaugh devises a plan.

"Mr. Dunmore always takes his lunch in the powerhouse, right?" Everyone nods.

"If you go in there then, what's he doing?"

"Snoozing," Chang laughs. "You can hear him snoring a block a way."

"Not only is he snoozing, but he always takes his keys out of his pocket, his watch off, and lays everything on the table beside his chair," Pooper continues. "What if we were to borrow the tower elevator key for a while?" He looks around. Our faces are blank but our eyes are black dots of anticipation.

"Well?"

"Who's going to get the key?" Bobby Witt asks. All fingers point to Pooper. He shrugs.

"Okay, okay." With that he races across the lawn to the powerhouse, and comes out in seconds with a stack of keys on a chain, raising them triumphantly above his head, then heads for the courthouse with Bobby, Kenny and Dick Tharp, Chang Benson, Phil Leahy and me racing to join him.

The elevator takes us past the fourth and to a fifth floor, which is well within the bowels of the tower. We all look up and see there's still a distance to climb to the courthouse bells, and even well beyond that to the courthouse clock.

"Did you think it would look like this?" Chang turns to Bobby. Bobby doesn't answer. He's too busy looking at the massive construction of this old tower. I'm disappointed. How could something so beautiful on the outside look so ugly on the inside? I feel as if an intruder into a giant's head like Brick Bradford was in The Herald comics. I colored that episode with crayons when I was four at my aunt Annie Dean's. Brick Bradford manipulated a giant robot against alien invaders. Here, however, I felt helpless surrounded by steel plates, rusty gears, and thick, greasy wire pulleys, the receptors and connectors of the tower's old and tired brain.

We have to climb up three flimsy ladders to get to the bells. They are gigantic and hang precariously in the center of the tower from wooden arches, which find me now thinking of a bodybuilder, massively muscular but not necessarily strong. Pigeons are cooing in the rafters. Their droppings are everywhere. To get above the bell level it is necessary to climb a twisting steel staircase. Once at that level, we crawl on our hands and knees to the edge of the tower, and lay there waiting for the bells to ring with our hands over our ears. When the bells ring, the thundering sound nearly breaks our eardrums.

"Mr. Dunmore will be waking up," yells Kenny Tharp, "we'd better haul ass to the powerhouse." He is ignored.

I agree but vertigo hits me and I am paralyzed to move. Meanwhile, the other guys crawl out and stand outside the tower and walk gingerly around its perimeter.

"Boy, this is something! You can see all the way downtown! Look! The stadium's right on top of us! The river, too. I can see people in the swimming pool! Wow! Wait 'til we tell the guys. Come over on this side! The jail looks tiny, so does the powerhouse. Oh, shit, there's Mr. Dunmore." Suddenly, this chanting delight hangs in the air as bodies fly down the ladders in panic. I've already descended to the elevator level, as soon as they went outside. Now, everyone is scrambling.

"Pooper, what are you going to say?"

"Nothing. I'm going to sneak into the powerhouse, and put the keys under the cushion of his chair, out of sight." He looks at Dick Tharp. "Does he look like he's missing anything?"

"No, he's getting on his power mower." Everyone breathes a sigh of relief. Pooper is incredibly cool under pressure. I'm impressed. I wouldn't be able to think if it were I.

We walk out of the courthouse as Mr. Dunmore's mower comes around the corner of the building. He stops the mower. We stop, too.

"Can I have my keys back now?" There is nothing to describe our shock. Even Pooper is speechless. "All you had to do was ask, and I'd take you up in the tower. I'm disappointed in you boys. Jack will be, too!" Pooper hands him the keys, and is about to say something when Mr. Dunmore is off cutting grass again.

*   *   *   *   *

Pinball machines had no appeal to me, but the guys constantly talked about playing them. Nick and Ewana Xidis owned Candyland and never seemed to mind that everyone won a zillion games playing this one pinball machine. Turns out it wasn't skill or luck. Somebody had drilled a hole in the side of machine, and controlled the tilt button with a coat hangar. How that was ever managed nobody ever said, but I had my suspicions. That could never happen at the Revere Candy Shop. The guys learned if you inserted your coin slowly and pulled the lever gently you could get your money back. It was easy to win games because there was a loose bumper in the machine. Pete Rastrelli didn't know this. If you won more than a few games, though, he'd pull the plug just the same. He'd put his hands on his hips, eye everyone down, and wait for someone to complain. No one did.

Mr. Rastrelli was kind of a father figure. He would call Cy Robb, the cop, who'd run you home if you were out after curfew, which was 10 o'clock. Amos and Pete Pallastrini, co-owners with Pete Rastrelli of the Candy Shop, were more relaxed. The Pallastrinis, both easy going, seemed at times to exasperate their partner, who constantly found it necessary to police the Fourth Avenue South entrance because so many exited that door without paying. As a ten-year-old, I only went there during the day and mainly for the free hot peanuts that always abated my hunger. I liked Mr. Rastrelli, who had a

156

number of names for me, but I doubt if he knew my real name. One time he'd call me "Slim," next time "Long John," and yet another, "Red" although I was blond. If the Candy Shop ran you out, or Cy Robb ran you home, most guys would go to Candyland, mainly because Nick Xidis never called the cops and didn't seem to notice how old or young you were.

* * * * *

August comes, my fingers are now fully healed, and I start playing again. Guys are happy to see me, mainly because nobody likes to catch, not even Dick Crider, who is a super catcher. It isn't a week after I am back playing that I am again victim of an accident. I couldn't find the catcher's mask in the jail cellar, so, I caught without it. I had done this before without any problem, but not today. We were playing an intrasquad game with me steady catch. Chang was batting, and he always takes a vicious cut at the ball. This time he missed, spun completely around, and caught me on the cheek with the barrel of the bat on his follow through. This produced an ugly split under my right eye with blood pouring down my face. It happened so quickly that it didn't hurt.

Head wounds bleed profusely, but with me even more so as I am a bleeder. I nearly bled to death when I had my tonsils and adenoids out when I was seven. Ever since then, doctors have been leery of operating on me, and my dentist puts me through all sorts of tests before pulling a tooth. I am now a bloody mess, but the guys stand around not knowing what to do. Our coaches are not about. If they were, they'd know what to do. Fortunately, a soldier stationed at Schick Hospital, renting from Mr. Yeager the plumber on the corner, and still in uniform just off duty, sees the accident.

The soldier watches us play nearly every day, and sometimes changes clothes and shags flies with us, or shoots baskets. What is most impressive with him is his quickness. I love to watch him move to the ball. They say that Joe DiMaggio knows exactly where the ball is going from the sound of the bat. The soldier is like that. He looks like an athlete with a lean square face, piercing gray eyes, and a strong slender athletic build. When he's in shorts and a tee shirt, I noticed a vein snakes up the middle of his biceps, and his calves flare out and taper to a runner's trim ankles. I can imagine him a soldier on the front lines leading the charge. He is terribly quiet, never talks about the war, or about much of anything. All any of us know about him is that he was wounded in the Pacific and is now stationed at Schick hospital.

"Anyone got a clean towel or tee shirt?" he asks. Phil Leahy rushes across the street to his house and brings back a towel. Dick Crider, an immaculate dresser, strips to the waist and offers his clean polo shirt. "You sure?" the soldier asks, not wanting to ruin a good shirt.

"Yeah, for Rube, yeah!"

"Then let's go!" The soldier motions for me to get on his gleaming Harley Davidson motorcycle. I've never been on a bike before. Hesitantly, I climb on.

"We're heading to the hospital, lad, so hold on tight!" With that, he rotates his right wrist on the handlebar and the motorcycle roars in response. I'm terrified. The bike seems to leave the ground as we take off. All this time I've had hardly a chance to think of the trouble I might be in at home for getting hurt again. The hair on the back of my head stands up as we breeze up North Third turning west on Thirteenth Avenue North to St. Joseph Mercy Hospital. The soldier stops at the side entrance, and lifts me off the bike. "You okay?" I nod.

"Let's get you fixed up."

The soldier immediately encounters a Sister of Mercy, one of the nuns running the hospital, dressed in white from her headpiece to her shoes. He explains my injury.

"I'm terribly sorry. There's no one on duty that can handle this emergency." The quiet soldier surprises me with his bluntness.

"This is a hospital, isn't it?"

The nun's slate blue eyes seem to narrow as if the eyelids have been loosely stitched. "Now mind your manners, young man. I'm sorry but you will have to go elsewhere." She puts her hands in her bib and walks away.

The soldier shakes his head, puts his arm around me, and starts to say something, then decides not to as we go out the door. I expect him to swear like my da, but all he says is, "Let's try Jane Lamb." The motorcycle roars back down Third Street, takes the corner at Seventh Avenue North roars south down Bluff Boulevard pass Mount

St. Clare College, past the rocky ridge of the bluff which shines golden in the sun, past Ikes Peak and Ravine Place to Jane Lamb Memorial Hospital. The trip takes only minutes. The bleeding has not stopped, and I am now drenched in blood with my shirt, pants and shoes an insidious red.

This time, the soldier stops at the front entrance to the hospital. Again, he puts his kickstand down, lifts me off the bike, takes my hand and proceeds through the door to the admittance desk, but unhappily with the same result. I wait for the soldier to explode. Instead he puts his hands on the desk splayed out past his shoulders and leans forward. "Sir, what do you suggest I do? You can see this lad needs immediate medical attention." The long cadaverous face of the admission's clerk bobbles up and down.

"Oh, I agree," he replies, his tallow-colored skin drawn up in furrows. "Indeed, indeed!" His chin is resting in his hands, his elbows on the desk. "Why don't you try the Wilson Building?" He regards the soldier gauging his familiarity with Clinton, which seems to say; *You're not from here, are you? You have the wrong accent.* "Several doctors have offices there. Quickest way is to go back down Sixth to Third Street and . . ." The soldier forces a smile, "Thank you I know the way." We roar down Fifth Avenue and I recall returning the stolen balls and shudder. Less than five minutes later, we are in the Wilson Building lobby, not an hour since my injury. The soldier looks at the paneled directory.

"How does a Dr. Leonard Nelken sound to you? He's an M.D. and does general surgery." He looks at me and I hunch my shoulders. "I take that as a yes."

"You okay? I haven't heard a peep out of you. Frankly, I'm losing my patience. No, not with you! With these hospitals! This doctor better be what we need, or," he breaks into a huge grin which closes his eyes, "or I'll have to sew you up myself." I cringe at the joke.

Several people are sitting in Dr. Nelken's waiting room. A nurse comes out and takes my name. She gives the soldier papers to fill out. He whispers in my ear. "We'll have to do this later. I only know you as Rube. What's your name?"

"Jimmy."

"Jimmy what?"

"Jimmy Fisher."

He puts out his hand and shakes mine. "Jimmy Fisher, you have one beautiful shiner," and runs his hand over my blond burr cut head. "I think we're in. The nurse didn't turn us away. Guess everything's going to be all right."

No sooner has the soldier said this, and the doctor comes out. He puts his hand under his chin, looks at me behind thick glasses, and says, "You're an awful good looking boy. Think this is going to hurt your chances with the girls?" The soldier laughs. I screw my face up into a pout.

"I'm not much for girls."

"Well, we're going to patch you up anyway so no one will ever know this happened."

"No scar, doc?" asks the soldier.

"No, I don't think so. How old is your son?"

This question throws the soldier for a moment.

"I'm not his father. Just happened to be there when the lad was playing baseball and was hit with a bat. Actually, I hardly know the boy."

"Ten. I'm ten." The doctor doesn't respond. He is too busy talking to the soldier.

"Oh, I see. Well, have his parents get in touch with me. No hurry. Regarding scarring, that's the beauty of youth. He'll heal up as if this didn't happen." With that he ushers me into his office, and stitches me up, talking all the time. "That's the best shiner I've seen in a while. Don't worry about a scar. You see the skin is tightly fitted over the skull, and when there is any blow to the face, the skin easily tears. That's what happened to you. You have a clean tear from the blunt surface of the bat. Now then, that's it," he says as he completes the stitching. He looks at his work. "Very good. It'll knit nicely. You can tell your friends you have seventeen new stitches in your face." He looks at me, moving his glasses down on his nose. "I think we'll get a picture of this so you can show the girls when you were not so handsome. Shall we do that?" I shrug my shoulders as he snaps the picture.

The good doctor takes a number of snapshots. He gives me a copy of one two weeks later when I come in to have my stitches removed. I still have the picture these many years later, thanks to my mother's album collection. The doctor was right. My face never scarred.

The soldier drives me home and meets both my parents at the door. My right eye and face are covered in a bandage. I stand behind the soldier as my da stands in the doorway behind my mother. "Your son had a little accident at the courthouse. He's fine. Dr. Nelken in the Wilson Building sewed him up. I'd call the doctor tomorrow, if I were you, to get the particulars." He looks back at me. "You have one brave son. He'd make a good soldier." With that he hops on his bike and leaves. My parents seem so stunned they are speechless. Neither of them even says thank you to the soldier.

No sooner is the soldier gone, and my father's lips are trembling, as are his hands as he attempts to light a cigarette. He doesn't explode. He doesn't swear. He simply sinks into his chair, the color leaving his face. "Dorothy, what're we going to do? Your son is a time bomb. He won't make it to an adult. I mean it. Disaster hangs over him like a cloud. Dorothy, I can't take it."

His head is buried in his chest, the cigarette precariously balancing on his lip with a snail of hot ash ready to fall on him. My mother comes over and takes the cigarette from him. She then comes over to me, where I am still standing, takes my face into her hands, steals a look under the bandage, and asks me how it happened. I tell her, leaving out that I never wore a catcher's mask, but explaining how Chang hit me when he missed the ball. I breathed a sigh of relief when she doesn't ask me to explain.

"Go sit on your father's lap." I look at her as if in shock. "Go!" Instead, I sit on the arm of his chair. I can smell his bad breath and he doesn't have bad breath. "Ray, Jimmy's going to be all right. I know what you're thinking. It's not the same."

"What?" My da's eyes look up as if in a daze. Red snakes are crawling across the whites of his eyes. "You're thinking about that time at Fairyland when that guy broke the bottle and stuck it in your face, when you nearly lost your eye."

My da's head goes back into his chest as he puts his hands through his hair.

"This is different, Ray. There was no malice here. No drunken bastard was out to maim Jimmy. This was an accident, a kid's accident. The soldier said the doctor guarantees Jimmy won't have a scar."

As much as I love my da, I also fear him. The only other time I ever saw him so diminished was that time at Martin Morris's when told he had bad credit. This was an equally confusing moment. Slowly, I move my hand until it is touching his shoulder. He puts his hand over mine, and starts to sob, his chest heaves with each sob. "Jimmy, Jimmy," he whispers almost inaudibly, "Sometimes you break my heart."

"I don't mean to, da."

"I know."

"I love you, da."

He pulls me into his lap, and buries his head into my chest, and wraps his arms around me. My mother stops smoking, and brushes tears from her eyes with her apron, then turns and goes into the kitchen to finish preparing dinner.

* * * * *

Chapter 12

Burnt by the Moon

*Troubles are often the tools by which
God fashions us for better things.*

--Henry Ward Beecher

My mind is sad that summer is gone, mainly because I didn't get a chance to play much baseball, always seeming to be hurt. I wonder what's next? I look at my palm. My mother says some people believe the wrinkles in the hand are a map of a person's future. That bothers me. Mine has a new wrinkle. When she was removing my finger splint, she jokingly said, "This is your heart line, Jimmy, this is your life line, which in your case is a single line, and I have no idea what that means, and this," she mockingly traced the new scar in my palm, "is your accident line. You have a new crease thanks to that curve ball that split your fingers. I wonder what a fortune teller would make of that," she added as she put out her cigarette rotating

the butt in the ashtray, then lit another, "and that cheek of yours, too."
She wasn't through in her inspection, placing her hand under my chin
and examining my face. It had healed, too, except for a thick scab
that extended from the base of my nose to near my temple. She
squinted at me through a plume of smoke.

"Jimmy, you are one slow healer." Then *sotto voce*, 'No scar?
That's what the doc says, huh? I hope for your sake he's right.'

This scar business didn't concern me until deputy Jim Gaffey
called me Scarface Al Capone. I ask my mother who Al Capone was,
but my da answered.

"Chicago hero of the south side."

"Ray, that's not funny. You know he's a gangster."

"What your mother's saying is that I could've ended up working
for him."

She then sent another column of smoke to the ceiling, which I
watched drift down, fade into a misty blanket, then disappear. I'm not
sure what they're talking about.

When I see Bobby Witt, I ask him with some embarrassment who
Al Capone is.

"A Chicago hood, a bootlegger who's now in Sing Sing." He
explains this as easily as if he's talking baseball. All these words are
new to me. How can Bobby know so much? To cover my ignorance,
I challenge him.

"Who says?"

"My brother Vern."

Vernon is getting ready to go into the Army Air Force. Bobby
adores him. Vernon is always smiling and is nice to us kids. He
seems to have a touch of mischief in his eyes. Maybe that's why
Bobby isn't so serious. Seeming to read me, Bobby says,

"Vern is always kidding my parents. My mom is very serious
while my dad thinks everybody is a little crooked. Vern makes my
mom laugh by telling her he's going to steal her from dad, and he kids
dad that the reason he doesn't attend Mass is because he's afraid he'll
be struck dumb once he enters the vestibule."

It must be wonderful to have an older brother, someone you can
confide in, and have tell you you're okay when you don't feel okay.

* * * * *

Finally, I arrive at school. We line up in front of St. Patrick's like we did last year, kindergarteners first to eighth graders last. I'm only a fifth grader but taller than some seventh and eighth grade boys. People think I should be more mature as if height and maturity are synonymous. Another complication with being tall is older girls look at you. I don't look back except in the case of Mary Jo Becker, who is in eighth grade. She is the prettiest girl I have ever seen. Her caramel-colored hair; chocolate-brown eyes and alabaster complexion compliment her talking lips, which are full in the middle and thin on the sides. I get warm all over just looking at her, which I do every day when we're standing in line to go into school. Last year I often took her bike out of the rack and wheeled it to her. She would thank me with her eyes, but no words.

"Little Jimmy Fisher's got a crush on you," I heard her girlfriend say. I'm not little, I'm taller than both of them, not sure what crush means, but I'm certain it's not flattering.

"Jealous, are you?" Mary Jo replies with a smile, and my heart sings. She is so kind. Pretty as she was last year, she's far prettier this year. I'm going to marry her when I grow up. She doesn't know it, but I am. I'm certain of it, that is, if I don't become a priest. She has an older brother at Clinton High, Bob Becker, who plays baseball over at the courthouse with Ripper Collins's team. He's left handed, and is not very big, but he's a good athlete, and nice guy. He doesn't know I'm going to marry his sister, but that's okay for now.

Jack Schuster is another guy who plays over at the courthouse a lot. He's rich. His father is a banker, and I see Father Finefield following his dad around like a puppy dog when he comes by the rectory. It's kind of funny to see the change in Father. Usually Father is the tyrant and sets the table as to how things shall be, but not when Mr. Schuster's there. Father is smiling, laughing, and cordial to St. Patrick kids as if this is his natural way. He stays clear of me, though, as I'm already a student of his game.

God! I hate standing in line. It seems like I'm in the military. Here come Father's two dogs, Rufus and Queenie. If they're not the mad duo. Rufus is a flaming red Irish setter and Queenie is a large blond cocker spaniel. Father loves to hunt, and they're his hunting dogs. They're interested in hunting something else right now, sniffing up girls' dresses. Bobby calls them the canine sickos. "Can you believe it?" he exclaims, as we watch the dogs go sniffing from girl to girl, against a chorus of squeals, dancing legs, and frantic pulling down of dresses, "Father must feed them saltpeter."

"What's that?"

"I don't know, but that's what Vern says." I just shake my head. Every time I ask him a question I'm more confused with his answer.

Sister Mary Cecile, the seventh and eighth grade teacher, is prepared for them. She has a rolled up newspaper in her hand, and gives the dogs a good thump on the snout when they approach the girls. The dogs whelp and look for their master, not seeing him in sight, they go back to the business of looking up girls' dresses. As the girls squeal and giggle, Sister Cecile gets increasingly energetic in her whacking, which finds the dogs retreating with their tails between their legs, certain to repeat the behavior the next day. The bell rings accompanied by the John Phillip Sousa's *Stars and Stripes Forever*, and we finally advance like little soldiers to our respective classes. Basketball! Finally, basketball tonight!

"Good morning students."

"Good morning Sister Mary Marguerite."

Sister is short and stout, and curiously, looks stern when she smiles, like a grimace. I wonder why. I notice things like that, which nobody else seems to see. I suppose there is a reason. I also am a student of people's hands. I believe you can tell more about people's hands than you can their eyes. Hands never lie. Father Finefield is fastidious about his appearance, but not his nails. He bites them. I notice that. I've never bitten my nails in my life. I'm not sure what nail biting means, but I don't think it is a good sign. My da bites his nails, but not my mother. So far I've never seen a nun who bites her nails. I noticed in third grade that Sister Mary Martina had broken nails. That's not the same thing. I don't know what broken nails mean either, but I don't think it's the same as biting your nails. One day I broached the subject of fingernail biting to Bobby as we go over to the courthouse. He looked at me as if I were weird, and knocked my cap off my head. "Rube, sometimes I think you have too many heads under your cap." We both laughed. It seemed funny at the time.

Sister Marguerite is not pretty like Sister Helen was, nor as relaxed. I sense, looking at Sister Marguerite, she doesn't have much room for cowboys, and if Sister Helen is correct, I'm something of a cowboy. She has been talking now for nearly an hour outlining her rules. I'm not paying much attention until she says,

"Anyone who dallies after recess, even for a minute, will lose privileges for a week." I'm something of a dallier.

"Ster, would that mean we couldn't practice basketball after school?" The question comes from Jim Rederer. Jim has a gift for asking provocative questions without being antagonistic. I envy him.

Sister attempts to smile, but it again is only a smirk. "What do you think," she looks at her roster, "Mr. Rederer?"

Not losing a beat, Jim replies, "I think I'd better not dally at recess." Laughter greets his rejoinder.

At lunchtime, I ask Bobby what he thinks of Sister Marguerite.

"What do you mean?"

"Nothing."

"Nothing?"

"Well, yes, something. Did you notice she can't really smile?"

"No."

"You didn't? Actually, it's really striking."

"Rube, do you ever relax? Sister's fine. We're new to her. She's new to us. Next thing you'll be telling me she has red hair like Sister Helen."

"What's that supposed to mean?"

"Nothing, just that all nuns look alike. They're meant to. That's why they wear habits. It reduces differences. Come on, you know that."

No wonder he astonishes me. He's so much smarter than I am. How can he know this? It can't be all Vernon. Some of it has got to be him on his own. What he says makes perfect sense. Maybe I'm imagining things. That's it. I'm imagining her facial muscles are not working right. And it works! When we return to class after lunch, Sister looks fine. I stare at her, and she smiles. Oh, no! It's back!

Sister Marguerite is much more organized than Sister Helen. She tells us precisely what she expects of us, the order of the subjects to be studied, and how much time she has available for students needing help. She is even available after school on Mondays, Wednesdays, and Thursdays, but only if scheduled at a day in advance.

167

"If you haven't signed up beforehand, forget it. I won't see you." This is meant to teach us responsibility. She cautions that there are no exceptions. "My aim is to make you all scholars," she continues, "masters of reading, English grammar, spelling, and arithmetic, and if you succeed, I guarantee not only will you be promoted, but will lead productive lives. One day you will remember this grade as your most important learning experience."

Her words mesmerize me. Wow! I can't believe my good luck. She says all the things I want to hear. Her eyes sparkle as she talks. Then she hands out our books. They are new, and have that wonderful smell of new books. I can't wait to tell my mother how happy I am. But something was to intervene in the afternoon of that first day to throw shock waves through my system and to place the rest of my life on mental alert. It happened innocently and without warning after the first afternoon recess of the school year. I was the last boy to bat at recess. It is the duty of the last batter to put the bat and softball away before returning to class. The softball had rolled across the alley into Mr. Clark's backyard. He is a brakeman on the railroad with my da. He tosses the ball back to me and asks how I am. We talk only a minute. When I finally come around the corner of the building, past Father Finefield's garage, and am about to enter the school's side door, three faces behind the door look at me tauntingly. Momentarily, I don't get it, that is, until I turn the door handle. The door is locked!

"Come on guys!" I yell. "It's not funny. Come on," I yell again terror seeping into my voice. They make faces at me stretching their mouths with their index fingers and sticking their tongues out, then they turn to go up the backstairs to class. I stand in absolute panic. My body is shaking. They're not coming back! The front door is locked! There's no other way in! This sends shivers up my spine. I'll be late for class! God! I'll be late! Sister won't let me play basketball for a week. All summer I've been hurt. Now I'm okay! Oh God! My mind rages. What am I to do? The doorknob is part of a large single bronze metal panel three inches across and nine inches long, bolted with three heavy screws across the top and bottom and six heavy screws on each side of the door panel. I grab the door handle with all my will and rip it out of the wood, bending the bronze panel a ninety-degree angle from its mooring. The guys hear the explosive wrenching of wood and metal and look down in disbelief. At that same moment, Father Finefield leaves the rectory and is walking toward the garage. His pace quickens as he hears the wrenching noise.

"What is this?" he says incredulously as he sees four-inch screws, like the corrugated teeth of a bronze tiger flaring out from the shattered wooden door, wood splinters everywhere, with an ugly gaping hole like a one-eyed monster where once was a solid door. "Who did this? Come, come, who did this terrible thing?" I am frozen in place, unable to speak.

"Jimmy. Jimmy Fisher," somebody yells from behind the door.

"What?" Father asks. "Who?" He looks at me, then quickly back at the door, trying to make sense of this. Clearly, he is exasperated. His lips quiver.

"Get me Sister Flavian immediately," he commands. Several boys fly up the steps to get the principal, relieved to get away. "This is despicable, outrageous!" He looks daggers at me, but strangely they are not accusatory. His powers have abandoned him. The whole situation is too incredulous. Sister Flavian hurries down the steps.

"Yes, Father?"

"Sister, do you see this?" She looks. A painful expression is in her eyes, but she says nothing. "This lot wants me to believe this boy," he points at me, "ripped this door to shreds all by himself." He looks to her to measure if her doubt is equal to his. Her face is an inscrutable mask. "It's clear Sister we're not going to get any honest answers here. I want you to put all these boys on report. All of them, Sister, until you get to the bottom of this! Suspend their privileges. You decide for how long. And please! Get somebody to repair this door immediately. We can't leave it like this. We have insurance, don't we Sister?"

"Yes, Father, but I'm not sure if it covers this."

"Well, look into it, and in any case, get the door fixed." He takes his car keys out of his pocket and turns to the garage. "And deal with these boys, Sister." He shakes his head in disbelief. "This doesn't reflect well on our school, Sister," his face not hiding the unspoken criticism, or on you Sister and your control of these miscreants. Sister Flavian says nothing, but her expression from my line of sight is one of patient obedience.

Sister Flavian is not only our principal, but also a devout nun, who is wise beyond measure. She interviews each of us boys separately, and establishes to her satisfaction that all share some guilt in the incident. Sister is quite accepting if not approving of the widespread inclination to perfect the art of lying. She knows under interrogation, even boys of ten never behave normally, that the stupid act intelligent, the intelligent act stupid; the guilty look innocent, and the innocent look guilty. That just occasionally, some boys act as they are and tell the truth as they know it, and of course, they're the poor souls who get caught every time. Knowing this, she assembles us in the sixth grade classroom after school. We wait for a lecture and severe punishment to follow, but are given neither. "I would have thought better of you boys. I'm disappointed and saddened. I'll leave it up to you to decide what you can do to make amends for this."

Her words still ring in my mind. In my interview, I tell her I did this terrible thing all by myself. I explain the circumstances. She looks at me with her compelling but sad eyes. There isn't a scintilla of disbelief. She understands the rage within me.

"You are an unusual boy, James, in that your body seems of the same resolute intensity as your will. You are a determined young man. I'm no psychologist, but I would pay attention to this strength that shelters your weakness."

I learned many years later that my intensity has a name. It is called "akathisia" (a-ka-theee-zha) and is derived from the internal sensation of acute restlessness. It is like the heat of a quiet volcano that suddenly erupts without warning when provoked by a combination of favorable circumstances. Akathisia suggests that this restlessness is just waiting for an opportunity to be engaged. It is a form of caged violence, when the soul erupts from the body and commands attention if only fleetingly. Emotional violence can be triggered by feelings of rage, fear or frustration. In destroying the locked door, I was displaying this. I was only ten, but what Sister Flavian said was to prove prophetic.

*   *   *   *   *

Sister Marguerite always has a bowl of candy treats on her desk for the winning team of a subject under discussion. Winners are giving a choice between a Tootsie Roll, sucker, or chocolate malted milk ball. I always choose a malted milk ball. We are learning the Latin Mass and practicing the altar boy responses to the priest in Latin. Sister pronounces the Latin words so distinctly that they seem like poetry. I can't understand why Latin is a dead language. It's so much more beautiful than English. I have trouble though pronouncing Latin words. They roll off the tongue of Jimmy Halbach, Dick Morris, and Jim Rederer as if they know what they mean. And Jimmy Halbach stutters! But I have no problem memorizing the Latin Mass, and know what the words mean by comparing them to their English translation on the opposite page in my mother's missal.

Coming home from school after the door episode, I enter the house to find it full of people, my parents, the two carpenters, the convalescing sergeant and his Dayton, Ohio girlfriend. I don't sit down. A chorus of conflicting feelings is yelling in my head, but fatigue is not among them, given I didn't practice basketball today. All are smoking. There is the smell of coffee and the incongruity of too many people pressed together with too little air. My eyes pass from empty coffee cups, cake plates to the monolithic smiles of surprise at my intrusion. Everyone stares but no one speaks until my mother breaks the silence. "Why Jimmy, you're home early!"

This catches me off guard. I feel I'm suffocating, force a smile, and then turn my back to them. "Going over to the courthouse, be back at five." With that, I escape into the fresh air, leap off the porch, hearing my da's fading cry, "Jimmy come back here!"

When I grow up, I know two things for sure. I'll never smoke, and I'll live in a house of many rooms filled with books from floor to ceiling, and be free of the heat of too many people. My feet fly over to the courthouse where they are playing football. Guys from all over Clinton come to the courthouse in the fall, guys like Bill Christiansen, Dave Holleran, Bob Petersen, Tom Pladna, Gary Stephenson, and Bob Becker. I've been playing tackle football with eighth graders since I was in third grade. Many of these guys are in high school like Gary Stephenson and Bob Becker, so are Gussie Witt, Jack Dunmore, and Lyle Sawyer. Bill Christiansen's father is an executive with Joyce Lumber Company, Dave Holleran's and Bob Petersen's dads are attorneys. Bill and Dave are sixth graders at St. Pat's and Bob is in seventh grade at Washington Junior High. These guys have helmets, shoulder pads, rib and hip pads, football pants, and football shoes with rubber spikes. The rest of us are dressed only in sweatshirts, jeans, and tennis shoes. Bill Christiansen is skinnier than I am, and not quite as tall, but likes to strut his stuff like he's a real football player. This gets to me. I don't have much room for dandies. "Rube, you can be on our side," Bobby Witt says as I race on to the courtyard, "we're on defense. You can play end."

How could I be so lucky? Christiansen is playing quarterback on the other team. He's calling a play in the huddle, and all those older guys are listening to him, can you beat that? He calls the signals, the center hikes the ball to him, and he follows his blockers around my side. I get knocked down, but get up and race after him, clipping him from behind with a body block that throws him against the jailhouse walk, causing him to slide against the building. He picks himself up, and looks daggers at me.

"That's dirty! Did'ya see that?" he looks about him for confirmation. Somebody says, "Come on, let's get on with the game!"

"Watch yourself, Fisher!" he says. "I mean it!"

I smile to myself hoping he'll carry the ball again. He does, only to the other side, the side nearest the gravel parking lot between the jail and the courthouse. This time no one blocks me, and I run parallel to the line of scrimmage with an angle on him. I hit him around the ankles, pulling his feet out from under him just as he's getting up speed with his face hitting the turf hard. Stunned, and a bit shaken, it takes him a few moments to recover. "Who hit me?"

"I did," I answer.

"That was a cheap shot. You play dirty, Fisher."

I shake my head. "It was a clean tackle."

"Think so?" he pushes me hard, and I lose my balance falling down. I get up and push him back. "Want to make something of it?" he says. I didn't. I was fulfilled just knocking him down to my level. People like Christiansen think they are better than people like me. They are more confident. Nobody can charm the good nuns more glibly, or find it harder to be sincere. I sensed quite early that nobody acts braver than when they are frightened, or happier than when they are miserable. Nobody can flatter you better than when they hate you than those who are the most privileged. Christiansen at least was up

172

front about how he felt. I had no problem with that. Nor did I have an appetite to fight him. I just liked the sensation of hitting him. It was acceptable in football to put a hurt on someone and feel the pleasure it gave, and not be seen as a tough, which I certainly wasn't. Hitting someone hard felt delicious. That is the only way I can describe it. But he was insistent on meeting me after school Monday. All weekend I pondered this. I didn't want to fight. Was I afraid? Perhaps. Did I want to hurt him? No, definitely not. All I wanted to do is knock him off his perch, and I did, and that was that.

If this day wasn't eventful enough, I come home to find the company gone, but purple drapes from floor to ceiling over the doorway to the little room off the living room. I pull the drapes aside to see a bed, vanity and mirror, ottoman and reclining chair and pictures on the wall. There is hardly space to move around. Everything looks used, but it's new here. The baby crib is gone and so is the radio.

"Mother, where's my radio?" The radio is our family's main entertainment. When I was little, I listened every weekday to my comic book heroes. Now I listen with my parents to *Bob Hope, Jack Benny, Amos 'n' Andy, Eddie Cantor, Fibber McGee* and *Molly, Edgar Bergen* and *Charlie McCarthy, Fred Allen, Red Skelton, Mr. District Attorney, Truth or Consequences,* the *Lux Radio Theater, President Roosevelt's fireside chats,* and the *Ave Maria Hour.* My da's favorite is *Fred Allen's "Allen's Alley"* with its host of characters, especially the salesman and the senator, and my mother's are the president's fireside chats and the *Ave Maria Hour.* They are mine, too.

She comes out of the kitchen looking as fresh and pretty as if she's ready for church. "The radio is in our bedroom. Do you like it?" she asks pulling the cord at the side of the drapes, collecting them together, and revealing the newly furnished room.

Her face is so expectant that I can't be truthful. "Where's Janice? Her crib?"

"In our room, too."

"Mother, what's going on?"

"Your father got all this furniture from a railroad buddy who was giving it away to the Salvation Army. You can't believe his excitement. You'd think he found a billfold full of money." She

173

patted her leg for me to sit on the sofa beside her, which was now in front of the drapes, before it was on the other side of the room. Two things I don't like, one is surprise, and the other is change, especially when not forewarned. She knows this and I can tell she is playing up to me. "There's something else I want to tell you."

"What?" I look at her suspiciously.

"The sergeant's girlfriend is going to live with us." I put my hands to my mouth in horror, pull my head down into my chest, seeing this she adds," for a little while."

"Why, mother? Why?"

"Because she needs a place to stay, and we can use the extra money."

"How long?"

"Oh, I don't know." She goes back into the kitchen and returns with her cigarettes. She takes one out, lights it, and stands above me with her hand under her elbow, smoking pensively, her profile frozen in my mind.

* * * * *

All these years later, I have a picture of that moment in my head. She looked more than beautiful. She was glamorous like a movie star, beautiful as fire. It was not the cut of her clothes, the texture of her skin, or her physiognomy. It was simply her attitude. The cigarette was always an extension of her, the embodiment of her alter ego. The way she held it, especially when she was thoughtful, added an extra dimension to her diminutive stature. Her 100 pounds was well distributed on a five-one body with a quietly graceful figure defined by a small waist, narrow almost boy-like hips, and shapely legs. This was the frame, but hardly the content of her indomitable spirit. Her essence was hidden in the mystique of the swirling smoke that encircled her like a majestic robe and then trailed off like a discarded thought. In silhouette, she appeared like a Vermeer painting viewed through a veil of gossamer. Her soft lines wrapped in fading colors were garment of her mystery not unlike Vermeer's lady putting on her necklace. His lady is frozen in a priceless work of art, while my mother's image is set in precious memory.

* * * * *

Part of me wanted to tell her about the door, but another part of me was angry. I said nothing. Deep emotions clashed in me. At moments like this, I felt that her mind and mine were extensions of each other. While I saw her beauty, I felt her pain, that she didn't like the course of events any better than I did, and that she, too, was powerless to act. I went upstairs to my room and pouted until dinnertime. How could I ever have Bobby over for dinner now? What would this do to our playing basketball in the basement? My life is terrible. I have nobody to talk to but my mother, and she seems caught up in loneliness herself. My sister, Patsy, and little brother, Jackie, are oblivious to all this commotion. They sit on the bed coloring away as if nothing has changed.

Somehow dinner finds all the people back. The two boarders, the sergeant and his girlfriend, and my parents eat in the dining room and we kids eat in the kitchen with Janice in the highchair beaming with happiness. I feed her and she looks back at me with those big beautiful blue eyes and I melt with love for her. Everyone in the other room is talking at the same time. When the dinner is over, my mother and the girlfriend do the dishes in the kitchen, and the men cramp together in the living room smoking and drinking coffee. Janice is back in my parent's bedroom in her crib cooing away, Patsy and Jackie are playing with her. I'm there too trying to play the radio, finally giving up because I can't hear a thing with all the noise. I go into the kitchen and the two women are working and smoking away, laughing and talking. The house is again a gray cloud of smoke, and so I escape into the basement to play basketball by myself. I don't want to be around any of them. Dribbling the tennis ball on the basement floor and throwing it through the coffee can cylinder gets old after a while. I go upstairs to read my comics. I pick out Howard Pyle's "Men of Iron," and transport myself into the year 1400.

* * * * *

I picture myself being among the rebellious nobles against King Henry IV, who has dethroned Richard II, and stripped noblemen of their property. Only Sir John Dale survives the slaughter. So what does he do? He stupidly yields himself to the mercy of the king, and of course the king has him murdered. Thus the "House of Falworth" is all but destroyed. But wait! Young Myles Falworth is determined

175

to redress this murder and these wrongs to his family. Thanks to many mentors, much courage, and a passion for revenge, he is prepared to meet the challenge. I float on a vicarious carpet, and leave my house and life, and enter another world where young Myles, blond, blue-eyed, handsome, and born in April like me, becomes an excellent swordsman and jouster destroying his enemies at will. And unlike Sir John Dale, even though in the flush of youth, he understands the devious ways of men, and beats them at their own game. He brings honor on his father's house, annihilates his father's enemies, and wins the right to ask for the hand of the Lady Alice to be his wife. I close the comic and look with anticipation to playing for coach Dean Burridge, my *Sieur de la Montainge*.

* * * * *

It is my bedtime, but I go downstairs anyway to get a glass of water, and find the sergeant and the girlfriend still here. Are they both going to stay all night? Where will he sleep? Not in her room! I look at her and smile. She smiles back. She is a tall woman, taller than the sergeant by a good four or five inches, must have been beautiful as a girl, but now seems to wear the signs of neglect. I wonder why. Is she afraid to be too pretty to the sergeant's ugly? He has a pinched-in face as if placed in a vice and squeezed into a horse-like shape with bulging eyes. She has an oval face with her eyes slanted and wide apart and with a long straight nose and lips that stretch nearly ear to ear when she laughs. What is especially pretty about her is her hair. It is the color of ginger, thick and curly, and glistens as it comes down over her eyes with her constantly pushing it away. She smokes her cigarettes with a holder like the president. I think she was educated in a convent school because she talks slowly and enunciates her words clearly with only a hint of a midwestern twang. The sergeant hardly pays any attention to her; instead follows my mother with his eyes wherever she goes. I saw him pat her on the fanny earlier in the kitchen, and she gave him a dirty look. She told my da about it, but he just smiled and whispered something in her ear, and she patted him on the head. I don't know what that's all about. So far I haven't seen him touch his girlfriend, not even an arm around her shoulder. You'd think it was his sister, or something. Could it be his sister? No, impossible. Someone so ugly couldn't have a pretty sister. No way.

The sergeant may have been wounded in the war, but he's not my impression of a soldier. He's small, has a widow's peak like a monk, and the hair that he has is combed across his balding pate. His eyes are like those of a muskrat with deep circles under them. He is always smiling as if he hears a private joke in his head. When he smokes, he smokes holding the cigarette vertically like some women do.

The two carpenters, who go to bed quite early, are both leathery looking, with weather-beaten faces, sinewy arms, calloused hands, and lithe physiques. Neither one seems to have an ounce of fat on him. The one carpenter has large blue eyes that seem full of knowledge. He hardly says anything at all, and gives out very little information when asked a question. His hair is golden like mine, but he has long sideburns that almost reach his chin. His chin is square with a deep dimple in the center. The only thing I don't like about him are his teeth. They are bad. The front tooth is chipped and all are stained yellow, like the fingers on his right hand. The other carpenter is a dandy. That's what my da calls him. He can't wait to get out of his work clothes and put on a shirt and tie, suit coat and slacks, and penny loafers, or when he goes casual, an open neck blue oxford shirt, matching cashmere sweater, gabardine slacks, and white buck shoes. He looks more like a college student than a carpenter. He has perfect teeth, and they are as white as ivory, and he smiles a lot to show them off. His hands, despite being a carpenter's, look as if his fingernails are manicured. His jet-black hair is burr cut, and his black eyebrows look like they are trimmed, too. He is shorter than the other carpenter with a slender build, round face and a weak chin. He is clean-shaven, so much so that I wonder if he shaves at all. My mother says neither carpenter is married, which she finds strange. Both are apparently in their late twenties, never been in service, as far as she can tell, so she wonders if they have been in trouble with the law. I wonder, too, but not my da. He seems to like all these people; maybe because they are helping to pay the bills.

* * * * *

177

School on Monday was a vague apparition with all the talk around me about my fight after school. People were betting on who would win. We couldn't fight on school property, so we met on the lawn of a house on Third Street and Third Avenue North.

"You want to box or wrestle?" I ask.

He pushes me. "Can you believe that?" He looks at his audience of fifth and sixth grade boys. "Chicken here wants to know whether we're going to box or wrestle." He pushes me again. "We're going to fight, chicken."

With that I hit him in the nose. He didn't react like Donny Costello did in fourth grade. Nor did his nose bleed. He hit me back in the face, making my cheek burn, and I grab him and wrestle him to the ground. We roll around until the owner of the house comes out and shouts us off his property. Then we head to another yard, and continue the fight. Again, we are shouted off the property. This continues until we are close to the bluff, and exhausted. Bruised, but not bloody, we call it a draw, and shake hands with little sincerity, and everyone scatters.

"Your jacket is ripped," Bobby says as we head for home, "all the way up the back."

I take off my new windbreaker, which is a lightweight tan coat, and a gift from my mother from money she earned sewing for neighbors. I am devastated, more crushed from this than the fight. What to do? "Oh, no! Bobby, I can't let my mother see this."

"Maybe she won't. There's a tailor downtown next to the Maid-Rite. Vern had his trousers fixed there. He's cheap, too."

I had fifty cents on me. "How much money do you have, Bobby?" He had a quarter. "Can I borrow it?"

"Sure, but why don't we see how much it costs?"

"You going with me?"

"Sure, why not?"

Bobby's show of support moved me. He was there for me, and made no big deal about it. "Won't you be late for dinner?"

"Rube, it's only three-thirty now. Come on, how can I be late?"

Three-thirty? That shocked me. The big fight lasted only a half hour. If I was hurt, I didn't feel it, my only regret was my ripped jacket. I loved it. Tan windbreakers were in style. It made me feel good. Having few clothes, those that I had were special and this was the most special of all. Bobby talked animatedly on the way to the tailor's about me tackling Bill Christiansen so hard in the game last Friday, but not about the fight. "Who do you think won, Bobby?"

"The grass," he said with a laugh, "you guys really tore up those people's yards."

"But the fight?"

"Rube, come on! You didn't hurt him. He didn't hurt you. The only loser was your jacket. That's it."

He was right of course; I just wanted him to say I won. The tailor's shop was so small that we walked right past it. It was sandwiched between the Maid-Rite and the furniture store next door. It wasn't much wider than the doorway. We opened the door and a bell rang. A little man pushed a frayed black curtain aside and came from the back room. He was hunched over, wore granny glasses, and had hair only on his ears and thick eyebrows that met in the middle like a gray bar across his forehead. All that was forgotten when he smiled. "What can I do for you boys?"

I explained about my ripped jacket, and that it was a present from my mother, and that she would be really sad to see what I had done to it. I didn't even ask if he could fix it. He took it into his hands, looked at the rip. "Somebody must have been angry with you, boy, they ripped the whole back away from the seams." I didn't say anything. Then thought,

"I don't have much money. How much will it cost to fix it?"

"How much do you have?"

"Fifty cents."

"That's exactly what it costs. Now, give me about twenty minutes and it will look as good as knew, except for the grass stains. You'll have to have your momma get rid of them."

Relieved, I smiled at Bobby. "Thanks for thinking of this." He ignored the compliment and pulled me back through the door. "Let's get a Maid-Rite."

"Bobby, you know I don't have any more money."

"I do, and they only cost a nickel."

So out one door and in the next we went. We were greeted with the wonderful aroma of sizzling ground beef in a long trough-like pan. The pan separated customers at the counter from the man behind it. He wore a white baker's cap and white apron with "Maid-Rite"

179

across it. The place was packed with people sitting on round stools. It was fun to watch him scoop up a ladle of hamburger and place it on a small hot square bun. He'd put several in a bag then pass it to the customer, or put Maid-Rites on a paper plate for the customer at the counter. My stomach growled with anticipation at the succulent taste of this treat as Bobby gave the man his quarter. He got five hamburgers, two for each of us, and we split the third. As I started to devour one, I got thirsty. Anticipating this, the man put two glasses of water in front of us with ample napkins.

By the time we had eaten the Maid-Rites and drank our water, my jacket was done. As the tailor had promised, it looked as good as new. I wondered if life could get any better than this, and it did. My mother noticed the grass stains, but nothing else except my scratched face. "Is that a new bruise on your face?" she asked.

"I don't think so," I answered, which was a lie hidden in some kind of truth.

"Well, let me take care of these grass stains. We can't have you wearing this jacket like that." Fall is such a wonderful god to me.

*   *   *   *   *

Fall gives way to winter, and if my history is consistent, winter is a harbinger of new troubles for me. This may sound paranoid, but I am always leery of the ghosts of winter. First, it seems to snow every day. Snow is all right when it is the crystal purity and whiteness of heaven. This whiteness is a mirage as mountains of dirty snow pile up quickly along the sidewalks and cling to my boots, and then the icy sidewalks and streets force me to step gingerly as if an octogenarian. Once home, I stomp my boots hard on the front porch. They never come clean. I am lazy and hate to take them off outside even though I'm supposed to. My mother is waiting for me, as she has every day this week. I know why. The ghosts of winter are hexing me.

"Well, do you have some good news for me?" I shake my head.

"What's wrong, Jimmy? There has got to be something wrong."

Nothing's wrong. Everything's wrong. What can I say? Sister Marguerite is a wonderful teacher. I am reading much better than I did in fourth grade, doing long and short division and the multiplication tables like a breeze. I even have mastered the Latin responses of the Mass, and can do the entire Mass without making a

single mistake. I love the Latin Mass. No one in my class is better at
Latin than I am. Yet I am one of only two boys in the fifth grade not
yet tapped by Father Finefield to be an altar boy. Can't he see I have
a prodigious memory for Latin, that Latin sticks to me like moth to
light? Christmas is around the corner, and today Father appeared in
our classroom for the final time this year. We are practicing our Latin
responses to the Mass when he enters. He smiles, sits down, places a
large envelope on his lap, then folds his arms across his chest, and
beams with the authority of his office, and listens with mock
attention. It is obvious he has heard enough. He stands, clears his
throat with that deep guttural sound of his, and laughs ceremoniously.

"Well, Sister, I see your students continue to make progress. That
is not why I am here today, however. I am here, Sister, to announce
that Joseph Zimmer is to be made an altar boy, and will participate in
the Christmas Masses. Joseph, if you would," he says beckoning with
his right hand palm up, "take this certificate and present it to your
parents, and this form and have them fill it out so that we can measure
you correctly for your cassock and surplice." He hands a framed
certificate and form to Joe Zimmer, and then shakes his hand.
"Congratulations, young man, you are now an altar boy. Your parents
should be rightly proud of you." Everyone applauds.

The sting of this applause rings in my ears as I tell my mother that
Joseph Zimmer, not her son, is to be an altar boy this Christmas.
"Jimmy, how can you ever become a Jesuit if you can't even make it
to an altar boy?" How, indeed!

* * * * *

Being an altar boy is the biggest honor of a fifth grader, and I am
the only boy not an altar boy in the entire class. This is like scourging
my mother at the pillar. She lives for this good news, and now she
must live with the infamy of my failure. I have a problem and I don't
know the solution. Father Finefield doesn't like me much, and I don't
like him much. Okay, that's a given. My problem is this: why is
Father's liking or not liking me relevant to my being a good altar boy?
Sister Marguerite, I know, has campaigned for me. She even told my
mother that I'm the best student in the class with the Latin Mass
responses to the priest. Shouldn't that be enough? Apparently, it is
not. How I wish now Vern were my big brother. I can't talk to

Bobby. He's an altar boy and says he hates it. I think he says that just to make me feel less miserable. Soon it will be 1944, and my private war with Father isn't going too well. I think when I go home tonight I'm going to reread my Classic Comic of Dostoyevsky's *Crime and Punishment*. Raskolnikov, a student residing in St. Petersburg, Russia, crushed by poverty, hopeless and forlorn, and guilty of a heinous crime, finds his way back to humanity. That ought to cheer me up.

* * * * *

Chapter 13

Mind and Matter

*As the firefly only shines when on the wing,
so it is with the human mind – when at rest, it darkens.*

--Letitia E. Landon

My mother is not through. She tips her head back and blows out smoke rings, savoring them as if emblems of her authority. She studies me. "Give the Jesuits your soul, Jimmy, and they will give you a brain." This finds me retreating into swirling wonder. My mother sensed from an early age my mercurial nature, which would come to define my life. Her duty, as she saw it, was to subordinate my temperament to a stronger authority. She believed the "Society of Jesus" would provide a more draconian discipline and more astute training than mere Catholic education.

Founded by Ignatius Loyola in 1540, the Jesuits complemented the explosive economic and political expansion of the 16th century by establishing themselves as educators – cultivators of human capital. She knew I had a passion to escape my subculture. This allowed the nuns to own me; the priests, too, and now she aspired to have Jesuit scholarship finish me off. But it was not to be.

* * * * *

Dread can eat a cavity into the soul and leave the detritus of confusion behind, turning a life into the dementia of betrayal. One day in my twenty-second year, still painfully devout, my mother became deathly ill with one of her massive mastoid ear infections. She beckoned me to her bed, and whispered in my ear. Her words ricocheting off the synapses of my brain like cataclysmic thunder, "Not still a virgin are you Jimmy?"

Not a virgin? What else would I be? The past five years had been focused on attaining a college degree. Nothing else mattered. Nothing! This is the way you programmed me, mother, I wanted to say. Your son is a grind, mother, a blunt instrument pushing back the darkness. Is this now a failing? Should I be ashamed? Have I misspent my youth? My mind, rattling like a cage of scurrying mice unable to purchase bearing, echoes in silent fear, *'Is there something wrong with Jimmy?'* Of course, mother, there is something wrong! I am a virgin! It shouts at me from the fissures of my mind in the voice of my da, *'You're not a fag are you Jimmy?'* Books, basketball and baseball displaced sensuous drive. My offense was that I turned off one passion and didn't turn on the other automatically. There are no words to convey how her doubt dislodged my psychic compass from its mooring, or how it threw my soul into perpetual turmoil. Catching my face in a book, my da would say, *'Jimmy, you don't know whether you're afoot or horseback. You're so full of bullshit you don't know whether you're coming or going.'* He was right. They both were. I was lost. I was a machine on automatic pilot. I had never rebelled, never questioned, and never doubted the truth of what was preached, taught or written for me to absorb. A ubiquitous sponge, I believed everything, trusted everyone, and belonged to no one, not even myself.

Women have been my learning vessel. Of the many callings that comprise the world, none requires as much sacrifice as the sisterhood of listeners. Men are good at talking, not listening. They are too busy telling and explaining. Only women are capable of understanding the nuances beyond silence, and my mother was a saint in that regard, as were the nuns. Nuns knew so much about me. This created an intimacy between us, which was all the more poignant for being impersonal. The sisterhood was so ingrained in them that there was no seam between them and being nuns, and that made them different if not better than any other person I knew with the exception of my mother.

The transformation of a young lady into a nun in the 1940s was a common experience among Catholic girls. After a year as a postulant, the novice made her first simple vows. She wore a wedding dress and walked down the isle of the motherhouse chapel toward the bishop-enthroned altar. The girl's parents were there, her mother proud, her father grim, watching his daughter dedicate her life to God, the bride of Christ. At a certain point in the ceremony, the young novices were led away. When they returned, they wore the habit of their order, and carried a new name. A plain gold band, a wedding band, was slipped onto their fingers to be a constant reminder of the solemn dedication of their life to Christ.

Nuns are not only special; they are the conscience of priests. They have a sly innocence in the way they storm heaven, an unworldliness that often goes hand in hand with financial wizardry. Handmaids of the Lord, as they are known, those that this tribute fits are now old or have passed on, as few new nuns being trained today have the same unworldly agenda. The irony is that no one thinks of nuns and their struggle with commitment the way they do of priests. My wonder is what I would be if I were young today without nuns of such commitment.

*   *   *   *   *

The last strips of an Iowa sun lay bravely dying on the western horizon. Trees curved from childhood, naked except capped with snow, are bent by the blustering wind. When the gust has gone, I wait, my back arched for the next assault. Suddenly, as if no will of my own, I turn east instead of west on my street and move away rather than toward my home. The courthouse clock chimes four times. I may never hear it again. 'There is no truth,' Sister Flavian says, 'that cannot be confirmed. No, my child, she would say, but the sins of others are a sacrifice to God. Your sacrifice.' A lone misguided bird flies away as I ponder her meaning, and come up empty. The sun is gone. As if in a fog, I turn south and walk toward downtown. The yellow haze of lights in the store windows against a winter's sky wink at me as I pass. Street traffic is light for this hour as the roads are slick, and snow banks on street curbs are four or more feet high. A policeman, his breath pouring out of his mouth like a charging bull, a halo of steam surrounding his cap, watches me curiously as I cross at Van Allen's walking south. I pretend not to notice. He remains quite still, like a statue, his eyes trained on the horizon, though the horizon is now obscure. Why is it I feel like a criminal when I have this secret I don't know how to share? Only this afternoon after school, Sister Flavian and Sister Julianne set off my paranoia. I can still see Sister Flavian massively sprawled out behind her desk, her eyes looking over her pyramid hands with a dint of pain in them. She was already prepared to return to the Mount. I know this because her shawl was draped over a chair, while she clutched a paper in her hands. Arcs of sweat ringed her eyes. Sister Julianne was stooped over her like a headwaiter, a stiff backed miniature tactician with silvery eyes and a crisp unfriendly look. She stretched out one hand towards the paper as if to recommend a specialty of the house. It seems my principal had already read the paper as she ignored the gesture.

"Yessss, Ssssister?" I said in a stutter, my eyes imploring what's this all about?

"Your little brother," Sister declared, "is on report," waving the paper in a fury, then quickly adding not to prolong my suspense, "for stealing milk money."

Before morning recess, second graders put a dime on top of their desks, and when they return from recess the dime has been replaced by a four-ounce carton of milk. "Sister Julianne noticed that several dimes were missing during the past week, and set out to find out why." Both nuns nodded to each other, then turned their attention back to me. Sister Flavian placed the report on her desk, then took up a pencil which she edged back and forth, top to bottom, bottom to top in her hand, practically mesmerizing me. "Your little brother was found scooping up the dimes as he left for recess with such skill that Sister Julianne could hardly believe her eyes."

"True!" Sister Julianne chirped in horror.

"When she confronted Arnold John, all he had to say was that he did it because the dimes were there. He showed no remorse, didn't feel he had done anything wrong." Sister Flavian's eyes were full of hurt, while Sister Julianne's enlisted only bewilderment at such blunt admission. As for me, I was still as ice but melting rapidly.

Sister Flavian's gaze moved over me slowly and then settled on my eyes without a word. It was reminiscent of the discomfort I feel every time I ask Father for the key to the school gym. This nun and priest could fry me with their eyes. I wonder if this is part of their training. "Well, James, what do you make of this?" The question astounded me. What was I supposed to make of it?

Sister Julianne straightened up and turned her eyes directly towards me, silver slits and quiet like a pointer's. My cheeks took on a queer color, a blushing red, painted high on my cheekbones. It gave me, I suppose, in my heightened state of nervousness, a slightly *Dorian Gray* look like his rotting portrait in the attic. There was nothing that I could say. Nothing I could do. What I needed was time. I begged for it, and Sister Flavian kindly granted me a stay until tomorrow. This is going through my mind as I saunter on past the business district, while my other mind is thinking what I should tell my mother about Jackie. It has turned much colder, the wind is getting up, and there is a promise in people's faces that the gift of warmth is not far away, but not for me. I am confined to my icy purgatory. A strange elation catches me. 'Til now I have been thinking too much about me. My little brother is in trouble, but my little brother hasn't had much of a life in his first seven years, living with relatives and never seeing his mother for the first five. The street sign says its 15th Avenue South with icy Beaver Slough close by. I can smell the river. It seeps into my pores and kin to me as much as my little brother. I am in South Clinton! Houses around me are mostly modest white clapboard with transparent substances tacked to their windows in lieu of storm windows to combat the cold, while chimneys bellow out smoke with the fragrance of burnt coal and wood. The streets are covered with snow with deep grooves like rails that cars must follow or become stuck. The sidewalks, too, have only tiny paths framed by mountains of snow. I cannot see the courthouse clock from here. I don't think I've ever walked this far before. It is a winter wonderland with virgin snow undisturbed by snowplows or shovels. I hear the voices of young people ice-skating in the Beaver Channel. The trees have snow for leaves and telephone poles look like giant white crosses connected by snow-capped wires. I forget the cold and kick the snow about. Then I realize, *I am late for dinner!*

What was I thinking? Oh, God, I'm in trouble now! I try to run but my legs are too stiff with cold. My tiredness hits me like a sudden virus. I feel it in the knees, the hips, my whole body. I turn and start walking north but my mind refuses to rest until I see the courthouse clock clearly. It is 5:20. Too late to panic. I think of Jackie. Then something remarkable happens. My mind says to me, 'this is a learning experience for Jackie. No more.' That's it! Doubt jumps in. 'Then why haven't you stolen anything?' I ponder this momentarily without an answer, and then my face breaks into a grin. I stole a box of baseballs, but gave them back so that counts under *not being caught*. Anyway, I'm a bore. Jackie isn't. He's an incurable little devil, that's for sure. Rebel is in his makeup. Everybody loves Jackie! So do I! Then I remember the funny stares of the nuns, knowing they must think the Fishers are quite an outfit. Well, we are! *'There are lace curtain Irish,' my da says, 'and there are shanty Irish. It's goddamn for sure we're not lace curtain.'* They probably think we're a poor and pathetic clan. My mind ricochets. No way! I surge with loyalty to my little brother and decide not to tell anyone. I'll pay him more attention. That's it! The nuns will be sympathetic to that, knowing I'm taking responsibility. It'll help, too, telling them Jackie's family history, of his traumatic first five years, and how I plan to be there for him. This is what I'll say, "Sisters, my little brother looks up to me like a god." No, no, not that! What else? How's this? "Sisters, my little brother idolizes me." That's better. Then I'll add, "I have influence on him." Ah, that's it! Good! "Sisters," I will say in conclusion, "You don't want this behavior repeated. Well, I can assure you it won't be. I'm taking responsibility for my little brother. What he said is what he meant. He didn't know it was wrong. There is no reason for my mother to know. She has enough worries." I can see them nodding their heads in agreement, knowing my mother has to deal with arrogant me, and deviant Jackie, with only the normalcy of Patsy in the middle. I'm at the Conoco Station of my block, cross the street and walk pass the courthouse, very satisfied with myself. It will be me, not my little brother on trial tomorrow, and it'll be me, not him, that gets the heat now when I get home. God! I would make a great martyr! I'll offer it up for the poor souls in purgatory.

And that is how it happened. Mother went to her grave never knowing one son was a juvenile delinquent in the second grade and the other played cute with a box of baseballs in the same year.

* * * * *

This was all hardly behind me when Sister Marguerite announced that samples of our handwriting were to be taken by Sister Cecile to determine who is responsible for the graffiti on the walls of the halls, and by the banisters between the second and third floors. In other words, it must be an upper classmen! I take a good look at these markings as we go to recess, and I am astonished to find them near identical to my own handwriting. How can that be? I didn't do this unless in my sleep. No, I know I didn't do it. So why does it look like mine? My heart is pounding so hard I think I might faint. Bobby Witt asks me what is wrong, but I can't tell him. Can't he see it is "my" handwriting? It doesn't look like his chicken scratches, so he is safe. My penmanship isn't much better but all my letters are formed with slanting loops precisely the way of this desecration, as Sister Marguerite puts it.

"Hurry, children, I need your handwriting now!"

Quickly, I write with my left hand, which makes all the letters slanting the other way, and without the severe looping. It is a more juvenile style, but what can I say? I even write my name left handed to give the sample some authenticity. I could kiss my da. It was he who made me right handed when I was a naturally left handed person. Now I have the benefit of being somewhat ambidextrous. I pass my handwriting in and breathe a sigh of relief. The culprit responsible for this vandalism is never found.

* * * * *

It wasn't only the Fishers who were inclined to deviancy. In March, Bob and Leo Kettleson snuck a pint of whiskey into school and hid it under papers on Sister Flavian's desk. When she found it,

189

she broke into uproarious laughter. We could hear her in the classroom with the door shut, her office being outside in the hall. She knocks on Sister Marguerite's door to share the practical joke played on her. I am sitting in the front and I can read their whispering lips. This is something I learned from my hard-of-hearing mother. I discern 'whiskey bottle' and 'desk' and 'under papers' as clear as a bell. Sister Marguerite's voice shakes with a repressed wobble as she whispers between clenched teeth. She obviously doesn't see the humor. I discern 'disgrace' and 'expel' and 'outrageous' from her, but Sister Flavian seems to listen with amused serenity. She touches my teacher's sleeve and laughs again. Our door is open only a sliver, but I can see her face. She has taken off her glasses and is wiping her eyes with a handkerchief. If anything, she appears more saintly than ever.

The Kettleson boys are overjoyed with not getting caught, but a bit confused with the turn of events. Nothing happens. No announcements. Nothing! Like the rest of us, they love Sister Flavian, but expected at the very least a wave of vexation at the boldness of the prank. The possibility of getting caught enlivens the juvenile mind, fueled by the first seepage of testosterone. The Kettleson boys considered pulling a similar prank on Father. Once the euphoria wore off they thought better of it, and thank God for that! The good priest with little sense of humor would have undoubtedly put us all under house arrest, meaning no basketball, and basketball is our life.

Even so, the ritual of having access to the gym on Saturday and Sunday mornings does not get any easier. Customarily, Father is having breakfast after saying morning Mass when I storm across the tundra through the rectory backyard and present myself at his door for the key. Our problem is that the sun starts to set early in an Iowa winter sky, and we're not allowed to turn on the lights. Being the designated key getter, and given the inevitable confrontation, it is like a movie that I hope will end differently, but never does. Eventually, the key is acquired, while Father turns a new shade of red as he hands it to me. *Playing basketball in the St. Patrick's gym on the weekends gave a constructive outlet for raging hormones and kept us out of trouble. The same can be said for ice-skating at the courthouse of a winter's afternoon. These activities occupied young minds in worthwhile and pleasant pursuits. There was nowhere to go and little to do during those war years. Father considered he was doing us a favor, while sheriff Petersen did it as an expression of understanding. In that sense, the sheriff was more of a priest than Father was.*

Once we clear the gym floor of tables and chairs left from bingo, and sweep the floor with compound, the gym is ready for basketball. We play at a fever's pitch knowing that by four o'clock we'll have to leave because of darkness. Nobody worries about lunch. Hunger is put on hold. Dean Burridge, Dick Price, and Red Lutz, all high school guys, show up this time and join us. That means I have to sit and watch them play against St. Pat's big guys like Jim Junker, Tom Clark, Jack Schuster, and Tom Christiansen. Our basketball court is not regulation, so these big guys fly up and down it like a shot out of a canon. Clark and Junker can hold their own shooting with the high school guys, and nobody out muscles Schuster. I love the guy. He's not afraid to mix it up with Price. It's fun to watch them crash the stage where the east basket is mounted. I'm thrilled while Bobby Witt pouts. He'd get killed out there, but he is so competitive he wants to measure up against these guys. When they leave just before dark, he still wants to shoot around. It's fun imagining where the basket is, until I have to return the key to father's thunder.

"You know what time it is?" The dressing down continues from the earlier encounter, but I shut off my hearing. I put on my martyr look, the one I've perfected for such occasions. I match Father's hostility with a blurred and sightless gaze, which only infuriates him the more.

One night, though, Dean Burridge switches on the lights. I panic, 'Oh no, I'm in big trouble now,' because I am responsible for the key. Turns out Dean knew Father was having dinner at the Schuster's, thanks to Jack Schuster sharing that information. I like deception, perhaps because I don't have the moxie to fashion it. We didn't get away scot-free, however, as a neighbor complained to Father of the lights being on until eight. The opera at the rectory door was thus prolonged the next time I sought the key.

When seventh and eighth grade boys were in the gym on weekends, only Bobby and I from the fifth grade got to play. Bobby had more finesse, and could already dribble like a Harlem Globetrotter, but I was better at mixing it up on the boards. My shooting was so poor that Jim Junker stopped scrimmage one Saturday, and blistered me with how lousy I was and promised never to choose me again for his side. I idolized Jim. Jim could hit from anywhere on the floor with an assortment of shots. I was destroyed. He was right. I was lousy. I felt so bad that I didn't go to the gym on the weekend for two weeks. Everybody thought I was sick. Only Bobby knew I wasn't.

*   *   *   *   *

One night I come home to be greeted by the boarders, the sergeant and his girlfriend, my uncle Arne, my parents and siblings. There was a strange aroma in the house. "Jimmy, the sergeant has a treat for us tonight," my mother looks at me waving her cigarette like a baton. "Oyster stew."

Oyster stew! The words still cause me to shudder. I got deathly ill that night after eating that oyster stew with a major headache. The headache was so intense that my sense of smell, sound, sight, and taste reached maddening levels. The cigarette smoke nearly blinded me with pain. Conversation and laughter were like hammers in my head. It was as if all my faculties were ganging up on me causing me nearly to collapse. This had never happened before. My da suffered mega-migraines. He would walk and moan across the house most of the night when hit by one. Such headaches would come to plague me as well. Did the oyster stew cause them? I didn't know. I only know that from that time forward I treated all crustaceans without exception as if they were poison.

*   *   *   *   *

Parents sometimes worry about things that have no substance. This is especially true when it comes to their kids. One afternoon I come home from school, and they are dressed to go out.

"What's up?" I ask simply. "Where's everybody?" I'm told Jackie is with aunt Helen. Alice Sullivan has Janice, and Patsy's staying overnight at Joan Dalrymple's house.

"So, where're you going? Who's taking care of me?"

"We have an appointment at four o'clock with Dr. O'Donnell . . . for you."

"For me? Why? I'm not sick!"

"We know that Jimmy. Dr. O'Donnell just wants to look at you."

"Come on mother that makes no sense. Why would he want to see me when I'm not sick? Mother? Come on!"

"Well, your father wants him to take a look at you." I look at him for comprehension, and not surprisingly, am disappointed. We seldom speak directly; usually through my mother as interpreter.

"It's no big deal Jimmy. Your father, ah, just wants him to give you a physical."

"What if I don't want a physical?"

"Goddamn it Dorothy, didn't I tell you?"

"Now Jimmy trust us. Trust me. We're doing this for your own good."

Terrible thoughts race through my head. Maybe I have an incurable disease from eating those oysters. Maybe I'm dying. I start to cry. "What is it mother? What's wrong with me? Tell me!"

"Christ Jesus will that kid of yours ever grow up? See that Dorothy? He's goddamn crying like a goddamn two year old." This makes my tears flow even more profusely.

My mother, coat and hat on, goes to the window and looks out with blind eyes. People have different ways of dealing with emotion. My mother's is to smoke slowly, and fill her eyes with a dark glow of indulgence, fixing them intently on nothing, like now, on the dirty window. She lights her cigarette with gloved hands, inhales slowly, and exhales even more slowly. The glow of the ash on the tip of her cigarette accommodates the movement of her hands, as she watches the ash fall into her open gloved palm as if into an ashtray. She turns and looks at me with those lustrous blue eyes.

"Jimmy do it for me, will you?"

That is all she had to say. We are connected at the hip. We walk silently to the Fourth Street bus stop, and stand like statues watching the bus descend the Bluff Boulevard hill. Nobody speaks during the bus trip to Seventh Avenue South, where Dr. O'Donnell has an office in his home.

His nurse greets us at the door, and takes me immediately into a room where she measures my height and weight, hands me a paper cup telling me to go into the bathroom and pee into it. I'm embarrassed but do as she asks and return with the cup full of yellow liquid. She takes it, then tells me, "This isn't going to hurt much," as she pricks my finger and places my blood on a little glass slide. She leaves with it, and returns with a stethoscope, and some apparatus with a bulb on it, and tells me she is going to take my blood pressure. She wraps a black strap around my arm, pumping a little ball until the wrap is uncomfortably tight, places the stethoscope in her ears, and the other end against the enlarged vein in my forearm, then gradually releases the pressure of the wrap. She follows this by taking my pulse, not once but twice. "You have a very slow heart beat. You by any chance an athlete?" I nod, having no idea how my heartbeat has anything to do with sports. I look over her shoulder and see this information is being collected in a manila folder. Then without ceremony she leaves. As if forgetting something, she pokes her head back in, "Doctor will be with you momentarily."

Momentarily is one of those *nonword words* I've become familiar with, as I am alone seemingly forever. The white, sterile room smells of disinfectant with all kinds of medical charts on the walls, a strange looking white enamel chair and a table with stirrups, and even a white enamel disposal. I push it with my foot and the top opens up. It becomes my toy of distraction until I knock it over with a crash. The nurse comes in, looks at the disposals contents all over the floor, puts on a pair of rubber gloves, returns the contents to the disposal, looks daggers at me, then leaves again without a word.

Dr. O'Donnell comes in finally. He is a large quiet man with a gentle voice, soothing manner and a cherubic face. Calm rushes in ahead of him and wraps itself around me like his white coat. "And how are you today, James?"

Seems a funny question to ask, especially when I might have an incurable disease of which I am not aware, not to mention having been pricked, wrapped, stretched, and made to pee when I didn't have to, but I lie anyway and say, "Fine."

"Your vital signs are also fine." He looks into my ears with an instrument with a miniature flashlight at the end of it, then into my eyes, mouth, and even nose. He has me say "ah!" when I open my mouth. Then he has me breathe deeply and hold my breath as he probes my chest and back with a stethoscope. He thumps here and there gently as he moves the instrument about. It is cold and tickles. Then he has me drop my pants, then my shorts, and has me cough as he cradles my balls in his hand, then spread the cheeks of my butt as he looks for something there. I would be petrified with fear if he weren't so matter-of-fact about it all. Then without preamble, he confides in me the purpose of this examination. "Your parents are concerned that you're on your way to being a giant, did you know that?" I shake my head. He smiles. "Let's join them now. Put your clothes on and the nurse will bring you to my office."

She takes me to Dr. O'Donnell's office, where my parents are drinking coffee and visiting with him. "Your son is fine," he says once I'm seated. "I've had a conversation with him and registered your concerns. I understand how these things can become troubling, so I thank you for bringing James in. Your son is indeed tall for his age. He is five foot nine and three quarters in his stocking feet, and weights one hundred and twelve pounds. All his vital signs are normal."

"But what about his height?" my da asks, fumbling with an unlit cigarette, the last in a pack which he crunches in his hand producing a crackle. "Hell, doc, he's already taller than me and he not yet twelve. My wife's six brothers barely break five-four. He towers over them and my brother, too. What's going on, doc?"

"What about grandparents?"

"Grandparents?" my da laughs. He puts the unlit cigarette in his mouth, then withdraws it. "Don't know. Didn't know my parents. Mother died when I was born, da took off for points unknown never to be heard from again, raised by my grandmother who was a little bitty thing."

"What about you Dorothy?"

My mother is so preoccupied with calculating her husband's mood that the question stuns her. She clears her throat. "Mother was four-ten, father six foot. He was a Norwegian with parents from Bergen, Norway, and she with parents from Dublin, Ireland."

"There you are!"

"With all due respect, doc, that tells me nothing. How tall is this kid going to get?"

"Hard to say, Ray. Could stop now, but doubt it. Some boys his age do. Suspect he'll be six-two to six-four or there about. Can't be sure. Hardly a giant. Can tell you this, though, he's a normal healthy young man."

"So you're saying not to be concerned?"

Dr. O'Donnell comes around his desk, and pats my da on the shoulder. "Ray, that's exactly what I'm saying."

My mother starts to cry. She takes out a tissue. "See, Ray, you were upset for nothing. You listen too much to your railroad cronies, implying *not enough to me*. She then lapses into silence. There is a particular intensity about clever people whose brains are under used, like my mother's were. Sometimes there is no way to control circumstances. Clever people are a great deal more at risk under the bright lights than their slower on the uptake company. This was now in evidence, and not missed by the good doctor.

"Dorothy, it's always better to error on the safe side. It was right to bring James in."

These words restore the swagger to my da as he rolls his shoulders as he gets up. "Hope his mind keeps up with his shoe size, doc," he laughs self-consciously. Dr. O'Donnell smiles wanly, but says nothing. Bill Knight put a bee in da's bonnet only a week before. "Jimmy's looking more and more like a freak of nature every day." The shock of this registered on my da's face, and ended in this worrisome adventure.

* * * * *

The winter of 1944 finds me becoming a shadow character, that is, I start to move away from the expected. Garrett "Pee Wee" Behrens, who lives four doors west of me, brings me to the Young Men's Christian Association, or YMCA. This opens a new world. Located downtown, the "Y" has a billiard room, ping-pong tables, a gym, gymnastic equipment, swimming pool, weight room, and an indoor track. High school athletes from Clinton, St. Mary's and Lyons High are always around. These guys talk to kids like us, and answer questions about sports. Bobby and I go to their games when our parents let us and these guys are our heroes.

I'm no good at billiards or ping-pong, can't swim very well, don't like to run, or lift weights, so I concentrate pretty much on basketball. They have a league for kids my age, and we play on Saturday mornings, which means I can play there in the morning and at St. Pat's in the afternoon. The basketball court is small, even smaller than St. Pat's, and there is an oval 110-yard track on the floor above.

You can sit on raised seats aside the south hoop and watch games below. It is an eerie feeling to watch the ball arch from the floor, come at you, and split the cords. It looks easy from that vantage point. It takes some getting used to the screeching sound of sneakers and the shrieking sound of the basketball as it comes off the backboard. Excitedly, I tell Bobby about the "Y," and am taken back when he chews me out.

"Don't let Father know you go there. You'll never be an altar boy."

"Why?" I gasp in total puzzlement. "What has that got to do with that?"

"Everything! Father says the Y's the devil's workshop and out of bounds for good Catholic boys."

"But Bobby! Dean Burridge goes there! He's Catholic!"

"Yes, and he's in high school. Doesn't have to deal with Father, does he?"

True. Still, it makes no sense. Only see fun at the "Y." Not religious. Never had anyone talk to me about religion. It's fun and I want Bobby to be part of it.

"Will you come anyway Bobby? Just once?"

"No," he says quietly. His quiet tells me the discussion's over. Bobby never does come to the "Y," not even in high school. So the "Y" begins my first shadow experience. I still want to be an altar boy, but I don't plan on giving up the "Y" to be one. I love playing basketball there, and can hold my own with everyone my age and older.

I notice something for the first time. Some guys play without tee shirts. They have well defined pectoral and stomach muscles, while I look like a board with pink nipples and sticks for arms. Bob Walding, who's always at the Y, isn't much of a basketball player, and he's a year older than me, but he has real muscles. I mention this to Bobby.

He laughs. "You're something else. Of course he's got muscles. He works out. Ever heard of doing pushups and sit-ups? I do them all the time, scissors, too. You don't get muscles just thinking about it. Fisher, you're really funny."

So, what do I do? That night I go home and do fifty pushups, and get Jackie to sit on my legs to do fifty sit-ups. Then I show him how to do jumping jack scissors. We're doing them when all of a sudden;

the downstairs door is pounded like it's about to explode, and then opened abruptly.

"Jesus Christ, what's going on up there? The ceiling is about to cave in!" I tell him we're exercising. "Well, you'd goddamn better stop it or I'll exercise you right out the goddamn window." He slams the door so hard it vibrates all the way to our room. My little brother looks at me in terror, as if to say 'now you've got us in trouble.' I put my hand to my lips then tousle his hair as he's about to cry. Through the door we can hear his deafening voice still yelling as he walks through the house.

"You tell me that goddamn kid of yours has brains. Well, I call him Mr. Stupid. How'd you like that? Kid just about fell through the ceiling. Hear me Dorothy? Your goddamn all-American just about ruined this house. Tell me, where'd we get the money to fix it? Goddamn it Dorothy. Goddamn that Jimmy." Then silence, my disquiet still ringing in my ears. Gazing out of the window I was suddenly assailed with the feeling that I would neither see nor hear with clarity, that my senses were being embraced and submerged by the cloying heat and the disembodied sounds of his wrath without a cause. I would never ever be comfortable around a raised voice.

Instead of feeling remorse, my mind thought of alternative places to exercise – the basement? Ceiling too low. The "Y"? Not in front of everybody. Downstairs when he isn't home? Might fall through the floor into the basement. I guess exercise is a bad idea. Guess I'll keep looking like a board with two pink nipples.

About that same time, I start to visit the Clinton Public Library. Similar to the ambitions of Thomas Wolfe who wanted to read all the books in his Ashville, North Carolina library, my goal is the same, starting with Catholic authors. A fast reader, I don't see this as such a daunting task. My uncle Leonard has suggested I read *Man, The Unknown* by Alexis Carrel. I am hardly into the introduction and find myself lost in the vocabulary. My mother reads books by A. J. Cronin. So, I decide to look for books by him. I find none. That seems strange. I begin to get discouraged. The librarian comes over, "Having trouble, young man?" I want to say, no, but instead remain silent. "What you looking for?"

Shyly, talking into my chest, I say, "Books by A. J. Cronin." She moves her index finger in a waving motion. "Come with me."

Now if I were nine inches shorter, I wonder if she would direct me to the adult book section. This is one of the few advantages to being tall. You are taken to be older, which means a more serious student, certainly not a fifth grader. We move to a wide but narrow chest of small drawers, and she pulls out one with "A, B, C" on its metal plate.

"Dr. Cronin writes novels, doesn't he?" she says mainly to herself, "so it will be in the fiction section. To find the book, let's check its Dewey-decimal number. Are you familiar with this system?" My head moves back and forth. She takes out a card, and there is his name *A. J. Cronin* at the top, a book titled *The Citadel*, with numbers divided by a decimal on the upper left hand corner of the card. The librarian's manner is so much like that of a teacher. She is unhurried as if she could be with me all day. I listen as we walk, not sure I understand everything she is saying. Then we're there! The book's spine is marked exactly as the card! She hands it to me. "Want to check it out?" I stutter. "Noooo, no, just want to look at it!" That's the last thing I want to do. I can just picture the reaction of my da if I come home with an armful of books. She smiles pensively, hesitates, and then leaves me alone.

The book looks and smells wonderful. I glance around for a place to sit. There are long mahogany tables with chairs in a reading room, and one table with nobody at it. I take the book there, breathe deeply, and feel at peace. I love the atmosphere of the library, the quiet and the warmth of the surrounding books. I'm not sure what *citadel* means so I look it up: *a fortress that commands a city*. I start reading and find the book is about a society doctor in London who abandons the rich to practice among the poor.

The library is the place I go after playing basketball at the "Y" on some Saturdays when St. Pat's gym isn't available. I'm especially attracted to novels because I identify with the protagonist. I do eventually wade through Dr. Carrel's *Man, The Unknown* finding man's still pretty much unknown to me at the end. I don't understand much of what I've read. That doesn't seem to be a problem. I had the same feeling when I first read the inaugural address of George Washington. I start *Moby Dick* but it is a slow read and takes several visits to finish. I know the story from my Classic Comics, which helps but, again, I can't get my mind around a lot of the ideas. I read parts of *Abraham Lincoln's Collected Writings* and think he sounds a lot like Herman Melville. They both write in complex sentences that I've come to love. It is the passion beneath the words that reaches out to me and keeps me reading when I'm not sure what they're saying. To be a writer must be like heaven on earth. To fill blank space with the passion in your heart, to come to this task alone and leave its prize behind must be like being born and never dying. Writers live in the shadows, too. I come to sense their company. I have to read fast because I cannot check out books. My da already thinks I'm mentally constipated. It's okay for my mother to read all kinds of books, but that's a woman thing. Guys don't sit around idly reading books. Guys do things! It would embarrass him mightily to have his railroad buddies catch me in a chair reading with a stack of books beside me. Well, I was safe here from everybody as part of my shadow existence.

* * * * *

The winter of 1944 refuses to give way to spring, and for some reason, I'm wrestling with God and death as I walk in the cold. Nobody has died in my family, or anything like that. I can't imagine the world without my mother. She is kind of my God, but she tells me that she wants me to be big and strong, true and straight, because she might not always be there. It is a bitter but still cold March night with the sky clear. I've been to a Clinton High basketball game at Washington Junior High gym, where the team suffered a first round regional loss to Davenport. I am walking along Bluff Boulevard, offering up the cold to the poor souls in purgatory, and thinking of my mother who has had a lot of pain of late, especially another terrible ear infection. This has knocked her off her feet again, confining her to bed for days. When these chronic ear infections reoccur, she walks around like a drunken person and she doesn't even drink. She tells me I will always have God if not her, and so I think a lot about God as I walk tonight, being not too sure what I'm thinking about or why. Then the movie "Song of Bernadette" pops into my head, and wonder if I will ever have visions like St. Bernadette. If I do, it'll confirm I'm some kind of saint. The cold really starts to get to me as I pass Mount St. Clare on the Bluff, and am about to turn east to home, only three blocks away when I see this light in the sky and I hear this music. I look around and I'm surrounded otherwise by darkness and cold. I don't know where the light or sound is coming from and I panic. I'm frozen to the spot, convinced that I'm about to have a beatific vision like Bernadette or possibly, the children of Fatima. Then I think nobody's going to believe me. I'll be examined, ridiculed, and hauled over the coals as delusional and harassed like the three Portuguese shepherd children of Fatima were. These uneducated siblings had six apparitions of the Virgin Mary in Portugal in 1917. Was I having an apparition? I don't want any of it. I put my hands over my ears, and my stocking cap down over my eyes, and stand there like a statue. Somebody in a car comes by and honks his horn at me that takes me out of my panic. "Are you all right?" the motorist asks. I say, fine, and keep walking toward Congregational Hill or Hoot Owl Hollow instead of toward home. Man, do I feel stupid. There's a display on the hill apparently left over from the holidays, and for some reason, nobody bothered to take it down.

In this heightened state of the ridiculous I come home to find a small light on in the living room and everyone in bed. I go to the kitchen and get a drink of water, then climb the creaking stairs as quietly as possible to my room. I turn on a little light by my bed and see my little brother caked in dry blood all over his hair, face and neck. I scream in horror, "Oh my God, oh my God, oh my God! Jackie's dead! Oh my God! Ohhhhhh!"

Lights go on. My da rushes up the steps. My mother follows. Pat and Janice are crying. "Oh my God! Dorothy! Oh my God!" My da howls like a wolf in agony as he looks at Jackie. Dorothy, how could this happen? Oh my God! Dorothy, what should we do? Ohhhh!" With all the lights on we can see the reddish brown substance on the bedspread, all over his clothes. I notice for the first time that he has school clothes on and not his pajamas. "I've called Dr. O'Donnell, Ray," my mother says, tears in her eyes straining to keep her composure, "he's on his way."

No one has touched Jackie, and now the focus is on me. "Goddamn it, Jimmy, what have you done?" his chest heaves in dry sobs while I stand in catatonic shock. My mother gets between him and me. "Well, Dorothy, somebody did it! Somebody had to get in here. It didn't goddamn happen by a goddamn ghost!" He is pulling his hair, walking around in circles, talking to himself. Chills are running up my spine and I haven't yet taken off my coat and stocking cap.

201

Dr. O'Donnell arrives. His face is full of concern but suspicion, too, as he climbs the rickety steps. He takes out his stethoscope and checks Jackie's heart. Then examines the caking on his body, rolls Jackie gently over and examines the back of his head with a small pencil size flashlight.

"Your son has a concussion. He's suffering from a subdural hematoma," he says with some anger in his voice, "the back of his head has taken a blow either from a blunt instrument or a fall. Can anyone help me on this?" I've never heard his voice so strident. Patsy hesitates then blurts out.

"Jackie fell off the stage at school, horsing around with Larry Morris. I saw it happen. I didn't tell daddy because Jackie told me not to, then daddy sent Jackie to bed without supper for coming home late."

"I've never done that before, doc," my da confesses in a sobbing voice, "never."

"That's true," my mother adds. "It's not the first time Jackie was late, and we were trying to teach him a lesson. I sent Janice upstairs later to have him come down for something to eat, but she said he was asleep.

"I brought him some cookies, mommy," three-year-old Janice confesses. "I felt bad that Jackie didn't get any supper." She snuck up some chocolate marshmallow cookies.

"That's what is covering him," Dr. O'Donnell explains, "not blood but chocolate from the cookies. He must have rolled in them as he slept. The bleeding is internal, and it is subsiding. I would give him a warm hand bath, which will wake him up, a children's aspirin, because he'll have a headache, and keep him quiet for the next two days. I'll come back to check on him then. In the meantime if you notice anything of concern, please call." With that he puts his instruments in his black bag.

"Thank God," my mother says.

"Yes, God was with us tonight, mother."

My da puts out his hand to shake the doctor's hand, who momentarily hesitates then extends his. "It won't happen again, doc," my da says, "it's not my way." I don't know if Dr. O'Donnell believed him, but it was true. That discipline was totally uncharacteristic of him. It was the first and last time anyone was punished by withholding supper.

* * * * *

Winter is a kind of death, especially an Iowa winter. It stubbornly holds on well into March when other parts of the country are experiencing the rebirth of spring. Death was on my mind when I thought I looked it in the face and saw the countenance of my little brother. Death is always beckoning from beyond. The undertaker contemplates his funeral, the rich man his destitute, the jailer his imprisonment, the debaucher his impotence, the priest his fall from grace, the executive his lack of power, the actor an empty theater, the writer the blank page. What are these but premature visions of dying?

For the child, it is the moment when his protective walls of comfort seemingly collapse around him and he finds himself no longer safe, exposed to and accountable on his own to the world. I wake up the morning after this ordeal to hear my parents in their bed confessing their failure to each other as parents. I hear my mother saying to my da with some resolve, "Ray, if I've learned anything, I've learned to live with being half finished. Finishing is not in our makeup. That's God's work. We're just constant starters to the end. Today we start again hoping the outcome is a little better. That's all starters can ever hope for. It's all that can be expected of them." My fears dissolve with her words, as I know spring is just around the corner.

* * * * *

James R. Fisher, Jr.

Chapter 14

Time to Awake

In me are people without names,
Children, stay-at-homes, trees.
They all conquer me
And this is my only victory.

--Boris Pasternak

An Iowa spring on the Mississippi River is a kind of war. It kills before it gives birth to new life. While another kind of war rages in Europe and the South Pacific, the swollen Minnesota, St. Croix and Wisconsin rivers pour recklessly into the Mississippi at its source and indiscriminately obliterate boundaries from Minneapolis/St. Paul to New Orleans. This rampaging god is wont to thunder past villages, hamlets, towns and cities swallowing shorelines up into its muddy soul. It demands the mettle of the most hardy of citizens in its path. It is no accident that Eastern Iowans have little time for idle talk or self-conscious posturing. They are direct, open, and often unapologetically blunt because survival has shaped them. They take no special pride in their lack of sophistication or downright earthiness. Nor do they have much time for east coast mimicking of European culture or west coast dalliance into hedonistic glamour. Spring keeps them edgy with reality, providing little inclination for pretense.

This mighty "Father of Waters" demands courage, sacrifice, stamina and resilience. Each spring it is the same, a saga of discouraging setbacks and spectacular triumphs as literally hundreds of volunteers build temporary dikes of sand bags, ceaselessly man chugging pumps, and make ready for a never ending succession of emergencies. Hundreds of families are typically forced to flee from their homes, while many businesses and industries suffer temporary paralysis, as they are turned into islands accessible only by boats. If this were not enough, often spring rains deluge the countryside with needed but excessive downpours. It doesn't end there, as the drudgery of clean up after the waters have receded faces these citizens when they are already numb with fatigue while the terrible threat of typhoid fever always looms over them.

* * * * *

The inaugural game of the 1943 season of the Industrial Baseball League was postponed until July because of spring flooding. This is repeated in 1944, as Riverview Stadium is again flooded with water from the Mississippi. Since baseball and spring are synonymous to the Courthouse Tigers, this is a huge downer. School is not yet out, and the nearly daily rains are adding to the water level of the park, making it impossible to even play catch at the courthouse. So, one Saturday in early May I am ecstatic when Dick Morris invites me to his "farm." Well, actually, it isn't a farm, but a home out Springdale Drive beyond Mount St. Clare. To my embarrassment, I've never actually been in the country. This would become the closest I would ever get to a farm, and I was excited. Dick's father, another Irishman, also works on the Chicago & North Western railroad as a conductor. But I think his first love must be farming. There on the outskirts of Clinton on a small one-acre plot of land, I found the nursery rhyme of "Old McDonald's Farm" in living color. First thing I notice is a brackish looking pig pen attached to a red barn with three gigantic pigs laying in the mud, a white wooden-framed chicken coop directly west of the barn is full of the cacophony of clucking white hens, while two strutting reddish brown roosters prance about the yard as if they own the place. I see ducks and ducklings quacking about as they waddle out of the barn and head for a man-made pond. In the barn, I see a cow in a stall contentedly munching on hay, and directly beyond the barn in a fenced in field is a baying chestnut colored horse with a white mane and tail being agitated by a couple of mangy rust colored dogs. Birds of all hues seem to be everywhere, on fence posts, top of the barn, on the horse's back, even eating out of the pigs' feeding trough.

It is obvious this is Dick's world. He impetuously climbs on a pig, grabs it by the ears with the sow squealing as they romp about the pen. I never knew he was so brave. He jumps off and asks me to ride her. I shake my head vigorously, no way! Come on, he encourages with a broad smile, it's easy. Yeah, for you maybe, but not for me. I was glad when his mother called to have a snack. She has prepared peanut butter and jelly wedges along with big glasses of cold fresh milk. I wonder if it's from Betsy. The snack is delicious, and I keep eating as she brings more wedges to the table. Dick laughs. "You'll get fat eating like that, wide and round as a pig." I put a wedge back on the platter. I'm finished.

Dick has one of those faces that is the map of Ireland, flaming thick red hair, a broad square face, wide mouth, long straight nose and enough freckles to bank them, and always a mischievous glint in his eyes. Bobby Witt's his best friend, too.

"Why didn't you ask Bobby to come?"

He punches me in the arm. "Guess I scared him off when I told him he'd have to ride Sally. Let's have some fun with him Monday and tell him you rode the sow."

"But I didn't."

"That doesn't matter. We'll just be kidding."

"Bobby won't believe you. He knows I'm a bigger chicken than he is."

Dick laughs so hard he looks as if he is going to up chuck his sandwiches.

"What so funny?"

"You! I never thought of that. But you're right. He'd never believe me." He laughs again. "Just the thought of you trying to ride Sally will crack him up."

It's always a little unsettling to be right when the rightness isn't exactly flattering.

"Come on, let me show you my room!"

Dick's room is shared with his brother Larry and it is huge compared to mine. Actually, it is like a picture out of a catalogue with pennants and sport posters on the walls, a tacked up picture of Dean Burridge and Clinton High's "Fire Wagon Five" basketball team cut out of the newspaper, a crucifix, a family picture of the Morris clan, and a bulletin board with snapshots, notes, and cartoons cut out of magazines. There is a small desk with a prayer book, some keys, and a charm bracelet. Twin beds display identical quilts in checkered green and gold patterns like St. Patrick's colors. I find the quilts quite beautiful and tell him so. He says his mother made them. I wonder how she finds the time. The floor is hardwood and it shines with a high gloss. Multi-colored throw rugs complete the warmth of the room. I ask Dick who makes the beds and keeps the room so neat. His eyebrows arch. "Who'd you think? I do!"

Dick has two sisters and three brothers, and the place looks like this? I can't believe it! It's downright impressive. Our house never looks this good even after my mother completes her cleaning. None of us are too good about picking up after ourselves, including my da. Seemingly noting my wonder, he says, "If you think this is something, wait till you see Vince's room."

It is on the other side of the hall, and he's right. The room is spectacular. You have to watch your head as a menagerie of hanging model planes of World War I and World War II vintage dangle from all quarters of the ceiling. They are balsam wood models, carefully constructed and even more carefully painted to be authentic replicas. I once tried to make a model plane. It was a complete disaster. "It's all Vince's," Dick says, "but me and my brothers helped a lot. Vince might not agree. He's strange that way. Fact is he'd be ticked off if he knew we were in here. Wants to be an aeronautical engineer."

"What's that?"

"You're kidding?"

"Nooo!"

"Rube, you always surprise me. So smart in school yet so dumb in other ways."

"So I'm stupid. Tell me, what is it?"

"It's the kind of engineering dealing with aircraft. I thought everybody knew that."

"Well, now you know everybody doesn't."

"Come on, I've got something else to show you!"

Still burning a bit, not because of my ignorance about aeronautical engineering, but because I disappointed Dick in not being as clever as he expected. Having older brothers and sisters must be like living through them.

"Where we going?"

"You'll see!" He says as he takes two steps at a time descending the stairs, crosses the kitchen and leaps from the porch to the ground. "It's my most favorite place." The excitement in his voice makes me wary.

He races across a field, and I follow. We are in open country. The eastern sky is more splendid than when I came. There are massive clouds, fantastically shaped and seemingly lighted from within by a golden fire. Another mass of clouds is a deep purplish blue, heavy with the threat of rain. It is shot through with flashes of lightning, twisting, sharp and brilliant. Above and beyond there are other weird shapes, incredibly beautiful and aglow with every color imaginable. "Dick, it's going to rain. I best be starting home."

"No it's not. See the rainbow? It's raining somewhere else. Besides, it won't bother us where we're going."

The sun darts in and out of the clouds like playing tag with God in a limpid sky, and towards the west, Dick is right, there is a pure golden light. Against this sky, over the tops of trees, the clouds dance to the music of thunder like a passing armada with the music fading to little more than a distant echo.

"Ta da!" he yells, and dances about as he comes to a small stream nestled in a heavily wooded area. "This is Mill Creek. Want to go for a swim?"

"I don't have a suit. Besides, I can't swim very well."

"It's not deep, and the water is surprisingly warm. Try it!" With that, he sheds all his clothes, stands naked for a moment on top of a rock, and dives in. He comes up quickly, spits out a mouth full of water. "This is great! Come on, chicken! Look, I'm standing on the bottom over here," he says as he treads water closer to the bank, splashing water at my feet.

No one on this planet is less of an adventurer than I am; yet since I'm taller, the shallowness of the creek is reassuring. So I carefully take off my clothes, fold my shirt, pants, shorts, and socks, and lay my shoes on top of them on the same rock from which Dick dove. I climb up on a downed limb that stretches out into the water and dive in. Immediately, I feel a wrenching pain on my side, splashing to the surface, I yell.

"I think I hurt myself."

"What?"

"I think a branch under the water cut me." As I climb up the bank, I look down to my groin and it is red with blood, and I'm bleeding profusely. This in itself is not too alarming as I am a bleeder. I put both my hands over my eyes to hold back the tears.

"Jesus, Fisher, how'd ya do that? Jesus, Mary and Joseph! Use your shorts to stop the bleeding. They won't show." Dick is still in the water.

The shock of seeing my blood makes me nauseous, but surprisingly, doesn't hurt much. I grab my shorts, which are under my shoes, and one of my shoes slips off the rock, and falls into the water. The current carries the shoe downstream as if it is a tiny boat. I look in disbelief. This isn't happening to me!

"Oh, no! Oh my God, no!" I look at the shoe helplessly with absolutely no desire to dive in after it.

"What's wrong now?"

"My shoe!"

Dick sees it and starts to swim after it, but is blocked by a tree limb. He goes under water and comes right back up. "I can't get through, too much debris. It's being carried away, about to go over the falls." We both watch the shoe disappear with a strange fatalistic resignation.

The bleeding has stopped, but there is a long ugly cut, like an appendix incision which now graces my left groin. He notices this as he comes out of the water.

"God, Rube, that looks awful." Then looking at me. "Are you all right?"

I shrug my shoulders as I put on my clothes.

"Well, the shoe isn't any good to you now anyway. Sole would come off for sure." Standing there naked as a jaybird with his hands on his hips, and always the jokester, he adds, "Could have been your clothes, then you'd had to walk home naked."

"Funny, funny! Going to catch holy hell for sure. My only other shoes are sneakers. What'll I wear to church?"

"I'd give you a pair of mine but you could only get your big toe in them." He laughs again. Then serious, "What do we do now?"

"Don't know." Some kind of calm comes over me that surprises me. "Get dressed, and walk with me a ways, will you?"

"Sure."

So I start walking with one shoe and sock on one foot and only a sock on the other. To change the subject, Dick says, "I wanted to show you something else, something nobody knows about but me. It's way out beyond Springdale Drive." He points to where the sky is turning orange and the trees look like a solid forest. I'm intrigued but cannot get him to say more. He leaves me at Bluff Boulevard, again says he hopes my cut heals okay, and that I don't get into too much trouble about my shoe. Actually, I am glad to see him go because I have to think. I need time and space. Have to sneak into the house somehow and get my sneakers on without being seen, then have time to think what to do next. My mother is in the kitchen making dinner and doesn't hear me when I come in. I yell "hi" and race up the stairs to my room. Fortunately, my da is on the road.

"That you Jimmy?" she calls from the kitchen.

"I said hi mother, didn't you hear me?" Then I come all the way down the stairs and open the door. "I'm upstairs," I yell again, "be down in a minute." My mother has always been hard of hearing, yet I constantly forget. Every time I do, I feel guilty and sad. She says it's not a handicap, just her cross to bear, and everyone has a cross.

"Got a job for you when you do!"

"Job? What kind of job?"

"I want you to take this bag of clothes to St. Patrick's for the Bishop's Relief Fund. I didn't have it ready when the man came by this morning. He said I could bring it to school this afternoon. They'll be there 'til six, so get a move on!"

"Yes! Yes! Yes!" I scream. St. Anthony, patron saint of lost causes, once again, you are there for me!

"What's that all about," she says as she comes out of the kitchen with the bag of clothes and sees me bouncing about.

"Nothing, mother. I'm just, well, just happy, that's all!"

Since I'm not known for eagerness, she is understandably suspicious, but then smiles. "Good, I knew I could count on you." She goes back into the kitchen and I drop my single shoe into the bag, and run with it to school. No one notices that I'm wearing sneakers until we are about to go out the door for Sunday mass.

"Jimmy, you know you can't wear sneakers to church. Now put on your school shoes."

"Can't find them Mother."

"Can't find them? What do you mean you can't find them? Now get them on or we'll be late."

"Looked but they're nowhere around. Honest. Think they may have gotten in with the church clothes?"

"Church clothes? Oh my God! Let's see. I put a couple pairs of Patsy and Janice's shoes that they'd outgrown, and a pair of your dad's that needed resoling. But none of yours. They're little more than rags by the time you're through with them. No. I'm certain."

"What's all the commotion? Thought you were going to Mass?" My da always appears like a moth to a light at the worst possible moment. He's coming up from the basement with a jar of strawberry jam in his hand.

"Nothing, Ray, Jimmy can't find his good shoes, that's all."

"Jimmy can't find his shoes. Now why doesn't that surprise me?"

"He can't go to church in his sneakers. Can he wear a pair of yours?"

"And stretch them out so far that I'll walk right out of them? Hell no he can't! Dorothy when you going to learn? If he can't find his shoes, he probably lost them, left them somewhere. You know he's half conscious most of the time."

"Now Ray that's not fair. Can't you see he's upset?"

"Jesus Christ, Dorothy, that kid of yours has you so flummoxed you don't see it, do you? The kid's lost his shoes and he goes to church in tennis shoes or he doesn't go at all. End of story. I guarantee you you can look now 'til sundown and you're not going to find those goddamn shoes. They're not here, Dorothy. Do you hear me, goddamn it? Trust me. Your kid's done a con job on you again."

Meanwhile, I look diligently with my little brother and two sisters for the non-existing shoes knowing the futility of the search. Not once did my mother stop to ask if what my da was saying had any credence. I wouldn't have lied. At that point, I would have cried and told the truth and played the sympathy card. I know he wouldn't hit me, just beat me up and spit me out verbally, like he always does. After a while, you get used to this, but not my little sister Janice. He is yelling now and storming around the house, aggravated that my mother doubts him. She is not listening but putting out her cigarette, and saying, "Let's go!" We leave the house and for Sunday Mass, leaving the turmoil behind to keep my da company. The shoes of course are never found.

*   *   *   *   *

Despite losing my shoe in Mill Creek, my fascination for the countryside will not quit, even though baseball is hitting a fever pitch at the courthouse. I must see Dick's secret place! It is the last day of May 1944 and the sun is very clear in the sky. There is a cool breeze from the Mississippi sweeping westward to the country beyond Clinton. It is a quiet morning and I am walking nowhere in particular, as I often do. My wondering is about the coming summer. Baseball is a given. So is my trip to Detroit to visit my uncle Leonard and to vacation with him at Higgins Lake along with cousin Robert and my uncle's aide Norb Bartos, as is our family railroad vacation across America. I'm also thinking of the Blessed Virgin Mary. This is the last day of her month. There are no people in the street as I walk toward the bluff with the morning sun to my back, warming my shoulders. Some cars pass by but they are mainly bread and milk trucks. Clinton people don't get up as early as farmers, especially on the weekends. It isn't going to be too hot a day, fortunately. I'm not too fond of the heat. Dust whirls about on the street as I walk. Each particle is like a separate universe spinning about with no awareness of other particular universes. Under a microscope, my uncle says there are millions of colonies of life in a single particle. We must be like gods to them. Awesome!

The rains have finally quit and now everyone is waiting for the water to recede so clean up can be put into high gear. I pass Mount St. Clare, which stands so regally above everything else, and wonder if the good sisters are praying for me. I'm somewhat puzzled by the whole concept of nuns, as much as I respect them, especially contemplative nuns that remain buried away in convents, walled off from the world. How can they understand me? Yet a part of me envies them as I envy Trappist monks like Thomas More. His "Meditations" are like honey, warming me all over as I swallow his words whole giving me a sense of his peace. Some nuns, like Sister Marguerite, seem neither in the world nor out of it, in a kind of limbo. I wonder if it is like that for most priests as well.

Every time I've go to the Mount all I see are nuns busily dusting, polishing, vacuuming, and bustling about like nervous bees. The place is so clean it sparkles but they keep right on working as if it were a pig's sty. Don't they ever relax? I wonder if any of them sneaks a smoke or a nip now and then. My mother is devout and she smokes like a chimney every waking hour of the day. She doesn't drink, but I wonder what she would do if she couldn't smoke. Probably drink like a fish.

Look at all the berries along the road! I've never eaten them but Dick has, and he's still with us. They do look delicious. I'll try just one. It's really good, like a raspberry but it isn't. I wonder what it is. I'm so ignorant of nature. This is the way to Dick's house, but I'm going beyond Springdale Drive where there are no houses. That's my plan. Funny, as you move away from the city the trees grow taller, broader and more majestic as if to say, You're now entering God's country! Just ahead is Mill Creek where I lost my shoe. I take a short detour. I'm in no hurry. Strange, seeing a place for the second time. I was so tense before and scared of the unknown. Now I sense the peace of the place, like an oasis, with broad trees forming a canopy of seclusion, and bright green bushes nestling around the rocks, while the creek itself runs cool with a fresh stream as clear as glass. You can see minnows playfully swimming about. I wonder if there are any fish. I sit on the rock where I lost my shoe, and listen to the sound of the stream as it gurgles by. It is pleasant, peaceful and dark here. The constant running water has a friendly sound as it splashes over rocks, and parts and rejoins itself over fallen tree limbs and passes through thick bushes at the water's edge as if they are transparent. Throngs of birds are fluttering about, filling the air with their chirping music, swooping down and landing lightly, prancing about, looking at me as if I'm an intruder in their sanctuary, taking a quick drink and an accompanying bath, then flying away again. I can see why Dick comes here. I feel strangely content, and surprisingly tired. I make a pillow of my sweatshirt and stretch out, and before I know it, I'm sound asleep.

When I awaken, the sun is no longer directly overhead but is sliding toward the west, which is still my objective. I take a BabyRuth candy bar out of my pocket and eat it ravenously. It is a bit sticky as the chocolate has melted. I wash my hands in the water and dry them on my pants. I am a little thirsty, but other than that I feel wonderful. Leaving this refuge, where I've found such contentment, makes me wonder about a contradiction in me. I hate nature for the bugs and the bites, but I love its music. I walk again going westward on Springdale Drive like explorers Lewis and Clark and finally come to the end of the paved road, and start trekking on a narrow dirt road. After some distance, maybe a mile, I come to a fenced in enclosure, the fence high with barbed wire curling on the top, two heads taller than me. Then I see a sign:

Federal Property
Keep Out!
Property of the United States of America
No Trespassing!
Violators will be prosecuted to the full limit of the law!
Signed
Commandant, United States Army

The hair on the back of my head comes to attention; a chill runs down my spine like someone has just dropped an ice cube down my back. My heart is on my sleeve. No one would ever believe Jim Fisher of all people would defy the law. I giggle. I wonder if I will be arrested, if army men in full military gear will come down out of the trees with fixed bayonet rifles and shout, "Halt or I'll shoot!" It is madness, but I revel in the danger and intrigue. I am Buck Rogers in the Twenty-fifth Century.

Oh! I know what this is! This is a prisoner of war camp that I read about in The Herald. It looks all but deserted. No, I see somebody. A football field away someone is leaning against the fence smoking a cigarette. He smiles and waves to me with his cigarette. I don't know what to do, but my feet must have a will of their own because I find myself closing the distance between us. When I'm only a few feet away, he speaks.

"Guten Abend!"

The voice is strong and forceful but, yet playful. I look at the man curious to see what a prisoner of war looks like. He's dressed in a gray shirt and gray pants with a number over his left pocket boxed in a white sewed on patch. He is also tall with blond hair the color of cornbread, and is young, about the age of my cousin Arnie Clegg who is not yet twenty. He has a strong trim physique with bold but friendly deep blue eyes, and a wide smile that shows white even teeth. He looks like he could be an American, but I know this language is German because I've heard it before when Father Sunbrueller gets excited giving Sunday sermons, and from one of my neighbors, too, who never bothered to learn English.

Du srichst wohl kein deutsch? Na gut, dann muss ich es halt mit meinen wenigen Brocken English versuchen. (You don't' speak German, no? Well, in that case, I must try my poor English on you.)

"Good evening, young man." *Du siehst genau aus wie mein kleiner Bruder. Wie heisst Du denn? Ach, Entschuldigung . . .* (You look like you could be my little brother. What's your name? Sorry . . .)

"What your name?"

"Jimmy, Jimmy Fisher."

He tosses his cigarette and claps his hands together. *Du bist deutsche Herkunft, nicht wahr? Fischer ist ein typische deutscher Name!* (You're German, yes? Fischer is a good German name!) He realizes again that he has lapsed into German, and shakes his head in aggravation, but I nod it's okay. For some reason I sense that he thinks I'm of German descent. Others have made the same mistake, spelling my name with a "c" which I know is German. I write my name in the dust in big block letters showing that there is no "c."

"No, no, I'm Irish. My people come from Ireland, not Germany."

He spreads his hands out, and smiles as if to say, "But of course." *Die Iren sind genau wie die Deutschen, wusstest Du das schon?* (The Irish people like Germans, did you know that?"). He corrects himself once again. "Irish like Germans, ya?"

Something happens that excites me. We are actually communicating. "Yes, that's true. My da liked Germans very much before the war, before Hitler." I look at him to see if he comprehends and he does, nodding as if to say, I'm not surprised. "Before the Nazis," I add belaboring the point.

"Ya, father right. *Aber der krieg wird bald vorbei sein und Dein Vater wird dann wieder Deutschland und die Deutschen gern haben* (But the war will be over soon and your father will be happy with Germany and the German people again).

None of this is comprehensible causing him to throw his arms up in frustration. He pauses. "Sorry, war over soon, ya?"

Ever since the fourth grade, thanks to the encouragement of Sister Helen, I've been an avid student of the progress of the war. For the past six months, The Herald has considered a European invasion of the Allied Forces imminent. I wonder if this German knows this, why else would he say that? Not knowing what to say, I shrug my shoulders and finally add, "I don't know. I'm only going into the sixth grade."

This statement clearly puzzles him. He scratches his chin. *Sechste Klasse, was ist das?* (Sixth grade, what is that?). The German hunches his shoulders in clear befuddlement, and then smiles again. "How old you?"

"Eleven." I flash my two hands than add one. "Going on twelve."

Nein, das kann nicht moeglich sein. Du siehst doch viele aelter aus, Du bist vielleicht sechzehn, nicht wahr? (No! Impossible! You must be much older, perhaps sixteen, yes?) Again confused by the language barrier, he nods in acknowledgement of this and raises his right hand palm down slowly from his waist to my height. *Du bist doch viel zu gross fuer einen Elfjaehrigen. Dann muss bestimmt Dein Vater sehr grossgewachsen sein, oder?* (Too tall for an eleven year old. Your father must be very tall, no?) Then adding, "Father tall?"

This is getting complicated. How do I tell him my father is three inches shorter than I am, and that my mother is just barely over five

217

foot? I don't know how to answer without making it even more confusing. I smile, and shake my head up and down, "Yes, my da is very tall," reaching far above my head, "like you." I point to him with a similar gesture to the one he used on me.

His face breaks into a marvelous grin that lights up his face, then he extends his hands as wide as they will stretch with his palms up, hunches his shoulders as if to say, "Well, there you have it!" Of course, the whole charade is a lie, and I feel a little sad about that. But looking at his grin makes the lie worthwhile. I make a motion with my hands that I must go. "Nice talking to you. You are Germany to me. I will take that with me," I say very slowly.

His eyes appear moist as he waves goodbye. *Auf Wiedersehen, mein Junge, ich wunsche Dir und Deiner Familie Gesundheit und alles Gute!* (Goodbye young man and good health to you and your family).

My da's railroad buddies are always trashing the Germans, saying they commit terrible atrocities. I look up the word atrocities and the dictionary says it means committing wicked and barbaric acts. I ask my da, what are the wicked things German soldiers are doing? He says he doesn't know. I ask my mother and she says the same. I ask Sister and she says it's not for me to worry about. I'm confused. They might think me unpatriotic if not a traitor for visiting a German prisoner of war. I know my mother, always protective, wouldn't understand how elated I am to have met this German soldier.

I wanted very much to see him again, and to ask him about his family, his home, and what he did when he wasn't a soldier, but I never got the chance. I went back to the fence a number of times and never saw him again. I found myself praying for him every day, praying that he would safely return to his country and be with his people again, that he would survive the war. I pray that he did. Everything I read, and everything I hear on the radio tells me to hate him, but I can't. I think in a way I love him like a big brother because I never had a big brother. And he is right. We look as if we could be kin.

Sometimes when I am about to fall asleep, I wonder if I dreamt all this, that I had never met him, that he is a figment of my imagination. Then The Herald has an article about German prisoners working at Pillsbury Mills, and how clever and hard working they are. There he is! His picture! Big as life! I breathe a sigh of relief. I'm not going mad after all. It is a secret I never shared with Dick or even Bobby Witt. Bobby's brother is fighting the Germans in Europe as an army air force gunner on a B-29 bomber. Should he ever be injured or killed, Bobby would never speak to me again. So, it is a secret I have carried for more than half a century, and it has had much to do with my trusting my own counsel, and what I know about people, and not relying on what other people tell me to think.

* * * * *

Even life in small Clinton is strangely cut off from the country. I'm thinking this as I quiet my heart and ease my trauma after yet another false step. I'm in my room and am thinking how man-made buildings have taken the place of hills and valleys, how the constant hum of traffic has replaced gushing streams. It is night and I wonder why I hardly ever look at the stars. We have our churches, libraries, taverns, movie theaters, beautiful clothes and our Fifth Avenues. There are people everywhere. A cloud passes across the sky, and who notices? Most people are too busy to notice anything. In the quiet of my room I feel a peculiar peace. Less than an hour ago I did not feel like this. I was on my way to Riverview Stadium with Bobby Witt and the courthouse gang. Clinton Foods is playing a doubleheader with Bridge and Iron Works. Wee Carlson is pitching for Clinton Foods and Warren Mason for Bridge and Iron Works in the first game. It is 6:30 and I'm in my room in this pensive mood and not at the ballgame.

Only an hour ago I was joshing with the guys on the way to the doubleheader. There were already a lot of people moving toward the stadium an hour before game time. The parking lot was half full, and I saw shaggers stationed around the perimeter of the ballpark as if military guards. It was a festive atmosphere and I was wild with anticipation. Without a word, once at the ballpark, Bobby Witt, Ken Tharp, Dick Crider and Chang Benson made for the seven-foot chain-length fence on the first base side. They mounted it swiftly as if negotiating a barrier in army maneuvers, causing the fence to yield in moaning, clanking sounds as they dug their sneakers into it, placed their pivotal foot on the spindly-wire top and leaped to safety on the hard cement surface inside the ballpark. The seven-foot drop was a

219

piece of cake for these athletes. Meanwhile, I watched. I'm far less agile than any of them, much less compact, a long drink of water, and to be honest, much less daring. They race up the ramp, climb to the top of the stadium seats and look down through the screen at me still standing there.

"Come on Rube it's easy!"

Not for me it isn't. Finally, my courage wells up, I grab hold of the fence in the diamond shaped gap of the wires, place my sneaker against it as they did, manage to get to the top, hesitate a moment, then imitate their leap to the surface below. Only it doesn't work for me. My pant leg gets caught on one of the wire spikes at the top, and when I leap, my body slams against the fence, upside down so hard that the imprint of the diamond mesh is on my face. Momentarily, I'm knocked senseless, too stunned to notice the guys are laughing so hard they're losing it. Then silence follows. I can't disengage myself, and I'm getting anxious.

"Well, what do we have here?" It is the deep voice of authority. I see a dark blue pant leg, a long dark blue pant leg. With force, I strain my neck in a cantilever move to see the voice is that of officer Robb, who is as tall as God.

"Good evening officer." What else could I say? One of my ironies is that I am wound so tight you could play music on my anxiety, but in crisis I'm as calm as a quiet sea. My guys are long gone. I'm alone in this ridiculous position. The officer's eyes narrow but he makes no move to release me from the fence. In the interim, my dangling has created a crowd.

"Good evening indeed," he says enjoying my humiliation. My face is now blood red like an inverted catsup bottle and all I can see is the bottom of officer Robb's arms folded across his chest. "My lad, do you have any idea the trouble you're in?"

"Yes sir, I do," I answer faintly, "I'm sorry, sir."

"I should run you in, know that? What will your parents make of that?"

Actually, I am beyond thinking because the blood to my head has cut off any notion of thought. Registering no reply, he unhooks me from the fence and lets my body fall to the cement. I break the fall with my hands, which burn and crumble into a heap. Slowly, I rise to my feet, feeling his hands on the nap of my shirt as he guides me out of the ballpark; people crane their necks to get a glimpse of this criminal, me!

"I'm feeling in a generous mood," officer Robb confesses once outside the ballpark, "Obviously you're not a smart ass." Then he looks down at me from that mountain on which his head is perched. I look up and imagine how silly his big head would be on a smaller body, then drop my eyes abruptly for fear he can read this. "If I ever catch you sneaking in again, I'll run you in. Hear? That's a promise. That clear?"

"Yes officer." It is so easy to say after spending a lifetime saying "Yes Sister," "Yes Father." There are advantages to a Catholic education.

"Now be off with you!"

With that I spirit my body home. When I get there, behind a cloud of smoke, I find my mother reading a book in my da's chair. "Home early." She looks at the clock. "Why, Jimmy, the game couldn't even have started yet. Anything wrong?"

"Yes, mother, I think I'm getting a migraine." With that, I retreat to my room.

* * * * *

It gets tiring hearing the latest exploits at the ballpark, which seem to be rehashed *ad infinitum.* "Did you see that stop by Chet Gaarde at third . . . how about that over the head catch of Bob Dalrymple in shallow left . . . don't forget Warren Mason fanning fifteen with pure heat last Wednesday . . . oh! how about Ed Hyde's dive into first the other night to keep a rally alive . . . say what you want, but nothing compares to that homer of Howie Boles over the scoreboard, that was awesome, must have traveled 450 feet . . . I like speed, loved it when Burridge stole home with the pitcher napping . . hey, did you guys see the House of David play the Negro League all-stars last Saturday, must have been 4,000 there . . . oh yeah, I did, went with my dad, those guys with long beards, you mean, weird seeing guys play ball looking like that . . . how about that long drink of water who pitched for the Negroes, he was all arms and legs and looked seven feet tall on the mound, he'd wind up, turn his whole body almost to second base and wham, it came in looking like a pea . . . pea my ass, you can see a pea, did you see the ball, no, course not . . ..funny, their catcher got hurt and couldn't play so they had to get a white boy from the Industrial League, what was his name, guy from Stebbens Market . . . oh yeah, Stebby Stebbens with Dupont . . . did you see his hand after the game, it was raw like a piece of liver . . . had the Negro pitcher autograph a ball for me, nice man, won't believe his name, Satchel Paige, if that ain't something, huh, says he's called that because he's a traveling man, like to see him pitch again . . . me too . . . and I thought Warren Mason was something . . ."

This was 1944 before Negroes were allowed to play in the Major Leagues. Satchel Paige would not play in the majors for many years, or not until he was long past his prime. Even with this handicap, he distinguished himself in the majors, playing for the Cleveland Indians and Chicago White Sox. I never got to see him pitch but remember how awesome he was to my fellow Courthouse Tigers.

Nobody says, "Sorry, Rube, you missed this or that, or oh yeah, sorry you can't go to the games anymore." No, they just lay it on as if I'm not there. Never felt more an outsider. Something has to give, but what? One night as the railroad cronies are talking, my da confesses, "My kid's big enough to earn a living but sits on his fat ass reading all the time." They laugh. Then Tony Tonzig says, "Ray, Jimmy could be working the ballgames. My kid is, and he makes couple bucks a night."

"No shit? But your kid is, what, fifteen?"

"Sixteen, but not as big as Jimmy."

Normally, whenever my da proposes anything, I already have a well thought out veto in my pocket before he gets through it. So, it shocks him when I say, "I'd love to work the games." Actually, working is the furthest thing from my mind. I can hardly contain my excitement. Won't officer Robb be surprised to see me?

So, with his permission against my mother's reluctance, I'm off to the ballpark at 5:15 to seek employment. I present myself to the concession proprietor, Mr. Quakenbush, his real name, who is a scrawny little man with a Mark Twain face with hair and mustache to match. After looking me up and down, but not asking my age, he says, "You'll make a good pop man." I'm given ten minutes of training, then he throws a couple of scoops of ice into a ten gallon bucket, adds twelve bottles of pop, and says, "Go topside and catch the early birds."

The bucket is extremely heavy, and makes my arm ache, and I haven't even started work. As soon as I get into the stands, I sit down and watch batting practice. Soon, I'm totally engrossed in the hitting.

"Hey! What the hell's this?" A voice explodes into my ear. "Get your ass off that bench and sell some pop or get the hell out of my ballpark." The veins in Mr. Quakenbush's neck look like angry snakes. "I've no time for this."

My face and ears are burning. I rise and want to cry, but instead walk away from him weakly chortling, "Get your ice cold pop here, only a dime, ten cents."

He comes up behind me and breathes down my neck. His breath is warm and smells of cigars. "Louder, like this," demonstrating with a squeaky voice. "Got it?" I nod. "Okay," he says, "and another thing, go into the box seats and push the bucket into people's faces. People are hot as hell and would love a cold drink." Again, he demonstrates. Of course, there are no people in the box seats so he looks a little ridiculous as he swings the bucket at the empty seats. "See how easy it is?" I nod again, but don't mean it. Satisfied, he hands me back the bucket. "It's a big game tonight. You should sell at least 100 bottles. Make you a dollar, penny for each. That's how generous I am." Then he turns and disappears into the concession warehouse under the stands.

For the longest time, I stand there. Every time I think myself clever something breaks my balloon. How am I going to watch the game doing this? My arm aches already, and I feel I'm getting sick. Maybe I can tell him that and tell him I'll come back tomorrow when I'm feeling better. At least I'll get to watch this game. But what if he says, "Forget it kid. You're not cut out for this," and escorts me out of the ballpark. Then I'll be back to square one. I hate life. I hate being poor. I hate adults. I especially hate scrawny little adults who breathe down my neck and smell like cigars.

"Hey kid," somebody yells, "over here." I turn and see four guys with two little boys in a box seat behind home plate. "Give us four cokes and two oranges." The man gives me a dollar.

"Sir," I say, "I don't have change for this."

"Forget it, keep the change."

I can hardly open the bottles I'm so ecstatic. I've just made, let me see, six cents, plus forty-cent tip, the same as if I sold forty-six bottles of pop. 'Yes,' I whisper to myself. 'This is great!' My voice takes on a new timber as I hawk my wares. I'm in the selling business.

By the time I check out I've made $1.12 plus 85 cents in tips for a total of $1.97, which I proudly give to my mother when I get home. She is equally surprised. My da wanders over to me. "Tony called. His kid made $3.00 tonight." I look daggers at him, then he breaks into a smile. "You did good Jimmy." I'm only twelve and I'm a family breadwinner. I'll be someone to reckon with for sure. The only problem is that I didn't see five minutes of the game.

When I tell Bobby about the money I made, he is even more impressed than my parents. "Wow! I never knew you could make that kind of money!" Then I tell him about Tony Tonzig's boy. "Made almost four dollars," I exaggerate for emphasis.

"Four dollars! Wow! Think I could get a job?"

"Sure."

Bobby never ventures into anything right away. It takes the entire summer for him to decide. It isn't until the All-Star Game in August that he finally accompanies me to the ballpark. Mr. Quakenbush gives him the same spiel, but he's a little less roughshod with Bobby. After I sold 112 bottles that first night, he couldn't be nicer to me.

To prepare Bobby on how heavy the pop is, I tell him to rest the bucket on the seats as often as he can. "Otherwise your arm might fall off." He laughs. But Bobby never sells pop, the biggest selling item. Mr. Quakenbush has him selling hot roasted peanuts in the shell. It's funny hearing Bobby say, "Get your hot hot roasted peanuts here, only a nickel five cents." No wonder the guys laughed at me when they first heard me hawking pop. Mr. Quakenbush also tells Bobby to go into the box seats, too, but he never does. I watch Bobby and can see from the first that he is having trouble trying to watch the game and sell, too.

The All-Star Game fills the stadium and bandstand to an overflowing capacity crowd of more than 3,000. Another thirty or forty can be seen watching from the incinerator beyond right field, which looks down on the ballpark.

I manage to sell 324 bottles of pop, and with my tips check out at $3.87, the most I'd ever made. When Bobby checks out, I am anxious to see how he has done. He made thirty-seven cents. The shock of this makes me want to split with laughter, that is, until I see his face. I had never seen his face like that before. He wasn't about to cry as I would, and he wasn't about to get angry, as I know I would, too. Mr. Quakenbush told him he should have made three times that amount. "Based upon what you sold tonight, son, must have had trouble making change," he assessed quite callously. "Let that be a lesson to you, son, people will cheat you if they can."

Bobby wasn't listening. His face was a map of pain, his forehead creased with worry lines, his jaw set like a vice, and all he said was, "This was a bad idea." I tried to give him a dollar of my own money, but he wouldn't take it. Then I told him, which was the truth, that some nights I made practically nothing, especially when I sold pop to a long line of people and the amount received back didn't match all the bottles sent down the row. Mr. Quakenbush said, "It happens. Just have to move on." I went on and on as we walked home spewing out Mr. Quakenbush's philosophy on enterprise, and how in the end, all things considered, things balanced out.

Bobby listened to me without a word. When we reached his house, all he said was, "See you tomorrow."

Bobby never sold at the ballpark again, never mentioned this experience to the guys, and I've never mentioned it to anyone until now. I've often wondered if that's why Bobby stayed as far away from commerce as he could get by entering the teaching and coaching profession. If my first night had been such a total disaster as Bobby's, I wonder what my life would have been like, certainly not as it has turned out, that's for sure.

*   *   *   *   *

James R. Fisher, Jr.

Chapter 15

The Relentless Wheel

Everything without tells the individual that he is nothing;
Everything within persuades him that he is everything.

--Xavier Doudan

"Jimmy we need to talk." These words greet my tired body as I come home from the ballpark after a 17-inning game. All I want to do is go to bed. It is 1:15 a.m. My mother's voice tells me bed is not an immediate option. I sit down fold one leg over the other, lean back in the sofa too tired to wonder why. The swirl of smoke from her cigarette, highlighted by a dull lamp behind her head, produces an eerie vision. What have I done now? Strange, but even upset has a malevolent odor.

"I listened to the game and know it just got over." Her delicate hands work and twist the cigarette like a miniature torch. "I'm not about to scold you, if that's what you're thinking. It's something else." She smokes deliberately. I watch the particles mask her face from the red glow of the cigarette then fade like a passing cloud revealing only the outline of her face, as if serene phosphorescence emanates from its own inwardness. Her voice registers concern, but I can't read her face, as the light is insufficient.

"Work is important in life," she says as she takes a deep drag on her cigarette, "but the right work. The right work for you right now is school. Your job is not to make money to help support this family. Your job is to get an education."

"I made $4.05 tonight."

"Jimmy, have you heard anything I've said?"

"Yes."

"What am I saying?"

"My job is being a student."

"What do I mean?"

"Mother, I'm awfully tired. Can we talk about this in the morning?"

"No we can't. I wish we could, but the right time is now."

A deep sigh escapes me. My head tells me truth is in the air. Truth is a terrible thing. You walk into it and it grabs you and pulls you to its meaning even if you're not ready.

"You're a good boy but have a high need to please. If you made $40 or $50 or $60 tonight, it wouldn't change anything. That's my point."

This irritates me. That's a lot of money. I can't even comprehend ever making that much money. Why would she say that? That makes no sense. My arms fold across my chest in defiance. I can barely see her. It's almost like being in the confessional only now a cloud of smoke rather than a sickening sweet odor from the lattice window separates us. I feel dizzy with a blackness darker than night with my mother's truth reaching out to my tired mind, which I fend off with malice. "What does da say about all this?"

"You let me worry about your father. My job is to keep you focused. That focus is school." She takes a long slow drag of her cigarette. "Tonight was your last night."

"That's okay. There aren't many games left anyway." This is true but I say it in defiance. I can't imagine not seeing the rest of the games.

"Jimmy, Jimmy, Jimmy."

"What?"

"Nothing. Give your mother a kiss and go to bed. We'll talk more about this later."

We never do. But I would never forget this brief conversation. She had a plan for me, less a destination than a journey. She was telling me, as I've come to understand, to travel is one thing, to arrive is quite another. If you're not on the right road, there is no chance you'll ever arrive where you'd like to go. She was also telling me that travel is constant arriving, and arrival that has no further destination is death. How strange to realize with that incomplete conversation she was placing a governor in me, a governor to monitor my drive these many years. I've never retired because I'm a traveling man, a man who is always a student taking on a new job and pushing myself into a new venue. Long ago I learned that work is not about getting, but giving, not about happiness, making money, or being successful, but everything to do with being useful. Work is not a means to an end but an end in itself, providing it is the right work. My mother had an insight into the essence of work. Rather than seek happiness in work, work and happiness are complete in and of themselves. When work is a means to an end, it ceases to be an end in itself. When we seek happiness in work, it ceases to be love made visible. We are neither connected to work nor to people. We are thus essentially incapable of love. Love is not a means to an end. Love is its own eternity. It took me a lifetime to understand this. When I use you and you use me, which we call a "relationship," we are important to each other only as a means to something else. So, we are not important to each other at all. My mother planned no derivative benefit to herself in launching me. It was her work. Happiness had nothing to do with it.

This perception escaped my da, and led to conflict between them, not because there was a lack of love, but because there was a lack of understanding. My da didn't want clarity. Clarity would upset the whole pattern of his daily existence. He was a railroad man. His son should be a railroad man, and his son's son. My mother was of an entirely different mind. She was a cold manipulator of the calculus of power, whereas my da was content to be its constant victim.

* * * * *

The next morning at the crack of dawn, I am over to the courthouse. We are playing the Chancy Cardinals on our field. Like the majors, we have batting practice, and infield practice. Then we all assume the role of groundskeepers, preparing the diamond for the game, running the lime bucket down the sidelines, securing the bases, raking the mound and infield, and putting up signs in the parking lot in left field so courthouse visitors won't park there during the game. The baseball season is officially over for us, but this is a game with our archrivals from the southwest side. They have great ballplayers in pitcher Ray Gilbert, and catcher Hans Andresen. Hans has such a strong throwing arm that the ball seems to explode from his arm when he throws to second base. Nobody ever steals on him unless it is a wild pitch, passed ball, or the pitcher spends too much time in the windup.

I had every intention of playing, but wasn't prepared for what was to greet me at home when I went there for lunch. The game was scheduled for one o'clock. Before I got to Judd's house, I could hear an unnatural roar sending shock waves through my system as if the Mississippi burst through the Clinton dam at Eagle Point and was about to swallow me in its wake. Coach Judd was in the yard looking to my house but saying nothing. I could see my two sisters and brother sitting on the porch swing, motionless as mannequins. Then I heard the resounding explosion of glass crashing against walls like clashing cymbals in an operatic rant. My da was on stage in this impromptu drama inventing new earthy expletives to register his eerie falsetto. Normally, he swore as naturally as he breathed but never like this. It torched the air and burned my siblings' ears.

"Daddy's mad at you Jimmy!" my little sister Janice cries as I reach the porch. "He's swearing a lot, too." She digs her head securely under Patsy's arm, while my little brother Jackie sits as stoically as a Buddha. Only his eyes betray the whirlpool of fear that pulls him deeper inside himself. My original plan was to get a quick bite to eat and return to the courthouse. When I left, my da was still on the road and wasn't expected until after lunch. Even when he came home early, his routine was to eat something and go immediately to bed. I wonder what provoked this. Me? What did I do?

No point in asking my siblings, or going inside, and absolutely no point in returning to the courthouse. My mother is in there with a madman, a madman not mad at her, but apparently at me. My da has never hit her. Nor has he ever broken anything before. His rage has been confined to noxious yelling and swearing. How is this different? Mr. Judd comes over. "Jimmy I wouldn't go in just now. Elsie and I have been watching your father. He hasn't hit your mother. Broken a lot of dishes though. Elsie wanted to call the police but I said wait. Never seen your father so upset."

Howard Judd is a large powerfully built man with a barrel chest, but a cherubic smile, and an earthy laugh that rumbles from the diaphragm like bumblebees in a dry gourd. He is a swimming coach with a national reputation, but quietly modest and always in control. More importantly, he is not judgmental. I sensed this in his calm. Often, when I think what makes a good neighbor, I remember coach Judd at that moment. His cool diminished my terror. Then, there is silence in the house. Coach Judd puts out his hand to me, which is as big as a catcher's mitt, and walks me to my front door. "Jimmy, I'll be here if you need me. Elsie and I are taking your brother and sisters to our house until you call for them. Understand?" I start to cry. He makes no move to stop me.

"Why, Mr. Judd, why does my da get so upset? What did I do?" Tears are coming down in torrents. He looks down at me and puts his hands on my shoulders.

"Jimmy, I doubt if it has anything to do with you. It's between your parents." Coach Judd is a wise man, but he couldn't have been more wrong. It had everything to do with me.

* * * * *

There are defining moments in every life, which never fade even with the passing of time. This was such a moment. Janice would never again be able to tolerate any degree of rage. Patsy would steal herself away as if it never happened. Jackie would feed on it to justify his cynicism, while I would become increasingly resentful of authority. There is a sense of abandonment, of being cut off from the umbilicus of family when parents fight. The impact is more painful than simple dread. With terror you can run and hide, but there is no escape from the sense of helplessness when the most important connection of life is ripped from your soul. You don't have to understand the horror, as I'm sure I didn't understand it at the time, nor did my younger siblings. You could see the fright in our eyes as we stared sightlessly at each other like deer frozen in headlights. Time stopped, and so did the rhythm of our souls. Wounds of the soul heal slowly if they heal at all, but worse yet, they leave invisible scars.

If an earthquake can reduce a house to rubble, rage can reduce its contents to smithereens. I could not believe my eyes. Broken dishes, lampshade bulbs, figurines, picture frames, cups, saucers, glasses, bottles, shattered candlestick holders and Catholic statuettes formed the new floor covering in the kitchen, dining room and living room. Only the busts of Jesus with the inscription "Ecce Homo" and Blessed Virgin Mary with "Santa Maria" remained on the walls. Everything else was stripped including the wallpaper, which hung in many places like weeping tears. Anything that could be broken was. It was as if the house imploded on itself, which in a way it did.

My mother quietly scrapes the floor of debris with a dustpan. A broom is too timid a tool for this mess. My da sits and smokes in the euphoric afterglow of rage, feeding on its emotional wreckage. This is when the false sense of peace takes hold and carries the mind beyond reality. It is the drug of calm that possesses the enraged and lasts through the night and produces the narcotic sleep. It will not last. By morning, regrets will come, along with apologies, and coin of that form. This too will not last.

It is sad to see, and sadder to realize that you are the cause. A man has such a marginal function in life when he measures his worth in terms of take home pay. The mind is forever in the cage of anxiety losing the battle paycheck to paycheck. The slightest upset to this precarious balance, forced to miss a trip on the road with a bout of flu, mother's need for a new hearing aid, or the necessity for medical or dental care for us kids, can throw a breadwinner against the wall. Why shouldn't he expect some income from his strapping son? What right does his wife have to put his son above contributing? How can she be so insensitive to his feelings as a man? When everyone out there is beating you up, why can't you expect safe haven at home, solace from this punishing anxiety? Why must you feel guilty for hating a family member who puts you in this predicament? I can imagine the conversation that took place that morning. He, tired, seeking sanctuary, walks into the buzz saw of my mother's declaration that "Jimmy is different. We must make allowances for him. We must put the focus on his education, not on him working."

Jimmy's different than I am? Is that what you're saying? He's a right arrogant sonofabitch. That's what he is, like your brother Len. Both think their shit doesn't stink. Jimmy walks on cloud nine without a goddamn care in the world. Dorothy you've made him that way! You've filled that kid so full of bullshit that he thinks he's clever when he's the thickest bastard I've ever known, but do you see that? No! You think he's a goddamn genius, God's gift to the world. Christ Jesus I cannot goddamn believe you Dorothy. You see him as a breed apart from the rest of us. From the rest of us, Dorothy, you hear me? You have any idea how goddamn stupid that sounds? I love you. But goddamn it, all I want around here is a little cooperation. Dorothy is that too much to ask? So Jimmy's only twelve. Well, goddamn it, what do you think I was doing at twelve? I was hanging out at goddamn hotels and hustling any way I could for a buck, that's what I was doing. I wasn't sitting on my fat ass reading goddamn books, or acting like I had a goddamn silver spoon in my mouth. I was working to stay alive. I had no mother, no father, and I was on my own. So, I quit school in the seventh grade. What choice did I have, I ask you? Why does he have to go to high school? He's already so constipated with bullshit it should last him a lifetime.

Just when he thought he was winning, while my mother let him rant on, I can imagine her launching her coup d'etat with a sinister comment that threw my da's composure off the Richter scale.

"Ray, you shouldn't compete with your own son. Someone might get the impression you're jealous of him, that you can't believe you fathered such a boy."

The logarithmic progression of earthquake rage apparently went from 1.5 to 8.5 on the Richter scale in a matter of seconds. It seems safe to say my mother hadn't heard anything he said. Blackness filled the void until nothing in the house that could be destroyed was left to be destroyed. What my da heard was that he was a failure, an extra board brakeman on the railroad that couldn't even hold a regular job, a provider she couldn't look up to, whereas she had a son, an Adonis, that would be educated and amount to something, come hell or high water, and despite him if necessary. She couldn't have driven home a greater sense of worthlessness if she had declared him a bankrupt person. For the rest of his life, which would be a scant thirteen more years, now only thirty-six, he would live with the memory of that day of lost dignity. Who knows when the death rattle begins? With my da, I believe it started that day. Was it my mother's fault? I don't think so. It was my da's for giving my mother such consummate power over him that mere words could destroy him. I would remember this and vow never to let any man or woman do like damage to me.

When evening comes, and dinner of sandwiches without plates and milk in a communal pan is passed around, my da says weakly, "Don't you have a ballgame?"

I look to my mother in confusion. She waves with her cigarette, go, and I do, relieved to be out of the house, but not wanting to see anyone I knew, at the ballpark or anywhere.

As I approach the stadium, a freight train blocks the crossing to the park. It slows to a speed of only about five miles an hour. Impulsively, I grab hold of the steel ladder on the side of a boxcar and ride the train as it passes Mr. Witt's railroad diesel refueling post, which is only one hundred yards from the stadium. Gradually, the clickydyclack cacophony of the freight car wheels increases as the train weaves its way north parallel to the Mississippi. I pass the O'Brien's house, where Bobby Witt's uncle and aunt live; Jimmy Keefe's house, too, a classmate of mine. Heads poke out of houses along the rail line following the train in kind of a hypnotic trance, until they see me hanging on. I smile and wave at their shocked faces. With a great roar the twin diesel engines pick up speed, and suddenly I'm conscious of danger. I can't ride the train very long like this, that's for sure. What'll I do? Why'd I do this? Will I be killed? Will I be missed?

Curiously, anger, not fear wells up in me. It's my parents' fault. They made me do this. Abruptly, the train slows again as it approaches the bend at the neck of Joyce's slough. With great relief, I jump to the ground safely, tumbling head over heels on the gravel bed beside the tracks, then, once the train passes, I cross the tracks again and plunge into the thick grass. My ankle hurts a bit, but otherwise, I'm fine. I look around and I'm in a veritable paradise. The grass is high and thick, trees are tall and strong, and it is like trudging through the thick underbrush and tangled vines of a jungle. I smell the water before I see it. Beyond Joyce's slough I also see Joyce's Island. It is like a quarter mile away and has a sandy beach, which looks pleasantly cool in the distance. If only I were a strong swimmer, which I'm not, so forget about it. I'll just have to stay on this side of the slough.

Clinton seems a million miles away, with its noise, dust and meanness. All of that is left behind while the clean evening air laps my face. It is a beautiful evening. The tangerine sky is behind me while tall slender trees sway in the autumn breeze. A long heavy-laden barge of several units loaded with coal moves down river against the evening sky and the dark trees. It is a lovely evening, calm and free. The water, once the barges pass, looks surprisingly still. The reflections of the trees are so sharp and clear on the water that it is confusing to distinguish the actual from the reflection. The setting sun makes the water transparent; the glow of evening is on its face, hypnotic in its quiet lapping of the shore. Even the whisper among the leaves seems to stop. From the meadow suddenly appears an animal – muskrat, beaver, rabbit? I don't know. The dark shadow drinks and disappears as silently as it came.

Early in the last century, this was a sawmill paradise as logs from the pine wood forests of Minnesota and Wisconsin were delivered to these mills in huge rafts pushed down river by tugboats. The Joyce Lumber Company was located where I now stand, approximately a mile down stream from the old Clinton-Fulton Bridge. Rafts of logs, some logs a foot to two feet in diameter, were customarily anchored a short distance upstream from the Joyce mill. When the logs were needed for processing, mill hands would take them out in small sections and float them into the slough as rafts, and thus on to the mill.

Clinton glory days of a hundred years ago are gone reminding me that nothing lasts forever. The silence of this mystery seems to hold the land. It seems to cover everything. Then I hear voices and move towards them. It is dusk but I have no sense of danger. I smell the aroma of burning pine, coffee, frying fish, and cigarettes. In a clearing not more than thirty yards from the rails is a hobo camp at the narrowest part of the slough. Three men are sitting around a fire with a coffee pot and skillet mounted on a makeshift stand over the sweet smelling blaze. One is rolling a cigarette; another is laughing and slapping his knee to the rhythm of the third man playing a mouth organ. I hesitate out of shyness but also with a fascination for watching the man struggle to roll a cigarette. As he lit it, he looks up and sees me. The other stops playing.

"Well, what do we have here?"

The mouth organ man pounds the instrument against his leg clearing it of saliva then says, "Join us? Drink coffee?" I nod. "Hungry? Got plenty of fish, cornpone, too." I shake my head.

"So it's just coffee. Don't have cream and sugar but it's good and hot." Then he extends his hand with a makeshift cigarette. "Care for a smoke?" I shake my head vigorously. "Well, plenty of time for fags." I've never heard cigarettes before referred to as fags. A disgusting word.

From a distance, these men look old in their shabby clothes and dirty faces. Now I see one is a boy not much older than I am. He is smoking away and drinking coffee like a veteran. I move toward him. He has a rough countenance, pockmarked face, and yellow teeth, with two missing in front. He looks stupid, but his eyes look old and knowing.

"You' all from 'round 'ere?" He speaks with a distinct nasal twang and an accent I've not heard before, almost but not quite like a Negro, but he's white. I nod. "Cat got use' all tongue?" he adds as he hands me a metal cup of coffee. It burns my lips when I try to sip it, and is so strong and tastes so awful I know I won't be able to drink it. I learn later that chicory added to the coffee gave it that terrible taste.

"No!" I answer with false gusto.

He takes a flask from his pocket and pours some liquid into his coffee. "Sweeten's it," he says with a toothless grin. I can smell the whiskey.

"Go easy on that, Quartlow!" says the older man, "We've got to catch the 11 o'clock. Don't want you pissed when it comes." The boy nods and puts the flask away.

"How old are you?" I ask, more or less just to make conversation.

"Don't know for sure, spect bout thirteen. What use all, sixteen?"

"Eleven but soon twelve."

"Holy shit, you 'ere that, Blacktop? Red 'ere's younger-n-me!" I was a full head taller than he was. Blacktop peruses me with a bored glance. To change the subject, I say,

"You remind me of Huck Finn."

"Huck Finn? Don't know 'em. Live round 'ere?"

"No, he's a character in a book. Mark Twain wrote it. Huck's adventures were on the river but I'll bet yours parallel his on trains. Had a wonderful life on the Mississippi with his friend Jim, a Negro slave he helped to escape from slavery."

"Man, ear 'em? Once he gets a rattling, he's like a runaway train."

The two men applaud his joke with laughter. Then the boy arches his eyebrows, tosses his cigarette into the fire. "No chance making his acquaintance. See, I can't read."

I look at him in shock and wonder, and hide it by picking up a blade of grass. I mean him no disrespect. It's just too horrible to contemplate. Not to be able to read, not to be able to follow *The Adventures of Huckleberry Finn* is nearly as sad as never having played baseball with the Courthouse Tigers.

"Do you think Negroes should belong to their owners?" I blurt out thinking about Huck and his bias.

He looks at me as if I've lost my senses. "No way! No way at 'all. Don't like Negroes called niggers though. Gets my backside up."

"Quartlow's pretty sensitive about niggers," one of the older men chimes in, "nigger saved his life in Mobile when he fell drunk into the river. Almost drowned, didn't you Quartlow?"

"Blacktop ya knows I's did, so why puts that in my face? Show some respect."

"Just kiddin." Then as Blacktop rolls another cigarette and looks to me. "That's why Quartlow prefers trains with no bridges over water in sight. Can't swim a whit." He smiles broadly, "Quartlow you're some case."

"Damned if that's not the truth," Quartlow replies with a stupid grin showing the gap in his teeth. "Trouble's always a following me. But I's just a kid, what's use alls excuse?"

The two older men give him a nod as if to say, point taken. They have craggy weather beaten faces, what you can see of them, especially around the eyes, as straggly beards cover the rest. They have old eyes, too, and gnarled knuckles that look as if they've been broken several times. But it is the eyes that are haunting. The eyes are weary and hooded by wrinkles at the corner and so dark that it is impossible to delineate between iris and pupil. The eyes of Blacktop are always moving, observing. He sits by the fire leaning slightly forward, and gives off the feeling that he's spring-loaded like an animal.

All three men are sinewy, muscular but pencil thin. None wears a belt. Clothesline rope holds up the pants of Quartlow and Blacktop. Good that it does, otherwise their balloon pants would be down around their ankles. Blacktop is a walking advertisement with Roosevelt and Willkie campaign buttons, a Democrat delegate button, and a "Buy Savings Bonds" button. All are pinned to his shirt along with five ink pens in his shirt pocket. The man with no name wears bib overalls and a bomber jacket. They could use new footwear, too, as cardboard fills large holes in the soles of their boots. Three gray bundles, about the size of large laundry bags, are neatly tied down with rope and now furnish them seats before the fire. The oldest man, who must be pushing thirty, the one that has not spoken stares me down.

"You studying us, boy?" he says finally. I shudder and turn my eyes away. "Never seen men on the road before?" He takes a deep drag on his cigarette and the butt is so small I fear it will burn his lips. Instead of throwing it away, he takes another drag on it, then spits out the tobacco. "Well, I'll tell you what, if you ever want real freedom, try the road. Will you remember that, boy?" I nod. "There's nothing like it is there, Quartlow?" He turns to Quartlow who smiles and puffs away.

"This is some place," I say honestly, but also to change the subject, "with an incredible history." The attention in their dark eyes slips through my hands like a fish. "Honest it is," I insist, feeling a chill in the air. Have I been disrespectful? Blacktop rescues me.

"Do you know the story of Joyce's Island?" he asks with a glint in his eye. I shake my head. The others repress their mirth knowing what's coming. "Well, it's some story. Care to hear it?" I nod.

"Joyce's Island's about a mile long give or take some, and pointed at both ends. Well, sir, one day my partners and me were fishing and hooked a large fish. The fish was so large, and moved so swiftly, we had to attach the line to that big tree over yonder. Didn't we fellows?" They nod while my eyes follow his to a giant tree. "But the fish swam away and turned the island completely around so the north end now points south and the south end north." The other two men can hardly contain themselves. Blacktop waits for my reaction. "What'd ya think of that?"

"I think it's a good story," I say calmly, "but I heard it before from my cousin Johnny Sturtz. He lives on Beaver Island, and that's one of Beaver Island's great fish stories. Only difference is Beaver Island is nine times as long as Joyce Island. Must have been one whopper of a fish to turn that island around, don't you think?"

Blacktop turns crimson and the two other men lose it. "Red's too clever for you Blacktop," says the man with no name. "Let that be a lesson to you," he continues laughing and shaking his head with delight, "boy's out flummoxed a flummoxer."

Blacktop runs his hands through his greasy black hair and pulls on his straggly beard. "Guess he has." Then grinning broadly, "But you've got to admit it's a dandy story."

"Yes it is. I first heard it when I was seven and my cousin seems never to tire of telling it."

"How'd ya happen on us?" asks Quartlow, "Way out 'ere'n nowhere?"

"I rode the freight from the ballpark."

"I'll be damned," declares Blacktop, "can't keep the boy on the farm, can we?"

"Want ta join us?" asks Quartlow. I look at each of their expectant faces, not wanting to offend, and then the man with no name speaks again,

"Best you run on home, boy! We've enjoyed your company." Then he points a gnarled index finger at me. "Don't be telling your friends 'bout this place. This's home to the likes of us. We'd be a bit upset if your kind destroyed our camp, catch my meaning?" I nod. "Now scat before you bring the law on us."

I turn and run and can hear them laughing as a fading echo. I rush through the heavy foliage and jungle-like growth of willows, as seemingly a thousand red-wing blackbirds are flushed out of the thicket, scamper up and over the tracks, dash between a couple of houses, unpainted and collapsing at their centers like underdone cakes. I am back in civilization. I stop. My heart is racing.

The three men gave me respite from my trauma, a kind of calm outside time and space. Now I am back in its confines. Their eyes were old and knowing, laughing with the gods. I think of my da's anguished eyes, eyes tied up in knots like snakes squeezing and suffocating them, distorting vision and killing insight. He is gripped with temporal concerns, while these men left such concerns behind in another life.

* * * * *

When I finally meander home, after walking for some time in a dream, it is nearly eleven o'clock. Darkness clings to my house while my recent companions still dance in my head. I marvel at their lack of urgency. They seem in rhythm with the universe without trying, like outlaws in the bosom of chaos with only the code of the stars to govern them. They are like Buddhist monks without the robes or baggage. I may forget them, but never their old eyes.

My mother is in the kitchen drinking coffee and smoking.

"Where's da?"

"Had to deadhead to Boone to bring back a troop train tomorrow."

"Oh! He all right?"

She smokes pensively with the plume rising to the ceiling like an Indian smoke signal. She watches it as if deciphering its coded message. "Whatever all right means. Don't want to talk about it. How's the game?"

"Okay," I lie, "only made a little over a dollar, all in change," which I send splaying across the Formica kitchen table in the music of spinning coins. It is the money I had when I left home to make change.

"Better keep it."

Does she know I didn't work the game? There is this conspiracy between us, which seems so natural if equally duplicitous, you protect my lie and I'll protect yours.

"Want something to eat?"

"What on?" I laugh looking at a dishes-less kitchen. She doesn't answer.

"Any chocolate cake left?"

In the Shadow of the Courthouse

Her face manages a faint smile like an old photograph. She goes to the oven, takes out the cake, and pours milk into a small pan. The floors have been swept and vacuumed with no evidence of the recent carnage. Only bare cupboard record the battle in their emptiness.

"You didn't have much dinner," she says with a forced laugh as she hands me the small pan of milk. Her brave upturn expression breaks against my face like a cool breeze. We're going to get past this.

"None of us did," I reply, immediately regretting it. I devour the cake, and then cut myself another even bigger piece. "How's everybody?"

"Fine. They're all asleep. It's you I'm worried about." She studies me with her puffy eyes, making no attempt to camouflage them with makeup. "Don't hate your father, Jimmy, he's a good man."

"I know that. I don't."

"Do you know he's a good man? Do you really know that?"

"Mother, he broke some dishes. He didn't break any of us. We know what he can do when he's really angry and hits someone."

Tears well up in her eyes. She reaches over and touches my hand, sobs uncontrollably, pushes her chair next to mine, then pushes my head into her bosom. "Thank you for that, Jimmy," her tears dripping down into my hair. "My son, the little old man."

"I'm not so little, mother. I'm as big as some men."

"True, you're not so little." She runs her hand through my blond hair. "Hope you don't hate me one day for your never being a little boy like other little boys. I wanted you so much to have that, but it never worked out for us."

"I won't ever hate you, mother," I say through tears, not understanding why I'm crying. In truth, I adore her. I will keep this promise, but not blindly. I will see her more clearly as the decades go by and love her despite the fatal flaws she passed onto me.

* * * * *

Just when I thought this business of my job being that of a student and not a wage earner was settled, my da comes off the road, eats his breakfast, takes his nap, and then comes over to the courthouse to corral me. I'm embarrassed to have him intervene in our game, and at

241

the same time surprised, mainly because he has never done it before. "What's up?" I ask dumbfounded.

"Just need you for a little while." I look at him suspiciously. "Need to check out something at the courthouse."

"The courthouse?" I don't believe him. It's got to be something else. What have I got to do with the courthouse? Now, I'm terrified. It must show on my face.

"It's no big deal. It'll only take a minute. It's just that I want you with me. Your mother knows I was coming for you."

"Why didn't she say something this morning?"

His eyes change. They become as flat as glass. He looks at my teammates who stand motionless, waiting, then back at me. He lights a cigarette. I notice his hands shaking. He tries to smile, but it doesn't work. Why do I provoke him so? I sensed anger surging through his body like a quick pain, knowing I am only moments from humiliating embarrassment. I leap to the sidewalk and walk sullenly beside him, which triggers a clenched teeth response.

"Don't ever defy me like that again in front of your friends, understand?" I nod. "Sometimes, I pray to Christ I could ..." He doesn't finish. He doesn't have to. His anger swells in me like a gas. We go through the massive courthouse doors, walk down the ancient hall, the wooden floorboards screeching as we walk. We then ascend the marble steps of the winding open staircase, which resembles those I've seen in movies, and come to the landing on the second floor, where an impressive gallery of pictures of Clinton County attorneys is framed on the wall. Mr. Holleran's picture is there. He's Dave's father, who is a grade ahead of me at St. Patrick's. I notice the Hollerans every Sunday at eight o'clock mass. They sit in the middle of the center isle, while we sit near the back in the left side isle. I study the family every Sunday. I guess it's one of my obsessions. The family is almost regal. There are three boys, Dave, Brent and Bob. They stand, sit, and kneel as straight as obedient soldiers. I wonder how they do it. They never fidget like I do. Of course, I'm way in the back where nobody notices. Mrs. Holleran is tall and elegant with a classic profile. I can imagine her face stamped on Roman coins. Mr. Holleran is equally handsome. He has a touch of gray at his temples, which gives him a distinguished look. And he's always so tan, trim and healthy looking compared to everyone else that I wonder how he does it. I know nothing about style and dress, but it is a style show to see their different costumes every week. My mother says Mrs. Holleran comes from South Clinton like she does. That is hard for me to believe because I've never seen anyone from South Clinton that looks like she does, including my mother. My da shakes me by the shoulder, "Goddamn it, Jimmy, get with it! We're here!" We are at the door of William A. McCullough, Judge Municipal & Juvenile Courts. I can't believe we're going in, but we are. Abruptly, I have severe pains in my stomach. I feel as if I'm going to throw up. My anger is as painful as the deep cut of betrayal. My own father is going to turn me in, but for what? For riding the train? He doesn't know about that! Nobody does! Then what? For provoking him to break all the dishes? If it's that, he's in as much trouble as I am. He did it. I didn't.

My da gives his name to the secretary and says we have an appointment. An appointment? Since when? There are Life magazines, Saturday Evening Posts, and Liberty magazines on a table. My da lights up and moves a metal ashtray to his side. He talks to the secretary as if they're old friends. How he can change his colors so quickly is beyond me. Then the judge comes out. He looks the perfect picture of a judge, round, short, white haired, open faced with kind eyes that seem to hide behind broad white bushy eyebrows. "Ray, good to see you. Come on in." Once we get into his office, he adds, not unexpectantly, "What can I do for you?"

"Well, Mac, I've got a problem." He turns and looks at me. "My boy here is growing like a weed as you can see, and they're three more like him at home doing their best to eat me out of house and home. And quite frankly, Mac, I'm having trouble making my bills. Kid here is big enough to work, but the wife has big plans for him, high school and all, so I'm between a rock and a hard place. And . . ."

"I'm sorry to interrupt, Ray, but I'm not quite following you."

"No, suspect you're not. Wonder what I want from you, right?"

The judge doesn't say anything but just leans forward with his hands clasped together on his desk and waits for my da to explain. Then the most disturbing thing happens. I never thought my da could surprise me. Thought I knew him like a book. My da starts to cry. My macho da who's not afraid of anyone in the world starts to sob.

"Mac, I'm over a barrel." He takes out his handkerchief and blows his nose. "I'm picking straws, Mac, and they're all short. You've known me ever since we were kids. Even helped me out of a few tight spots when I was young and stupid. I've not forgotten." He can't go on. He just sits there crying uncontrollably, his chest heaving with periodic giant intakes of air, expelled in equally giant sobs. I'm paralyzed to do anything. The judge's posture doesn't change. This, I trust, is not the first time he has seen male strength running out of a man like sawdust. Weakly, he continues almost in a whisper. "I don't know where to turn. Thought you might have some ideas. How I might get some social service help, some welfare, Jesus Christ, something. Make any sense to you?"

"Ray, are you asking me to advise you on qualifying for welfare?"

"Yeah, maybe." Much of his composure is back as well as his belligerence.

"But Ray, aren't you working on the railroad?"

"On the extra board."

"What does that mean?"

"I take runs when guys are on vacation, there is an extra train, somebody is sick, or they need an extra body, stuff like that."

"Do you work much, I mean, do you work close to a regular forty hour week?"

"More like a fifty, sixty hour week. Get paid half as much when I deadhead as when I work a full run."

"Ray, about how much did you make last year?" My da tells him.

The judge shakes his head. "Ray, that's well beyond the cutoff point for welfare benefits. I'm quite certain in any case that you would not qualify with that income. No. Not at all. I'm sorry."

"Had to ask."

"Perhaps I could recommend a financial counselor to help you and your wife with your budget."

"Judge, I don't need no goddamn counselor to tell me how to spend my money. Mac, I don't have enough goddamn income. That's the point."

The judge seems to bristle a little every time my da swears, but he doesn't interrupt. He watches my da rise from his chair walk around the book-lined office punching the air with his index finger like a politician on the stump and going into a familiar harangue. The litany of woes is old fare for me so I hardly hear a word but wait for us to be thrown out. Before that happens, judge McCullough's secretary intervenes announcing that the judge's next appointment is here. It immediately settles my da down. He apologizes for the outburst. The judge's head, I notice for the first time, rests on his shoulders like a bowling ball on a shelf, unmoving and displaying no emotions. Perhaps relieved that we are going, he apologizes for not being able to help, while I feel like a fifth wheel in this confusing charade. We leave the courthouse without ceremony, walk past the guys scrimmaging.

"Da, I left my sweatshirt here," I say as we are even with the jail.

"It's all right. You can stay. I'll see you at dinner." He doesn't smile, but he doesn't frown either. He keeps walking home. I watch his narrow shoulders sag and I feel more love for him than ever before. He did a brave thing with the judge. He knew it was hopeless going in, but he needed to share his pain with someone on the other side of the tracks, if for no other reason then to let them know he exists. What the judge saw was authentic Ray Fisher, warts and all, and not an obsequious pretender. He saw the father I see every day, the real McCoy. Regarding his actions, obviously it was not a well thought out plan to go to the judge, but it was an explicit acknowledgement that his son's main job for the foreseeable future would be that of a student, while he would remain the family provider. Dignity was on display that day. It was my da's finest hour.

* * * * *

James R. Fisher, Jr.

Chapter 16

A Broken Wing

Of all bad things by which mankind are curst,
Their own bad tempers surely are the worst.

--Richard Cumberland

Born the last day of 1908, my da seemed always a day late and a
dollar short. On his fourteenth birthday, in the middle of eighth
grade, he decided he had enough education, and quietly quit school
for good, electing to find his way in the world without a smidgeon of
protest from anyone. How anyone could be less lucky is hard to
imagine. His only skill, acquired hanging out at the Lafayette Hotel
in Clinton, and then later at the Palmer House in Chicago, was that of
a bellhop.

It was the "Roaring Twenties" following victory in World War I,
a time when the Blue Danube Waltz was put aside for upbeat New
Orleans jazz, Dixieland music and for wild jam sessions on Chicago's

east side. Young women, who finally had the vote, dressed provocatively as flappers in coonskin coats or yellow slickers, smoked cigarettes boldly on the street, swore like men, and worried only about the next party. It was a period of wild binge drinking, vulgarity, corruption, and gaudy vitality. Rumble seats in cars were the rage and dress hemlines rose above the knee. Folks danced to the music of Clinton's own Wayne King in Chicago, whose theme song was written by another Clintonian, Emil Flindt. The Aragon and Trianon ballrooms and the College Inn were popular Chicago places to let it "all hang out." And "Nola" was made famous by the Coon Sanders band with Vincent Lopez playing piano. People everywhere were humming or singing "My Blue Heaven," "I'll See You In My Dreams," "April Showers," "Linger Awhile," "Yes, We Have No Bananas," "Barney Google," "Toot, Toot Tootsie," and "Ain't We Got Fun."

It was a perfect world for a swaggering, pugnacious, skinny Irishman, who looked twelve, swore he was eighteen, was actually sixteen. Famous people stayed at the Palmer House in Chicago where he landed a bellhop job: John and Lionel Barrymore, Lillian Gish, D. W. Griffith, Al Jolson, and even President Calvin Coolidge. "All were poor tippers," my da was fond of saying. This contributed to his smoldering bias toward politicians, celebrities and other high rollers. With such a background in his youth, little gems of life's lessons would be proffered for my benefit at unexpected times. He'd be dressing to go on the road and say, "Jimmy ride with me to the station." He always looked handsome and clean-cut in his black well worn but carefully pressed Chicago & North Western brakeman's uniform, with a freshly laundered starched white shirt, black tie, and highly polished black shoes, the one garment that identifies a person more than any other. A black vest, which was not regulation, completed his attire. The vest gave him a chance to show off his gold plated Hamilton railroad watch with its golden chain. The chain curled across his vest to his watch pocket. One of his idiosyncrasies was to take the watch out, clip open its golden cover, study the dials, and then announce the precise time to the second. It is hard to imagine a more defining talisman.

Already the Clinton winter afternoon had taken on the misty pinks and yellows of evening as we walked past the courthouse. The clock chimed five times as the bus approached. Once on the bus, the routine never changed. He'd stretch out on the seat, light a cigarette, and offer me one of his homilies, looking beyond me as if his muse was holding up flash cards. I always planned to write these down for my children, but never got around to it.

* * * * *

Today he had sin and sinners on his mind. "You know about mortal and venial sin?"

"Yes, of course I do."

"Well, I'm going to tell you something you don't know. People like us are only capable of committing venial sins. We lack the opportunity and imagination to be mortal sinners."

"Then who commits mortal sins?"

"People who can afford to."

"Like?"

"Like bosses, bankers, politicians, presidents, priests, popes . . ."

"Priests, popes?"

"People in power that can punish people like us without breaking a sweat."

"But that's immoral."

"No Jimmy, that's business. Can you imagine people like us committing mortal sin? People like us are never in a position to commit mortal sin. Let's face it, if we were, we'd commit them, too."

He smokes in a lofty manner, and then smiles with satisfaction. I turn away feeling I'm on the horns of a dilemma. Swearing is a mortal sin. Not attending Sunday Mass is a mortal sin. Getting violently angry is a mortal sin. Destroying property like breaking every dish in the house is a mortal sin. He is guilty of all these mortal sins. Yet he claims he is not a mortal sinner. How can that be? What can I say without him exploding in my face? I know how quickly his calm can erupt to anger, so I pray he doesn't ask me to reply. He doesn't. We stop to pick up several people downtown. An electric van is scrubbing the gutter across the street. In Van Allen's display window, a young girl is fitting clothes on a mannequin. She wears boots of heavy felt and shuffles about the window like a prisoner, holding one plastic arm and feeding the sleeve of the dress along it, then the other. The girl is small and springy with pink cheeks and blonde hair that looks green in the window's light. I put my hand to my lips and blow her a kiss. She must feel my eyes. She turns and looks at the bus with the stance of a cheerful pugilist. I duck my head down, then look back. Her smile is quick and compelling. She's very pretty, but not a girl. She's a woman.

"Ordinary people like us are incapable of committing mortal sin. We're too busy just managing to survive."

"Then what exactly is a mortal sin? Who commits them?" I ask, knowing I've missed something, hoping this doesn't make him fly off the handle.

He tosses his cigarette on the steel grated floor of the bus, steps on it, and takes on the look of the storyteller. I notice a lot of other butts on the floor. Disgusting! Oblivious to this, his eyes glisten with the satisfaction that comes to a storyteller with a captive audience.

"Mortal sins are committed by people who use people like us to satisfy their ends. Politicians, employers and bankers caused the depression, a mortal sin. Who suffered for it? Venial sinners like us. It's a mortal sin for a company to close a plant without giving workers fair warning. It's a mortal sin for that same company to claim bankruptcy and fail to pay the wages already owed these workers."

I look at him in disbelief. This only causes him to smile. "I know, it's hard to believe, but it happens. It's a mortal sin to expect people to live in darkness simply because they can't pay their utility bill. Why? Because there's no work. It's a mortal sin for governments to declare war on each other then send their venial sinners to fight. And it's a mortal sin for priests and popes to do nothing about it. Mortal sins, Jimmy, are always committed by the wealthy and the powerful on the backs of the powerless, venial sinners like us."

"That doesn't make sense." I look for him to explode, but instead he lights another cigarette and actually looks radiant.

"It doesn't, does it? Well, who do you think dies in wars declared by mortal sinners? Mortal sinners? Not on your life! Venial sinners die on the battlefields, Jimmy, to satisfy the pride, greed and corruption of mortal sinners. They are out to protect their interests at little cost to them, but at the ultimate cost to us, our lives. Mortal sinners create patriotic slogans to exploit venial sinner pride. I'm going to Boone now to bring back a troop train of amputee veterans from the South Pacific, a whole train load of amputees, do you hear what I'm saying? The greatest sins these young men ever committed were all venial sins. Venial sinners' interests are never on the table.

"No one, Jimmy, ever gets to the top of anything without a huge capacity for sinning, and I'm not talking about venial sins. Sinning is one of the basic skills required of high rollers. Most of us don't have the foggiest notion how to be mortal sinners." He examines the flaming tip of his cigarette, and taps the ash off. "Maybe we have too much conscience."

"But that's not what I learn in school."

"I know. School is not about life. That's too bad. They teach you all about heaven and hell, but our lot as venial sinners is all about Purgatory, never about hell. Our hell is on earth. Mortal sinners have to wait for theirs." Perhaps recalling his Baltimore catechism, he laughs so heartedly that a heehaw erupts from his diaphragm. "I doubt if most of these bastards ever make it to Purgatory."

* * * * *

Crime existed, but on such a small scale that a community today would consider Clinton statistically crime free. The Clinton County Sheriff's Department had a chief and three deputies while the city police department had a chief and fifteen officers to serve and protect a community of more than 33,000. The salary for sheriff Ky Petersen's in 1945 was $2,200 with deputy sheriffs Chris Stamp, Jim Gaffey and Ed Mulligan drawing $2,000 annually. The city police salaries were comparable.

People in Clinton, Iowa listened to KROS radio, read The Clinton Herald, Davenport Democrat, or Des Moines Register, checked books out of the Clinton or Lyons library, or read Look, Life, Saturday Evening Post, or Time magazine, hung out at one of fifty-some neighborhood taverns with friends, cheered on their favorite team in the Industrial Baseball League, or played on their company's softball team, swam at the Clinton Municipal Pool, had family outings at Eagle Point Park, parked their cars on Main Avenue in Lyons or Fifth Avenue in Clinton on a Friday or Saturday night, and watched the shoppers, attended concerts at Clinton High, Lyons High, St. Mary's High, Mt. St. Clare Academy or Our Lady's of Angels Academy, attended one of the high school teams' football, basketball or

American Legion baseball games. Clintonians played bingo at their local church or attended a movie at "Bank Night" held at the Capitol, Rialto, Strand, or Lyons Theatre. Women wore their best to Sunday church services with more than fifty different churches in which to worship. Men had their private card games, played pool at Clinton Billiards, bowled at Clinton Recreation Lanes, or Odeon, fished in one of the many sloughs and lagoons of the Mississippi. During duck season, several sportsmen maintained permanent blinds on the river's hundred or more islands, or shot pheasants in Clinton County's countryside. Many regulars made it a habit to have breakfast once a week with cronies at Reynolds Cigar & Restaurant. Their wives preferred lunch downtown at Ford Hopkins Tea Room, while their kids hung out at Marcucci's, or Rastrelli's candy emporiums, or at the soda fountain at Milo John's Walgreen Drug Store. It was a community very much involved in the war, but still able to keep the war at arm's length.

Some went dancing at the Modernistic Ballroom to the music of Wayne King, Jan Garber, Ted Fiorito, Clyde McCoy, Dick Jurgens, Sammy Kay and Lawrence Welk, or hung out at the Am Vets, Eagles, Elks, Legionnaire Club, Izaac Walton League at Ikes Peak, the German Club at the Odeon in Lyons, June Van Meter post of the American Legion, or Turner's Athletic Club. Then, there was the Masonic and Moose Lodges, the spiritualist camp at Mount Pleasant Park, which overlooks Bluff Boulevard, the Women's Club downtown, the 18-hole golf course at the Clinton Country Club and the Kiwanis 9-hole links, where many Courthouse Tigers first learned to play golf with special proficiency, especially David Cavanaugh and Phil Leahy.

Seemingly, ninety percent of all men and ninety-nine percent of all women smoked. Women had clubs, church bizarres, and played cards and talked about their kids, husbands, or other loved ones in military service. In the main, men and many women on the home front worked long hours in Clinton factories, which were running at 150 percent of capacity in support of the war effort. With World War II victory on the horizon, the tempo was beginning to change to a new rhythm and momentum. It was not about to return to the lackadaisical insouciance of the prewar years but to a new kind of frenzy and collective hysteria. On the cusp of a world about to explode in maddening change, I was in the sixth grade at St. Patrick's School. Things were happening to and in me that were increasingly confusing. Looking back, I realize it was a remarkable time to be alive.

* * * * *

Sister Mary Gertrude is our new teacher. She is much younger than the other nuns and doesn't look fully in charge. I tower over her. She has an open tranquil face that resembles the statue of the Blessed Virgin in church, and seemingly has the same quiet strength of my mother. Her eyes are bright and inquiring behind rimless glasses. There is a touch of mystery about her. She has alabaster skin with a straight nose, strong chin, white even teeth, and full lips, and is petite like my mother with a similar incongruous round face for such a slender form. She starts the class with no preamble simply asking each of us to tell a little about ourselves. I follow Bobby Witt, who stands and says, "I live across from the courthouse, play baseball there, like to play basketball here." He shrugs his shoulders, "That's about it," and sits down. He says nothing about his parents or his brother. Sister nods to me and I stand up.

"Bobby is the best athlete and most popular boy in our class. He's smart, too, and has a big brother who's a gunner on an Air Force bomber. His father works at the railroad refueling station across the tracks from the ballpark, and his mother makes the best apple pie this side of heaven."

Bobby glares at me. I look away. This non sequitur is sufficient to ruffle Sister. She takes her hankie out cleans her glasses, then says in a calm voice. "Now what exactly does that . . ." she looks at the class roster sheet, "James Fisher, have to do with you?"

"Nothin ster."

"Nothing, Sister."

"Nothing, Sister."

"So what about you James?"

"I'm Irish, my da works on the Chicago & North Western railroad. He's a passenger brakeman. My mother is one of the prettiest women in Clinton. I have a little brother and sister in school here with a little sister at home." I move to sit down. She motions with her hands for me to remain standing. I oblige.

"Why do you call your father da? I'm curious. I've never heard that expression before."

"I don't know. Guess he likes me to call him that. Maybe its because we're Irish." I shake my head. "Never thought 'bout it."

"What is it like to be Irish? I thought you were American." Everyone roars with laughter. My face reddens. Here I am trying to make an impression and already I've fouled up. I feel humiliated. "Now children that's enough. James is an Irish American, aren't you James?"

"Yes ster, I mean yes Sister."

"James share some Irish with us." With that simple statement, she defuses the taunting and erases my rancor.

"Like what?"

"Like anything."

"There's this poem my da likes to sing when he's in a good mood. Don't know it by heart but it goes something like this, Oh patty dear and did you hear the news that's going 'round, the Shamrock is forbid by law to grow on Irish ground, St. Patrick's Day no more will keep, its colors can't be seen, 'cause there's the terrible bloody law against the wearing of the green . . . something like that."

"Bravo!" she says, and claps her hands, motioning the others to join her. They do so half-heartedly. I look to her to see if I can sit down, she smiles, and nods. As I sit, she adds, "You'll have to tell us more about your Irish in the future."

At recess, Dick Morris says, "Fisher you're something. Already you're snowing Sister." He laughs and so does Bobby Witt. Dick feigns Sister's voice in a squeaky falsetto, "James you'll have to tell us more about being Irish in the future."

"Fish why don't you try that con on Father," Donny Costello says poking me in the ribs, "maybe he'll make you an altar boy."

Oh! That hurts and Donny knows it. "Just kiddin Fish, I know how bad you want that. Maybe this year, huh?" Donny's a good kid and means well so I just shrug my shoulders. I've all but given up hope of being an altar boy, yet it's embarrassing to be the only boy in the class that isn't one.

"Made it up didn't you, Rube?" Bobby beams, changing the subject. He turns to the guys. "He's always making stuff up like that."

"Don't try that on us Rube. It's a con job," says Dick Morris, "Bobby's right. You're a comedian."

"I think you mean chameleon," corrects John Knoerschild, "meaning he's adept at changing his colors as the situation demands." Everyone finds that terribly funny, surprising John with his new found popularity.

Bobby touches his index finger to his lips, and strikes the air. "Score one for John."

"John, John, John," goes the chant as recess ends.

"Regarding the iambic pentameter of the Irish poem," John continues as we return to the classroom, "James didn't make it up. Worse than that," he pauses in his perfect diction for dramatic effect, "he bastardized it."

"Who cares?" cracks Super Halbach. "It sure put Sister in a good mood."

Super was right. The afternoon lesson on geography was turned into a John Knoerschild theater. John enlightened us that Saint Patrick did not convert Ireland to Christianity, but organized the Christianity that already existed among Irish peasants. It was the princesses that remained pagans. His great accomplishment was the conversion of Irish kingdoms to the Christian faith. Listening, it was hard to imagine John a boy like the rest of us. He was obviously not Irish, but seemingly omniscient. It was rumored his ancestors were Jewish and converted to Catholicism. I wonder now if he knew as much about Judaism, a religion my mother favored, as he did about the Irish. "If I wasn't Catholic," my mother was fond of saying, "I'd be Jewish. Jews have steel in their spine like Catholics and don't waffle on divorce or family." As a boy, John looked remarkably like the English don and philosopher, Isaiah Berlin. I made this startling connection with a picture of the youthful Berlin in Michael Ignatieff's 1998 book *Isaiah Berlin: A Life*. Berlin was Jewish and escaped from Russia early in the 20th century. John didn't escape from anywhere, but spoke with the same authority I have come to appreciate in Berlin. I would have traded my athleticism in a minute for half of John's brains.

Sister used our enthusiasm for the topic of Ireland to weave geography into the discussion and place the subject in our lives. "I have a confession to make," she says as the session ends. We all look with anticipation. "I was born in St. Patrick, Missouri, but didn't live there long, a place I'll bet you've never heard of." We shake our heads. "Well, it doesn't matter. It doesn't exist anymore, but I do." We all laugh. What a marvelous way of getting us back on track with a bit of disclosure.

Sister Gertrude was a good teacher and the honeymoon was to last well into the winter. It was getting to the Davenport diocesan tournament time and Bobby Witt and I were on the eighth grade basketball team along with Bill Christiansen, a seventh grader, Jim Junker and Tom Clark, both eighth graders. We were having the final practice before the Davenport Diocese Tournament. Coach Dean Burridge, who was finishing up his starring role at Clinton High as a junior, was holding the final practice that night to drill us on our plays. All I could think about throughout the day was basketball. I could smell the basketball, feel it in my hands, hear it bouncing on the hardwood floor, then feel it leaving my hands in an arc and swishing through the net. I could see myself getting the rebound with seconds to go, passing to Bobby and watching him lay in the winning basket. Each subject was dreamlike. The last period was an oral drill of vocabulary. Euphoric in anticipation of basketball practice while having a special love of words – I read the dictionary for fun -- I was expansive, almost deliriously happy. I'd raise my hand for each word but Sister ignored me every time. I was getting bored, anxious waiting for people to respond and suddenly found myself blurting out,

"Eccentric means to be different, odd, not in harmony with others."

"Are you defining the word, James, or describing yourself?" Laughter follows. She looks sternly at me, her expression not touching her eyes, which appear clouded by streaks of gray like wisps of smoke. Were I more perceptive, I would have known I was in trouble. Sister rose to her feet and strolled languidly to the window and affected to study the drab houses across the street. There was freak thunder about, and the indefinable smell of tension that precedes an Iowa winter rain. Without turning to the class, she speaks, "James do you remember my instruction at the beginning of this drill?"

"Yes, ster."

"Yes, Sister."

"Yes, Sister."

"Which was?"

"Wait to be called on."

"Exactly. Now can you restrain yourself?" I say nothing, dropping my glance to the floor. I am upset, but have no idea how this compares to Sister's. "Let us continue. Now this is a word you hear all the time, but probably don't bother to think about, liturgical. Katy Newhouse, how would you define liturgical."

Katy, a pretty girl, stares at Sister Gertrude as if asked to define Einstein's theory of relativity. Everyone looks away including John Knoerschild, which surprises me, another warning sign I missed.

"Liturgical refers to the eucharistic ritual and the defining moment of the Mass," I exclaim with a smile so spare that I know at once I am in trouble, but can't stop myself, "which is the transubstantiation, or the changing of the bread and wine into the body and blood of Christ."

"James I find your impertinence disruptive of the class and disrespectful of me." Sister's anger smoldered within her like an unwholesome fire, her cheeks reddened beyond pink, more like rouge. "I have no other recourse than to hold you after school to write on the board 200 times I will not interrupt my fellow students when they are called on to recite." There is a collective gasp with everyone letting out breath at once. It is unusual for Sister to be so resolute. It is more her style to have a student reconcile bad conduct with a class apology, and little more, but she is not through. "When you have completed that assignment, I want you to sit at your desk and write a 500-word essay of apology to the class and to me, expressing your remorse for being so impolite. Is that clear?" Her eyes narrow as she manages a smile like a crack in old plaster. "I'm very disappointed in you James."

My body shudders as if about to have an epileptic seizure. I rise from my seat without volition. My mind is unable to comprehend my predicament. My anger is like shards of broken glass cutting through my heart. Basketball practice is obliterated! Vision of coach Burridge crushes through my blindness. I hear, "No room for smart asses!" In trouble. Disrespectful to a nun. No tournament trip. Second highest scorer. No matter. Out. Caput. Through. No longer here. Heart races. Blood boils. Anger rises in a heat never felt before.

Beside my desk there is an inanimate collapsible wooden folding chair. I pick it up like it is the object of my fury; raise it above my head, my face on fire, my eyes dots of madness. I look in the direction of the window, to Sister, to my classmates and I see only blackness. Time stops in a freeze frame of tension and chaos.

Sister Gertrude stands speechless, shivering like a thin dog in the cold, hands to her mouth, her face the color of chalk. Violence is not anticipated. Her eyes read madness, what will he do? Throw the chair? At me? Out the window? Oh my God!

Seeing her vulnerable, defenseless, exasperated, something snaps, blinding anger lifts from me like helium gas replaced by deflated fear the taste of rusty knives. Unexpectedly, I'm aware I have a chair in my hands, above my head, embarrassed, I want to say something, tell everyone it's a mistake, it isn't me, it's someone else, this isn't happening, I can explain. But I can't. The chair is placed gently on the floor as I collapse into my seat, fatigued, queasy in a swoon. The heat of the room makes me nauseous. I watch the pat, pat, pat of my own sweat fall on to my desk. I try to say something, but Sister, now in control, extends her hand, palm up, shakes her head. A deep pall pervades the classroom like an indrawn breath. The class is dismissed. We are alone in silence. She stands looking down at me clinically. I am in a seat too small for my big body, looking like a white protoplasmic glob with various diseases at work on the inside. Neither of us have been here before, strangers in a land of primitive emotions with only our souls tethered to 500 million years of violence and survival on this hostile planet.

Is violence genetic? Cultural? Life's primal expression? Violence was when I destroyed the school door, when my da broke all the dishes, when he knocked my uncle through the door. We call it temper, but could it be more primitive? Creative destruction? Destructive creation? To kill or be killed psychologically is that the question? Anger has been more friend to me than enemy, more galvanizer to action than not. I've come to know how to use anger to survive. It all started with how Sister handled this incident.

I go to the board and start writing my lines. We still have not spoken to each other. She leaves the room and comes back with her black shawl over one shoulder, her black gloves in her hand, ready to return to the Mount. I plan to write the sentence 300 times, or 100 more than she asked, but I don't mention this.

"The janitor knows you're here. He'll clean around you. So, it'll be up to you to turn off the lights. Good night James." I nod. She leaves. No lecture. I feel worse. It is dark outside when I finish the lines, and start my essay. Writing comes naturally and it goes more quickly than the lines. The janitor has been here and gone, and now I've four handwritten pages in less than a half hour. I count the words on one page, 150. That makes about 600 words. I quickly reread what I've written. It's good, really good. I think she'll like it, may even save it. God, how arrogant I am!

My confidence regained, I bounce down the back steps of the school and hear a basketball bouncing in the gym, with the lights on. That's odd. I stop, curious, open the door. Coach Burridge is alone shooting around. I watch him drive to the basket, dribbling with total control of the ball. He leaves the floor, the ball rolling off the tip of his fingers, kisses the backboard gently, then spins through the net. Poetry in motion. His dark hair in Greek-like curls frames a broad brooding forehead. He has a pinched, rosebud mouth that pleads and denies. His eyes, round with hurt, are haunted by thick eyebrows that conceal a private horror he will never share. He wears a judicious frown on his face as he looks up to see me. The moment is etched in my mind like a painting these many years later.

"Been waiting for you. Hear you're in trouble."

I nod, relieved that he knows. Hope rises in me like heat from a radiator. Am I getting a second chance? Reading my face he quickly dashes that expectation.

"You'll not be going to Davenport," he says matter-of-factly, "but I think you know that." I try to meet his eyes, but can't. My face is expressionless, my body straight as a stick, yet I feel crushed. "But that's not why I've stayed to see you." I feel a lecture coming on. He understands my weariness.

"You've come a long way since fourth grade, but I've seen these demons in you before. Maybe it's because I'm fighting them myself." He tosses the ball to the other end of the court. It bounces against the stage and starts rolling back toward us, then stops at center court. "Anyway, I hope you've learned something. Fisher, there're good demons and bad demons. Good demons serve you. Bad demons destroy you. No point in trying to get rid of them because you can't. They're part of you. If you want to be successful as an athlete, you'd better know what demons are in charge. That's all I've got to say."

Coach doesn't wait for a reply. Grabs the ball, walks away in that slightly stooped forward walk of his, hits the lights, puts the basketball away, and leaves. I follow. The door locks behind us. He goes toward the front of the school, and I out the back and down the alley, passing Franny Hendrickson's house where I can smell dinner cooking, realizing I could eat a horse.

* * * * *

Walking to school the next day with Bobby, there is no mention of the incident, my missing practice, or my writing of lines. He has a little carry on bag with him as the team is going by car from school to Davenport. I break the silence.

"Who you riding with?"

"I think Billy Christiansen's dad."

"You think? You don't know?"

"Well, yeah, with him."

"Bobby, it's okay. I screwed up. I know that." I give him a soft poke in the arm. "Score a hundred points."

He laughs. It's clear he didn't know what to expect from me, like I might be some kind of ogre. God!

"Coach Burridge was really upset with you. Said if it was up to him he'd have expelled you. Said there was no excuse for you acting like a moron." How could I tell Bobby about my conversation with coach after that?

"You going to talk to Burridge?" His eyebrows curl like a question mark.

"Yeah if I get a chance," I reply, holding back for some reason. One of my da's homilies pops into my head. People never tell the same story twice. How could they? They are one person here and another person there, one person now another person then. Plus people say one thing and mean another. If that weren't bad enough, they tell a different story about the same thing every time they tell it. So, take anything you hear with a grain of salt. People lie because they wouldn't know the truth if it bit them in the ass. You got to always read between the lines. That's what is really meant. Coach

260

Burridge talked to the team one way and to me another. But that's okay.

"What will Father Finefield do when he finds out?"

I stop walking. God! Never thought about Father! Hits me like a punch in the stomach, forcing me to bend over in pain as if with a side ache. Think I'm going to throw up. Brace myself against a tree.

"You okay?"

"No!"

"What's wrong?"

"Nothing. Everything. Don't talk to me!" Bobby is never in trouble. Everyone likes him including Father. How would he understand? My whole world is collapsing around me. Will I be allowed to stay in school – maybe; could I be expelled – yes; do I have any chance to be an altar boy – no; will Father delight in making my life miserable -- absolutely. I feel awful.

"The shit will hit the fan when Father finds out! Know that Rube?"

God! Will he not let up? "Yes, I know that Bobby." How could someone so kind be so cruel? That bothers me, but not as much as hearing Bobby swear. Bobby never swears! Never! I don't know what to think, say. He looks so serious, so concerned, and he doesn't seem to realize saying . . . shit . . . hurts me. Anybody. But not Bobby!

"Bobby, it's going to be all right. Really! Wait and see! Everything will be just like always, except I won't be playing tomorrow." I laugh. Bobby joins me. It must be the Irish con in me that waxes banal when nothing else works, but it does get Bobby back to being Bobby.

"Think so?"

Actually, I wasn't thinking. Was shutting down. Did wonder what he thought of me now. What could he say? I'll never know. Bobby draws a line and words never cross it. We are at school and panic shakes me as if tottering on the edge of a cliff. Would Father pull me out of class, draw me aside with principal Sister Flavian, and say, "James Fisher I think you should find yourself another school." I can see the delight in his eyes and the relief in his face as he says these words. Would Sister Flavian look up at me with hurt eyes, and say, "I'm sorry James I think it is best for everyone."

It didn't happen! Nor did Sister Gertrude ever bring up the subject again! Silence covered the classroom as I entered, settling around me like fine dust. And then it vanished, dispelled with the normal chatter of another day.

St. Patrick's basketball team lost in the first round to Sacred Heart of Davenport 28 – 16 with Jim Junker scoring half St. Patrick's points. Bobby scored two free throws. The guys came back talking about his ball handling and dribbling. And Burridge said Sacred Heart's coach liked Bobby's aggressive defense.

"The crowd really liked Witt," echoed Jim Junker, "he must have stole the ball a dozen times."

"Three times," quipped Billy Christiansen. "I stole it twice." Billy also scored a basket.

The rest of the scoring was from Tom Clark, who did most of the rebounding. Always modest, he added, "We could have used you Fish."

The star of Sacred Heart was Skip Green, who would go on to play at Davenport Central, make all-state and help coach Paul Moon to consecutive Iowa Scholastic High School Basketball Championships in 1948 and 1949.

* * * * *

The first sign of spring in Clinton is not when the groundhog sees its shadow. It's when the sport pages start to be filled with baseball. On March 31, 1945 The Clinton Herald has the great news that Bobby Dalrymple, all-star shortstop for the Collis Company and 1944 batting champion in the Industrial League is in spring training with the Chicago White Sox at Terre Haute, Indiana and is doing okay. Dalrymple is Clinton's hope of finally having a major leaguer. Hope springs eternal on that front, and it's just around the corner. I am still a student at St. Patrick's by the blessing of the good Sisters of St. Francis, and this spring and summer promise to be quite eventful.

* * * * *

Chapter 17

Spring Eternal

April is the cruellest month, breeding
Lilacs out of the dead land, mixing
Memory, and desire, stirring
Dull roots with spring rain.

--T. S. Eliot

Schick Army Hospital is in full operation in April 1945 with more than 2,000 patients and medical personnel on board. Our two carpenter boarders are still here, why I don't know. They must fix things that get broken, because the facility is totally constructed and operational. My da says they are "finishing carpenters," whatever that means. The sergeant's girlfriend from Ohio is back, too. Why he doesn't marry her is beyond me. The house still fills up with relatives and friends practically every evening.

263

School is winding down, and courthouse activity is picking up. It feels so strange to replace a basketball with a baseball. A baseball is so small in comparison. You feel as if you could throw it to the moon once it's in your hand, but only Dick Tharp can do that. Everyone is bigger than they were last year. I'm taller than Lyle Sawyer, nearly as tall as Gussie Witt, and not much shorter than Jack Dunmore, who is slightly over six feet. I like being tall, but wish I were a little heavier. I eat like a horse yet only weigh 132 pounds. That's not much on a five-ten frame.

Food is one place my da refuses to cut corners. We eat ground chuck and not hamburger, butter and not margarine, lean roasts and not fatty cuts, and lots of fresh vegetables, mashed potatoes and gravy. He likes whole milk with the cream on top, white bread and freshly sliced lunchmeat and oatmeal and cream of wheat instead of dry cereals. His favorite fruits are apples and oranges, so we always have them on hand, apples from our trees in season, and Florida oranges. He likes fried potatoes and hot dogs, but they don't agree with him, so they're out. Fowl is not a favorite, not chicken, turkey, goose or duck. So we often have roast beef, mashed potatoes and gravy on Thanksgiving and Christmas. He also loves grilled cheese sandwiches and hot tomato soup, peanut butter and jelly sandwiches, and buttered bread sprinkled with sugar.

The only time we as a family ever eat out is confined to vacations, and then mainly in cafeterias. Snacking is not a Fisher thing either. However, most kids in the neighborhood hit the A&W Root Beer stand across from the courthouse for a snack, or ride their bikes down to Rastrelli's or Marcucci's for a cherry coke, CMP sundae, or chocolate malt. Not me. For one, I don't own a bicycle, for another, I've never developed a taste for carbonated drinks. I like ice cream for sure, but what I like especially is being alone.

Since my da is a railroad man, I like to go to the railway café in the depot and watch people coming and going. Max and Mable, the cook and waitress there, know me as "Red." They never seem to mind that I never get on a train. I usually time my visits to see the 11:30 train. I order a cup of coffee and Mable always suggests I try a bacon and egg sandwich, an omelet, or a grilled cheese. Once I had Max make me a grilled cheese and it was out of this world. The cheese melted in my mouth and the toasted bread tasted like fried butter. It costs a quarter. I seldom have that much money, so I make do with a cup of coffee, which costs a nickel. The wonder is how this place stays open. Few people coming off trains or waiting for trains ever come in. Mable places my cup in front of me as I sit on a counter stool, and pours the dark rich liquid into my cup with a kind of sublime reverence, the aroma steaming up and tickling my nostrils with mellow intoxication. I love coffee and have been drinking it since I was five. She returns the Pyrex pot to the burner, and then begins to wash glasses behind the counter. I drink my coffee wondering who could have dirtied all that silver and glassware she's washing.

Beneath my feet, as I put the cup to my lips, I feel a faint tremor in the floor telling me the 11:30 is coming in and will soon be throbbing on the tracks. It is a passenger train. Normally, I would be sitting on a bench outside looking at people through the train's clouded windows. As it slowly rolls into the station, I study the faces as they pass by. Some appear sleepy, others bored, some bent over books and newspapers, everyone looks exhausted. I haven't finished my coffee so I observe what I can through the café window. It isn't much, just the loading of a few large crates by two men in gray uniforms and red caps on a flat bed freight handler, then disappearing from sight. Two soldiers get off, and one civilian gets on right in front of me. With the train now at a complete stop, I make out the faces in the car directly across, which is heavily shadowed. They seem unaware that the train has stopped. I wave and no face turns toward me. This is also a mail train, so the stationmaster, who always seems to appear out of nowhere like a genie, is busy with the mailbags, pushing them somewhere down the platform that I can't see. In a matter of minutes, the train lurches forward once, then again, trying to get underway, finally chugs out with no announcement of its arrival or departure. The two soldiers who got off look tired in their crumpled uniforms. It saddens me that no one is there to meet them. They don't seem to mind, shaking hands and departing on foot in opposite directions.

Now it is quiet enough to hear the tick of the regulator clock on the café wall. Mable goes back to the counter and stands there, hands in pockets, still looking out at the empty tracks. She looks pensive, a new word I learned and immediately associated with my mother, and

265

now Mable. She then returns to her post at the end of the counter, looking out the window, smoking a cigarette. A flare of sunlight opens like a fan across the glass and lights her apron as if it were white flame. I drink my coffee and wonder what she's thinking. It seems as if her thoughts rise to the ceiling with the smoke of her cigarette. Her left hand supports her right elbow, as she holds the cigarette close to her lips as if to embolden her courage. Courage? Hmm, I wonder.

She would think me crazy if I told her I could read her mind, which of course I can't, but I sense her mood. I have that knack. I don't know where it comes from. Something is troubling her, I'm sure, and it's written in her cigarette smoke. Courage comes to mind. I wonder if a person can be courageous without knowing it. My mind falls back to an earlier time. I see the hard angry face of my da, the face he showed when I split the wood of my sled (was I six or seven?) when he wouldn't fix it and I tried to fix it myself. He picked up the hammer and threw it at me. The hammer missed but I looked at him defiantly without budging. Was that courage? I don't think he intended to hit me, but was frustrated in not being good at fixing things. Surely, there must be courage other than physical courage. Perhaps no particular act is itself courageous. Gliding down the icy hill at breakneck speed above the courthouse on Hoot Owl Hollow would hardly be courageous for an Olympic skier, but for a clumsy novice like me it might be. Courage must be relative, like beauty. Recalling my defiant eyes looking into his agitated face of blazing anger, knowing that his anger was meant for me, being immaterial whether the hammer struck me or not, was perhaps a courageous act, not simply a display of physical courage, more likely an expression of mental resolve that I would stand my moral ground whatever the consequences.

Mable comes back and refills my cup with coffee. I smile and thank her.

"You live 'round here?" she asks as she pours.

"By the courthouse," I say turning my head in that direction.

"Like trains, do you?" she smiles broadly showing uneven teeth with a gold filling on a front tooth.

"Yes, I like trains, but I like this café more, mainly because it's quiet."

266

"That's strange coming from a boy." She studies me suspiciously, plunging her hands back into her apron. "Would think this is the last place you'd want to be."

This puzzles me. Why would she say that? "I like being alone around people, like here," I confess, and then grin sheepishly. "It's kind of like being in church without hearing all the coughing, if that makes any sense." Her expression tells me it doesn't, so I continue. "My da is a passenger brakeman. Sometimes I meet his train coming from Boone. Waiting one day," I hesitate her eyes appearing somewhat glazed over, but decide to continue anyway, "is how I found this place, liked it, so I return whenever I can, especially when . . ." I stop again. Mable's look is unsettling. "Not making much sense, am I?" I force a smile.

"You never meet a stranger, do you?"

"What do you mean?"

"You're talking so easily to me and you don't know me, that's what l mean."

"But I see you all the time. I know your name's Mable. That you call me Red, but that's not my name. My name's Jimmy, Jimmy Fisher."

"Well, I'll call you Jimmy from now on."

"Can I ask you something?"

"Yes."

"Why are you so sad?" It has unintended consequences. She turns from me, and pulls her apron up and wipes her liquid green eyes. I never thought a person could be so pretty with her back to you, but she is. Her hair is the color of an orange sunset in a mannish cut exposing a sun burnt neck. She has slender shoulders and a short back tapering to a tiny waist. Bravely, she turns and looks me in the eye.

"Were you not so young I would find that cruel." Her eyes are red and mascara drips down her cheeks.

"I didn't mean to hurt you."

"I know. I know." She tries to smile. "But you did just the same."

We look into each other's eyes. There is pain in hers. Concern in mine. A feeling rises in me that I don't understand. I feel queasy as

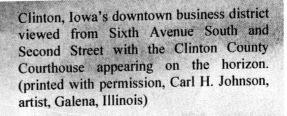

Clinton, Iowa's downtown business district viewed from Sixth Avenue South and Second Street with the Clinton County Courthouse appearing on the horizon. (printed with permission, Carl H. Johnson, artist, Galena, Illinois)

if I could faint. She puts a hand on mine and it must blister hers as she withdraws it quickly.

"Are you all right?"

"Yes," I lie. I want to press my head in her bosom and feel her warmth. I want to hold her close to me, why I don't know. She senses my edginess.

"Well, I must get back to work." With that, she moves to the other end of the counter, picks up a cloth and rigorously wipes the counter that's already sparkling clean.

Guilt races through me, and I don't understand why. What have I done wrong? Is she mad at me? I want to ask her, but my courage fails. I don't think I'll come here for a while.

*   *   *   *   *

I decide to walk home rather than take the bus, so I head up Third Street and decide at the bridge at Eighth Avenue South to walk over to Second Street and take the more scenic route through downtown. It's longer, but there is more stuff to see, and the courthouse is always on the horizon as it is centered on the street. I walk past Marccuci's and smell the mixed aroma of roasting peanuts, frying hamburgers, and brewing coffee. I'm not hungry as my stomach is knotted with confusion. I look in the transparent door of the Clinton National Bank and wonder if I'll ever have any money, past Reynolds's and the Clinton Cigar Store and smell the sweet blend of tobaccos, past Van Allen's and look at the splendidly dressed mannequins in spring fashions in the store's windows, on past Boegel's Clothier, then Rastrelli's and am hit with another whiff of roasted peanuts, surprised in not being tempted to purchase a dime bag, but my need is not for food. My eyes glide across the street past the Strand Theater, Bender's Music Shop, and the magazine shop next door. I pass Becker's Café, Burken Brothers Clothier, Beil's Studio, and am just about to cross Second Avenue North with Haas Grocery directly ahead, when I spot the most beautiful woman I have ever seen. She is about to cross the street to my side at the corner.

For a moment, I stop dead in my tracks and just gape at her. She is as cool as ice cream as her body dances to the rhythm of her smile. I can't believe my eyes. Can anyone be so beautiful? She walks toward me because I am now at the corner in her line of sight. No longer pretending to look elsewhere, I feast my eyes on her totally, wondering if she's an apparition. Her jet-black eyebrows are arched in curious pleasure seemingly enjoying my catatonia. She has hair the color of coal and the deepest black eyes I've ever seen, which sparkle like diamonds. A long straight nose is tipped with delicate nostrils and divides her face in perfect symmetry. Her cheeks are rosy with prominent cheekbones displayed in a whimsical smile, encompassed by rich red lips framing perfect white teeth, like a dental ad in *The Saturday Evening Post*. She puts her tongue between her teeth and looks at me teasingly as she approaches.

"Naughty boy, didn't your mother ever teach you not to stare?"

Before I can answer, she closes the distance between us. I am suffocating. The air is perfumed with her aroma, but it is her body that is disturbing. My eyes caress her bosom. She has a chest you could rest a book on, and her tight red sweater is so daringly cut to reveal deep cleavage. I can hardly breathe. The sweater angles down to a wasp like waist and continues uninterrupted into a jet-black skirt that hugs her hips like another skin. Her womanly hips dance to their own rhythm as she walks. They talk their own language. I notice her legs are shaped with bulging calves that splay out the way a baseball bat does, then like a bat, tapering to incredibly delicate ankles that match a bat's grip. She wears flamingly red patent leather high heels that match her scarlet sweater. Now abreast of me, she breaks her smile into a glorious salutation.

"Hi there, handsome, how are you?"

"Finnnne," I say, wishing I didn't stutter.

Momentarily, she takes me in from head to toe, then says, "Bye now!" and waves me off touching her hand to her lips and blowing me a kiss. My face is on fire. Cruelly, she breaks the spell and destroys the moment, heading with the same leisurely walk toward downtown. I still do not move. I can't keep my eyes off her retreating figure. How could anyone look equally beautiful from every angle? Her shoulder length jet-black hair flipped up at the ends bounces off her shoulders as she walks, with her long slender neck winking at me with each stride. I wonder how anyone with such slender shoulders and arms can support such a gorgeous bosom and still walk erect. A shoulder strapped red purse toys with me, too, as it passes back and forth through her left arm, while her tiny waist twists ever so slightly as the cheeks of her behind move up and down with each step of her pumps. Those legs! Beautiful as she is, her legs are heavenly. I feel as if in a swoon just watching her calves and nothing else. I have an itch I've never experienced before, the itch that I felt if only briefly with Mable. This is not right. What's happening? I'm a boy and she's a woman. She's got to be at least twenty something, all grown up, and I'm . . .

I yell to her back. "I'm seventeen going on eighteen."

Without turning her head, but erupting into a joyous chuckle, "Of course you are."

Humiliated, and angry that God gave me such a baby face with this big body, I stand there watching her disappear down the street wondering if I have committed a mortal sin. If I told Bobby Witt what I saw, he'd laugh at me. Will I have to tell this in confession? How will I know? Am I a voyeur? Came across that word when I was studying the "v's" in my dictionary: one who seeks sexual stimulation by visual means. Is that what I'm doing? Not sure what "sexual stimulation" means, but have a strange feeling I'm guilty of it. I wonder if the lady in red and black sees me as disgusting. I feel unclean. Terrible.

Why did I make myself older? Did I believe I could fool her because I'm tall? How stupid! Anyone can see I'm just a kid. What would I have done if she had encouraged me? I don't want to think about it. I touched her body with my eyes. I'll admit to that. So is that what's troubling me? Did I sin doing that? If I did, I don't know what sin it is. I only know I shouldn't, wouldn't, can't. I don't look at girls my own age that way. Why? Is it because they don't have any shape to them, all straight up and down? They don't even have butts and they're flatter in the chest than I am. Their legs look like sticks stuffed into shoes. I know in time God will whittle these sticks into some shape. Then there are their faces, full of freckles, noses spread out like putty, eyes too small or too large, too close together or too far apart, and they always have that dumb expression on their faces, I know what you're thinking! They don't have a clue anymore than I do about them. I'm convinced they practice flirting in the mirror. They walk around with that knowing smile on their faces as if I'm thinking about them. Fact is, I don't know what I'm thinking.

Shazam! I remember the magazine shop I passed earlier. I feel a surge of excitement -- nudist magazine *Sunshine & Health*. That's what I need. I retrace my steps downtown, dash across the street at McKinley & Hummelgaards, sprint down to the magazine shop, slip into the store, grab a Captain Marvel comic, then head for the section displaying adult magazines with *Sunshine & Health* on the top shelf easily within reach. I study the nude pictures. There are naked women and naked men of all ages, naked children, too. People are frolicking in the water, playing on sandy beaches, lounging in canvas chairs, playing badminton, volleyball, and even tennis. Some are sitting in their living rooms reading, preparing meals in the kitchen, or sitting around a dinner table eating, naked! Disgusting! Naked people are not nearly as interesting as I thought they'd be. Certainly not as exciting as the beautiful lady in red and black. What a wonder she is! Thinking of her again makes my heart race. It must take courage to walk around naked. People look horrible without clothes. Come to think of it I don't look too good myself with my dinger hanging down, my bony shoulders, naked ribs, and my pelvic bones sticking out. Somewhere I read, "Clothes make the man." Well, they must make the woman, too, because I can't imagine the woman in red and black looking anything like this naked. I wonder if people are disappointed when they get married and see each other naked for the first time. Something to think about.

Daydreaming, I'm startled. "Hey kid! That's against the law! This is the adult section. Can't you read the sign, adults only?" I gently put the magazine down with the Captain Marvel cover showing, obviously not fooling him. "Ought to turn you into the police. Give you a record. Want that? How you going to explain that to your parents, huh? Now get your ass out of my store."

Thank God there're no customers. Won't be coming back here soon either. Maybe he'll be dead when I do. Looks at least forty with triple circles under his eyes, jaundiced skin, a purple spider web of broken blood vessels mottled on his bulbous nose, and silver hair slicked back with gel, giving it a yellow tinge to match his stained teeth. Ugly!

* * * * *

As I stumble home, my heart is still pounding. What's going on? It started lately and won't let up. It's not as if I'm asking for all this new tension. It happens! I mean, if anyone likes a tension-free existence, it's me. That's why I like being alone, no one crowding my space, telling me what is or what's not, just going about my merry way with nobody the wiser. Yet, might be something terribly wrong with me.

The distance between the magazine shop and the courthouse dissolves as I find myself trudging up my front steps without remembering a single thing between there and here. I open the front door, oh no! It starts all over again. The devil must be resting in the middle of my head. The sergeant's girlfriend is ironing her pinafore just off the living room in nothing but her bra and panties. I stand in the doorway in shock as if in the glare of a car's headlights. I've never seen a person undressed, not my mother or even my sister. The bra barely covers her nipples and her panties are sheer and transparent. I can see a blond mound of hair in her pubic region like in the *Sunshine & Health* Magazine. It looks thick and coarse.

"Hi, Jimmy, we didn't expect you home so early." Obviously. She takes in my stupid look as if to say, *Haven't you ever seen a naked woman before?* I am struck speechless. Her smile says, *Feast your eyes as long as you like as I'll soon be dressed.*

Covering my embarrassment by looking at the floor, noticing the carpet needs vacuuming, I say, "Wwwherrrre's everybody?"

"Well, my boyfriend's at the base, your mother's at Cramm's picking up some groceries, Patsy's out playing with Joan Darymple, Janice's taking a nap upstairs, and God only knows where your little brother Jackie is."

"What about da?"

"Got called on the road. Left hours ago."

"Apologize for catching me like this, but nobody was here, and well, hell…"

"IIIIttt'sss okay, rrreaallly."

Quickly, she pulls the dress off the ironing board, throws it over her head in a ballerina like move, and her breasts grow full to fill the flat surface with their pouting eminence. She places her hands again on her hips, and looks at me provocatively, "How'd I look?"

"GGGGooood." Actually, fantastic.

"Good?" she says with arched eyebrows, "That's all?" I want to say delicious, but say instead. "Ttthhe dress fittts you weeelll, pretty toooo." She's a good-looking woman, not beautiful like the lady in red and black. I've seen her looking at me before, smiling nicely, and feeling embarrassed. She's doing it now, then ruins it by picking up a cigarette, lighting it, inhaling deeply and blowing smoke through her nostrils. I wonder if she smokes as much as my mother. With the cigarette between her lips, she adjusts the hem of her dress while still talking. Don't women know how obscene this looks, talking with a cigarette dangling from their lips? I see an ashtray on the ironing board that tells me this is only her second cigarette. Were it my mother the ashtray would be overflowing. Mystery solved.

"Why don't you go in the kitchen and get a glass of milk or something? I have to take this off again and fix the hem."

"OOOkkkay," I say reluctantly. As I go into the kitchen, I still see her bra and panties in my mind. Even the peanut butter and jelly sandwich doesn't erase this. All this stuff today has given me a terrible headache. I think I'm going to be sick. It's cruel to be a boy when every way you turn; women are in your face making you feel a pain you've never felt before. Thank God she's out of sight. Still, stuff dances wildly in my head, sad Mable, the lady in red and black, nudists, now the sergeant's girlfriend. I am exhausted, and need a nap.

Blame it on April showers! Happened because it rained today and we couldn't play ball at the courthouse. Reason I was out walking. Don't get much out of sitting around shooting the breeze, talking baseball, arguing who's the greatest, oiling baseball gloves, playing Dick Crider's baseball game, having deputy sheriff Stamp bring out vintage submachine guns supposedly used by bootleggers like Al Capone during Prohibition, talking to the prisoners, arm wrestling, electric taping coverless baseballs, putting tacks in broken bats and taping them, checking Courthouse Tigers' batting averages, going over individual statistics kept for us by Bob Collins, reading the sport pages of The Des Moines Register, or climbing to the clock tower in the courthouse. None of this appeals to me. Would rather be alone as I was this morning.

"I've a headache," I tell the sergeant's girlfriend, "going to take a nap." I smell her soapy fragrance as I brush past her climbing the stairs to my room. I find no peace there. All I can think of is wasp-like waists and large pouting breasts, soft shoulders, long tapering necks, sensuous smiles, perky faces, and now the flaming hair of the strawberry blond downstairs, whom I hear singing. I'm miserable. She's happy. It's not fair. What's happening to me?

After a restless sleep, I wake with a start. My dinger is hard as a rock. Terrified, I know something must be wrong with me. I go downstairs to the bathroom with a sweater wrapped around my waist to cover my embarrassment. For the longest time I can't pee. My dinger won't let me. It seems the hardness won't go away until it's ready. I wait. I hear her still singing. Must have slept only a few minutes. Finally, I can pee. Once I start I can't stop. I flush for fear she can hear me peeing. I flush again wondering if I will pee forever. Finally, I'm empty, feeling much better. I smile at her as I go back upstairs. She looks radiant with her hair piled on top of her head in a bun. She could do much better than the sergeant that's for sure. I go back to my room, pick up my Classic Comic *Men of Iron,* and read once again how young Myles, although badly wounded, out jousts the hated Earl of Alban, Lord Falworth's bitter enemy, to win the hand of the Lady Alice de Mowbray. I am ecstatic in his triumph.

My dinger is soft and quiet now. I'm naked in bed with the comic in my lap. I lift the comic and look at it. My dinger looks ever so much like the trunk of an elephant with the crown of an eyeless snake thanks to the cruel surgery of circumcision. In any case, it's ugly. I sit upright in my bed looking at my dinger wondering too, if I've committed some kind of sin just observing it, wondering too if it's a mortal sin or a venial sin. I can't wait to talk to Bobby Witt about this new problem.

* * * * *

As we're walking to school Monday, I can't seem to broach the subject. Each day my courage wanes. It's the same all week. Then on Friday, after we've both gone to confession, feeling pure and light headed, I blurt out,

"Bobby, something's terribly wrong with me." I don't tell him about my adventure the past week, but I do add, "I might have an incurable disease. Could be dying."

"Dying? Come on Fisher get real!"

"My dinger gets hard as a rock sometimes. Happens when I'm sleeping. When I'm just standing around doing nothing. Embarrassing to have this bulge in my pants. Happened when I was walking Betty Timmer home from the Knights of Columbus milk bar. Bobby, think I should go to the doctor's?"

"No. It's normal, stupid."

"How do you know?"

"Vern told me." He laughs holding his gut and shaking his head.

"What's so funny?"

"You! You're really stupid, you know that Fisher?"

"So I'm stupid. You've said that before. That doesn't help. What's going on?"

"Had a wet dream yet?"

"A what?"

"Wet dream."

"What's that?"

"You wake up and you've got all kinds of gooey stuff in your shorts."

"That's sickening."

"No, it's not."

"Is that like peeing your pants, wetting the bed?"

"No, it's different."

"How do you know? Has it happened to you?"

"No, not yet, but Vern says it will, so be ready. Told me to write him when it does."

"Why does it happen? You know?"

"Vern says your dinger has a conscience of its own. When it wants to throw up, it will and you can't do anything about it."

"What does that mean?"

"Just what I said. Vern says if you don't pay attention to it, don't stroke it now and then, and let it throw up when you're in charge, it's likely to throw up when you don't expect it to, and that can be embarrassing."

"Dooo yyyyou dddoo thhhat? Ttttoucch it III mmmeaann."

He laughs. "Wouldn't tell you if I did."

"But Bobby that's a mortal sin."

"Who says?"

"The Bible does. It's in the story of Onan, 'bout spilling your seed on the ground."

"I know. Vern says that's just a story in the Bible, says it doesn't count."

"But it does Bobby. You know it does. Bible says we must preserve our seed for marriage."

"Show me where it says that?"

"Maybe I just heard it. Don't remember for sure."

"See! You're not sure. Fisher you're not even interested in girls."

"I know." Bobby doesn't know though how women torment me a hundred years older than I am.

"Vern says it's healthy for your hand to get acquainted with your dinger when it starts to act angry like that. That's why it gets hard. If you don't, you're going to have gooey stuff in your shorts for sure, and how are you going to explain that to your mother when she goes to wash them? Vern says mothers don't want to know about such things. Means their little boy is growing up. And mothers never want to know about that. They put it off as long as they can. That's what Vern says. So giving your dinger a rubdown now and then saves your mother that embarrassment."

That night instead of being comforted by Bobby's words, I'm terribly disturbed. Bobby is so wise and I'm so ignorant. I can't get this stuff out of my head. I sit in bed with the moonlight coming through the window, and look at my dinger. It's at peace at the moment, quiet, just lying there like the head of a snake, clean, natural, not bothering anybody. I don't want to touch it. But I do. Boy! It springs angrily to my touch like a snake snapping at its prey. I can't believe it. I must tie my hands behind my back. I can't do that. What would my mother think if she comes into my room at night while I'm sleeping and sees me that way? I must think pure thoughts.

Why is it I've suddenly noticed women? I still don't notice girls. I'll say a thousand Hail Marys. Her month is just ahead. On the tenth Hail Mary my snake goes miraculously back to sleep and so do I.

* * * * *

The only person I believe who is more ignorant about life than me is John Knoerschild, our class prodigy. I make it a point the following week to walk home with him after school. He seems amused at the prospect, as I seldom interface with him. It's not that I purposely avoid him but rather that I seldom understand what he's talking about, and don't have that much in common with him. So, to make conversation as we walk, I ask him what he's reading. It seems a safe question because he's always reading some book, and for sure, not a comic.

"Herman Melville at the moment," he declares with a kind of aloof disdain.

"Who's he?"

"You've never heard of Melville? Shame on you! He's one of America's greatest authors."

"Really? Where does he live?"

"He doesn't live anywhere. He's dead." John shakes his head, blows a loose hair from his face, obviously having great fun at my expense, but it's okay. I know I'm out of my depth.

"Oh! What's he written?"

"Lots of things. Most people know him for *Moby Dick*, but I prefer *Benito Cereno* and *The Encantadas*, two of his less well-known works."

"Could I understand him you think?"

John stops, puts his index finger to his chin, screws up his face, his horn-rimmed glasses so thick it seems his dark eyes are swimming behind the lenses. "Perhaps."

"Perhaps? Is that a yes?"

"Well, for one, Melville doesn't read like your comics. For another, you're always throwing some kind of ball around," the corners of his mouth turn up, "then again, you show promise." His eyes behind those lenses look like little bicycle wheels racing at dizzying speed. *"Bartleby*! I should have you read Bartleby! Perfect! It'll remind you of your relationship with Father Finefield."

Now I'm curious. "It will? What's it about?"

"You must read it James to find out. I'll tell you this much. It's about a man who refuses to bend to authority and convention." My clueless expression provokes him to add, "He's a man who wanders into a scrivener's office one day and everything for him stops."

"A what office?" I had no idea he had given me a powerful clue in saying "everything for him stops," as I asked the wrong question being thrown by the word "scrivener."

"An office where public documents are copied. That was common in law offices in the 19th century." He shakes his head. "I won't say anymore."

"So, why should I read it?" still persisting.

John removes his glasses, rubs his eyes, then puts his glasses back on. "Melville's a moralist. Morality seems important to you."

Not knowing how to respond to this, I divulge, "*Moby Dick* is in my comics. About a white whale, isn't it?"

"Egads!" John throws his arms up in exaggerated dismay. "James, Moby Dick is not a fantasy comic. Not *Superman*! It's a morality play of good and evil personified in the quest of captain Ahab, yes, to kill a giant white whale, but much more. A comic book! I don't believe it!"

"So I read comics. I don't have books," I say defensively. I don't understand a word of this. It only takes John seconds to go beyond my depth, leaving me feeling silly and stupid. My shoulders slump, as I kick a stone as if it's a football just missing a passing car. My vulnerability doesn't escape John.

"Walk home with me and I'll loan you the book."

"The book?"

"*Bartleby*."

With a little boy pout, I acquiesce. We must look like quite a pair. I'm ten inches taller and forty pounds heavier than John. There's absolutely no chance in hell of asking him about my dinger. He has this magnificent brain, but is fragile, slightly built, and walks bent forward with a loping gate like an old man who must propel himself forward or fall on his face. His bright eyes under those thick lenses are trusting and innocent. Perhaps his dinger sleeps all the time and causes him no anguish. Maybe that's what it's like to be intellectual; the animal in you sleeps all the time. It would be cruel to wake this monster, so, I say, "Okay, let's go."

I'm anxious to see his house. The house is a two-story white Tudor style bungalow with green trim that John says was built the year Calvin Coolidge was assassinated. We enter an ornate living room furnished with a Queen Anne camelback couch and two matching chairs and a Duncan Phyfe furnished dining room. John rattles these names off like a tour guide, pointing to a numbered reprint of Leonardo de Vinci's *The Last Supper* on the living room wall, along with a wooden crucifix blessed by Pope Pius XII. A signed picture of His Holiness is framed in the dining room.

The most commodious room in the house is adjacent to the living room and is beyond ornate. It is spectacular. I've never seen such a room. It is dark and meditative with mahogany paneling and floor to ceiling bookcases on three walls with a large rustic fireplace cut into the east wall. The parquet floor shines with a rich luster complemented by Indian throw rugs. These are colorfully positioned flanking a roll top desk with an Empire chair, and a Steinway piano in the center of the room. A drop-leaf table sits beneath a large bay window, which is piled high with assorted books, magazines and papers. The drapes to this window are pulled, holding out the afternoon western sunlight. Reading lamp stands and black leather chairs are situated in opposite corners with a platform rocker and a world globe on a wooden stand in another. John takes measure of my astonishment.

"We seldom have company," he confesses, "and since the arts are important to us, we spend a lot of time here." Just then John's sister, Marilyn, races into the room. She's a freshman at Mount St. Clare Academy.

"John, can I see you a minute?" John shrugs his shoulders and leaves the room. I hear her voice rise to a piercing shrill. "Not supposed to have anyone in the house, especially when our parents are gone. John, you know that!"

"He's in my class. Wants to borrow a book."

"My God, John! You're not supposed to loan our books. Where's your mind?" The door closes and I don't hear them anymore. I wander about the room.

Beside the drop-leaf table is a small stand with an expensive looking record player and a rack of 78s. Names on the jackets are mostly unfamiliar: Schoenberg, Debussy, Verdi, Mozart, Bach, Beethoven, Wagner, Berlioz, Dvorak, Grieg, Mahler, Vivaldi, Liszt, Schubert, on and on. No Bing Crosby, Frank Sinatra or Glenn Miller, my folks' kind of music.

Browsing through the books I see an eclectic collection on one wall: James Joyce's *Ulysses* and *The Dubliners*, Sherwood Anderson's *Winesburg, Ohio, Collected Poems of Edna St. Vincent Millay, Poetry and Prose of William Blake*, then I spot a collection of

Melville and see the *Bartleby* book. It's a slender leather bound volume in a transparent cellophane jacket with the title *Bartleby The Scrivener* in italics. A picture in the center of the cover is of a roll top desk open with an inkwell and quill pen, displaying a document half written with the author's name at the bottom. I open the book and see that the text is preceded by a portfolio of photographs of lower Manhattan that were taken in the mid-1800s when Melville worked as an officer at the Customs House in New York. The book has the smell, the feel and the texture of age, of a well-cared for and very rare book. I imagine the book is a collector's item and is priceless.

When John returns, I thank him for the tour and say I cannot take the book. His eyes narrow ever so slightly and one corner of his mouth turns down, "Why?"

"John, we both know why," and with that I leave. That library and study has remained a vivid picture of tranquility in my mind and an example of John's reckless generosity. It would be many years before I would read *Bartleby*, a book that still haunts me with its message. Bartleby reached the point beyond despair where there is no longer hope or any appetite for life. I didn't learn anything about my dinger, but I did learn that common sense doesn't always go with brilliance.

* * * * *

This mental confusion is all but forgotten, as it is a sunny Saturday, the second of the month of April 1945, with a good pickup game going at the courthouse when a chartered bus pulls up at the curb. A short man with curly brown hair steps off the bus, and comes over to our game. He is dressed in a crumpled suit, and looks a bit fatigued. He watches our game for several minutes, then says,

"Would you boys possibly do me a huge favor?"

"Depends on what it is," answers Dick Crider boldly with a sly smile.

"My name is Les Brown and my band is playing at the Girl Scout's Annual Ball tonight. We've been on the road for some time. Thought it might be good for the boys in the band to stretch their legs and get a little exercise. Wondered if you boys might let us play some softball with you?"

Crider looks at Bobby Witt. "Sure," Bobby says, "have any equipment?"

"Matter of fact we do," replies the bandleader. "We really appreciate this."

The band members are a delight. They are all ages and sizes with various degrees of athleticism. One fellow has a wooden leg and he pitches for them. Everyone calls me "Red." Phil Leahy, who is one of our best players, is overlooked because of his size. Phil takes it in good humor. Chang Benson, Dick Dunmore, Walt Ferguson, Pooper Cavanaugh, Chuck Holm, Jim Holle, Bobby Witt, and Dick Crider make up our team, along with me. It is great fun with a lot of laughing, kidding, fumbling around, and even a little baseball.

When it's our turn to bat, I notice the bus door is open. A pretty girl is sitting on the steps of the bus smoking. Her legs are crossed and she's humming some song to herself. I walk over to the bus and say "Hi!"

"Hi!" she replies but turns her head aside, obviously not interested in talking. She is a strong athletic looking woman with hair the color of Iowa corn stalks, which curls around her bare freckled shoulders in a strapless sky blue summer frock. Her face is covered with freckles, too, and she has wide rather insolent blue eyes reinforced with a strong but attractive jaw line. She is handsome rather than pretty, her freckles making her look younger than I expect she is. I learn later that her name is Doris Day, that she is from Cincinnati, Ohio, just twenty-one a week ago, and a singer with the band. Several times in the hour we play I look over and see her still sitting in the open doorway, smoking, and seemingly bored to death with the little boy fun she has no recourse but to endure.

That night more than 2,000 Clintonians are present for the dinner-dance held at the Modernistic Ball Room. Les Brown and his Band of Renown are a big hit. But even a bigger hit was Doris Day according to The Clinton Herald. The newspaper said she was besieged with autograph seekers during and after the ball. Reading this, I wondered how she masked her boredom.

* * * * *

If there is anything that can take you out of yourself, it is death. Two deaths also occurred in April 1945, which broke up our games at

283

the courthouse, one was a national tragedy; the other was a neighborhood one. *President Franklin Delano Roosevelt, the nation's 31st president, died on April 12, 1945 in Warm Springs, Georgia of a massive cerebral hemorrhage after complaining of a terrible headache. He celebrated his 63rd birthday only the previous January 30th. My da was on the road when the president died. My mother quickly bundled us up and walked us off to church. I had never seen her so convulsed with sorrow. Father Finefield conducted an evening Mass, and the church was filled beyond capacity, something I had only seen before at Christmas. For the next month, my mother maintained a prayerful vigil in our home for the president's departed soul. We were all expected to be participants. On Friday, April 13, 1945, the day after the president died, we weren't allowed to play, which was difficult for us to understand, especially Jackie who was only eight. We attended Mass again on that Friday morning, and then listened to the radio all day with commentaries from Edward R. Murrow and others on what this loss meant to the national war effort. Murrow's voice was soothing but his words were laced together with meaningless jargon. I didn't want him to stop talking, and yet he didn't reach my heart. Vice President Harry S. Truman of Missouri was sworn in as president on Friday. My mother was horrified at the thought of this "lightweight" taking the place of her president. "God help us now," she kept repeating.*

Meanwhile, the United States Ninth Army, according to The Clinton Herald, was only 45 miles from Berlin. I thought this news would cheer her up, but she waved me away with her cigarette. It seemed strange to me for a person to be so sad about a person she had never met and didn't know. This strangeness was compounded when my da came off the road, and he was equally morose. We had to be as quiet as church mice around them for what seemed forever. I swore I'd never get emotional like them.

That all changed with Polly Gore. I knew and liked her. One day we were playing at the courthouse when somebody yelled, "Little Polly was hit by a car!" Polly lived at 506 North Third Street, or just a stone's throw from the courthouse. She was only six-years-old. A pretty, chubby little girl, I often would see playing in front of her house when coming home from school at St. Pat's. She bubbled with happiness. On this day, however, she ran into the street and was struck and killed by a taxicab driven by Lloyd Renkes, who lived in Fulton, just across the river from Clinton. Polly darted in front of his cab and bounced down the street to land near the corner of Fifth Avenue North. The courthouse gang arrived just as Polly's father, Bill Gore, took her crushed body into his arms. Racked with grief, and powerless to do anything, he held her like that until the police arrived. I marveled at his composure.

Polly looked so beautiful and peaceful in her father's arms, as if she were sleeping, but it was apparent as coroner Ed Martindale arrived that she was gone. Polly was only two years older than my sister Janice. Thinking of this, I wished for a miracle, and started to sob uncontrollably. It wasn't fair. God, where were you?

We hear Mr. Renkes speaking to a policeman. He says he was going about 25 miles an hour, and had just passed the city street sweeper when he saw the little girl directly in front of him. Gussie Witt and Jack Dunmore, shake their heads. "That's about right," Gussie tells Jack. "He's telling the truth as he stopped within 50 feet of the collision."

Polly has a sister Beverly about the same age as my sister Patsy, and a brother Richard about the same age as my brother Jackie. This hits me hard. 'They're a family just like mine' I say to myself. 'It could be our tragedy but for the grace of God.'

The death of the president quickly recedes into my memory, but not the death of Polly Gore. I remember it as if it were yesterday. Polly was playing with a friend on the east side of the street, or across from her home, when her mother called her to dinner at 4:35 p.m. Her mother was standing in the doorway waiting for her and saw it all happen. Nothing can compare to that horror. Nothing. May her soul forever rest in peace.

* * * * *

Cruel April is giving way to calming May, the month of the Blessed Virgin, and to the hot summer ahead. Still, April has been a wrenching month, particularly this April. The Clinton Herald reports that 136 Clinton area servicemen have died in combat in the European theater alone, and that 5,418 men and women from the Clinton area are now serving in the Armed Forces, 4,087 in the army and 1,331 in the navy, coast guard and merchant marine. I read this in the newspaper and walk to the wooden monument at the courthouse corner of Second Street and Sixth Avenue North, and touch the names of my family members and friends listed there, all fortunately still alive, and pray that God keeps them safe in the last months of this war. I look at the monument. It is shabby and a disgrace. The paint is peeling, the names are fading, or coming loose from the wood, and for some reason tears start falling down my cheeks. Were my name on this monument, I would want it etched in marble, never to fade, never to be forgotten. I hold the newspaper clipping of this listing in my hand, read each of the 136 names, touch them and say a silent prayer of thanksgiving for their sacrifice. I don't understand war, even less than I understand life. To die in some God forsaken place before your life has hardly started seems terribly unjust and unfair. I don't buy all this patriotism. Words! Anger wells up in me as I try to deal with my confusion. I promise myself I will never take a moment for granted and will not forget my debt to all these brave souls.

"What you doing there, lad?" a man says as he gets off the bus.

"Nothing," I say, embarrassed at being caught mooning over this monument.

"See my name there?" he touches a name, and smiles. "Out now. Getting married." He musses my hair. "It's a good year for the U S of A." With that, he walks toward Seventh Avenue North with a decided limp.

"Sir, what's your name?"

"Call me Hap, Hap Wilson, short for Happy."

How could we lose the war with men like him? I smile to myself. The gloom lifts. Yes, it's going to be a good summer.

$$* \quad * \quad * \quad * \quad *$$

Chapter 18

Dictating the Inferno

No sound of grief except the sound of sighing . . .

--Dante, Inferno IV

"James, James, James," Sister Flavian says, her dark eyebrows jumping over the frames of her bifocals. "I see you're in trouble again."

"Trouble, Sister?" I answer as if I have no idea what she's talking about.

"Miss Donaldson informs me you've embarrassed her in class, and not for the first time."

Miss Naomi Donaldson is a student teacher studying at Mount St. Clare College, and teaching us social studies one day a week. She's a knock out, and we can sit wherever we want when she teaches. I always sit in front of her desk, where she either stands or sits on its edge with her gorgeous legs crossed. She's elegant with black shiny hair cut short, a perky face, and the bounce of a whippy girl in her late teens but moves in a way that speaks only of class. I imagine she comes from one of Chicago's first families on Lake Shore Drive. Typically, she wears figure-hugging cashmere sweaters. Her nylon thighs swish a little when she goes to the blackboard, making the hair on the back of my head stand at attention. I can't keep my eyes from drifting over her. She is half my size and I feel I could read a newspaper through her clothes. Whenever she notices my slack jaw looks, she blushes with her cheeks turning as red as if she has just completed some vigorous exercise. She tries to give me her steely look but I must have my own, because she always turns away, until one day she says,

"James, now stop it! Stop looking at me like that!"

Stop what? The declaration shoots past me like a wild animal in the night leaving me stunned. What have I done? I am suffering and can't look her in the eye. My chest feels as big as a cathedral roof. If I open my mouth, there'd be a chord from an organ with all the stops pulled out. When social studies are over, Sister Gertrude comes back in the classroom. Miss Donaldson whispers to her. Sister nods as if to say, I understand, careful not to look my way, but I know it's about me. Sure enough it is. Now, after school, I'm sitting in the already empty kindergarten classroom on a tiny chair before St. Patrick's principal and my favorite nun, Sister Mary Flavian. She is sitting behind Sister Mary Julianne's desk looking down at me in this ridiculous tiny chair with my knees up to my chin. God! I wish Sister had an office! I know why we're here. The room's in the basement, been empty since noon, and the coolest spot in school, plus no one's likely to barge in here unannounced. I sit there in a white T-shirt, jeans and sneakers feeling guilty of some crime beyond my comprehension. Sister seems to be studying my blond reddish hair parted on the left, moving her eyes to my sad face with its limited range of expression. I feel as if my head is a specimen in a bottle. My mouth barely opens when I attempt to speak.

"Illll eeemmmmbarrassed Miss Donaldson?" I say finally, valiantly clothing myself in an innocence I don't feel. The walls of the classroom are covered in drawings and sketches, pinned to the polished wooden frames of the blackboards on the three bulwarks that encapsulate me. "These children are sure good artists, Sister," I observe using my charm to make conversation. No reply. I comb my hands through my hair with them flapping like startled birds in an attempt to seem humble. This doesn't work either.

"Have you ever touched Miss Donaldson?" Sister stares down at me like a judge in a criminal court.

Say what? My mouth opens two millimeters more than a clam's, which must resemble Edvard Munch's "Scream." My hands clasp automatically over my ears desperate to shut out this shattering accusation. I feel broken inside without Sister saying more, as if I were a spider wearing my skeleton on the outside. What could Miss Donaldson have said? Have thought? If I've touched her, it has only been with my eyes. Where's the crime in that? Sister Flavian gives me a look I can't hold. Despite my jeopardy, I'm thinking how I might salvage something from this situation. I know Sister likes me. I'm the boy always in trouble with authority and she's a rescuer. Before I can compose a reply, Sister explains,

"I mention this because Miss Donaldson asked me, 'Why is it he's always looking at me that way?'"

"Hhhooww aaammm I looking at her Sister? IIII don't mean to..."

Sister, with hooded unreadable eyes, the shadows already showing through her glasses with pouches under them, perhaps from lack of sleep, her skin so taut and raw looking that you'd think she'd spent a night in a blizzard, and this is practically summer, interrupts, "Miss Donaldson's exact words, 'He looks at me as if he's looking through me.'" Sister Flavian takes off her glasses and rubs the bridge of her nose with her thumb and forefinger. "You make her so uncomfortable she says she hates to teach at St. Patrick's."

Wow! This is wild! And I thought Miss Donaldson liked me!

"BBBuuutt wwwhhatt dddooess . . . hhhooww aaammm I supposed to be looking at her? Aasskkk her tttthat Sister!" I sense some flaw in Miss Donaldson's accusation; some hint of Sister's doubt causing her to hold back total judgment of me. Yet, she remains resolutely direct.

"Sinfully. She feels you are looking at her sinfully, undressing her with your eyes."

Now I understand. But this only ups my anxiety. The two ventricles of my heart ice up. The blood is only going through in thin spurts and the oxygen in my breathing is hard to find. I stand up and shake all over fearing, I'm about to faint. *She thinks I'm a peeping Tom! Am I?* Sister motions for me to sit down. I do so, feeling slightly better for the exercise.

"She says you think you're being cute, but you make her feel cheap, that you don't respect her."

This is so shattering I lapse into silence. If there is one thing I've learned from my da, who never knew his mother, is that women are divine, to be put on a pedestal and worshipped as the mothers of us all. From Sister's facial expression, my stomach automatically tightens. There is something indigestible going down, a painful wind ballooning in my bowel wanting to get out. Seeming to sense my perturbation, Sister says,

"This will go no further than us. My desire is for you to understand your effect on people." My belly grows quiet. Sister still keeps me off center with a look that reads *probation doesn't suggest innocence.* "Miss Donaldson said the other day you looked so sad that she felt compelled to ask you what was wrong. You said that you missed her wearing cashmere sweaters now that the weather had warmed. Everyone laughed, but she felt humiliated. Do you think that was an appropriate comment?"

"No, Sister."

"Respectful?"

"IIIIII dddinnn't mmmean . . ."

"I'll ask you again, did you think it was respectful?"

"No, Sister."

"Then why did you say it?"

"I guess because I thought it."

"Everything you think you say?"

"Yes, Sister. I mean no, Sister."

She looks at me with those sorrowful but beautiful blue eyes in that squat peasant frame, and even though I'm not yet thirteen, I know I'm in the presence of holiness.

"On the other hand," she continues, "I've noticed since you came to this school you have a fire in you. That is good. Such fire kindles all passions. Now, I'm reminded you don't fully understand the passion in your vision. You don't recognize how threatening visual intrusion can be."

"No Sister that's not true," I protest weakly, still gazing down at my hands. "It's nothing like that," I add lacing my fingers together, turning them inside out. *Passion in my vision? Threatening visual intrusion? I have no idea what she's talking about.*

"Yes James. I'm afraid it is. Your eyes are the windows to your soul. Now they are exciting you and you are in danger of saying provocative things, embarrassing things, things you don't totally understand, things that will get you into a lot of trouble. You are now becoming a young man."

A what? "No, Sister. I'm just a boy. I like being a boy. Honest I do."

"It is 'yes Sister,' young man, and neither you nor I can do anything about it. The passion in your eyes goes with the fire in your soul. These fires don't register the same intensity with us all. For some, self-restraint is easy, for others it is not. You have a compulsive nature. It shows. These fires emanate from within. Channeled they can be a force for good. That is my role, to see that the corners of your mind work for you, not against you. So I'm not going to punish you. I am asking you to be considerate of the feelings of others, especially of Miss Donaldson."

What a relief! I'm euphoric, words dance out of my head. "But why am I like this, Sister? Why do I say things like this?" Am I baiting her, or do I want an answer?

"Why?" She ponders the question a long time, playing with her rosary beads. "I suspect it is because your energies are coming together, and yes, overwhelming you, forcing a transition in your body and soul that you would prefer not to understand. You must decide whether you're going to be master or slave to these forces. In control, you will harness these fires and light them in others, enabling them to be better people. This is called leadership, James, and you have a lot of it in you, but I sense that you don't like it very much, do you?"

"I don't understand, Sister."

She ignores this. "You don't like to be out in front of everyone, isn't that true?"

I shrug my shoulders. "I guess, Sister."

"Why do you think?"

"Ah, I don't know Sister."

"I think you do. You don't want the responsibility."

"No, Sister."

"You don't want to disturb your comfort."

"No, Sister."

"You don't want the notice."

"No, Sister."

"You don't want the ridicule."

"No, Sister."

"And you don't want to fail, especially that. You prefer to be in the group whispering into someone's ear what he might do, rather then be in front of the group leading the charge. This is especially true of you with Bobby Witt."

"What?" This awakens me. Up to this point I have hardly been listening. Why bring Bobby's name into this? He's done nothing wrong.

"Bobby Witt. He's your leader."

"Yes, Sister. But he's everybody's leader, captain of our basketball team."

"No, James you know that's not true. You are the captain. Dean Burridge named you captain and reported that to me."

"Well, yes, but everyone sees Bobby as the captain anyway. He's the best player and the most popular boy. Everyone likes him. Not everyone likes me." I laugh nervously, "Guess I'm captain in fact, but Bobby's captain in spirit."

"It's not funny James, not funny at all. You think Bobby Witt has more leadership ability than you?"

"Oh! Yes, Sister!"

"I don't think so."

"You don't think so?"

"No. It's not that Bobby Witt isn't responsible, or that he minds leading. His focus is on developing as an athlete."

"Yesss? Wwwhhhat's my focus, Sister?" I feel terribly confused.

"To understand everything, and then to save the world. No one can do that. The only one you can save, James, is yourself. I sense you're not doing it very well. That's why we're having this conversation. Do you understand what I'm saying?"

"Not completely, Sister," I answer honestly. I lace my fingers together again and roll my thumbs. "No Sister. Truthfully, I don't think I understand you at all."

"Well, we'll leave it at that." She rises, takes her shawl from the back of the chair, even though its late May and terribly warm outside, picks up her briefcase, excuses herself and turns to go.

"Sister! May I walk you to the Mount?"

Surprised, she says, "You would like to do that?" I shake my head. She smiles her radiant smile that lights up her face like magic. "Well, come along then. Sister Gertrude is waiting for us now." I forgot nuns never travel alone. But that's okay.

"Sister, can we talk about something else?"

She laughs shaking with mirth. "Oh, yes!" And that is what we do. I talk about the Chicago Cubs all the way to Mount St. Clair and the Cubs' chances to win the National League Pennant, while both nuns listen with knowing smiles on their faces. When we reach the Bluff, Sister Flavian looks at me with twinkling eyes and thanks me for the company. Sister Gertrude does as well. I watch as they climb the treacherous steps to the convent door, knowing they're not talking but already praying for me. How can I fail with them on my side?

*   *   *   *   *

The last day in May we receive a surprise visit from Father Finefield. He is in an expansive mood, greets Sister Gertrude with a smile, and then turns to us, "Good morning, children."

"Good morning Father Finefield," we respond in unison.

"I see a lot of happy faces knowing school is about over." He laughs with a chortle that rises from deep in his diaphragm with a pleasant guttural resonance. Still beaming, he adds, "Would James Fisher please come to the front of the room?"

What have I done now? Sensing my discomfort, he queries me, "Know the meaning of the word *gospel* James?"

"Yes, Father, 'good news'?" Where is this going?

"Well, I bring you good news. You are being made an altar boy." The class breaks out into a cheer. Everyone knows that I've wanted to be an altar boy since the fourth grade. My face breaks into a tight smile, angry at being snubbed so long, jubilant that it's finally happening. I try to remember how Sister Flavian instructed me to behave, but my memory fails, so I just rock on the balls of my feet studying my scuffed sneakers.

"What do you have to say James?" I think, *this is long overdue,* but say,

"Thank you, Father."

"Well I hope you can say that after you complete this little oral examination of your Latin." He laughs again, while everyone looks at each other. Their faces seem to say, Father has never done this before, why now? "Do you know the altar boy Latin responses to the Mass, James?"

"Yes, Father," I say without hesitation.

"Well, class, we'll see about that, won't we?" He chuckles; his eyes water slightly, his cheeks reddening. "Altar boys, listen carefully. You'll be the judge of that." Tension stretches like taut wires across the room, but for some reason I'm completely relaxed.

Unceremoniously, Father begins, *In Nomine Patris, et Filii, et Spiritus Sancti. Amen. Introibo ad altare Dei.* He waits.

I respond, *Ad Deum qui laetificat juventutem meam.*

"Have you any idea what that means, James?"

"Yes, Father. You made the Sign of the Cross and said, 'In the name of the Father, and of the Son, and of the Holy Ghost, Amen. I will go to the altar of God.' And I responded, 'To God, the joy of my youth'."

He continues,

Judica me, Deus, et discerne causam meam de gente non sancta: ab homine iniquo et doloso erue me.

I respond again. *Quia tu es, Deus, fortitudo mea: quare me repulisti, et quare tristis incedo, dum affligit me inimicus?*

Without prompting, I say, "You said, 'Give judgment for me, O God, and decide my cause against an unholy people, from unjust and deceitful men deliver me.' And I responded, 'For Thou, O God, art my strength, why hast Thou forsaken me? And why do I go about in sadness, while the enemy afflicts me?'"

"Well, well, well," Father looks to Sister Gertrude. "You have trained James Fisher well Sister, my congratulations." Sister nods in appreciation but says nothing. I resent this oral examination and pucker my lips defiantly, which fortunately Father misses as he is looking to the class. "How many altar boys here know the English meaning of the Latin responses?" Only John Knoerschild raises his hand. "Besides John." Every other boy in the class studies the initials curved into his desktop as if high art. "Interesting. Very." He then launches into his standard altar boy speech.

"Altar boys are like Disciples of Christ and have the apostolic role of assisting the priest in his sacred duties in the celebration of the Mass . . . It all starts with being elected an altar boy. For that I bless you all, and especially James Raymond Fisher, Jr. as he joins this select company. Now kneel and I'll bless you, In nominee Patris, et Filii, et Spiritus Sancti. Amen."

Making the Sign of the Cross over us, Father is gone with the swiftness with which he came. Never once did he acknowledge the girls in the class or their role in the Mystical Body of Christ. We would have no priests from this class, no nuns, no monks or brothers. Dickie Van Ah in the class ahead would become a priest, and Phyllis Morris in the class behind would become a nun.

* * * * *

Perhaps because I have had such a long anxious wait to be an altar boy, I don't mind being used by Father Finefield. I serve 7 o'clock weekday masses, not only for June, but all summer long. He apologizes for other boys canceling, but he senses I am not disappointed. Far from it, I'm happy for the opportunity. Besides, it gives me an early start at the courthouse that I might not otherwise have. The longer day improves my baseball skills, especially my hitting.

Taking communion every day keeps me in a state of sanctifying grace and keeps my demons at bay, well, at least most of them. Wanting to stay in a state of grace, and having a volatile personality makes it difficult. I don't swear I just kind of swear. It's a safety valve of sorts. I say, "jiminy crickets" instead of Jesus Christ, "gosh darn" instead of goddamn, "heck" instead of hell, "baloney" instead of bullshit. I don't even say "BS" because that's an abbreviation for bullshit. There's no logic to my sanitized language, but using it lightens my spirit and gives me some balance for the rest of the day that I might not otherwise have. Even after taking communion today, however, I'm still on fire. My unease with Father is so great that I want to break something. My da comes to mind. Holy mother of God, I'm like my da. Mother of Mercy, pray for me!

After Mass, I go home, have three bowls of cornflakes with sliced bananas, milk and lots of sugar. I hope my mother doesn't mind. It's the first time we've had bananas in the house all spring, and I just ate two of them. I also have four pieces of toast with heaps of butter and currant jelly, and two glasses of milk. I put an apple in each of my front pockets and decide I'm not playing baseball at the courthouse today. My mother is still asleep, my da is on the road, and only Patsy is up. She eats like a bird, saying she loses her appetite watching me eat. I love her. She is as tiny as a bird, herself, but that's where the comparison ends. Whereas I'm flighty, she has her feet firmly planted on the ground. She never gets lost in the details.

"Where you going?"

"For a walk."

"Not to the courthouse?"

"No."

"Why not?"

"Because I just want to take a walk."

"Where to?"

"I don't know."

"Can I come? Please!"

"Next time, all right?"

"Promise."

"I promise." She gives me a hug and I feel in heaven. I'd take her along but I want to be alone today.

One beauty about Clinton is that it is seven miles long but only three miles wide, so where I live I'm less than two miles from the country, an easy walk, and one I find myself doing now as I go past Mount St. Clare, then west on Springdale Drive, snaking my way out across Elvira Road and into the countryside. Here the city quickly gives way to the country, where the grids of geometric county roads intersect, and where dust is a hurricane of color as cars streak across the golden roads. I watch a car on the crest of a hill zoom towards me. Dust bellows out of the car's wake like a giant squirrel's tail as it passes by. The corn on either side of the road sways gently in the breeze, giving the fields a sense of heaving life, as if the ground itself is breathing. I have a feeling of moving through a landscape whose topography is altered with every puff of wind. In Iowa's corn country, it's not the hills or rivers that delineate the land, but the grain itself, the solid blankets of yellow stalks and green leaves that ceaselessly shift and sigh. Occasionally, an entire field will cease to respond to the breeze in a moving wave and rise up all together, holding its green leaves in concert like a mirror to the light and the field will flash for only an instant like a burst of illumination from a nearby star. Then, the light will blink out and the restless emerald carpet will resettle itself upon the land. Watching this miniature nova in a field of grain is like being transported out of body to somewhere else more pleasant and reassuring. Perhaps that is why I like these walks.

Never having been a country boy, I still love the country. Walking down the dusty road I can hear the long green leaves saw and scrape against each other, producing the music of stress and relief like a mantra. I engulf myself in this music knowing the quiet sounds of the earth are never quiet; knowing too that the smell of the dirt and the sun on my neck are things to be relished. An Iowa summer sun is a different sun in the country than it is in the city. It is more radiant, more a companion, and more an extension of everything living. It is easy to see why the Indians worshipped the sun. It is difficult to see why anyone would do otherwise. There could never be a more generous or more searingly cruel god than the sun.

Unexpectedly, I'm on the verge of tears. Everything around me is so orderly, so beautiful. I don't know if I'm weeping for this demanding beautiful landscape, for the reserved people who inhabit it, or for my tarnished innocence that seems to dwell here. I feel a chilling thrill haunting every wind shaped contour, every faded crumbling barn, every rust covered abandoned piece of farm machinery.

The strident cawing of crows disturbs my tranquility. A black crow drops from the sky like a black handkerchief, wings fluttering frantically. Others break off the engagement in the sky and swoop down after it, swift as avian arrows as they disappear from my sight below the level of the corn. I climb over the fence and roam through the corn stalks. In the middle of the field, I discover crows are plunging into the yellow darkness of the corn. I try to imagine the solar radiation absorbed by their pitch-black bodies in the full sunlight

297

on a day like this. It is a miracle they aren't baked, but all I hear from the baking cornfield is screaming, cawing. The suspense is too great. I have to investigate. Around a fluttering circle of crows I see them pecking at a downed crow. It is still alive. A crow hops towards it, takes a stab at it, then hops back. Another crow hops forward and repeats the act. Crows were being crows, emboldened by the waning resistance; they stayed longer, pecked harder, and with more effect. In violent parody of an elegant dance, the birds in the circle surged inward, struck at the helpless victim, then hopped back to their place, beaks wide open, screaming hatred or triumph or bloodlust. After several minutes, the downed bird in the circle appeared resigned to its fate, folded its wings next to its body, and let its head drop, accepting each blow without protest, its beak still open, panting, until it expired. The crows pecked at it, still cawing in raucous chorus, until it fell on its side, pecked on it until the only motion in the victim was caused by the force of their blows, pecked on it so that its inert body danced sideways in the dirt, recoiling from each blow as if it were a rolled up black sock being used by children for a ball, pecked on it although it was dead and still, pecked on it well beyond death in something of a elegy to nature.

It's strange. I don't like to swim, don't like boats, but I like being near water. I'm now walking along Mill Creek. The confluence of the creek's waters creates eddies and turbulence, which is music to my ears. Mill Creek extends well beyond the Clinton county line west and empties into the Beaver Slough east, flowing into the Mississippi. I follow Mill Creek west for some distance, grow incredibly tired, and am forced to lie down. I take my two apples out and eat them with pleasure. Lazily, I watch two sticks float slowly downstream. A field of soybeans is behind me. Through the trees I can see the stalks of corn glistening on the other side of the creek. I sit silent. A crow flies overhead, cawing, followed by a blue jay squawking in outrage. I hear other birds less obtrusively singing and chirping. A meadowlark sings in the far distance, and something less melodic cheeps nearby. A sparrow? A high-pitched trill sounds close at hand. It is a red-winged blackbird. I am astonished at the number of different birds that fills the silence. I put my head down in the weeds. The sun strikes me full in the face, making lights dance behind my eyelids. I hear a car pass on the road, feel the bridge rattle in protest. A cloud crosses the sun and I feel the difference on my face. A cicada chirps from the tree line. A breeze rustles the weeds and I recognize the leaves of the soybeans slapping one another. A branch groans slightly overhead. I lift my head off the ground. I hear a loud chirring noise. It's a squirrel. I watch its spastic darts, stops and scampers. I sink deeper within myself while allowing my senses to expand outward stretching to encompass miles. I hear birds nearby, cars on the dusty roads in the distance. It is like shifting bands of radio stations in and out at will. I feel kin to Indians who own this land we borrowed, and never gave back. On that note, I fall asleep.

It is near twilight by the time I wake up and head for home. The sky is heavily overcast with angry clouds storing up the rising heat and damp of the day, and lights from farmhouses stand out like flickering beacons far out to sea. I am lost. I feel like Huckleberry Finn on a raft on the Mississippi, drifting through a sluggish muddy section of the river, only it's not the Mississippi, but a sea of cornfields. I walk, kicking the golden dust of the country road, not in panic, but in a kind of resolve that being lost is a natural state for me. I imagine myself being propelled by an angry current toward a maelstrom of rapids, and like a hero in one of my comics searching the jagged coastline for a low hanging tree branch to grab to foil certain death. Instead, a farmer yelling from a nearby tractor shatters the irenic moment. I can't hear what he's saying. He cuts the motor. "Lost young fella, are you now?"

Improbably, I put my arm up over my eyes to ward off a sun already starting to set. "You look like a city boy." I nod my head. "Clinton is it?" I nod again. "How in tarnations did you get way out here?"

"Walking."

"Walking?" The farmer takes off his cap and rubs his head with it. His face is brown but there is a white line about an inch below his hairline on his forehead. It makes him look funny. I hold back a laugh.

"Well, son, it's getting dark and you're better than four miles or so from town. Look hungry, too. Are you now?" I nod.

"Well, let's get you up to the house. The wife will fix you some supper. Call your people. After you've eaten, best I run you into town. How's that sound to you?" I shrug my shoulders. "Okay."

He laughs slapping his cap against his leg. "Boy, for a minute there thought you a mute. Just kind of scared, are you now? Out here in this godforsaken country." He adds with a touch of sarcasm.

"No, sir," I say vigorously shaking my head.

He starts the tractor again. "Guess I would be too." He motions for me to hop on the fender. I do. "We'll soon get this sorted out, now won't we?" The irenic moment doesn't die, but takes a different turn.

I've never had food that tasted so good, homemade bread, homemade butter, and breast of chicken sandwiches, fresh milk and homemade apple pie with homemade ice cream. The farmer beams as I eat.

"Martha, he eats like a farm boy, wouldn't you say?"

"Lordy, he does indeed," she agrees. She is as round as a butterball while the farmer is as tall, lean and gnarly as a birch pole, and just as brown.

Neither of us talks as the farmer gives me a ride back into Clinton. I don't know cars but his is an old one. I'd guess it was made long before the war, but it runs as smooth as his tractor. He must be a good mechanic. The car radio is tinny with a kind of music in which everybody is twanging. Wonder if John Knoerschild knows this music. The farmer pulls up to the curb in front of my house, and says,

"Did you learn anything today out our way?"

I think about the mayhem of the crows, serenade of the birds, the bubbling brook, the swaying corn and soybean, the vibrating language with my ear to the ground, but say only, "Corn sure grows tall." He reaches over and opens my door. "As tall as an elephant's eye, as the song goes, don't you know?" I thank him, slam the door, and he is off with a wave.

My mother is waiting. She puts a match to her cigarette, draws a deep breath, tips her face towards the ceiling and releases a cloud of smoke. "Now what story are we having for your country folly?"

I try to sound glib. "Just walking. You know how I am. That's where I ended up."

She answers with a prolonged sigh, as if my voice taxes her patience to the limit. "It is after eight and you've been gone since early this morning. How do you explain that?" She smokes, seemingly doing nothing but exhaling, mixing her slump-shouldered sighs with random puffs and openmouthed pants. It is as if the only thing holding her together is smoke and breath control. She steadies herself against the coffee table, rapping it with her ringed finger. "Something's wrong. I know it is. You don't do something like this unless something's bothering you." She examines her cigarette, puffs on it, leaving a red mark on the white end, blowing out the strange strong smoke. "Tell mother what it is."

The light outside darkens and brightens as clouds crash across the clearing sky, bringing showers, which beat against the side of the house like nervous fingers dancing on a table. "See, you could have got caught in this and caught your death of cold. I don't know." She waves her cigarette as if in surrender and collapses onto a sofa chair, "You beat all."

"I'm okay, mother, really I am. Just took a walk and got lost. That's all. Nice farmer fed me and brought me home." Tiredness creeps across my face, "Can I go to bed now?"

She rests her chin on the heel of her hand and smokes dreamingly, which makes her eyes look particularly green. "Yes, that's a good idea. Have to serve Mass tomorrow?" I nod. She gives me her cheek to kiss. I do, and escape to my room. The rain on the roof and window is soothing music; delicious sleep is not far away.

* * * * *

On Monday, August 7, 1945, I read in *The Clinton Herald* that yesterday "President Truman reveals a U. S. Army Air Force bomber dropped an atomic bomb on Hiroshima, Japan." I never heard of such a bomb or such a place. On Thursday, I read that the day before, Wednesday, August 9, another atomic bomb was dropped on Nagasaki, Japan. Each bomb, according to The Herald, was a single missile 2,000 times the blasting power of the largest bomb used previously in the war. I try to fathom this destructive power and the reason for it.

I listen to my da's railroad buddies celebrating these bombings with a kind of excitement I hadn't heard before. "Understand it leveled Hiroshima to the ground, and all their *papier-mâché* huts with it," says one. "Not a Jap standing," says another. "Did even a better job at Nagasaki," says a third. "Heard on the radio tens of thousands killed and tens of thousands more critically wounded in both attacks," says a fourth, "and we didn't lose a flier." Finally, my da concludes, "Won't be long now."

"Thank God for that!" they echo as one.

"Does Japan have that huge an army in those two cities?" I ask innocently, seeing that as the only justification for such an attack. All eyes turn to me in stunned silence. Usually, they don't even notice me. Then they break into uproarious laughter. Their eyes go watery. Fists to the eyes stay their tears; legs kick the floor until the house shakes, and some even hold their stomachs in raucous hilarity. I didn't mean it to be funny. What's so funny about tens of thousands of people dying? Does war make people like that? I ask my mother who is in the kitchen reading. She says, "You wouldn't understand." I ask my da after his railroad buddies leave. He says simply, "It saved thousands of American lives." Both answers are inadequate.

I go to the Clinton library; look up the population of the two cities; both are at least ten times the size of Clinton. I sink into a library chair in the reading room and cry uncontrollably. Faces look at me disapprovingly. I don't care. I don't want to ever grow up. Even kind people can grow cruel.

That night I have a dream. The world is collapsing, folding under its own weight and crushing all within. In the heart of the world, I stand, sensing rather than seeing the immense pressure of a world falling inward. I hold my arms out to withstand it, like Samson in the temple, blinded and betrayed, a giant under whose legs scurried an indifferent populace. "It's coming!" I yell, but no one seems to hear. I realize I am holding the pillars of the earth in place for myself, not for anyone else, they don't care, only I care. Yet, I yell again. "It's coming!"

"What's coming?" my mother says, looking down at my sweating body. Now awake, I pull the covers to my neck, trying to hide my embarrassment.

"You okay?"

"Just dreaming," I say, lying on my back, bending my knees to keep the pressure of the blanket from my body. She kisses me on the head. "Better put on a dry T-shirt, catch your death of cold."

"Yes, mother."

I have exploded in my shorts with a sticky viscous discharge with a sickening smell, like Bobby warned. He said it would happen if I didn't masturbate, that according to his brother Vern, wet dreams are natural, and bring relief. Far from relief, I feel terrible. I cry, stifling sobs for fear of waking others. Sin is the name of my agony. How am I going to serve Mass and go to communion? I know what. I'll say the *Second Sorrowful Mystery of the Rosary*. That will be my Penance. A dreamless sleep follows before I finish the first decade.

* * * * *

James R. Fisher, Jr.

Chapter 19

Follow the Yellow Brick Road

You road I enter upon and look around,
I believe you are not all that is here,
I believe that much unseen is also here.

--Walt Whitman

The summer of 1945 is here. All the faces are a year older and bodies a year stronger as they rush to play baseball at the courthouse, led by Gussie Witt, Jack Dunmore, Lyle Sawyer, Bobby Witt, Dick Crider, Phil Leahy, Bill "Chang" Benson, Dick Morris, Dick and Kenny Tharp, Sam and Russ Annear, Walt Ferguson, Rock Carver, Jackie Fisher, David "Pooper" Cavanaugh, Jim Holle, Dick Dunmore, Bob and Thiel Collins, Bob Becker, Gary Stephenson, Ramy Baker, Ray Jorgensen. New guys are Chuck Holm, Alex Grayes, Garrett "Pee Wee" Behrens, Bob "Carnegie" Andrews, Hod McKenna, Don "Gigger" Kinney, Smiley Carlson, Jim Junker, Art and Eddie Sheller,

Ed Goene, Ollie Stearns, Billy Lutz, Dave Peterson, Billy Christiansen, Dave Holleran, Jack Schuster, Clarence McArdle, Tom Clark, Bob Leuders, Don Schumacher, Charlie Sloppy, Johnny Burken, Dave and Jim Keefe, and many others. They weren't all destined to be Courthouse Tigers, but they all gave the courthouse neighborhood a light and electricity that brightened the day for everyone. It was their time, and this was their place.

The routine differs little with last year except now there is a Junior-Junior League organized throughout the city by the Clinton Parks & Recreation Department for boys nine through twelve. Teams are formed at Sino Park in Lyons, the courthouse, South Clinton, Iten Field, and Chancy Park. Each team plays the other on a home and home basis. The Courthouse Tigers will go undefeated with a record of 10 and 0, and be crowned city champs with Sino Park's Muffy Sox finishing second at 9 and 1, and the Chancy Park Cubs third at 6 and 3. The Courthouse Tigers were undefeated last year in Bob Collin's League, when there was no adult involvement and no formal championship. Times are a changing.

Courthouse Tigers Win Over All-Stars 1 to 0

The Courthouse Tigers Defeated Junior-Junior All-Stars in a well played game yesterday that concluded play for this group for the season. The Courthouse Tigers had won both halves of the summer league and concluded with an undefeated season. The stars threatened in the fourth when they rapped out three hits but each time the runners were erased on attempted steals. The Tigers counted the winning run in the fifth on a single by Fisher, a hit by Cavanaugh, which sent Fisher to third, and a steal of home by Fisher. Holm fanned six and allowed six hits for the Tigers while Stamp gave up six hits and whiffed 10 for the All-Stars. Fisher and Cavanaugh led the Courthouse Tigers each getting two hits. (The Clinton Herald)

The passion is high for baseball throughout the city. I have often wondered why Clinton hasn't produced a bevy of major league baseball players. Several have played professionally in the minor league system of major league clubs, including Gussie Witt, Jack Dunmore, Bob Dalrymple, and Ray Gilbert. Some have even been invited to the major leagues for a "cup of coffee," but never for an extended career. Perhaps it has something to do with the short season. In Clinton baseball is essentially a June/August affair, and even at the courthouse, intensive play doesn't get underway until well into June, or after school is out. It is the same throughout Iowa. Even so, Iowa produced Bob Feller from Van Meter, which is only a fork in the road and not listed on the atlas. He threw his first pitch in the major leagues for the Cleveland Indians at the age of seventeen and struck out a dozen batters.

Clinton had its own Bob Feller in the halcyon days of the 1940s. It was a short scrawny kid named Dick Tharp. He was a right hand version of the diminutive left hand Hal Newhouser of the Detroit Tigers. He had arm strength that defied physics. Velocity wasn't measured in the 1940s, but as a boy Dick Tharp could throw with as much velocity, I believe, as could Feller at the same preteen age. Tharp was practically unhittable, and he wasn't wild. He played for the fun of it, never thinking of baseball as a career, and unfortunately no baseball scout came to Clinton to discover him. Were he to have been born a generation later, even growing up in this frigid tundra of a limited baseball season, chances are he would have shared a common heritage with Iowa's magnificent "Rapid Robert" Feller. So much of life is a matter of chance, governed by time, place and circumstance.

* * * * *

Sometimes the greatest moments pop up out of nowhere. It's a slow day at the courthouse. Only Gussie Witt, Jack Dunmore, Walt Ferguson and me are there, sitting around shooting the breeze. "Got an idea," Jack Dunmore says, "let's catch the Cub's doubleheader in Chicago Saturday. What do you think? They're playing the Phillies."

"Great! I'm for it!" adds Gussie Witt. "How about you Rube and Fergie? Want to go? Passeau and Wyse are pitching." Gussie is always full of the latest baseball news. Claude Passeau is the leading pitcher in the National League, and Hank Wyse is not far behind. The Cubs are headed for their first National League flag in seven years, piloted by Jolly Chollie Grimm, who took over from Jimmy Wilson last year.

Just like that, Shazam! Fergie and I take off for home. My da's sitting in his favorite chair reading the just delivered Clinton Herald. The newspaper smells like fresh ink. He looks up. "You find a hundred dollar bill somewhere?"

This startles me. "No. Why?"

"Don't have your normal long face. So what's up?"

307

This knocks the wind out of my sails. No time to calibrate his mood, no time to ask Patsy to ask him if I can go. All blinders are off and I have to face him with no chance for deception. "No, ah, well, ah Gussie Witt and Jack Dunmore want to take Fergie and me to the Cubs doubleheader in Chicago Saturday, and I was . . ."

"Let him go Ray!" my mother says as she floats in from the kitchen. It always astounds me. She has a serious hearing problem but seems to hear whatever she wants to hear whenever she wants to hear it, like now. "Isn't that what you keep telling me, the boy needs to get his ass out into the real world? It'll be an adventure for him, Ray. He'll be with Gussie and Jack. You like them both." Remarkable. Just like that, my mother effortlessly pulls my da's strings. In fairness, he's always talking about how lucky we are to have them looking after us at the courthouse. Knows their dads and likes them both. "Good people" is the way he puts it. Most people to him are assholes.

He puts down his paper. "You can go," he says. Just like that! No long pause, no conditions, no warning, simply, "You can go." I'll never figure him out. Once I think I've got a good reading of him, he breaks the code, like now, only this time in my favor. Parents! No, "We don't have the money"; No, "You're too young to be traipsing about the country"; or the usual no, "No, period!" I'm too ecstatic for words; afraid I might break the spell.

He reaches over, takes out a cigarette from a pack, lights it, and takes a long drag, looks to my mother. "Dorothy, should be able to get them all round trip passes to Chicago. Suspect it'll save them a couple bucks," he adds blowing out a stream of smoke in celebration of his power, an unfamiliar joy.

*   *   *   *   *

As many trains as I've been on, and as many family trips that we've taken by rail, this is truly a first, an adventure without adults! We are free to do as we please! What could be greater? I can hardly sleep, waking at 5 a.m., putting on my white T-shirt, blue jeans and white athletic socks and sneakers, and wearing my red Courthouse Tiger baseball cap. I've already consumed my third bowl of corn flakes with homemade canned peach slices, and thinking of a fourth, when I smell the cigarette smoke before I see my mother. Her first words shatter my morning.

"You're not going to Chicago looking like that!" This is a battle I can't win so I don't put up a fight. Dutifully, I put on a blue shirt with a collar with enough starch in it to walk across water, a pair of dark blue khakis, blue socks and my best black shoes. "Put this on, too." I make a face, as she hands me a white cotton cardigan sweater. I put it on even though it'll probably be 90 degrees at the game. I look like I'm ready for church. I still have on my baseball cap. "That's got to go, too. You're not wearing that disgustingly dirty cap to Chicago." True, it's soiled with sweat, oily grime and dirt, and more black than red, but it's precious to me. Again, no protest, I put it down, but later slip it into my pocket. Mother gives me $7.00 to spend, $2.00 for the grandstand seat at Wrigley Field, and the rest for meals and treats. It is the most money I have ever had, and well beyond what I expected. My da is feeling especially generous. Why, I'm not sure. Chicago is his favorite place on earth. Perhaps that's it.

We meet at the courthouse at 6 a.m., catch a bus at 6:10, and are at the railroad depot by 6:30, plenty of time to catch the 7:10 to Chicago. The guys get cold drinks and I get a coffee in the depot café, where I introduce them to Mable and Max. Mable takes a shine to Jack Dunmore, but he doesn't seem to notice. Max talks Gussie's head off. I can tell Gussie is humoring him, as Max knows less about the Chicago Cubs than I do. While we are waiting, a freight train buzzes through the depot without stopping. Often, when I'm in the café, I notice trains going very quickly by like that. Everything close to the tracks becomes a blur, like it does now. I discovered if you blink your eyes quickly you could stop the motion for an instant, actually freeze the image like with a camera. I tell the guys this as we anxiously wait for our train. They look at each other with blank expressions; shake their heads, and then Gussie laughs,

"Rube, that's a good one," mussing my hair and knocking off my cap. Fergie and Jack laugh, too.

"Do you ever shut down Rube?" Jack asks with a gentle smile.

I squirm, but persist. "Try it sometime. Yyyyooou'll see it really works."

If they only knew, it doesn't just happen to me with trains. Sometimes when things seem to be coming at me close to the speed of light, my mind's eye blinks to stop the motion, freezing my muddle, like when Sister Flavian asks me if I touched Miss Donaldson. The shock went through me like electricity. Is it so odd to stop things, to blink? Don't the guys do this, too? They probably do, but don't know it.

Once on the train, it's so frigid I'm glad I have a sweater. I'm the only one that does. Fergie is dressed like me, so I don't feel bad, but Jack and Gussie are dressed like they're slumming at the courthouse – sleeveless sweatshirts, jeans and scruffy sneakers and Industrial League baseball caps. I envy them. From a window seat, I watch the landscape roll by like a motion picture. It is a symphony of colors with fields of yellow corn stalks and green soybeans in perfect rows. There are white and brown Guernsey, brown Jersey and Black Angus cattle in pastures or under trees to stay cool, earthen hogs and pink piglets slopping in mud to do the same, or poking their heads out of their little wooden igloos. Ashen silos, crimson barns, pasty farm houses, bottle green tractors are also interspersed with towns of white clapboard houses with black shingle roofs which whiz by with names like Morrison, Dixon, Franklin Grove, Ashton, Creston, DeKalb, Geneva, Wheaton, and finally Chicago. Chicago is 138 miles by rail from Clinton. Along the way, I look at open fields as possible baseball diamonds. All this open country is overwhelming. There are never enough places to play baseball.

We pull into the Chicago and North Western terminal at 9: 30. The depot is spacious like a cathedral with large Romanesque pillars, polished marble floors, bellowing loud speakers announcing train arrivals and departures, and like a Norman Rockwell painting, seemingly miles of long mahogany benches occupied by tired travelers, people sleeping with newspapers over their faces, mothers breast feeding their babies, servicemen checking their orders or playing cards, and little kids rough housing as if they were home.

We leave the station. It is a bright sunny morning. The immensity of Chicago hits me immediately, and is quickly diminished by a squat man with a round face and a handlebar mustache and a ridiculously tiny cap on his head hawking fruit from a portable stand on the corner of the Michigan Avenue Bridge. Gussie buys a bag of white grapes from him. "How much?" he asks.

"Half-a-dalla," replies the man with a foreign accent.

"Half-a-dalla," Gussie laughs. "Okay," and gives the man two quarters. Gussie keeps repeating "half-a-dalla" as we walk downtown until Jack says, "Gussie we get the point. Chicago is a foreign country." And we're Iowa hicks I say to myself.

With time on our hands, the game hours away, Fergie says, as we cross State Street, "Why don't we take a boat ride?"

"Boat ride? Where?" I ask.

"Back there at the bridge," Fergie replies with excitement in his voice, "didn't you see the sign?" None of us did. Sure enough, back at the bridge the sign reads,

Wendella Sightseeing Boats – Narrated cruises daily: 90-minute cruises at 10, 11:30, 1:15, 2, 3, 4:30, 7 and 8:30; and a 2-hour cruise at 7:30 p.m.

It is almost 10. We hurry down the steps to the level below the street where the boat is waiting. The Chicago River is flat and narrow, not even as wide as Beaver Slough. I'm not impressed. It's hard for me to pay the 75 cents for the ticket. The morning breeze once underway is barely able to stir the worn pennant flying from a halyard on the mast. Astern, we stand looking at the Chicago skyline with the sun flickering playfully off the skyscraper windows. I recognize the Tribune Tower. The guide points out the Chicago Board of Trade, Merchandise Mart, the Wrigley Building, and the Chicago Mercantile Exchange, talking in a staccato voice and never dwelling very long on any one landmark. We move through downtown and then pass through the locks letting us into Lake Michigan. From this vantage point, we see the stretching big shoulders of downtown Chicago in contrast to the tarnished industrial buildings along the Chicago River we just passed. I suppose this is from neglect during the war. Newly painted commercial signs on these crumbling facades signal redemption. These bright signs advertise beer, cigarettes, Wrigley gum, and the consensus sentiment, "God Bless America!"

Overhead, a cloudless sky has the morning sun already burning through an industrial haze, churning up flecks of silver in the vessel's wake. I stand watching in wonder. One cruise boat is coming back as we are going through the locks into Lake Michigan. The guide explains how the locks work by water displacement as he cuts the engine and we rise as the other boat descends through the locks. I am mesmerized as we pass Soldier's Field where the college all-stars play the champions of the National Football League, who last year were the Green Bay Packers. We pass Naval Pier and the Metropolitan Museum, and make our turn back at the Adler Planetarium. People are everywhere and appear like little dots, as does the traffic on busy Lake Shore Drive. I can see why my da loves Chicago. Around us and seemingly as far as the horizon, there are a zillion white sailboats and yachts with another zillion tied up to the docks as we pass. How can this be? Luxury crafts were not manufactured during the war. I wish someone could explain this to me.

It is lunchtime when we leave the boat. We vote to skip lunch until we get to Wrigley Field and instead take a ride on the famous "L" (Northwestern Elevated Railway) around Chicago. I like the idea, even though I'm a little hungry, because I love hot dogs, and Chicago hot dogs are supposed to be the best in the world. We board the State Street subway at the Cathedral corner and ride down to the Loop, where, after an exhausting climb from the subway to the L, we find a Ravenswood Line train waiting for us. We arrive at the Lawrence Avenue terminal at Lawrence and Kimball and discover that the Ravenswood L (The Brown Line) goes nowhere. Nonetheless it provides a fascinating jaunt through the Chicago Loop as Lawrence and Kimball are in the heart of the city. The ride is not merely a journey to nowhere; it is also a journey through places where no one goes.

Having loaded passengers at the Merchandise Mart, the train turns abruptly a couple of times, as if to throw off those who might be trying to follow it, and then slides along the thin borderland that separates the Gold Coast from the slums. To the right are the pastel luxury apartments near the lake, to the left the grim red brick buildings of the projects. Then the train eases its way across North Avenue by St. Michael's Church, and into what a passenger beside me says are the German and Swedish neighborhoods with DePaul University abutting the track. I tell him my uncle Leonard once taught at DePaul. He nods approvingly, but says nothing.

It is a strange feeling as the L slips through bathroom windows, sneaks down hallways, creeps out through second-floor doorways, and roars off with a furious rumble that no one seems to notice or mind. I am exhilarated by the conversation of the man sitting next to me. "I'm a motorman on the Blue Line," he says, "and take the loop L once in a while just for atmosphere." He looks at me, "What do you think of it?"

"I like it."

He smiles. "How would you like to live next to it?" I shrug and drop my shoulders. "Well, I live by the Blue Line and I can tell you the noise is family to you. When the train thunders by, it shakes the windows and light fixtures before it slips in and out of your house. It's likely to be company to you when you leave your bed and go to the bathroom at night, and sometimes gives you the feeling like it's exploding right into the commode. My home, I can tell you, is like living on an earthquake fault line."

"Wow! I don't know if I'd like that."

"You say you and your friends are going to the Cubs game?"

"Yes."

"Well, when we return to State Street, transfer to the Red Line from the Brown and take it through Grand, Chicago, Clark & Division Street, North & Clybourn, Fullerton, Belmont and get off at Addison. Wrigley Field is right there at Clark Street and West Addison Street. Can't miss it. I've got to get off here. Can you remember all that?"

"Yes sir," I say not wanting to disappoint him. Only "red line" and "Addison" stick.

"Well, so long," the motorman yells over the screaming wheels. "Have a great time at the game. Nice talking to you." He stands, waits for the doors to open, and is gone. I watch him disappear into the crowd and beam; Chicagoans are the nicest people in the world. My buddies who look lost in the big city gawk at me with stupid grins. I sit back and put my arms behind my head, and smile contentedly.

"What's got into Rube?" Gussie asks.

"Nothing," I reply with a twinkle in my eye. "Just happy. That's all. Man told me the way to Wrigley Field. Need to get off at the next stop and transfer to the Red Line."

We make the connection and the L train plows north across the city, through the stops the motorman mentioned, rattles from side to side, grinding hard on the tracks in the subway tunnel and then climbs the steep steel hill at the point north of North Avenue where it rises out of the tunnel and becomes the elevated train again with only two more stops before Wrigley.

*   *   *   *   *

We step off the train, descend the steps to the street, and there is a huge marquee

Wrigley Field
Home of
Chicago Cubs
Games Start One Thirty

Blue pennants with large red "W's" fly inward from the curved second deck of the stadium as you look up at the entrance to the ballpark. Inside on the esplanade are blown up pictures of former and present Cub greats. Throngs of people are entering the park through multiple gates. All the seats are painted a bright green. Green ivy also covers the brick outfield wall in front of the bleachers. Center field has no bleacher seats but is a solid garden of rich green shrubs that stretches from the wall to a massive scoreboard high above the field. I ponder this. Jack anticipates my question,

"Wonder why no stands out there? Well, that's so batters can pick up the ball. Otherwise, in a sea of white shirts batters would experience snow blindness giving the pitcher an unfair advantage." I nod. It makes sense.

Our seats are in the third deck on the first base side of the field, the home team's side. It seems as if we are looking right down on the Cub players warming up. Great seats! I look up. There are three decks above us. We all get programs and learn that Wrigley Field is one of the oldest ballparks in baseball. We also learn it plays no night games, having donated the lighting equipment that it had purchased for night games to the War Department on December 8, 1941, the day after Japan attacked Pearl Harbor. We also learn that on April 26, 1941 the Cubs became the first team to play organ music in major league ballparks; and that Wrigley seats over 38,000 and was enlarged to that capacity in 1926. It looks today as if every seat in the park will

314

be filled. The program also reports that the 27 by 75 foot ("Green Monster) scoreboard in centerfield is manually operated just like in Clinton. Across the street behind the left field bleachers, a two story building on Waveland Avenue is already crowded with thirty or more people. Fans there are called "ball hawks" as they wait with long fishnets to catch homeruns hit over the left field bleachers. It reminds me of big games at Clinton's Riverview Stadium. At least a score of people collect atop Clinton's incinerator driveway beyond the right field fence to watch the ballgame. They have a bird's eye view of the whole stadium.

I'm the only guy not keeping score with my program. I'm too excited. Afraid I'll miss something. The starting line up and batting order for the Cubs is announced on the public address system. The guys dutifully write it down: Don Johnson, second base, Peanuts Lowrey, left field, Phil Caverretta, first base, Bill Nicholson, right field, and batting clean up, Andy Pafko, center field, Stan Hack, third base, Lenny Merullo, shortstop, Mickey Livingston, catching, and Claude Passeau, pitching. The only change scheduled for the second game is for Hank Wyse to pitch and bat 9th. "I'm starving," I tell Gussie. All I've had to eat is your grapes. "Aren't you guys hungry?"

"Yeah!" they echo. Then Jack puts it to me fatherly. "Rube wait 'til the hot dog guy comes around." I make a long face. "Well, you could go to the concession stand, wait in line forever and miss batting practice." I jump up. My stomach decides. I head for the concession stand with Fergie joining me. "Want us to bring back something?" Gussie and Jack look at each other. "We'll wait for the guy to come around."

There are a lot of people at the concession stand. "Watch this," I tell Fergie, "my da taught me how to crash a line. Follow me." I worm my way to the front, where people are politely waiting their turn. "Four hot dogs with everything," I yell at the top of my lungs. One of the concession guys immediately tends to the order. I look for Fergie to be impressed. Instead, his eyebrows arch,

"You going to eat four?"

"No, two for you and two for me. Is that okay?"

"I guess."

"Two dollars," the guy says. I hand him a dollar and wait for Fergie's dollar. "And two waters," I add.

"I don't want water. I want a coke," Fergie complains.

"One water and one coke," I say, and give him Fergie's quarter and a dime tip. He takes the dime, looks at it, shakes his head, and fills two cups three quarters full of ice, pouring water in one and coke in the other. "That'll be fifty cents."

"Fifty cents for the coke?" Fergie asks.

"And the water," the guy returns. Fergie looks at me confused. Again, my da's mind kicks in. The guy's doing a number on a couple of what he considers 'hayseeds.'

"Give him another quarter Fergie. I'll give you mine when we get back."

Gussie and Jack are feasting on hot dogs, hamburgers, potato chips, and beers. And beers? They're not old enough. They both smile with contentment. We're all in our element. "You missed Nicholson in batting practice. Put eight balls into the stands," Gussie reports.

I'm sorry we missed that, but I feel better having eaten my hot dogs. "Gussie, when the hot dog guy comes around again, will you get his attention? Want two more hot dogs."

Fergie pokes me, "And a glass of water. Rube's a water drinker. Costs as much as a coke here, doesn't it Rube?"

"So?" I say defensively. "So I don't like cokes."

"It's okay Rube," says Jack with a devilish grin, "we'll get you a beer next time around." Everyone laughs.

The Cubs win both games of the doubleheader over the lowly Phillies, 4-3 and 12-6. Bill Nicholson has a homerun in each game, and Phil Caverretta goes 3 for 3 in the first game. He has to leave the first game in the 8th inning after colliding with Bill Nicholson chasing a foul ball down the right field line. To our disappointment, Caverretta doesn't play in the second game. The p.a. announcer assures Cub fans that he'll return to the lineup in a few days. Hank Sauer, recently acquired for the pennant drive, plays first base in the second game for Caverretta and gets two hits, including a homerun.

Phil Caverretta will go on to win the Batting Championship with a .355 average and the Most Valuable Player in the National League. The Chicago Cubs will complete the regular season winning 98 games while losing only 56, the best winning percentage in the majors for 1945 and will play Detroit (American League Champions) in the World Series.

* * * * *

On August 15, 1945, The Clinton Herald ran this editorial following the unconditional surrender of representatives of the Empire of Japan to General Douglas MacArthur on the American battleship, the U. S. S. Missouri:

Peace on Earth
Peace on Earth!
Short words but beautiful ones. Words which for so many long, weary years could not be heard above the din of shellfire, the screams of the dying or the hymns of hate chanted by those who would rule the world. Words, which suddenly become a glowing banner in the heavens when a strange race of little people with a strange religion bowed their heads in defeat.

Truly we have witnessed a miracle. We with all our skepticism, suddenly stand awe-stricken and humble in the face of this momentous event.

Peace on Earth!

It should mean more than merely the end of a struggle for supremacy on the battlefield, of death and desolation, of separation from loved ones, of numerous trials and tribulations at home. It should mean that we now are ready to embark on a great and strange adventure of friendship among nations and of respect for the wishes of those whose political and religious beliefs are not identical with ours. It should mean that we at long last have learned the futility of war.

Let us not adopt any high-sounding but false slogans. Let us not say that "our boys have not died in vain." We have no right to say this until we can prove to God himself we know how to wipe out forever the lust and greed, suspicions and misunderstandings, which brings war down on us periodically as a plague. Then, and only then, can we face toward the thousands of unseen graves across the sea and say, "Johnny, we have kept faith with you."

Let us forget about making the world safe for democracy. Instead, let us strive for a world, which is clean, honest and law-abiding for all people, regardless of race, color and creed.

And so as we Americans go on trial let us enter the doors of Clinton's churches and offer our prayers of thanksgiving for the end of the holocaust and ask for divine guidance in shaping the future course of events.

Over 35 million people died in World War II. Among the Allies, the U.S.S.R. or Soviet Union with 18 million dead, suffered the worst. Poland comes second with 5.8 million. Yugoslavia lost 1.5 million, France, 530,000, the British Commonwealth, 466,000, the U.S.A., 298,000. German deaths totaled 4.2 million, the largest of the Axis powers. Italy lost 395,000, and Japan, the last to surrender, lost 1.97 million.

* * * * *

All this excitement, and school too, makes me feverishly happy. I am now a seventh grader, an upper classman, and a student of Sister Mary Cecile. For three years, I have watched her move about with consummate authority. She sees that all grades line up smartly and march orderly to their respective classes daily from the sidewalk in front of St. Patrick's school. She flows. Her St. Franciscan habit flares out like dark angel's wings as she whistles by checking out the line. Then her regal face breaks into a wide smile as my stiff rectitude melts her no nonsense presence. I want to smile back, but resist, holding on to the illusion. I hear she is tough, but fair. I like that. I also hear that she doesn't make friends with you, but instead tries to bring out the magic in you. I like that, too. Sister Flavian is a saint, but I feel more comfortable with a person with a few possible cracks in her porcelain, a person like Sister Cecile, who reputedly is in your face and on your back if you try to play both sides of the street, which I do occasionally, but doesn't fault you for trying. So this next year should prove interesting. Her first words to me, "You're a tall one. Don't make me have to whittle you down to my size." She's about five-two.

"No, sister. I'm looking forward to being in your class."

318

"Don't try to romance me either." I smile and say nothing. She smiles back. It is the beginning of an unforgettable experience. We're both driven personalities and not always in self-understanding ways. As I get to know her, I find I'd go to war for her, but all she wants is for me to be the best I can be. It's a truce of sorts, as I find it increasingly hard to imagine her in a cloistered life. She seems a person who defies walls, ceilings and definitions, a person of action, who needs freedom to breathe, more a take-charge leader than a spiritual follower. If women could be priests, Sister Cecile would be a good one. Some people are meant to run things, others to be run by them. Sister leaves no doubt which category fits her. I don't know if love is the right word to describe our relationship, but it may be.

Two things I've come to discover motivate me, one is anger, the other is love. Anger finds me stepping outside the crowd to declare what I think. Love compels me to rejoin it. If I didn't have love, I'd have nothing but noise and blow to offer. Now in the seventh grade, this Manichean dualism is taking hold of my personality and giving it form, thanks to this remarkable nun.

We are not a month into the term when coming back from lunch I hear the World Series on the radio in the classroom. Mel Allen's melodic voice is calling the play-by-play and the discordant music of the crowd in the background makes my heart beat faster. Bobby Witt is as surprised as I am, but none of the eighth graders are. "What's going on?" Bobby asks Jim Holle, an eighth grader.

"Owl" as Jim is affectionately known because of his inscrutable frown says,

"What's it sound like?" And then moves to his desk.

The game is just underway and we all sit attentively, girls too, even though some of them look bored, and listen to the game for the next thirty minutes. Then the game is turned off without ceremony and afternoon lessons pick up where they left off. During the World Series broadcast, however, Sister Cecile is totally engrossed in the game hovering over the radio, listening with dreamy eyes not unlike those of my mother when she is listening to the Cubs. Sister's a sport's fan! How could I be luckier?

Class routine is to have the seventh grade study while the eighth grade discusses its lesson plan. I've never experienced this before, and at first find it hard to concentrate. Then I find myself evaluating the eighth grade discussions and rating oral presenters. I discover I associate beauty with brains, not physical perfection. Eighth grader Jackie Stolle, for instance, a freckled face bespectacled Chicago girl, boarding at the Mount, becomes a ravaging beauty every time she nails an answer, while the prettiest girl, also an eighth grader turns out to be less so for not.

It doesn't take long to recognize Sister's manner of teaching. She gravitates toward excellence. That means John Knoerschild and Patsy Kelly assume starring roles from the opening day. Sister relentlessly prods John to be more specific with his answers while he entertains himself dancing around her questions. "What do you mean John when you say there are two answers to the problem? Give them both and we'll decide if you're grandstanding." Sister Cecile is unsettling to John. He's not used to being challenged. "John," she continues, "you have far too much sense to settle for being a dilettante." It is the first time I've heard that word, but not John. He bristles with anger, but says nothing. When I look up the word in the dictionary I can see why John was upset. *Dilettante: a person with a superficial knowledge, a dabbler*. Wow! Sister couldn't have hurt him more!

Patsy Kelly has the measure of Sister from day one. She calibrates Sister's mood of the moment, and Sister is moody, and then stays well within those discrete boundaries. In a way, she is an echo, using Sister's words back to her. This causes John to ventilate a gasping, 'egads!' throwing his arms up in mocked exasperation. Eventually, the rebounding-like responses become too much for him. "Now Sister, where have I heard that before?" mimicking Patsy's unconscionable parroting of Sister's words. As for Patsy, she demurely folds her hands in her lap, drops her eyes in silence, and waits for Sister to come to her defense, which she invariably does. It is fun to watch the word play between these three, and makes the class period fly. Having stimulating characters in class taught me an important lesson: stay close to people brighter than you. They are the best teachers.

Nearing the end of the day, the radio is again turned on and we listen to the later innings of the World Series. After school, Bobby and I rush home to my house to hear the end of the game. It is a wonderful seesaw series with the Tigers winning, then the Cubs coming back to win the next day, game after game. It is not easy to tell whom Sister is for until she comes into class following the 12-inning sixth game, beaming, "The Cubs are still alive!" Not for long. Two days later Detroit wins the final game of the series and the World Series, four games to three. No mention is made of the Cubs' seventh game loss. Bill Christiansen catches me before class. "Stay loose, Fisher. Whatever you do, don't bring up the game." Good thing he warned me. The subject was on the tip of my tongue. After all, baseball is only a game. I know passion for sport can get intense. My mother is a die-hard Cub fan, and she goes into a silent funk when they lose. Sister too? Well, I guess I better not find out.

* * * * *

There is already the icy bite of winter in the air at Halloween. Differing this year is a clammy seriousness across the community. The war is over. The focus has shifted from the common good to self-consciousness. Patience has died and the postwar world has been born with all its demands for change, not tomorrow, but yesterday. The haughty throb of "compare and compete" is in the air. Autonomy is the first casualty in the guise of imitation. Provincialism is the second casualty as it is neutered with the broad brush of "one size fits all." The guys at the courthouse are unconscious of these silent invasions. They are too busy winding down from football and turning their attention to playing basketball. Thanks to sheriff Petersen, the basketball court has been graded and rolled and made ready for extensive use.

Sheriff Ky Petersen's Mardi Gras Parade is bigger and better than last year's. The Courthouse Tigers acquire a flatbed truck and make a float to pay tribute to the sheriff and his deputies. They also display the team's 1945 Junior-Junior Summer Baseball Championship. It isn't much of a float as floats go, though Ky, Chris Stamp, and Jim Gaffey say they love it. That's good enough for us. Placards of Ky's campaign picture are acquired, which are huge, nearly life size. And these are just of his face.

We make a three-sided box-like facing of these placards and attach them to the truck's cabin. The idea is that parade spectators can then see the sheriff's face from every angle as the float passes. On top of this box is a crude facsimile of a red baseball cap with "The Courthouse Tigers" across the brim. A makeshift two-sided 4 by 6 foot flag has been created with the caption "Thank You Ky" across the banner. It is held in place by a pole secured to the truck's cab. The Courthouse Tiger colors of red, white and blue bunting are draped around the truck bed covering the wheels. We ride the float with a glove, bat or ball in our hands, waving to the crowd. Our uniform, if you can call it that, is a white sweatshirt (too cold for T-shirts), blue jeans, white sneakers and a red baseball cap. Chris Stamp surprised us with a "Courthouse Tigers" banner, which is at the back of the float. The banner is far more professionally done than any of our efforts, and makes us swell with pride.

*   *   *   *   *

Chapter 20

Phantasmagoric Dream

A. I like Superman better than the others because they can't do everything Superman can do. Batman can't fly and that is important.

Q. Would you like to be able to fly?

A. I would like to be able to fly if everybody else did, but otherwise it would be kind of conspicuous.

--From an interview with a 12-year-old-girl by Katherine Wolfe & Marjorie Fiske, "Children Talk About Comics"

It is really cold out. Bobby Witt and I missed the bus and are walking to Washington Junior High gym, more than a mile and a half away to see Clinton High play Sterling High of Sterling, Illinois, a community just 30 miles due east of Clinton on the Rock River, which empties into the Mississippi at Rock Island. We must look almost like identical mummies wrapped up as we are. You can hardly see our faces, red stocking caps pulled down to our eyes, the same red scarves wrapped around our mouths, identical dark brown parka jackets with our collars turned up, red earmuffs, black leather gloves, and double pants -- gray sweatpants inside blue jeans -- something my mother invented and Bobby's mother copied. I clap my gloves together with ecstatic glee.

"Bobby, isn't this great? I love winter! It's my favorite time of year."

"I thought the fall was."

"That too."

Bobby squints at me and responds with an icy quiver. "You're crazy. Know that? Wouldn't miss the bus if you'd been ready. God, you're always late." He shakes his head in disgust batting his arms across his chest in an attempt to beat out the cold, his breath forming an icy cloud as he walks.

"Not always," I reply, my cheerfulness gone.

"Always!"

How could I tell him that I had to wait 'til my da left for Boone before I could ask? Bobby wouldn't understand. His life is not complicated. If I told him, he wouldn't believe me. Think it just an excuse. How could he? He's free as a bird. Look closely at me, and you can see my caged bird eyes.

"What do you think was wrong with Burridge against East Moline?" I say to put this behind us.

"What?"

"I said . ."

"I heard what you said. Do that all the time, don't you? Get in a pickle and try to change the subject. Fisher, you're always late! Always! Next time I'm not waiting." Bobby stamps his feet for emphasis kicking up the light snow as if he were stomping on my lateness. "What about Burridge?"

"Had only five points. Pieper, Price and Petersen carried the River Kings. Each had eleven. Weren't for them we'd of lost."

"I know," he agrees quietly, "listened to the game on the radio."

"You did? Why didn't you come over?"

"Fisher, we have a radio too you know."

"But you always come over!"

"Well, I didn't so it can't be always, can it?"

"Guess not. Still mad at me for being late?"

"Naw, not really. You're just a doofus. Got to accept that."

It's strange how fast the cold can leave. Bobby is Bobby now, and we can hardly feel the cold except in our nostrils and drying lips, and a little bit in our eyes. Otherwise our bodies are warm from the fast pace of our walking.

"Watch Burridge!" he says excitedly as we approach the gym, "he'll burn the nets tonight, fly to the basket with his Sterling defender standing flatfooted. Wait and see!"

Yellow light flares out of the gym like patches of sunlight on the slippery ice-covered concrete walk in front, slick from past melting and freezing. The blare of the Clinton High band interrupts staccato-like as the gym's double glass doors open and close with people rushing through them. We mesh with the steaming crowd, at least thirty people to the rear. It's funny looking over people's heads. They appear on fire as clouds of vapor pulsate from them into the dark night, while flashing red fire sticks between their lips fill the air with the rich aroma of tobacco. Everybody seems to be puffing away in two directions like steam engines with us in the caboose.

"Next you'll be saying he can leap buildings in a single bound. Coach Burridge is great, but I don't know. Listened to the Sterling game against St. Mary's. They sound pretty good. Got good ball handlers."

"You doofus. That's Sterling Community. Different school. St. Mary's doesn't play Clinton competition. And don't sell Burridge short."

"I don't. Coach's my hero." Embarrassed with my error about Sterling High, I add, "Anyway, should be a good game. I'm excited." Wanted to add, 'not as much as you,' but I never am. We get excited about different things.

"The River Kings will bury them with the fast break," he continues, "you'll see. Sterling will wish they never came across the river to play the Fire Wagon Five."

As we push through the doors, we're hit with a blast of heat. It stuns me. Not Bobby. He's laughing. "Shouldn't even be playing these bums." He's already got his game face on. The tiny gym that seats about 800 is already overflowing with raucous fans. People are sitting in the aisles of the permanent stands above the temporary bleachers. That is where we'll have to sit, thanks to my being late. There must be close to a thousand here. Maybe I'm almost as excited as Bobby. I hope coach Burridge is indeed Superman tonight.

The game turns out to be a war. I love basketball, the poetry, athleticism, the blazing speed, quick feet and ball handling of Herb Boegel, the magical touch of Dean Burridge, the husky rebounding of Dick Price, Leroy Watts, and Therol Petersen whose size and girth explode onto the boards as if pulled there by magnets, the ballet moves of Dean Pieper who tucks his legs up, flying under the basket to make reverse lay-ups. Incredible. Defying gravity. Nothing like it. But this night, move for move, Sterling High meets finesse with finesse and then some. The last four minutes of the game shake the gym to its rafters with the devastating roar of the hometown crowd. Sterling has their Burridge in a guy named Kenny Gould, who can shoot with either hand, dribble like a Globe Trotter, and wiggle away from double coverage with ease to score or pass off to an open teammate. He's awesome.

The game goes into overtime 39 - 39. In the overtime Petersen puts in a rebound and Sterling's Wolfe makes a free throw to give Clinton a one-point edge. Here play gets rough with Petersen ejected from the contest for fighting. Sterling's Linton shoots the technical foul to tie the score with a free throw. Then Burridge and Gould collide at mid court for a double foul. Burridge, who had tied the score during regulation play with a free throw in the last second to put the game into overtime, commits his fifth and final foul, making him ineligible to shoot the free throw. Coach Rashke calls on Ron Kramer to shoot it for Burridge. The tension is maddening. Gould shoots first. Without hesitation, he calmly makes his free throw toss. Kramer is tentative. You can feel his apprehension as he wipes his brow, dribbles the ball several times, takes a deep breath, dribbles some more, and then finally arches the ball to the basket. Time freezes. Everyone holds their breath. The ball leaving Kramer's hands is so flat you can count the seams. It strikes the front of the rim, rolls around, then off the basket with the gun going off a second later. The final score: 42 – 41 in favor of Sterling.

For a moment, there is the death pall of disbelief, then pent up frustration erupts into pandemonium. The promise of an undefeated season is gone; an upstart upsets the invincible River Kings. Superman has left the building. Madness follows. I am standing at the railing of the visiting team's locker room when bedlam erupts. A pretty blond Clinton cheerleader jumps on the back of Sterling's Gould as he leaves the court riding him like a bronco holding on to his mane of hair. Then a big blond guy, who I recognize from his picture in The Herald as a tackle on the football team, leaps down from the stands, and grabs Gould by the neck and starts punching him in the face. I freeze in astonishment. This isn't happening. This isn't the way a game is supposed to end. The crowd is growing increasingly rowdy with people pushing me so hard against the railing that I think it might give way with us all pouring onto the floor below. I feel near panic. I think I might be smothered. I can hardly breathe and suddenly start to fear for my safety. Where's Bobby? I can't turn my head to check. Finally, it is so bizarre that my mind shuts down as if I'm not there, only observing it from the comfort of a movie house. I don't faint but do go into a kind of swoon. Across the court, I can see coach Burridge, round shoulders, hairy arms and massive black curly hair, standing there momentarily. His olive complexion looks almost ashen, his eyes downcast as he slumps through the gym doors to climb up the steps to the home team locker room off the lobby. He is not part of the melee, nor is any other River King player. Ordinarily sane and responsible students and adults have become a collective rabble. Now the mob rules. People are throwing things, upsetting the timekeeper's table and chairs and heaving them onto the court. Everyone seems to be shouting profanities, language I'd never even heard my da use. Burridge looks up at me as he passes through the doors into the lobby, but I can only blink my eyes, as my arms are pinned to my sides. I don't think he sees me anyway.

And then it is over. Two police officers appear while the two high school attackers mysteriously melt into the crowd and the Sterling players disappear into the locker room. The whole affair probably didn't last more than thirty seconds, but it seemed like an eternity. I am trying to understand why after such a great game in which clearly the best team won, how a handsome football player and pretty cheerleader could be so consumed with madness that it triggered this

327

insanity. I look for something in the newspaper the next day, and find only an antiseptic account of the game. It is as if what I saw never happened. Now, after the game while waiting for the bus, Bobby is very quiet and so am I. We are cold again. It is well below freezing, and after 10 o'clock. But the cold I feel is a different cold than before. It is the cold of palpable loathing. Why so hateful? Why beat up a tired, defenseless player, who has done nothing but display incredible skill on the court? Why couldn't the fans say, 'you beat us at our own game, played our Fire Wagon Five style of basketball better than we did. Good going!' Why is winning so important? I wonder what Bobby is thinking. As we get on the bus and feel the blast of heat, I ask him,

"How could that happen Bobby?" The plea in my voice is an attempt for solace.

"It's coach Rashke's fault," he says matter-of-factly, "pure and simple."

"What?" I answer, astonished. "How could you blame the coach?"

"He started the second five, didn't he? Didn't play Lutz either, did he? So Lutz is a little banged up. He's still the best defensive player on the team. Gould would have been shut down, I guarantee. Good players play hurt. Still, could have done better than Kramer. Missed that crucial free throw, didn't he? Now tell me, Kramer was the best free throw shooter on the bench?" He looks at my puzzled face. "Agree, don't you?"

I am too stunned to answer. I don't handle pressure well, and can see me missing that free throw, too. Bobby is different. He thrives on pressure, and thinks the rest of us should as well. What about the brawl? Didn't he see the same attack on Sterling's best player that I saw? He was sitting right next to me. Where did he go? His mind is always on basketball strategy, a twelve-year-old coach, mine is on behavior, a twelve-year-old shrink. Who says best friends have to be on the same wavelength?

* * * * *

School the following Monday is a welcome respite from this turmoil. I can't take my eyes off Sister Cecile as she moves about the classroom with graceful energy handing out the day's assignments. She feels my eyes, turns and smiles.

"What," she says, loud enough for the rest of the class to hear, "fire lights your eyes with such brilliance this morning, James?"

"Nothing, Sister. Just happy to be in school," I reply candidly. This is followed by a hush.

Sister puts her hand to her face in mocked surprise. "I feel faint. A dedicated student!" Both seventh and eighth graders erupt in laughter.

She raises her hand. "Enough!" Then she walks over to my desk. Quietly, she whispers, "There's more isn't there?"

My head drops and I nod, then I look up at her with pained eyes, tears I can't hold back start to roll down my cheeks. She shrouds me with her black habit so no one else can see, waits for me to wipe my eyes with my hand, and then while still shielding me from view, continues, "Seventh graders, open your books to page 75 and read to page 82. I want everyone to be able to explain the Wilmot Proviso and why it is important. Eighth graders, I hope you're prepared for our math drill." She bends down to me. "We'll talk after school." She claps her hands and heads for the blackboard. "All right, a volunteer to explain the first problem in our homework assignment." Four eighth grader hands go up. I raise my hand, too, with a frown on my face. She comes back to my desk.

"Sister, I've got basketball practice after school!"

Warmth in her countenance gives way to an instant steel coldness that sends shivers up my spine. Quickly, I recover,

"Yes, Sister. Right after school."

The warmth is back. "Fine." She sashays away, the black veil of her habit opening up like the wings of a raven. I have trouble reading the assignment as my eyes are still moist, my spirits complicated by my weakness for tears. Good going, Fisher. Now you're going to miss practice! Sometimes I hate myself! Only girls cry. So what does that make me? A big baby! Thank God I'm at least big. Otherwise, I'd be called a sissy and thrashed every day. I only hope nobody saw my eyes. At lunch Bobby doesn't mention my humiliation. But instead, a rarity for him, he makes an apology.

"I was too hard on Kramer. It wasn't his fault that Clinton lost. He only had one free throw in the game and missed it. Burridge had eight and missed four, can you believe that? When I saw that in the paper, I nearly croaked. Burridge!" He shakes his head. "Could have won the game if he'd made only two more free throws. Shouldn't miss free throws. Nobody's guarding you. Amazing!" He shakes his head again.

"You going to share this analysis with coach tonight?"

He throws his hands in the air. "Think I'm crazy? Of course not. That'd be stupid! Besides, it's over and done with."

"Bobby, will you tell coach I'll be late? Got to talk to Sister Cecile after school."

"You in trouble?" he looks at me suspiciously. "What was that all about with her swarming over you like a ghost?"

"She wasn't swarming over me."

"Then what was she doing? Everyone was whispering. Wouldn't say anything to me because they know we're friends."

"It was because ..."

"Yeah?"

"Because . . . nothing. I'll tell you about it later."

"Yeah, sure you will, like you always do."

I want to tell Bobby, but know he won't understand. Cry? He'd say something like, 'grow up you big doofus! Boys don't cry. They get mad and fight.' So, why not lie and tell him a story? It isn't as if I don't lie. I lie all the time, but never well, and never spontaneously like my mother can. She can invent a plausible story on the spot. My da tells his railroad buddies, "When Dorothy talks about Jimmy, divide it by four, subtract one hundred, and believe half of that." His buddies laugh knowingly. He never exaggerates, not even in his mind. I do all the time, though mostly in my mind. These exaggerations even top my mother's. Though I guess I get the talent from her. I dream of making 90-foot shots to win basketball championships, and our basketball court isn't even 70-feet long. Things like that. In my dreams, too, I'm a great pressure player, like Superman, invincible. But then I always wake up.

It is a relief to me after school that Sister Cecile has her shawl and gloves on and her briefcase on her desk. This isn't going to be a long session. She sits down behind her desk with me in the first seat in front of her. She notices the classroom door is ajar, scrapes her chair on the floor as she pushes it back to rise. I watch her close the door gently, and then turn the lock. The scraping chair jars me and the click of the lock reduces me to raw nerves. What now? She comes back. Sits on the desk. Smiles that beautiful toothy grin of hers. I have never seen a more radiant, intelligent face. If I were a painter, I'd be obsessed with capturing it.

"Can I tell you a little story?" she says, removing her gloves and shawl.

"Yes, Sister."

"There was this boy I knew, a sensitive boy, a bright boy, a serious boy, too serious. He wore his heart on his sleeve and worried about everything. His radar was always on, passing over his world, feeling the pain, confusion, and brutality of his world, absorbing all of this until one day, he couldn't even get out of bed. The weight of the world immobilized him. He couldn't eat because his stomach ached with chronic disappointment. Then one day, as he was being helped by his mother back to his bed after going to the bathroom, he stumbled over a chair, knocked it against the mantel and a book on the mantel fell at his feet. He picked it up and a Holy Card fell out. While his mother was tidying his bed, he slipped it into his bathrobe and put the book back on the shelf. When she had left the room, he took the card out. It was a picture of St. Francis of Assisi surrounded by animals on one side, and this prayer on the other:

> *Lord, make me an instrument of your peace,*
> *Where there is hatred, let me sow love;*
> *...where there is injury, pardon;*
> *...where there is doubt, faith;*
> *...where there is despair, hope;*
> *...where there is darkness, light;*
> *...where there is sadness, joy;*
>
> *O Divine Master, grant that I may not so much seek*
> *...to be consoled as to console;*
> *...to be understood as to understand;*
> *...to be loved as to love.*

I waited for her to say more, but she just sat there and stared at me. It made me uncomfortable. I tried to read her eyes, which were clear and blue and yet distant. "What happened?" I said finally, unable to maintain silence. "Did it inspire him? It would me. Did his sickness lift from his bed? What Sister?"

"He died."

"Died?" That was incomprehensible. Died? How could he die? I buried my face in my hands. I didn't want Sister to see my anger. I felt tricked. I was waiting for Irish glee, not Norwegian gloom.

"Everyone, including his parents, believed he was a hypochondriac and was faking his illness, that the illness was psychosomatic. They tried to cure his illness with words, even his doctor thought his problems were mainly psychological."

"Then St. Francis didn't help."

"Oh, I think he did. He was clutching the Holy Card when he passed on. His priest found it when he gave him Extreme Unction. Unfortunately, it was after his death as no one thought him in a life threatening state."

"Pardon me, Sister, but that's a very depressing story. I'm not sick. And I'm not dying. I'm just very confused. People make no sense to me."

With her hands on her beads, she waited, her eyes telling me to go on, and then I started to bawl. At first I tried to hold it back, but couldn't and so let it go entirely. Her eyes never left me. They seemed to encourage the release of my pent-up feelings, feelings I thought beyond stupidity. Then finally the deluge ceased and I shuddered as if I had caught a chill. Talk followed. I tell her through my sobs of the upsetting experience at the basketball game. She doesn't interrupt. When I finish, I feel strangely relieved. Then I am flooded with a kind of euphoria. "Sister, am I too sensitive? If I am, can you help me correct it?"

Her head arches back in a throaty un-nun-like roar. It is like a diva hitting a high note and shattering glass, but in this case shattering the last remnants of my composure. I don't know what to think. It is a kind of intimacy I've never experienced other than with my mother. "Oh by the grace of God, no, my child. Heavens no! Hold on to that! That's your secret weapon. That's the vehicle of your calling. James, James, James! That is why I wanted to talk to you. I knew you were in pain. Your pain is quite visible because your pain is sincere. Your strength is your sincerity. You are not afraid to show it. Can you imagine what this means? James, you're not afraid of love. Do you hear what I'm saying? Have you any idea what that means?" She takes a handkerchief from her habit, removes her glasses, wipes them dutifully, gets up from the desk, puts them back on with studied care, puts her handkerchief away, then turns to put her shawl and gloves on with her back to me.

"Love is the answer to everything. Love is built on sensitive souls and there are never enough in the world. Never. It is the only truth." I sense her mind is drifting away from me. So I ask,

"Sister, do you think I could get a Holy Card like the one you mentioned?"

She turns but only revealing her profile and hands me a Holy Card without meeting my eyes. "Take mine. It's yours to keep." I can see a tear welling in the corner of her eye. Then, without saying good-bye, she flies out of the room. I sit there in a daze for several seconds, and then reread the card. A wave of peace passes through me. Is this love? Is it that simple? I look at the clock above Sister's desk. It's too late for basketball practice, and too early to be with others at home. I walk down to the Mississippi waterfront and read the card to the icy wind, imagining a flock of invisible doves whirling around me. I feel the warmth of being cared for, and feel blessed to have Sister Cecile as a friend. The courthouse clock strikes once, the half hour. I turn from the river and look up at it. It is 5:30. Yes, mighty sentinel rising in your green helmet to the sky, you are my friend, too.

* * * * *

After three patient years of coaching, Dean Burridge honed the modest talent of St. Patrick's basketball team into a regional power. No other junior high team in Clinton's history to that date so dominated the region, as did this team. It was unique in the sense that St. Patrick's "Fighting Irish" failed to have a legitimate sixth man. Substitution was not an option. Out of 17 seventh and eighth grade boys, coach Burridge culled out five bona fide players who could compete with anyone at that level. It was an accomplishment never given much attention. Basketball was king in this frozen tundra in 1945. Yet, St. Patrick School in a demanding regional schedule never lost a game, winning the Fulton Tournament, the Davenport Diocese Tournament, and the Clinton Catholic Parish Tournament, as well as beating its archrival Washington Junior High three times, and the

Clinton High School freshman team once. This basketball season would prove the personal high point in my athletic career, although I would play many more years of football, basketball, track and baseball. It is another reason why December 1945 was so sweet.

Coach Burridge had recruited me out of the fourth grade when I had no knowledge or interest in basketball. Instead of making me into a replica of a small forward like he was, he assessed what I could and couldn't do and built me into the player I became by the seventh grade. Obviously, he did the same with the four other starters, but with a difference. They were all natural coaches-in-the-making, and would one day seek that as their profession. I was at best a reluctant athlete from the start with no inclination to coaching. The best players in my experience are usually self-coaches.

Dean Burridge's coaching achievements are even more impressive when measured against the fact that he was a full-time high school student in his senior year, and one of a handful of premiere Iowa high school athletes. Add to this the fact that his team was now vying for a Clinton High first, an Iowa High School Basketball State Championship. Then reflect that he had been grooming this handful of players since they were eight and nine-year-olds into a synergistic and unbeatable unit. Such is what makes for legends in coaching.

At six foot and growing, I was the tallest player on the team in December 1945 and played center forward. Although a seventh grader, coach Burridge built his offense around me. He taught me to use my upper body strength to advantage in rebounding and either hand in scoring. He did this by schooling me in the pick and roll, where I would screen for Bobby or Bill Christiansen, then pivot for the basket where a bounce pass to me would lead to an easy bucket. Likewise, he adapted to the player's strength of eighth graders Bill Christiansen, Jim Holle and Bing Shepherd. Christiansen, like Bobby, was already a complete player with skill in ball handling, dribbling, finesse shooting and defense. What handicapped him was his slight build. Jim Holle was built close to the ground and already stocky. He was also scrappy and unselfish, a good ball handler, dribbler and defensive player. He often stole errant passes and led the fast break for easy two-pointers. The most dedicated player had to be Bing Shepherd. He worked hard to score, harder to get open without the ball and was a demon on defense. Never flashy, he always provided that bit of extra to win. Like Bobby, he used his athletic intelligence to compensate for a young body still developing. And also like Bobby, he had quick hands and feet. But if there was one player coach Burridge singled out for attention, it was I. He taught me to use my big body to block out for rebounds, which meant opposing players had to reach over me to get the ball, often fouling, which in turn led to frequent trips to the foul line. I shot at least 50 free throws every night with Super Halbach retrieving the ball for me and alerting me to variance in my shot.

Foul shooting came in handy in the championship game of the Fulton Tournament where I made eight for eight free throws in a 26 – 24 victory over Washington Junior High. The eighth grade class of WJH had more students in it than St. Patrick's entire student body. Coach Ed Rashke of Clinton High's varsity squad made it a point after the game to meet with me.

"That was an impressive exhibition of free throw shooting," he chuckled, "Burridge teach you that?" chiding coach Burridge who was looking on with a grimace. Coach Rashke was a surprise, first for being there, and then for not looking like a basketball player. He had a kind face but was as broad as a barn with powerful shoulders on a five-ten frame, weighing at least 220. He had a football player's build, and that was the sport, I learned later, in which he excelled at Illinois Normal. "Wish I could get your coach to shoot free throws like that," he said still eyeing the coach.

With that innocent introduction started his recruitment efforts of all five of us for his Clinton High basketball program. It seemed every time we turned around, he was at one of our games. Being Catholic, we also saw him at Mass on Sundays. And the following spring, it was never a surprise to see him at the courthouse watching us play baseball.

In December 1945, although only a seventh grader, coach Rashke along with coach Burridge drove me to the Washington Junior High gym to display my shooting skills to Clinton High's sophomore basketball coach, Dick Pollack. Burridge would feed me the ball and have me drive to the basket, shoot reverse lay-ups under it with my right and left hand, then shoot 18-footers facing the basket from the corners and around the key. I hit a phenomenal number of these shots in this exhibition, and received so many accolades that I was truly pumped up. I went home that night and told my mother I might be one of the best all-around athletes my age in the nation. My da, hearing this, exploded from the bathroom – I didn't know he was home.

"Jesus Christ!" he yelled throwing his hands into the air, "you, Dorothy! You did this! I don't goddamn believe it!" With that he rushed out of the front door, forgetting he only had on his undershirt, and it was winter.

"It's all right Ray," my mother said, when he sheepishly came back in the house his lips shattering, "don't worry your mind about Jimmy. Life will deflate him soon enough. We don't have to be part of the gang that does. Face it, your son is special."

"But Dorothy . . ."

"Don't but Dorothy me. This is only the beginning. He's not like you and me. Get used to it."

Shaking his head, waving his arms in total surrender, he again disappeared into our tiny bathroom, still murmuring earthy expletives that sounded like a man being tortured.

* * * * *

The Clinton Herald had me totally captivated with the phantasmagoric dream of being a "Golden Glove Champion." My uncle Frank was a former Golden Glove Midwestern flyweight champion. He boxed as Frankie Farrell. His picture had been on the front page of the sports section of the Chicago Sunday Tribune on February 17, 1929. It must have been a hex as he took sick and was unable to fight for a Golden Glove crown. Perhaps because of that history, I was particularly intrigued reading night after night about the coming tournament. The courthouse area's own Clarence Clare was entered to fight in the light heavyweight class. A senior at Clinton High, Clare played on the River Kings 1945 football team as a tackle.

My uncle Frank taught me how to jump rope, shadow box, and what type of boxing gloves to buy. He told me to run ten laps a day around the courthouse block just inside the sidewalk, and to do 10 slow pull-ups, 50 push-ups and 100 sit-ups every morning, afternoon and night. My da allowed me to buy the official Golden Gloves at Rod Fitch's Sporting Goods. I was so excited I could hardly stand it. At six-foot and 142 pounds I was in the welterweight class, which meant I would be boxing people with much shorter arms. My uncle was only five-four and when we boxed he could hardly put a glove on me.

"You box left handed," he said the first time we sparred. I had no idea I did. It was natural for me to keep my left glove back and to lead with my right. "How do you explain that?"

Once again, I had to share the history of how I became right-handed. "Your power should be in your right," he added, and it was but boxing, with my right glove back and leading with my left felt awkward. My uncle just shook his head. "Get your friends at the courthouse to box. Take on all sizes, even boys bigger than you to get a feel for your weakness."

This I did, learning it wasn't amusing to be knocked off your feet. A boy my own weight was usually shorter and couldn't reach me with my long arms jabbing him at leisure. This made it fun. I told my uncle about this.

"You're not going to knock anyone out. Few knockouts occur at your weight. Scoring points is the key to winning."

This puzzled me until he showed me how "hits" were scored as points by the judges and could lead to winning a bout. It was surprising how tired I got in a three-minute round. Even with all the courthouse training, I couldn't do three-rounds with a minute between rounds without feeling exhausted. When I told my uncle, he laughed. "Imagine going fifteen rounds with Joe Louis." I couldn't.

All December, I trained religiously for the Golden Gloves, and each time I presented my da with the entrance application where he had to sign for me, he would say "Later." The Clinton Herald announced that training sessions would be held at the Clinton High School gym starting January 9, 1946 with the actual fights to be held in the Modernistic on February 19, 20, 21 and the finals to take place on February 23. I'd go to sleep at night dreaming of myself as a Golden Glove Champion. I would look at myself in the mirror at my well-defined biceps and chest muscles, my flat stomach, all products of my rigorous training schedule and imagine what a striking picture in The Clinton Herald it would make showing me making a left cross on my opponent. It never occurred to me that I might get hit and hurt, or that this might interfere with my basketball career. The appeal of boxing was totally romantic, like I was a comic book hero. Then,

January 9, 1946 comes with the Golden Glove Tournament the headline story.

With anger in my eyes, I approached my da. "If you don't sign me up today, I won't be able to fight. This means everything to me. Everything!" I repeated in a choking voice. My mother was in the kitchen and said nothing when I looked to her for support, hiding behind a waft of smoke. She then came in the room and lit his cigarette with hers. He opened The Herald to the sport's page, and held it out to me. "Did you look at these entries?"

"At the entries? No, why should I?"

"Do you see anyone listed your age?"

"I didn't look."

"Well, the youngest is 16 and the oldest is 26."

"Guess who you'd have to fight?"

"The 16-year-olds?"

"Take a look at the entries. There're right here." He showed me the enclosed box listing the entries on the sport's page. I smiled. "Only Clarence Klare and Bob Dippo are taller than me and both are heavyweights. I wouldn't have to box them."

"Jimmy this isn't funny. You'd have to fight two 26-year-olds and several ages 20 to 22. Men! It's right here! Can you imagine what they could do to you?"

"But da, look! They're five-three, five-four, five-five and only one's five-eight."

"My size," my da stated bluntly.

Immediately, I had a horrible epiphany. My da was 37, five-seven and weighed about 148 pounds. He could kill me! I shuddered with that prospect, overwhelmed with fear. These guys could kill me! It never entered my mind. I was living a comic book dream.

"But why, why did you let me train for this?" I started to cry. "Why get my hopes up of being a Golden Glove Champion like uncle Frank? I don't understand."

"You have this exaggerated sense of yourself. I can't remember when you didn't." He drew deeply on his cigarette, holding its smoke deeply in his lungs, exhaling slowly. It formed a circular cloud, which fascinated me. He'd never done that before. "I thought, maybe, just maybe, somebody over the courthouse would ring your bell a couple times too many and that would be it. That is why I let your uncle encourage you. When that didn't happen, thought maybe I'd let you enter and have your bell rung in preliminary training, and your uncle said there isn't any boxing at the beginning of the training with sparring partners. It is all work on the bags. Then I asked him if he thought you could really get hurt. He hesitated. Then I rephrased it, 'Would you let Donnie fight in this tournament if he were Jimmy's age?' Your uncle shook his head, no. That was good enough for me. "I don't want you hurt, Jimmy, what I want is for you to get your goddamn head out of the goddamn clouds. I thought this might be the way."

In my memory, he had never connected so many words together into a coherent argument. He was smoking furiously, puffing away like my mother did routinely, lighting a cigarette on the end of his butt, which I'd never seen him do before.

"I knew you would be disappointed. I apologize for misleading you." He paused and looked to my mother. Now, I got it. It was a conspiracy.

"They're in the hutch Ray. Want them now?" He nodded.

"I've purchased two tickets for us to attend the Golden Glove finals on February 23rd. Best I can do." Overcome with emotion, I swallowed him up in my arms and pressed my face against his, the heat of his cigarette on my cheek. "I love you da! I love you!" My mother looked on wiping her eyes, and I felt his tears melting into mine.

* * * * *

Chapter 21

Glacial Change

Gene Autry, famed cowboy singer, expounded his own ideas on politics when in Washington recently for a visit. "Christopher Columbus," he said, "is the first New Deal Democrat. He laid down the whole philosophy. Columbus left Spain and he didn't know where he was going. He discovered America, and didn't know where he had been. And he did the whole thing on borrowed money!"

The Roving Reporter, "Readin' Over My Shoulder"
(The Clinton Herald, July 5, 1946)

The tapestry of memory, like early light diffused by fog through a garland of gossamer, can stretch across time and space as if an Impressionistic Monet. That was to be my A&P supermarket experience – life changing, yet incredibly bizaare. I can still hear my da. "Bill Knight was talking to John Whelan. Told him they're looking for sackers at the A&P."

"So?" my mother curls her cigarette around the ashtray as if outlining a new design.

"Thought this might be a way for Jimmy to pick up a couple bucks."

"Ray, Jimmy's not yet thirteen. I'm sure you have to be at least sixteen to work there."

"Goddamn it Dorothy he's bigger now then most men."

"So?"

"So whose to know how old he is if he doesn't tell them."

"You want him to lie about his age?"

"You goddamn right if he has to. Doesn't have to volunteer his age."

"That's still lying Ray. You know they're going to ask. You want him to lie."

He rolls his shoulders, his nose and chin almost meeting as he screws up his face. Lights a cigarette. Draws deeply on it. "Yeah, I suppose I do. So what? All he does is eat, sleep and throw some goddamn ball around. Never home. Never does anything around the house 'less you goddamn threaten him, then does a half-assed job. You goddamn right! Lie if he has to."

"Hear that Jimmy? Your father wants you to lie about your age. Next thing he'll want you to start stealing for us."

"Now Dorothy that's not goddamn fair." His shoulders slump into him to make him look almost womanly. My mother, who hates weakness, bolts upright.

"Here, here, Ray. I'm sorry. Know you mean Jimmy no harm. Know we need some help around here." Then she turns her head to the kitchen "Jimmy!" I have the door open a crack peeking at them from the kitchen. "I know you've heard everything. Come here!" I do.

"It's Saturday. Don't care what you're doing. Want you to go to the A&P and apply for a job."

"But mother you said . . ."

"Don't but mother me. Clean up. Put on your best shirt and pants and go down there now. And don't wear those sneakers or that damn baseball cap. Hear?"

"I'm supposed to be . . ."

"You're not supposed to be anywhere but where I tell you. Now get a move on!"

"You want me to lie?"

"You heard your father, if you have to."

"But mother it's a sin. I'll have to go to . . ."

"Don't go there Jimmy! Don't get my dander up. Don't play that holier than thou business with me. That's beneath you. Not raised you to play games with me. Your father's right. We treat you with kid gloves. Now scat!"

I look at my da who sits there meekly smoking, a pacifier cigarette between his lips, curled around himself in the chair like a wounded animal, not looking at either of us. There is no triumph on his face, just pained reality.

* * * * *

The A&P Supermarket is next to the Machael Oil Company and Oldsmobile dealer. The store is jam-packed this Saturday with wall-to-wall people. All four registers are humming, tabulating purchases with long lines of shoppers behind them waiting to have their groceries processed, while blocking the aisles. I notice at least twenty bags of groceries against the front wall with people's names stapled to the groceries for "late pick up." Just beyond the registers to the right as I enter the store, is a box-like open office with an apparently elevated floor as a man and woman stand in it peering out over the heads of shoppers. I guess that's where I'll find the manager. I walk over to the office and look up. They either don't see me or prefer to ignore me. I just stand there. Finally the door snaps open and a man descends to the floor. He looks up at me, not quite smiling, but doesn't say anything. He has a round likeable face with a deep five o'clock shadow. He has thinning black hair combed straight back like my da's, but is a few years younger, and piercing not quite smiling dark blue eyes, which appear as if entertained by a private joke. I like him immediately. This feeling causes me to smile and say in almost a cocky voice,

"Looks like you could use some help."

He laughs through his teeth making a hissing sound. I've never heard anyone laugh like that before.

343

"You sixteen?"

There it is, right off the bat, boom! Without missing a beat, I say, "Going on seventeen." Where'd that come from, I don't know. One day I will be going on seventeen and that's not to say I'm sixteen now, is it? Let's face it, it's a lie.

"Big body and pretty face, huh?" he says, "Bet you have to be a scrapper with that handicap." He hisses again. I say nothing. "Got a white shirt and bow tie?"

"Not with me but I can get them."

"Get them yet today and you're hired, but we close at six and it's noon now. So when am I going to see you?"

"As soon as I can get my stuff. Thank you sir." I bolt for the door exhilarated.

"Name?" he yells over the hum of the registers.

"Jimmy Fisher. Live by the courthouse."

"Well, Jimmy Fisher mine's Sam Spalding. Come back here a second! How much can you work?"

"Only Saturdays."

"Still in school?"

"Yes, sir."

"Well, it'll have to be just Saturdays then. Nine hours, eight to six with an hour off for lunch. Pay you sixty-five cent an hour. You didn't ask about pay, but that's it. Any chance of working nights to stock shelves?"

"Nights? Stock?" All these questions!

"Yeah, sometimes have to stock at night. Store traffic too great to restock the shelves during the day." His hand spans the store, "Like now. Saturdays don't allow such luxury. So, can you?"

"IIIIII'lll hhhavve to check." This is going too fast. Much too fast. I shake his hand quickly. It is dry and firm. Mine is moist and soft like a dishcloth. He doesn't seem to notice, just hisses and moves on. I try to think who he reminds me of and decide it is Sam Spade in the movies.

* * * * *

I'm back by two o'clock white shirt and black bow tie. Sam Spalding puts me immediately at one of the registers to sack. The checker is wild looking; her hair a thick tangle of coal-black coils that frame a heart-shaped, strawberries-and-cream face. Blossomy breasts strain against her green and white striped uniform with the "A&P" logo in red on a pocket above her left breast. She wears her uniform skintight and I can see her stupendously long legs gleaming with nylon stockings. She is tall like a model, at least five-eight or up to about my chin. I've never seen a more exotic-looking woman in my life, not even the one I saw last year. Her emerald eyes greet me,

"Welcome to A&P! Anyone ever told you how cute you are?"

"No, ma'am."

"No, ma'am," she laughs showing bright even white teeth. "No, ma'am that a lark! Believe me! I'm no, ma'am. Name's Colleen, Colleen O'Hara. Call me Colleen, okay?"

I nod. She does this while making the register sing, passing the food to me with staccato speed, faster then I can put it into paper bags.

"Make the bags double," she whispers. "Saves you a lot of trouble."

I go to put five double-bags into the lady's cart. "No, no!" the lady says, "Hold these for me to pick up." I stare at her. "Well, dear God in heaven, aren't you going to ask my name?" She looks at me as if my hesitation is too much to bear.

"Yes, ma'am," I say with poised marker.

"My name is Mrs. Isaiah Soelpaestine. I'll pick it up by four."

I stand there dumbfounded. I have no idea how to spell either name. "Well, aren't you going to write that down?"

"YYYYeeesss, ma'am. HHHHooowww do yyyyouu spell it?" She tells me. It doesn't register on my brain. "Ccccouullldd yyyouu repeat that?" She does. I still don't get it right. She takes up the marker, "My word! Youth today!" And writes her name.

"There! Now don't damage my goods, hear?"

"No, ma'am," I say, and gently put it with what seems like about another forty bags now across the front lobby almost blocking the door. I find it unbelievable that people would allow their food to be bandied about like this. What happens to the perishables? Disgusting! I know why I'm being defensive. I hate being stupid, but am all the time. She spelled out her name clearly and yet it didn't register on my brain. Now why is that? It must be some mental deficiency. I'll have to work on it.

345

* * * * *

My shyness was camouflage for my social ineptitude. I loved working at the A&P, but did not love people. I loved stocking the shelves, unloading boxed goods off conveyor belts from semi-trucks, and even working long hours at night to restock shelves for the next day. People are aberrations. I tolerate them like background noise in a River King's basketball game. They are not there at night when I'm stocking. This is usually done on Sunday nights before the Monday rush, and on Friday nights in preparation for Saturday's pandemonium. By nature, I'm a hard worker, not much for small talk. I take satisfaction seeing the shelves restocked. Work however makes me quite tired on Mondays in school and hurts my basketball practice. I never tell coach Burridge why.

I've always needed a lot of sleep, and often wouldn't get home from the A&P until 12:30 or 1 o'clock on a Monday morning. Much as I loved the A&P, I didn't like sacking groceries. I didn't like the way some customers treated checkers, challenging their totals, asking them to redo entire orders, or once orders were totaled having items subtracted because they miscalculated their funds, or insisted on talking to checkers while the order is being tabulated, then scolding checkers when mistakes are made. People seldom act adult. What I hated most of all however, was putting names on bags to be picked up later. I butchered people's names. A customer's name might be Smytherson and I'd write "Smithsomething" on the bag in my scribble. Guys would bust a gut examining my labels. People always got their groceries but were never too pleased with the spelling of their names. I did my best to correct this shortcoming. But when tired, and close to exhaustion in the eighth or ninth hour of work, automatic handwriting took over.

Another problem was also developing. Coyness is often disguised attack equal to a retreat into shyness. Colleen was increasingly sharing intimate details about her self and asking me personal questions. Quite frankly, I wasn't equipped to deal with them, and I resented the intrusion. You have a girl friend? No. You have big hands and feet. Yes, so? Bet you've got a lot of secrets. No. What kind of fantasies do you have about girls? None. You have fantasies, don't you? Yes. About what? Playing basketball. You're kidding? No, I'm not. Yes, you're kidding. You just don't know you are. She informed me that she was nineteen, on her own and originally from Decorah, Iowa and was working her way down to Florida. She dropped out of high school in her sophomore year, picked up with a road band "that went nowhere," left that and found herself in Dubuque for a while waiting on tables and got to Clinton too tired to go any further and so ended up at the A&P. "Clinton's a jumping place if you know where to look." She dared me to ask where with fluttering long eyelashes. I didn't. But her carefree personality was nonetheless intriguing to me. I wanted to ask her if she was Catholic, with a name like "Colleen O'Hara," but never got the nerve. I was afraid she'd laugh at me. She seemed to flirt with everybody and to have a joy of life, which was foreign to my experience. I liked her, in a way, but feared her in another for reasons I didn't understand. Did she accept that I was going on seventeen, or didn't it matter to her one way or the other? I never learned the answer but suspected it didn't.

One night, as we were cleaning up after closing, the assistant manager and meat manager were kidding with her. "Hey, I could take you both on and spit you out like confetti," she said coquettishly eyeing them challengingly with her hands on her hips. She looked provocatively beautiful. They both laughed with arched eyebrows. "Shouldn't talk that way in front of the boy," the assistant manager said, noticing me sweeping nearby, "might corrupt him."

Colleen gave a throaty laugh. "He's old enough to watch if he likes."

I quickly disappeared down the aisle. Later, I saw the three of them leave together, smoking cigarettes with Colleen's arms through each of theirs, looking like the Three Musketeers. I didn't see them again until the following Saturday, but couldn't help notice everything had changed, a kind of polite formality instead of the spirited banter of a week before. The luster, too, had gone out of Colleen's eyes. She looked much less pretty. Even make up couldn't conceal her darkness. She never kidded around with me again, and by the next Saturday, she was gone. I hope she made it to Florida and found what she was looking for there.

* * * * *

One of the boys working on Saturdays with me was John David of St. Mary's. John seemed to know something about everything including what impressed manager Sam Spalding. He was a good worker, but not any better than I was. Where John differed is that he could sweat on cue. He could blink his eyes and be drenched in sweat while I wouldn't even appear exercised. It didn't help that John was making a quarter more an hour than I was doing the same stuff. Sam would come by and compliment John on his hard work and say, "Fisher, learn to work like David and you won't have anything to worry about." What's to worry? I'm working as hard as he is if not harder. John smokes and I don't. John takes a lot of breaks and I don't. John is a great gabber with customers and I'm not. Dear God in heaven why can't I sweat like he does?

I'm taller than John, but he outweighs me by more than fifty pounds. Maybe that's why he sweats so much. He's also seventeen. I like John and am amused with him. He tells me he's an "A" student at St. Mary's and I believe him. When I ask him where he's going to college, he answers sarcastically, "Why go to college when you can make a good living as an electrician?"

That makes no sense to me. Why an electrician? He tells me that with a trade, he'll always have work, and not be diddle dawdling his time away in some university making no money and only learning to talk pretty. It dawns on me, money is important to John, but money is deceptively described as a kind of work. Is that the way I see things? Being useful is important to me, but how do you describe usefulness? In terms of money? No! In terms of work? No! Then how? I guess I don't know.

We're trimming lettuce in the back room, and Sam throws his car keys at John. "Got my new Oldsmobile today from Machael's. Needs to be waxed and polished. Think you can handle it?"

"Can Fisher help? Got a date after work and I won't be able to stay over."

"Sure." With that he leaves whistling.

The Oldsmobile is one of the first produced after the war. It is steel gray with a blue interior and smells new. I can't imagine why he wants it waxed and polished, as it looks fine to me. But Sam, who lives in Rock Island, and stays in Clinton during the week must want to impress his family. We work hard and fast on the car because John wants to be out by six, and Sam didn't give us the assignment until five. I wax. John polishes, sweat dripping down from his face and his white shirt soaked though to show his undershirt. He has the radio playing full blast. I don't like his music. It's country-western, but I don't say anything. It's John's assignment. I'm just helping. He looks at his watch. "Damn it! I knew this would happen! Finish up will you? Turn off the radio and give Sam the keys, okay?"

Before I can say anything, he's gone. I finish his polishing and sit in the driver's side to turn off the radio, and take the keys from the ignition. My family has never owned an automobile. Nor have I ever been in the driver's seat before. I turn the key to remove it and the car, which is in drive on the automatic transmission, moves forward. I am terrified. I poke one dial and after another in hopes that the car will stop but it doesn't. I know there is a brake on the floor so I put my foot down hard on a pedal. The car leaps forward and then explodes into the parking lot, just as a Largo-Marcino Group Produce Truck moves into view. I hit the truck's side panel on the driver's side going about 30 miles per hour. It caves in the side of the produce truck and pushes the whole front end of the new Oldsmobile accordion-like into a steam hissing pile of junk, while scaring the belly be Jesus out of the truck driver but not injuring him. It is unbelievable, how moments ago this automobile was so beautiful and is now reduced to crinkled rubble.

At that precise instant, captain Ed Clancy of the Clinton Police Department comes out of the A&P, assesses the situation, and races around the wreckage, to pull me out of the car, and handcuff me with my hands behind my back. I'm so terrified I can't speak or cry. The police officer doesn't say a word but ushers me towards his police cruiser when Sam Spalding comes out of the store. For a moment, his face shuts down as he surveys the damage to his new automobile. Then seemingly torn between outrage at the condition of his beautiful prize and terror at seeing my handcuffed body pushed down into the backseat of the cruiser, he shakes his head yelling, "No! No! No!" at the top of his lungs.

Captain Clancy yells back, "Everything's under control, Sam," putting his large hand out as a sign of reassurance. "Caught the culprit in the act."

"No! No! No! Ed! You don't understand! This boy works for me!"

"He was stealing your car Sam!"

"No! No! Ed!" Sam says, pushing his hands through his thinning hair, "He was washing it."

"Washing it?"

"Yes, and waxing it too if you can believe that."

"But, but . . ."

"Ed, I don't think he knows how to drive."

"You're kidding?"

"No, I'm not. He's a good kid. Good worker. St. Pat's boy — goes to your church." Turns to me. "I'm right, aren't I?"

My head is buried in my chest. I'm terrified. My lips quiver but nothing comes out. I'm crying, my chest is heaving but there are no tears, no sound. I want to curl up and die. Then one of the most touching moments of my life occurs. Sam comes over to me. Turns to the police officer. "Please, take these damn things off. Please." Sam says in almost a whisper as he looks disapprovingly at my shackled wrists.

Undaunted, captain Clancy declares, "That mean you're not pressing charges?" as he removes the handcuffs, shaking his head incredulously.

"Yes! I'm not pressing charges!"

"But Sam, if you do, chances are you won't have to pay your deductible. Otherwise I'm sure you will. Just advising you as a friend. Know how these insurance deals work."

"It's all right Ed. I'll pay the deductible."

"You're sure?"

"I'm sure."

"Okay, then I'll treat this as if it never happened. File a report that your car went into automatic drive and reamed the produce truck. I'm sure I can convince the Largo-Marcinno people to go along with this. If they have any questions, I send them on to you."

"Ed, if it gets more complicated then this, I'll have them contact my insurance company."

"This'll make your premiums go sky high, Sam, know that?"

Sam shakes his head, "I suppose," still in apparent aftershock.

Captain Clancy goes over and talks to the truck driver while Sam puts his arm around me and walks me back into the store, which is now closed. "Are you all right?" he asks. Not how could you do such a stupid thing? Not what am I going to tell my family? No stomping up and down, no swear words, only "are you all right?"

"IIIIII'mmm ssssorrry Sam," I sob.

"I am too," he says honestly looking into the distance. "The important thing is you're okay." I'd never truly loved another man other than men in my family before that moment. But I felt genuine love for Sam Spalding, which has lasted a lifetime. Every time I get angry with someone I try to recall how he acted in that climatic moment. My gratitude and amazement has never dimmed.

* * * * *

Confirmation is an important milestone in Roman Catholicism. It is the third ritual in the rites of passage from Baptism to Holy Communion to Confirmation. In Confirmation, Catholic children confirm their belief in the doctrines and dogma of Roman Catholicism and submit themselves to becoming "soldiers of Christ." Much preparation is required for this passage, as the diocesan bishop puts questions to those being confirmed regarding matters of faith and morals before an assembly of parents and friends. Each child takes a saint's name to be added to his or her Christian name. I took the name of St. Aloysius Gonzaga because I liked the sound of his name, only to learn years later that Irish author James Joyce took the same name when he was confirmed. Like first communion, we are all dressed in our Sunday best, with Bishop of Davenport Ralph L. Hayes presiding. Bishop Hayes recently had his picture in The Clinton Herald. I was pleased to see he looked in person like his picture with a mane of white hair, a handsome Irish face, complemented by a deep melodious voice. I couldn't picture a bishop looking any other way. He asked such questions as, why are you Catholic? What do you believe? Why do you believe it? He would look around the room and smile and then stare at someone until that person finally stood up and answered. Answering the bishop's question shouldn't have been an ordeal as we were well rehearsed, but I still sunk deeper and deeper into the pew seat with each question. Not Dickie Van Ah. Dickie is our equipment manager on the basketball team and tiny, but with a confident voice. His hand goes up for every question, even before Bishop Hayes can get the question out. Finally, the bishop turns to him. Dickie stands up and answers with the same eloquence as his questioner. I am impressed and so, apparently, is the bishop, who studies Dickie for some seconds. "Excellent!" the bishop says. Small wonder that Dickie Van Ah became a priest.

"Now children," the bishop says as he is satisfied with our preparation, "please come to the altar rail and receive my blessing along with your sponsors."

My sponsor is Leon Cavanaugh, a devout Catholic and my da's best buddy from childhood. As I am blessed by the bishop, making the Sign of the Cross on my forehead, repeating my chosen saint's name, and am about to return to my pew, horrified I look up and into the smiling face of Sam Spalding, one of the sponsors.

After the Confirmation, he comes over to me in the school gym where we are having refreshments, "Either you're the oldest kid ever confirmed at St. Pat's, or you're not sixteen. What is it?"

"Sam, who you sponsoring?" I ask to deflect his question.

"My nephew. Let me ask it another way. What grade are you in?"

"Seventh."

"Seventh?

"Yyyyyeeesss sir. Arrreee yyyouuu going to fire me?"

"You're twelve or thirteen, which?"

"Thirteen now," I lied. "Well are you? Going to fire me?"

The hissing laugh between the teeth follows. "No, I'm not going to fire you. How could I? You're one of my best workers." Then he pats me on the shoulder. "Think I always knew but didn't want to think about it, that car mishap for one, your innocence for another. Like that about you." With that he leaves with his nephew. We never discuss this incident again.

* * * * *

March madness is an annual Iowa mania that builds as the regular basketball season concludes and tournament play starts. The Clinton Herald has been stoking the boilers the entire 1945 - 1946 season for a Clinton High School Basketball State Championship, and now these boilers are producing the superheated steam of maddening expectations. The early Sterling defeat has been erased from memory, as the River Kings haven't lost a game since, finishing the season 22 and 1. There isn't a Clintonian that doesn't carry a picture in their mind of the "Fire Wagon Five" made up of Dean Burridge, Dick Price, Red Lutz, Therol Petersen and Dean Pieper outfitted in firefighting gear and raging through the streets on the hook and ladder to ultimate victory. The Clinton Herald created this metaphor by having these players pose in firefighting rubber raincoats and pointed helmets in a fire station on a fire wagon to imprint in the minds of Clinton sports fans the imagery of the "Fire Wagon Five," and the newspaper succeeded. Expectations were at a fever's pitch.

The River Kings haven't let their fans down winning the Mississippi Valley Crown and their Regional, and now they are set to claim the coveted prize of Iowa High School Athletic Association Basketball Champion as they travel to Iowa City, a prideful member of the final "Sweet Sixteen." Enrollment of final 16 teams ranged from Danbury's 42 to Clinton's student body of 927. Clinton's first round opponent is Ames High, last years State Champion.

Bobby Witt and I can hardly control our excitement as the State Tournament nears. Then we get the surprise of our lives. Sister Cecile announces on Monday that Paul Holleran and Paul Christiansen, parents of Dave Holleran and Bill Christiansen, teammates of ours, have organized to take us to the Clinton-Ames game on Wednesday, March 20. "The game's not scheduled until 9:30 p.m. which means you won't get home from Iowa City until early Thursday morning," Sister Cecile states, "so don't worry about attending Mass before school. We'll all pray that you have a safe trip. Now let us get to work with our studies."

She is obviously thrilled to present us with this wonderful news, but hides her emotions in a business-like manner. She is amazing!

This was my first trip to Iowa City, a sparkling clean university town 90 miles southwest of Clinton, and once the state capital of Iowa with a population of about 33,000. Walking into the field house was more overwhelming than when I entered Wrigley Field last summer to see the Chicago Cub's play. Situated on the University of Iowa campus, the field house looked dark and dreary from the outside, a soot coated dirty brick façade without architectural splendor, appearing more like a heap of bricks piled box-like to create an arena without much thought to form. Once inside, my whole attitude changed. It was a rocking place with more than 14,000 fans hovering over a brilliantly lighted basketball court, which was seemingly in the bottom of a huge pit with glaring lights flaring down on the court like blinding sunlight. A distraction, however, was the placement of huge steel structural support beams every thirty or forty feet, which blocked a clear view of the basketball court if you found yourself seated behind one. I made certain that I wasn't.

We arrived just as Danbury was defeating Crawfordsville. I couldn't help but notice the tall skinny center of Danbury. "God, look at that guy! He towers over everybody on the floor," I comment, "but doesn't look like he weighs much more than a hundred pounds." I check my tournament program. He's six-four and weighs 150.

Bobby laughs, "Looks like Icabod Crane!"

Just then he makes an impressive hook shot, "But shoots like Kentucky's Alex Groza."

"If you say so." Then he points to another player. "Look at that little guy for Danbury! He dribbles like me. If he were a Negro, he could play for the Harlem Globetrotters." He laughs in clear admiration. Bobby's as excited as I am.

"He does, doesn't he? He's No. 3, same number as Burridge," I add, then looking at the program, "if we win, Bobby, we'll have to play Danbury next."

"What do you mean 'if'? We'll cream Ames."

"Remember they were State Champs last year."

"Well, it's our turn this year. Wait and see!"

The River Kings do win beating, Ames 43 to 37, but I didn't think coach Burridge played too well. He missed three out of four free throws and made only four baskets. The guy who looked really great was Leroy Watts. His rebounding was spectacular and he led the fast break for Petersen to get easy baskets. Price was sluggish too, didn't score a basket. I wondered if the River Kings were nervous. I didn't share this with Bobby. He would have called me a "spoil sport."

* * * * *

Bobby and I are having bets with each other on the point spread or by how many points Clinton will whip Danbury. We are camped out around my radio. My mother has made us a fudge cake and poured us big glasses of milk, and we can hardly wait for the game to start. I say the final score will be Clinton 55 – Danbury 45. Bobby says the score will be Clinton 65 – Danbury 25. He is right about Danbury's score but wrong about Clinton's because Clinton scores only 24 points. The Clinton Herald eats humble pie with the headline, *Clinton Defeat Rated One of the Biggest Upsets in Iowa High School Basketball History.* It shakes the foundation of our confidence. It couldn't happen. Defeat was not in our vocabulary; especially to a team so small it's not even in the almanac. Danbury has only 728 people in its entire town compared to Clinton's 33,000 citizens. It doesn't compute. Hank Dihlmann does his best to make sense of the loss, pointing out the great stalling ability of Dick Reicks, the rebounding of Elton Tuttle, and the surprising scoring of Jack Barry.

Providence would not find Dean Burridge its superhero, but Bob Freeman of the Iowa City Little Hawks. On the next night, Friday March 22, 1946, Iowa City faced and defeated Danbury by the identical score of 25 – 24, earning a right to face Le Mars High School, who defeated Waverly 35 – 29 to play for the Iowa State High School Basketball Championship on Saturday March 23. That game would prove one of the most spectacular comebacks in Iowa tournament history as Bob Freeman scored three baskets in the last 50 seconds to erase a 40 – 35 deficit to win 41 – 40.

Rather than stalling out the last 55 seconds of the contest, the Le Mars quintet elected to add to their margin only to have Gene Hettrick grab the rebound, feed to Freeman who raced down court to score from the key, making the score Le Mars 40 – Iowa City 37. Now with 30 seconds on the clock, the Little Hawks go into a full-court press. The inbound pass goes awry, intercepted by Freeman who dribbles past two defenders, pulls up and scores from 20 feet: Le Mars 40 – Iowa City 39. Le Mars takes a time out to settle down and set up a play. Center Don Johnson inbounds the ball to Eldon Clement, who throws down court for Bill Haas, Le Mars best ball handler, but Freeman intercepts the pass, and with time running out crosses the time line, puts the ball up and scores. Five seconds are left on the clock with the score: Iowa City 41 – Le Mars 40. Time expires as Johnson inbounds the ball to Haas. Superman is in the building, and it is not Dean Burridge! It's Bob Freeman of the Little Hawks! Burridge makes the all-tournament team, and first team all-state. Leroy Watts, who never started, makes third team all-state. None of the other River King starters are named to an all-state team, but all receive honorable mention honors.

* * * * *

At another level, honors are coming to our St. Patrick's basketball team with our picture with coach Burridge prominently displayed on the front page of the sports section of *The Clinton Herald* April 3, 1946 in recognition of our fabulous season, The Herald noting "the most brilliant record in the history of the school." This is followed with the same picture and write-up in the May 1946 issue of the *Catholic Messenger*. My mother is ecstatic. She can't put her hands on enough newspapers. Then 10 days later *The Clinton Herald* runs a picture of St. Patrick altar boys with palms in our hands with the caption "First Peacetime Palm Sunday Since 1941 Will Be Noted Here Tomorrow." In the picture are Father Finefield along with Bing Shepherd, Jim Rederer, John Knoerschild, Dick Morris, Jim Holle, Jim McComb and me. My mother goes on another newspaper buying spree. She lives for this.

* * * * *

Just before the end of the 1946 school year an informal father-son dinner is held in the school gym for the basketball team of the St. Patrick's Shamrocks. All the fathers of the basketball players are invited. My da has never seen me play, and has never shown any interest in the game. When asked to attend, he says he is "too busy." But my mother cajoles him into attending. In the short three-block walk, he smokes but doesn't talk. When we reach the side door to the school building, several fathers are already standing around smoking and talking. My teammates are gathered apart from them. As we approach this assembly, I break through our bitter silence. "You go over there," I say pointing to the other fathers, "I'll see you later inside and make sure we sit together."

He looks at me in what I can only describe as terror in his eyes, a look I can remember seeing only one time before. "I can't talk to them. What will I talk about? I have nothing in common with that crowd."

He is referring to Paul Holleran, a prominent Clinton attorney, Paul Christiansen, a lumber company executive, James McComb, owner of an auto supply company, and Edward Holle, a large paint contractor. First surprise, then resentment rises in me. I say with

356

contempt in my voice, "You have me in common with them and I'm a better basketball player than all their sons put together."

He flicks his cigarette, shakes his head in disgust and swears under his breath, not loud enough for anyone else to hear. But before he can turn tail for home I announce, "Gentlemen, I would like to introduce you to my da, Mr. James R. Fisher, Sr. Da this is . . ." and I rattle off their names as if strangers to him. My bravado is as contrived as my conceit is disingenuous. If he only knew, but obviously doesn't, I am as much a hider as he is. Still, it is strange to witness the reaction of the group. Their collective expression is almost hostile lending credence to my da's reluctance. My introduction seems to freeze the air with an unwelcome frost. Quickly, attorney Holleran recovers, forces a smile to disguise the group's unease, and breaks the ice with, "Well, Ray, how's the railroad treating you?"

"Fine Paul," my da answers groping for another cigarette, "working pretty steady now with veterans coming back home from the west coast."

With that I remove myself, still watching him light his cigarette and putting on his civil mask if slightly askew. It is troubling to observe. It is the second time I've felt miserable for him, and I wondered why.

Fortunately, Father Finefield's housekeeper calls to us that the dinner is ready, that Father will soon be joining us. Inside the gym the place is decked out in green shamrocks and green ribbons streaming from the west basketball hoop and along the walls. The east hoop has been taken down to set up a table for dining on stage. The bingo tables we tear down every Saturday and Sunday to play basketball are now covered in white paper trimmed in green and gold, and I notice the head table on the stage has name placards to identify who will sit where – Father Finefield is to sit in the center with coach Dean Burridge and Paul Holleran to his right, and Paul Christiansen, and basketball coach Ed Rashke of Clinton High to his left. As I am studying this arrangement, in walks Father Finefield ceremoniously accompanied by the two coaches.

Father Finefield gives a brief welcoming of players, parents and coaches, along with special appreciation to Mr. Holleran for his generous contribution to the financing of the dinner. He tells us how proud he is of our team, but I don't remember him ever attending a game. Then he gives the thanksgiving prayer before dinner.

The meal is not one of my favorites – fried chicken. I like everything else -- mash potatoes and gravy, cold slaw, milk, coffee, wheat buns, and hot apple pie with ice cream for dessert. Jim Rederer is happy to eat my chicken.

After dinner Father Finefield gives the thanksgiving prayer, and then turns the meeting over to coach Burridge. The coach talks briefly about how important chemistry is to a team, "and this team had chemistry." He then introduces his high school coach, Ed Rashke. Coach Rashke says that he recently learned an important lesson, "It doesn't take a big school to make a winning basketball team." Everyone laughs. They know this is self-deprecating humor in reference to Clinton's painful loss to little Danbury at state. Then to leave no doubt as to the sincerity of his sentiments, he concludes, "I've watched these kids play as much as I've been able, and they have had something you can't teach, and that is a 'can do' spirit that Danbury showed us at state."

Some parent yells, "Here! Here!" Polite clapping follows.

Then Paul Christiansen speaks. A large tall man and careful dresser with wavy steel gray hair, a handsome face, and horn rimmed glasses, a classic Roman nose, and a strong although slightly indulgent face; he has a comforting yet compelling voice, a voice used to command. I still remember his remarks all these years later.

"I've had the privilege of seeing this rag tag bunch of Catholic kids put St. Patrick's School on the map. I've watched them play every game, across the county, down in Davenport in the Davenport Diocese Tournament, across the river in Fulton in their tournament, and even out at Clinton High School against their frosh team. And the single thing that seems to have stuck out in all these contests, yes they played well, and yes they pushed themselves to be just a little better than everybody they faced, as coach Rashke has pointed out, but that's not what stuck out for me. It was how ridiculous they looked. They were the only team that didn't have uniforms." Everyone laughs heartedly.

"But could they play! No team was any challenge to our kids, and everywhere we played we were the smallest school with only ten boys out of a total of 18 boys available in the seventh and eighth grade that were capable of playing basketball. Imagine that!

"They went over to Fulton and won. They went out to Washington Junior High and won. They went up to Lyons Junior High and won. They went down to St. Mary's and won despite Father Vincent Morrissey's praying on the bench for a miracle." More laughter. "I would look at the well designed uniforms of our opponents and then look at our kids in white tee shirts and green shorts, and I would bury my head in embarrassment at our bazaar costumes." Again laughter.

"Then it finally dawned on me. You don't become an original by comparing and competing against some arbitrary norm, by imitating and envying what you're not and what you don't have. You become authentic, something special by discovering that small seed of difference that is yours, and coach Burridge was able to identify that seed and grow it into a Shamrock, into a team, into these champions." Applause.

"And I thank him and I thank you, each and every one of you boys for the honor you have bestowed on St. Patrick's and the pleasure you have given us. Thank you and God Bless!"

He receives a standing ovation. I only wished that Sister Cecile could have been there to share in the celebration. She was the spirit behind that seed and its nurturer.

* * * * *

Change was inevitable and I didn't want any of it. The past year was the most idyllic of my life. All of this would be shattered, not in a single instance but in a maddening glacial like movement into the future, a future of increasing riches and diminishing peace, of fortuitous good fortune and reduced freedom. I sensed this incipient loss as a boy, but fortunately wasn't wise enough to understand it, or I think I might have gone quite mad. The world I would increasingly occupy was in the process of making madness the norm.

* * * * *

James R. Fisher, Jr.

Epilogue

Epiphany Two

What is time? The shadow on the dial, the striking of the clock, the running of the sand, day and night, summer and winter, months, years, centuries – these are but the arbitrary and outward signs – the measure of time, not time itself. Time is the life of the soul.

--Henry Wadsworth Longfellow

The year's eight through thirteen are an eternity. These years stay with you a lifetime. Born in innocence and run through by reality, these years make an imprint on the soul that has a bearing on the way you walk and talk, think and behave, believe and problem solve for the rest of your life. You are unconscious of anything happening other than what at the moment meets your fancy, but you are getting a report card every day because in life school is never out.

You can't rush nature. The body has its own internal clock as to when the bones and muscles, cartilage and tendons are ready for the test of stress. The mind is another matter. I pushed my body to its limits the summer of 1946 while my mind remained in low gear. After coach Burridge organized a tryout with the Dupont team of the Clinton Industrial Baseball League, I worked with a vengeance to improve my throwing arm, toughening my hands doing yard work, and developing my muscles with intensive exercise. I also continued to study the catchers in the Industrial League, and practiced throwing the baseball the same way they did, not with my back and legs like pitchers do, but by simply putting the ball behind my ear and snapping my wrist the way catchers do, not realizing the tremendous strain that was putting on the tendons of my elbow. I would use Dick Tharp and Chang Benson, Phil Leahy and Bobby Witt to catch my practice throws to second base, always with this unnatural movement of my arm. In our Courthouse Tiger games, I would throw the ball

361

back to Bobby, or whoever was pitching, as hard as it was thrown to me, always with the mind to perfect my throwing arm. If anyone successfully stole a base on me, I felt a grave sense of incompetence, not realizing that most bases are stolen on the pitcher. To say I was obsessive compulsive is to put it mildly.

Then about the middle of August I noticed a pain in my right elbow that raced up my arm to my shoulder when I would throw. I told Bobby Witt about it, but not my parents. Bobby said, "You're not supposed to throw as hard as you can as soon as you touch a baseball doofus. You're supposed to warm up gradually. Limber up the muscles." I never did. I've had only two speeds, stop and flat out.

* * * * *

On Wednesday, September 11, 1946 at lunchtime at St. Patrick's school, playing touch football in the cinder playground behind the school gym, I go back to throw a long pass to Joe Zimmer, and there is a loud snap. The football goes straight up in the air like a soaring canon shot and then fizzles to the ground. I scream in a mind wrenching cry, "Oh my God!" cradling my right elbow as if a fragile ornament. Then horrified, I look at my arm as it swells and becomes discolored. In less than a minute, it is twice, then three times its normal size until the swelling between my shoulder and hand grows inconceivably to the size and shape of a small football. The shock temporarily obliterates the pain, as I grow oozy with Bobby Witt and Dick Morris rushing to support me. Still no one says anything. Finally, Donny Costello says,

"Better get him to Father for help."

With that the guys take me to the parish house, ringing the back porch bell, the same bell that so many times has led to confrontations between Father and me for the key to the school gym. Several minutes elapse before Father answers the door.

"Jimmy Fisher's been hurt Father," Donny says breathlessly. "Hurt real bad."

Father looks at me with undisguised disdain, and then at my swollen arm. "How in the hell did you do that to yourself?" his face contorting into an ugly mask.

Hearing Father say "hell" jolts me. "IIIIII ttttthhhhrrrrew tttthhhhe football and this happened Father," I say stupidly, holding out my grotesque looking arm for confirmation.

His expression indicates he clearly wishes to be somewhere else. "What do you expect me to do?"

The four of us look at each other speechless, and then Dick Morris says, "Think we need to get him to the hospital Father."

"That's not possible," Father replies, and then realizing how insensitive it sounds, "I mean I have an appointment, an emergency house call. Perhaps," he looks to me, "you can get your mother to run you there."

Even with all the pain and embarrassment of getting hurt, I am utterly astounded. Father knows my family has no automobile. He knows my mother doesn't drive. His remark is beyond impudence. It is blatantly offensive. I feel disgust rise in me, which again abates the pain. To my astonishment I hear myself say with venom in my voice, "But Father you know we have no car, now don't you?"

Sister Cecile rescues the situation from getting more ugly. Only minutes before, she arrived back from the Mount where she had taken lunch, was apprised of the accident, and went into her action mode. I can still see her flying across the space between the school and the parish house her black veil flaring out with a bundle of white towels cupped in her arms across her habit. "It's all taken care of Father. I've had a girl go to the Costello's. Mr. Costello has agreed to run the boy to the hospital." She turns to me. "We'll make a temporary sling of these towels to take the pressure off your arm." She expertly forms the sling and carefully places a noose about my neck. "That should do until we get you to the hospital."

Ashen faced, Father Finefield stands as impotent as a track star with a broken leg. No longer the focus of authority, but clearly relieved, he recoups imperiously. "I place matters in your hands Sister. See that the boy gets proper attention and report back to me tomorrow."

"Yes Father," she says dutifully and ushers me from the scene, down the alley behind the church to the Costello's just north of the church on Third Street side, where Mr. Costello is waiting.

At Mercy Hospital, it is obvious the hospital is not prepared for an emergency, reminding me of the same situation four years earlier when the soldier powered me on his motorcycle here after I was hit with a baseball bat at the courthouse splitting my cheek open under the eye. Then a nurse approaches. "Dr. Amesbury is here making his rounds. Should I get him?" The nun in charge nods. I breathe a sigh of relief.

Dr. Amesbury is a tall, dark cerebral looking man with a kind face and gentle manner, and fortunately for me, an orthopedic surgeon. The first thing he says seeing my arm once unwrapped and taken from my makeshift sling, "How are you dealing with the pain?"

"Fine doctor." In a peculiar way with my elbow now bigger than a football and already turning an ugly purple, I am so much in shock that I seem beyond pain. All I can think of is what my da will say when he sees me. Like Father Finefield, he doesn't like surprises. He will be torn between wanting to punish me for this stupid thing and worrying about the hurt it'll cause my mother. Then he'll go into a deep depression worrying about how he's going to pay for this. My mother will only worry about my arm.

"Let's get you down to x-ray," Dr. Amesbury says, "and nurse I'd like him in a wheelchair."

She brings a wheelchair around, guides me into it, and then hands me a paper cup and a capsule, "Take this for pain." I do.

The X-ray laboratory is in the basement of the building down a dark dank hallway where the lights seem to flicker. I think of a dungeon. In the room I'm left for more than a half hour and it is cold and quiet, all I hear is a beep, beep, beep of some code through an intercom system, wondering what it means. I try to measure the beeps to see if different codes are being communicated, but again become drowsy. I'm startled awake when the x-ray technician comes in and abruptly moves me. She is pretty, and as chipper as an apple-cheeked summer girl, tall, blond, a kind of bizarre beauty with a strong jaw and sky blue eyes, but a little on the heavy side. Her nametag says she's "Hilda." I think of a Milk Maid pictured on a dairy product.

"We have to get you out of this to take some pictures," she says, putting her arms gently under my shoulders as if I'm an invalid and lifts me out of the chair. She smells like flowers. I'm directed to sit on a long steel table with a huge glaring eye above it. "Lie down and put your arm here like this hon," contorting her figure to demonstrate how as if she's on the table. I comply but almost laugh because she looks funny doing it. The table is so cold I sit up.

"First time?" she smiles. She is really pretty. "I know," she continues with happy eyes, "kind of a shock is it?" She doesn't wait for a reply, but drapes a heavy metal-containing leather cloth above and below the damaged elbow. "Now I'm going to go over there," she points to a little alcove hidden from the table, "and take a picture. Hold your breath until I say, okay, okay?" I nod obediently but cannot see the connection of holding my breath and taking a picture of my elbow. We repeat this activity for nine additional x-ray pictures. My arm now really hurts, despite the painkiller. Why all these contortions? Sensing this, she says, "You will feel more comfortable in a little while." She winks coquettishly. For the first time I want to cry but don't. I wonder if it is her kindness or her beauty that's so unsettling.

"The doctor will be with you shortly once he sees the x-rays." With that she is gone and I miss her immediately. I'm left in this cold room with a clock above the door as my only company and watch the second hand go around and listen to its hypnotic ticking. After several catnaps, I hear Dr. Amesbury's voice coming down the hall. I feel anxious and hungry. It must be dinnertime. The doctor comes in with a book under his arm. "Are you by any chance an athlete?" he asks.

"Yes doctor," I answer.

"I thought so. Well, this is an athletic injury. But I've never seen it in a boy your age." He opens the heavy book with the title *Gray's Anatomy* to a previously marked spot. The page shows an illustration of a bone, anterior and posterior views. In the corner of the page is a small sketch of a skeleton with the humerus bone of both arms highlighted. "The bone you injured is the humerus," he says, tapping the page, "a very important and sturdy bone. You have torn away the medial epicondyle, trochlea, greater and lesser tubercle from your right humerus at the elbow joint," he traces on the page the precise area of the fracture. The words are Greek to me, but he continues as if I understand every word. "Your right humerus indicates a longitudinal fracture splitting off the medial epicondyle. This tells us the fracture is the result of the constant twisting of the arm with great force. The tension between muscle and bone can grow acute, and bone doesn't always win the struggle. You apparently fractured the bone sometime ago. Have you been in any pain before?"

"Yes doctor. All summer."

"What sport do you play?"

"I'm a catcher in baseball doctor and do a lot of hard throwing."

"Ah, that's it is it?" He pauses and rubs his chin. "That explains a lot. Yes." He studies me. It is like looking into the face of God. I totally trust him and know he will make me well. "There is a slim chance, now mind you I must emphasize this, a slim chance that placing your arm in a cast with the ligaments and muscle still attached to the fractured piece, which is a good size I might add, it may naturally move back to its normal mooring and reattach itself to the humerus. This is not at all certain but it needs exploring, otherwise we'll have to surgically wire the piece to the humerus, which means a bit of radical surgery, detaching the piece from the muscles, ligaments, and tendons, and thus of necessity requiring a protracted period of physical therapy.

"I'll explain all this to your parents, but right now I'm placing your arm in a plaster cast and sending you home, would you like that?" he concludes with a smile. Before I can say anything, he adds, "You'll need to take these capsules for pain every four hours as it's going to get a bit uncomfortable." He hands me a bottle. After he completes putting on the plaster cast, he says, "This is a serious injury. I must emphasize that. It means refraining from any physical activity. Some call it 'tennis elbow,' which is not quite accurate, but it does happen to tennis players and some baseball pitchers. So we know something about what is involved." Strange, but his talking to me as if I'm an adult gives me confidence I won't need surgery. I am wrong.

Two weeks later on September 25 I am back in the hospital taking more x-rays and submitting to another examination. In the interim I have been doing my schoolwork writing left handed which surprisingly is more legible than with my right. My mother is with me this time. Dr. Amesbury explains to her that surgery is necessary and that he would like for her to sign papers to admit me to the hospital on Friday after school.

"Whatever you say doctor," she replies.

I can tell this is hard on her because she has us walk home, a good mile, rather than take the bus. She doesn't talk, just smokes and once in a while squeezes my good hand. When we're about home, she says, "We'll get through this Jimmy."

The hospital experience other than the surgery is a joy. My arm is in traction and I'm immobile and totally dependent on the nurses. They visit with me, bring me treats, and extra meals when it is something I like. Hilda visits me too, and I learn her nickname is "Happy." It fits. I have a roommate from Preston who has had an emergency appendectomy. He is older and hates the confinement. I love it. Mother brings me books and I discover how much I truly love to read. She comes every day. The hospital Catholic Chaplin visits me too along with several different ministers. They are all nice. I'd never talked to a minister before. Some have Roman collars but purple vests, others wear ordinary suits. A group of Jehovah Witnesses visits me, too. They give me little books to read. I like them best because I can feel their passion.

The biggest surprise is Sister Cecile. She comes one day after school along with eight of my classmates. Considering this is more than a mile walk out of her way, I am moved by it. I want to tell her I love her, but say only, "Thank you for coming Sister," with a tear in my eye, which she pretends not to notice.

"Here is your homework," she says matter-of-factly. "Bobby Witt has offered to bring the future assignments to your mother to bring to you." Bobby is at basketball practice and not in the group. The guys and gals sign my cast, and then leave with me forgetting to thank them for coming.

It isn't until November 13 that Dr. Amesbury removes my cast. I am not prepared for what I see. I have an ugly ten-inch scar on my right elbow that looks like a butcher did the cutting while in a drunken stupor. More than fifty years later you can still see the holes where the stitches were made to secure the wound. But what is truly devastating is that my arm has atrophied to less than six inches in circumference, smaller around than my left wrist. I start to cry, loud deep sobs looking at this grotesque freak of an arm, not realizing until I start to cry that it is also deformed. I can't bend it! It is permanently shaped at a 45-degree angle, the exact inclination of my cast. "Doctor, what have you done to my arm? Mother look at my arm! Look!"

"Now get hold of yourself young man!" Dr. Amesbury says rather sternly, which is uncharacteristic of him. "We explained all this to you before, and to your parents. The arm required radical surgery. I told you that. I told you it meant stripping away the ligaments and muscles from the floating piece and reattaching it with wire to your humerus. This was necessary to make certain that it grafted properly. I also told you it meant that we had to keep you immobilized much longer than normal with a broken arm. That was why your hospital stay was so long. Now, it is up to you. You decide whether you're going to have a crippled arm or going to regain the full use of it. This as I told you before will require extensive physical therapy."

The heroes in this physical therapy are my mother and Clinton High's coach Ed Rashke. Every Saturday over an eight-month period (November 1946 to July 1947), coach Rashke gives up his Saturday mornings to give my arm electric shock stimulation to exercise the atrophied muscles. This is done at his shop at the high school. Meanwhile, during this same period, there is a nightly ritual at home. I soak my arm submerged in an Epsom's salt solution at a temperature of 110 degrees Fahrenheit in a ten-gallon pan for thirty minutes. Then for the next hour I carry a ten-pound bucket of bricks around the house. At the end of this period, my mother measures the perpendicular from my wrist to the table with my upper arm flat on that surface. She records the date and value in inches. At first the arm is counter flexed and no perpendicular can be measured. But over the next 120 days my arm goes from a counter flexed angle of 135-degree to a flexed angle of 45-degree. Obviously, we are not there yet but real progress has been made with my arm inching its way to being extended flat on the kitchen table surface.

* * * * *

With my arm only about 35 degrees from being straight, the next phase of my physical therapy involves my mother handing me the ten-pound bucket of bricks with my upper arm flat on the table and my hand extended over the table's edge. Soaking the arm in an Epsom's solution still precedes this therapy. The strain of this extension is excruciatingly painful. At first, I can only hold the bucket for seconds, but gradually this grows to a minute, then two, and so on until I can hold it for nearly five minutes. Sweat pours off me, but off my mother as well. Slight progress keeps us at it.

Where the perpendicular once was nonexistent, with the arm curled back towards the body, steady but slight improvement has been noted for months now. We were ecstatic when we first could measure the perpendicular. Now it is like an athletic contest with victory on the horizon. We suffered a minor setback when I started to play basketball when my arm was not ready. My mother figured we lost a month for that indiscretion, but she never said, "I told you so." But now a quarter inch improvement a night is not unusual. By mid-June 1947, or over 200 days from the start of this physical therapy, my extended arm is less than five inches from being flat on the table's surface. We are nearly there! I'm not going to be a cripple!

* * * * *

Philosopher Arthur Schopenhauer points out that when you reach an advanced age and look back over your lifetime as I have, there can be seen a consistent order and plan as though composed by a novelist. Events that when they occurred seemed accidental and of little moment turn out to have been indispensable factors in the composition of a consistent plot. Schopenhauer suggests that just as an aspect of ourselves of which our consciousness is unaware composes our dreams, so, too, our whole life is composed by the will within us. My life began the day I met Bobby Witt and it was changed forever when I broke my arm. It forced me out of my routine as primarily a jock into a world of deeper reflection, a world that was always beckoning me, a world of books and ideas, a world that has led to this book. What stirred me the most were the writings of Emerson, especially his essay, Self-Reliance. Its message would prove consequential as the next six decades would put a strain between self and reliance to the point of near estrangement, not only for my generation and me, but for all succeeding ones. It took the death of my friend, Bobby Witt on August 27, 1990 to jar me out of my reverie, and to reflect on what made us, us. Lads and lasses of my generation who rose out of the rich soil of our birth would march through the maelstrom of wars, scandals, corruptions and new paranoia to have careers, marry, have children and grandchildren as they partnered to the dance of life in an atmosphere of death. They bled the blood of their time and its color and consistency are now lost to Time's memory. But what is time? Time, as Longfellow reminds us, is the life of the soul. The soul connects us all to each other, the living and the dead. I learned this at the courthouse at the feet of the philosopher Bobby Witt who only wanted to play baseball in the Major Leagues.

*   *   *   *   *

About the Author

James R. Fisher, Jr., Ph.D., has had a distinguished career as an international corporate executive and organizational/industrial psychologist. Dr. Fisher is author of seven books including *The Taboo Against Being Your Own Best Friend*, and hundreds of articles, most recently the *Fisher Paradigm* ™, a breakthrough concept in the genre of organizational development. He lives in Tampa, Florida with his wife, Betty. This is his first novel.